MEDICAL
MANAGEMENT

MEDICAL
MANAGEMENT
A PRACTICAL GUIDE

Edited by

Hameen Markar MBBS (Sri Lanka) FRCP (Edin) FRCPsych
MPhil (Edin)
Retired Medical Director, Bedfordshire & Luton Mental Health NHS Trust and
South Essex Partnership Foundation Trust (Bedford & Luton); formerly Associate
Lecturer, Department of Psychiatry, University of Cambridge

Geraldine O'Sullivan MB BCh BAO (National University Ireland)
MD (NUI), FRCPsych, Diploma Company Direction (IoD)
Executive Director – Quality and Medical Leadership, Hertfordshire Partnership
NHS Foundation Trust

HODDER
ARNOLD
AN HACHETTE UK COMPANY

First published in Great Britain in 2012 by
Hodder Arnold, an imprint of Hodder Education, a division of Hachette UK
338 Euston Road, London NW1 3BH

http://www.hodderarnold.com

British Library Cataloguing in Publication Data
A catalogue record for this book is available from the British Library

Library of Congress Cataloging-in-Publication Data
A catalog record for this book is available from the Library of Congress

ISBN-13 978-1-4441-4540-3

1 2 3 4 5 6 7 8 9 10

Commissioning Editor: Caroline Makepeace
Project Editor: Joanna Silman
Production Controller: Avril Litchmore
Cover Design: Julie Joubinaux

Cover image © iStockphoto

Typeset in Minionpro 11 points by Datapage (India) Pvt. Ltd.
Printed and bound in Great Britain by CPI Group (UK) Ltd., Croydon, CR0 4YY.

What do you think about this book? Or any other Hodder Arnold title?
Please visit our website: www.hodderarnold.com

CONTENTS

Contributors

Mark Agius MD
Visiting Research Associate, Department of Psychiatry, University of Cambridge; Associate Specialist, South Essex Partnership, University Foundation Trust; Research Associate, Clare College, University of Cambridge, UK

Raja Badrakalimuthu MBBS, MRCPsych
ST 4 Psychiatry, Cambridge and Peterborough Mental Health Trust

Paul Cosford BSc(Hons) MSc MBBS(Hons) MRCPsych FFPH
Director of Health Protection Services at the Health Protection Agency; Honorary Senior Fellow in Public Health at the University of Cambridge

Paresh Dawda MBBS DRCOG DFRSH FRCGP FRACGP
Medical Director ACT GP Super Clinic, Ochre Health; previously GP Principal – South Street Surgery and Teaching Faculty – NHS Institute for Innovation and Improvement

Trish Donovan ACMA CGMA
Director of Finance, North Staffordshire Combined Healthcare NHS Trust, Stoke-on-Trent

Duncan Empey FRCP
Group Medical Director, BMI Healthcare, Brentford, Middlesex

Julian Flowers MRCP FFPHM
Consultant in Public Health Medicine; Director, Eastern Region Public Health Observatory & Quality Intelligence East

Matt Fossey BSc MSocSc DipSW DipMHStud FInstMH
Senior Associate, Centre for Mental Health, London; Honorary Lecturer, University of Nottingham; Independent Healthcare Consultant

Peter Graves MBBS FRCGP
Chief Executive of Bedfordshire & Hertfordshire LMC Ltd and GP

Simon Gregory BSc MBBS DRCOG DFRHC DCH M Med Ed FHEA FRCGP LoC SDi
Postgraduate Dean, East of England, Cambridge; Visiting Professor, Norwich Medical School, University of East Anglia and Anglia Ruskin University

Anton Grech MD MSc MRCPsych
Chairman and Consultant Psychiatrist Psychiatric Service Malta; Lecturer in Psychiatry, University of Malta

John Hague MBBS DRCOG
Partner, The Derby Road Practice, 52 Derby Road, Ipswich; Board member Ipswich and East Suffolk CCG

Elizabeth J Haxby MBBS MA MSc FRCA
Lead Clinician in Clinical Risk, Royal Brompton Hospital, Royal Brompton and Harefield NHS Foundation Trust

Jacky Hayden FRCP FRCGP FAcadMed
Dean of Postgraduate Medical Studies North Western Deanery and Manchester University

Sajeeva Jayalath MB BS(Hons) MRCPsych
Consultant Psychiatrist and Clinical Director, SEPT providing services for Luton, Bedfordshire and Essex

Hameen Markar MBBS (Sri Lanka) FRCP (Edin) FRCPsych MPhil (Edin)
Retired Medical Director, Bedfordshire & Luton Mental Health NHS Trust and South Essex Partnership Foundation Trust (Bedford & Luton); formerly Associate Lecturer, Department of Psychiatry, University of Cambridge

James IDM Matheson BA(Hons) MBBS DMCC
Academic Foundation Doctor, Academic Foundation Programme, Royal Lancaster Infirmary; Catastrophes & Conflict Forum, Royal Society of Medicine; Faculty of Conflict & Catastrophe Medicine, Society of Apothecaries, UK.

Ed Neale BSc MB BS FRCOG
Consultant Obstetrician and Gynaecologist and Medical Director, Bedford Hospital NHS Trust

Peter Old LLM FFPH MFFLM MRCGP
Medico-Legal Adviser, Medical Defence Union

Geraldine O'Sullivan MB BCh BAO MD FRCPsych
Executive Director Quality and Medical Leadership, Hertfordshire Partnership NHS Foundation Trust

Sheila Peskett MA FRCP
Group Medical Director, Ramsay Healthcare UK, London

Alastair Scotland FRCS FRCP FRCGP FFPH
Director of the National Care Advisory Service (NCAS) (retired)

Philip Sugarman MSc MBA PhD FRCPsych
CEO & Medical Director, St Andrew's Healthcare, Northampton; Visiting Professor, School of Health, University of Northampton; Honorary Senior Lecturer, Institute of Psychiatry, King's College London

Sylvia Tang MBBS MRCPsych
Medical Director, Camden & Islington NHS Foundation Trust, London

Jayaraman Thiagarajan FRCA FFICM MBA
Consultant in Anaesthesia and Critical Care, East and North Herts NHS Trust, Lister Hospital, Stevenage

Preface

Health services across the world are under pressure to become more effective and to deliver better quality care for less in the face of increasing demand related to demographic changes, the emergence of ever more expensive treatments, and government pressure to limit the spend on health.

In the United Kingdom, it is no different with healthcare going through one of the most turbulent periods in its history with the controversial Health and Social Care Act 2012 heralding big changes in the configuration of healthcare organisations responsible for commissioning and provision of care. Reforms involving the development of commissioning groups, abolition of Primary Care Trusts, increasing competition with the concept of 'any willing provider' and the need to make cost savings amounting to 20 billion pounds by 2015 pose significant challenges. Such substantial savings can only be achieved through a considerable reduction of both managerial and clinical resources. Therefore, the biggest challenge for all of us working in healthcare is to optimise the use of available resources and provide a clinically effective and safe service within limited resources. General practitioners and hospital doctors have been thrust to the forefront of this challenge and given the responsibility of both commissioning and delivering these services.

We all agree that clinicians need to remain at the heart of leadership and management of the healthcare system. But how well equipped are doctors in the UK to take on this challenge? Doctors are trained to be clinicians and have very little management training as undergraduates. Therefore, the majority are most comfortable within their own area of expertise and often have problems in understanding and dealing with management issues that require entirely different training and skills. Most doctors who choose to go into medical management have little knowledge or experience of matters such as commissioning, financial processes, managing people and dealing with under-performance, how to manage meetings or function at board level. These are skills most of us learn on the job through years of experience.

There are a range of books covering management in the corporate and business sectors but little has been written on medical management. We developed the idea for this book because of this dearth of books that comprehensively cover the various aspects of medical management in both primary and secondary healthcare. We felt that there is a huge need for such a book particularly at a time when doctors are taking a more prominent role in managing healthcare. We hope that this book, in which almost every chapter is written or co-authored by an experienced medical manager, will be of benefit not only to doctors engaged in management but also for a much wider audience including undergraduates and non-medical managers.

The book has two main sections: general management in healthcare, and specific issues. The former includes chapters on project and change management, patient safety and quality, health outcome measures, leadership styles and skills, human resource management for doctors and information technology and innovation in the NHS. The second part deals with specific topics such as the role of the medical director at board level, the challenges for a clinical director, doctors in difficulty, financial issues for doctors and enhancing personal effectiveness. We have been very fortunate in recruiting several experienced medical managers from a range of specialities to contribute chapters on a variety of settings such as acute care, mental health, general practice and private health care. We have also had expert contributions on topics such as commissioning, clinical governance and patient safety.

This book is mainly related to English policies and healthcare configuration within England and is especially relevant to doctors working in the NHS and private health sector in the UK who have an interest in management. However, the principles of management are relevant irrespective of jurisdiction or professional background. There are therefore several chapters that will be of interest to a much wider audience including non-medical managers in healthcare, medical and nursing undergraduates and doctors working outside the United Kingdom.

We would like to thank all our contributors for their effort and cooperation in making this publication a reality. We are both psychiatrists and have considerable experience in management within Mental Health services. We are particularly grateful to all our non- psychiatric colleagues who have made such useful contributions enabling comprehensive coverage of all aspects of medical management including general practice, public health and acute care. Finally, we owe a great deal to Joanna Silman and Caroline Makepeace at Hodder for their help, advice, encouragement and co-ordination of the entire project. We have immensely enjoyed editing this book and we hope it will prove a valuable and comprehensive source of information for all our colleagues.

Hameen Markar and Geraldine O'Sullivan

PART 1

Management in the NHS – general issues

Chapter 1

Healthcare management – an overview

Peter Graves

Introduction

Doctors in management roles, such as medical directors and clinical commissioning leads, as well as those in a range of leadership positions often find themselves caught in the crossfire of arguments between their clinical colleagues and the organization's managers – the former wanting to provide the most effective available treatment and the highest possible quality of care for their individual patients, irrespective of cost, and the latter striving to hit output and outcome targets while being constrained by budgets and financial restrictions. At the same time, these doctors are having to manage significant changes within their organization, not to mention the politically driven reforms of the National Health Service (NHS).

It is becoming more and more apparent that strong medical leadership is essential to secure the sustainability of the NHS. In view of this, this chapter sets out to discuss some of the dilemmas faced by doctors in management roles and the reasons these dilemmas have come about, by examining:

- the importance of the quality of healthcare, including the uneasy balance between what has been described by Donabedian[1] as 'optimally effective care' and 'maximally effective care'
- the ever-rising costs of healthcare to the taxpayer
- the political drivers that have led to numerous NHS reorganizations over the last 25 years, all of which fuel this debate (outlining the changes in the NHS that have taken place since the late 1980s and the reasons why change has been necessary)
- the 'purchaser/provider split' and the 'internal market' with competition, which are here to stay for the foreseeable future
- why those closest to the patients (mainly doctors; GPs in particular) have been placed firmly in the 'driving seat' of commissioning in the latest reorganization.

Healthcare quality

Quality assurance in healthcare: a strong driver for political change

Quite rightly, the best available healthcare is an expectation of those receiving and paying for it, *but it is expensive*. Meanwhile, poor-quality healthcare is soon identified by the media and castigated by all, including politicians and those who dictate the budgets. Many medical disasters and lapses in care, highlighted by the media, have led to significant political pressure to make changes. As doctors take on management positions, they are expected to take on responsibility for the quality of the service provided by their department, organization and, by implication, their colleagues too. Inevitably, medical managers get embroiled in the performance concerns of colleagues, an area I do not cover in this chapter.

Avedis Donabedian dedicated his life and career to understanding and improving healthcare, through his research into and teaching about the quality of healthcare. His work and publications had a worldwide impact. His final book, *An Introduction to Quality Assurance in Health Care*[1] (which he wrote during his last, physically debilitating illness), was published in 2003 after his death. It is a testament of his commitment to improving the quality of healthcare.

While his work has been refined and developed over the last 10 years, for those new to medical management and the quality agenda it is a brilliant summary of the issues and complexities of quality assurance in healthcare and an excellent introduction to the subject. It sets out the criteria for measurement and monitoring of healthcare and highlights the difficulties involved in pursuing high-quality care. For those already well versed in this area, his book contains nothing new but it pulls all the fundamental principles under one cover and reaffirms the importance of constantly striving for improvement in quality.

Many people, especially doctors, continue to argue that the quality of healthcare is far too subjective and abstract to be measured and monitored, and that managers only measure that which can be measured, ignoring the subjective, but equally important, unmeasurable, complex elements of healthcare, including some outcomes from general practice and mental healthcare. I believe that wider use of patient-reported outcome measures (PROMs) could help to redress this to some degree. However, it is an indictment of the healthcare sector, according to Appleby and Devlin,[2] that the NHS was the first provider to make wide use of PROMs data to assess health outcomes – and even that was not until 1 April 2009, despite evidence to show their usefulness a long time before this.[3]

Nevertheless, it remains our duty as doctors and medical leaders to strive to find appropriate measures to improve quality and achieve better outcomes for our patients and many chapters in this book focus on quality issues.

Optimality – 'maximally effective' vs 'optimally effective' care

It is impossible in one chapter to give full justice to the life's work of Donabedian but it is useful to introduce some concepts in order to help understand one major debate faced by medical managers.

Donabedian argued that quality in healthcare is the product of two factors: the science and technology of healthcare, and the application of that science and technology. Quality is then characterized by seven potentially measurable components: efficacy, effectiveness, efficiency, optimality, acceptability, legitimacy and equity. A summary of the definitions of all seven components is set out in Box 1.1.

> **Box 1.1 Components of quality: definitions (reproduced with kind permission from AUAC and OUP)**
>
> 1 **Efficacy** – the ability of the science and technology of healthcare to bring about improvements in health when used under the most favourable circumstances
> 2 **Effectiveness** – the degree to which attainable improvements in health are, in fact, attained
> 3 **Efficiency** – the ability to lower the cost of care without diminishing attainable improvements in health
> 4 **Optimality** – the balancing of improvements in health against the costs of such improvements
> 5 **Acceptability** – conformity to the wishes, desires and expectations of patients and their families
> 6 **Legitimacy** – conformity to social preferences as expressed in ethical principles, values, norms, mores, laws and regulations
> 7 **Equity** – conformity to a principle that determines what is just and fair in the distribution of healthcare and its benefits among members of the population

When faced with finite budgets and serious financial constraints, all clinicians must be engaged with the quality agenda and the continual endeavour to achieve the best quality of care alongside optimal productivity. However, it is often difficult to persuade colleagues that this is the case. In order to explain this debate, I will focus solely on optimality.

Donabedian defines optimality as 'the balancing of improvements in health against the costs of such improvements'. As a clinician, it is easy to assume that the more money that is spent on a healthcare programme, or the more resources given to an individual patient, the better the likelihood of a successful outcome; treating cancer patients is a good example. All too frequently, however, this is not necessarily the case. A very simplistic example concerns the delivery of a vaccination programme. Theoretically, if it were possible to vaccinate 100 per cent of a target population against a particular illness, spending more money on this programme wouldn't improve outcomes that are dependent upon the efficacy of the vaccine.

Figure 1.1 shows this graphically. Hypothetically, if a fully efficient clinician, providing the best care possible, is given successively larger amounts of resources, then the outcome benefits of the care provided could be measured against the expenditure (as shown in the upper graph). Initially, the rate of improvement in outcomes is faster than the rate of increase in resources available. Eventually, irrespective of further increases in resources, the rate of improvement in outcomes flattens off; there is no further outcome gain for continued expenditure – shown by line B on the graph. Donabedian calls this the 'maximally effective' point. Clearly, this is the point that most clinicians aspire to reach in respect of the patient sitting in front of them.

In health economics terms, by comparison, it is hypothetically possible to express health improvements minus the costs (as shown in the lower graph in Figure 1.1). It can be seen that, at line A, the lower graph reaches a point of inflection, which is significantly lower than the maximally effective point (line B). This second point (shown by line A) is what Donabedian calls the point of 'optimally effective' care. I believe that this is the level of care that healthcare managers and politicians, who rarely face vulnerable patients on a one-to-one basis, and who try to persuade clinicians to achieve the best outcomes for the maximum number of patients within the resources available, are aiming for. As a clinician myself, I propose that this is a rather 'utilitarian' view.

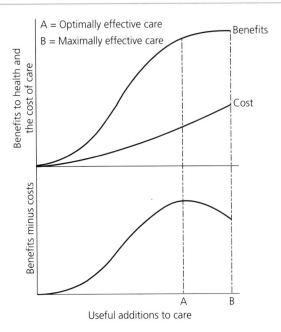

Figure 1.1 Hypothetical relationships between health benefits and costs of progressively more elaborate care, when care is clinically most efficient. A, optimally effective care; B, maximally effective care. (Reproduced with kind permission of AUAC and OUP.)

It is this difference between providing 'maximally effective' and 'optimally effective' care that creates the tensions between clinicians and managers (not to mention politicians) and is responsible for one of the dilemmas facing doctors in management roles, who can see both sides of this argument.

In order to help guide clinicians towards providing optimally effective care, the National Institute for Health and Clinical Excellence (NICE) was set up in England and Wales on 1 April 1999. Its aim, according to its website, is to 'provide guidance, set quality standards and manage a national database to improve people's health and prevent and treat ill health' and to ensure that 'everyone has equal access to medical treatments and high quality care from the NHS – regardless of where they live in England and Wales'. Similar bodies exist elsewhere in the UK, including the Scottish Intercollegiate Guidelines Network (SIGN) and Healthcare Improvement Scotland (HIS).

The quality agenda is, of course, much more complex when ethical, legitimate and social factors are also taken into account. Donabedian goes on to discuss these issues in his book. A typical example might include preventing deaths from pneumonia by instigating a mass vaccination programme that has significant economic impacts on other health or social care systems.

Healthcare costs: a brief history

Since the launch of the NHS on 5 July 1948, the cost of the NHS to the taxpayer has been a source of controversy – one that medical managers cannot avoid. It was always thought that the costs of healthcare would drop (or at least, would not rise) as the health of the nation improved, thanks in part to the NHS. But this has never proved to be the case. Indeed, in its first year the NHS is purported to have over-spent its £140 million budget by over £130 million. The £276 million spent in 1948–49 (equivalent to over £7 billion in 2007–08 prices) represented 2.3 per cent of gross domestic product (GDP) at the time.[4] There was a 57.9 per cent increase in expenditure in 1949–50, increasing the percentage of GDP to 3.5 per cent. According to the Office of Health Economics (OHE) estimates for 2010–11, this has gone on rising since, reaching approximately 9.16 per cent of GDP in England by 2009–10. This equates to a combined figure of £2,024 per capita in England, compared with £1,977 in Wales, £2,226 in Scotland and £2,008 in Northern Ireland (figures adjusted by the GDP deflator at market prices) and £4,690 per household, compared with £4,503 in Wales, £4879 in Scotland and £5075 in Northern Ireland.

The cost of the NHS across the UK has escalated to well in excess of £100 billion (£89.9 billion for England 2009–10)[5] but has been capped at £114.4 billion in 2014–15 (see the *Spending Review 2010*: departmental expenditure limits[6]). To put this into perspective, this *Spending Review* also shows that the total expenditure on health (which includes a number of other areas over and above the expenditure on the NHS) exceeds the government's revenue from income tax (see Fig. 1.2).

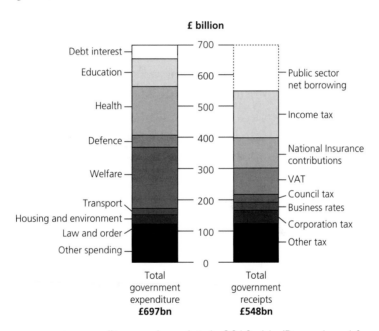

Figure 1.2 Total government expenditure and receipts in 2010–11. (Reproduced from the *Spending Review 2010*[6].)

With the NHS budget capped at this level, commentators equate this to requiring £20 billion in efficiency savings between 2010–11 and 2014–15, equivalent to a 0.5 per cent budget cut in real terms.[7] In the same article, Timmins goes on to argue that the squeeze on finances is greater and longer than any faced by the NHS since the 1950s, and at the same time the numbers of elderly and vulnerable are rising at rates never seen before.

Over 80 per cent of the NHS budget currently goes towards commissioning of services from acute NHS hospital and mental health trusts as well as primary and community care. Therefore, because every time a GP makes a referral or writes a prescription significant resources are spent, it could be argued that the most expensive piece of equipment in the NHS is the GP's pen!

For this reason, *Good Medical Practice*[8] (General Medical Council) places a responsibility on all doctors to utilize resources appropriately, stating that 'in providing good care you must…make good use of the resources available to you'. As a result, GPs, in conjunction with other clinicians, have been given increasing responsibility for commissioning of services for those living within their locality.

It is essential, therefore, that medical managers have some understanding of the financial flows and pressures within their own organizations and within the NHS as a whole, in order to understand the necessity for the constant drive for efficiency through reform. This chapter necessarily skims the surface of the finances of the NHS to develop the arguments; there are more details in Chapter 12.

Healthcare politics

Drivers for change

Some of the drivers for healthcare reforms have already been highlighted, namely:

- the necessity to improve quality and outcomes for patients
- the constant drive to improve efficiency
- a drive to increase productivity (in relation to healthcare, a term rarely defined by those who use it).

Of course, the overall list of drivers is much longer, and includes:

- the rapidly increasing expectations placed upon the NHS by the users of the service
- an inexorable increase in demand (felt by healthcare systems across the world, by no means unique to the UK), fuelled by better-informed patients
- ongoing research and development resulting in an ever-increasing number of highly expensive investigative procedures and treatments
- a demand for medical solutions to social problems
- unacceptable inequalities in health outcomes and life expectancy, both geographically and across social classes
- improvements in social and economic factors in the developed world leading to different health challenges, such as obesity and increased alcohol intake
- an ageing, and therefore more vulnerable, population, with more long-term chronic conditions that can be better controlled by more effective interventions – this is, I propose, the strongest pressure on social and healthcare systems at this time.

This list is by no means exhaustive, and I am sure that the reader will be able to add many more. While most of these are pressing drivers for change now, many remain unchanged since the inception of the NHS in 1948. This chapter, however, considers some of the answers to these pressures proposed by politicians since the mid-1980s and compares the solutions implemented by the governments of the day with the recent proposals for reform.

The prelude to the NHS reforms during the 1990s

A number of significant problems faced the NHS during the 1980s. These included increasing waiting lists and times, ward closures, staff shortages and serious difficulties admitting emergency patients, particularly during the winter months when stresses upon acute hospital wards were at their highest.

There was also perceived to be an unacceptably high variation in performance and outcomes for patients not only in different areas across the country but also between neighbouring hospitals. Further, there were no incentives for doctors to control their own working patterns or to modify clinical behaviour; the dominance of hospitals over GPs and their patients went unchallenged.

Margaret Thatcher also believed that lowering public expenditure and taxes produced a healthier economy, resulting in a cut in real terms in NHS funding. NHS staff believed that the NHS was suffering significantly from insufficient resources and, as a result, became more and more dissatisfied, leading to a staffing crisis over the winter of 1987. In this way, exacerbated by increasing demands, the NHS was heading for disaster.

To compound the pressures on government to act, the media publicized more and more shortcomings in the health service, including the case of a child in Birmingham who had life-saving surgery cancelled due to a lack of intensive care nurses. This resulted in the announcement of a wide-ranging review of the NHS to be carried out.

The 'internal market'

At the time, Thatcher's Conservative government held the strong belief that market forces and competition, as seen in industry, drove up quality and improved productivity – the weakest would and should fail – and that this would be the case in the public services too.

The results of this review were published in June 1989 in the white paper *Working for Patients*,[9] which was influenced by Professor Alain Enthoven, a visiting US economist, as well as two English economists, Professors Alan Maynard and Nick Bosanquet.

While maintaining the fundamental principles of the NHS, namely access to care based upon need, free at the point of contact, the white paper set out the following key proposals for the NHS:

- improvements in value for money
- rewards for higher efficiency and quality
- greater patient responsiveness
- the move towards a degree of independence from government control of hospitals by becoming 'NHS acute hospital trusts'.

Most importantly, however, the white paper made two further proposals that have underpinned government policy ever since:

- The function of purchasing should be separated from the provision of care – the 'purchaser/provider split'. It was proposed that health authorities would receive direct funding based upon a weighted capitation formula to purchase primary, community and secondary healthcare for their populations.
- The new NHS acute hospital trusts should compete to provide services, with competition based on efficiency and quality.

Thus the 'internal market' was formed. As it was possible for health authorities to purchase from private providers outside the NHS, and GPs had been providing services as independent contractors since 1948, some preferred to call it a 'quasi-market'. Dixon[10] also gives a much more comprehensive history of the political situation and the changes within the NHS than is given here.

GP fundholding

At the same time, it was recognized that in some of the most efficient industries – notably the Toyota car company in Japan – they had discovered that giving operational responsibility to 'shop-floor' workers resulted in better decisions (particularly regarding the purchase of components and raw materials). It was therefore felt that if those responsible for prescribing and referring patients to local trusts – namely GPs – took direct responsibility for their own budgets, they might be able to reduce referral rates and, consequently, hospital activity and costs. It was also felt that GPs were more likely to be able to influence hospitals to make changes in clinical activity.

With a degree of discretion within the white paper, *Working for Patients,* it was possible for some GP practices to volunteer to hold a devolved budget (directly sliced from health authority budgets) and purchase a number of services from local acute hospital trusts. Because implementation was piecemeal and hurried, evaluation was not put in place at the outset. However, it did show some early successes, thought to be helped by the fact that the scheme started with volunteer practices, which were given funding for the necessary management and administration, as well as incentives to reduce referral rates. Goodwin[11] undertook a full and comprehensive review of the literature. He also compared fundholding with other models of commissioning, including health authority purchasing, locality and GP commissioning, and total purchasing.

Some benefits of fundholding identified by Goodwin are as follows:

- Initially the rise in prescribing costs was lower in fundholding practices than in non-fundholders, although this was not sustained. This might have been because there was a lot more prescribing information available to practices, enabling discussion and debate between doctors about prescribing habits.
- Fundholders were able to procure more practice-based care and clinics run by consultants in the community.
- Providers were more responsive to the influence of fundholders.

However, he also identified that:

- there appeared to be no difference in the rate of increase in referrals of fundholders
- a two-tier system for patients to be able to access secondary care developed between the patients of fundholders and the patients of practices on whose behalf the health authorities purchased care.

Labour government changes

Within months of coming to power in 1997, the Labour government condemned the initiatives of the Conservative party, especially the internal market and fundholding, highlighting the increased bureaucracy created by the former and the two-tier service created by the latter. In a speech given on 9 December 1997, Tony Blair, the new Prime Minister, claimed that Labour would replace the internal market with 'integrated care' and put 'doctors and nurses in the driving seat' of the NHS. He committed the NHS to driving up quality standards by 'comparing not competing'.

The results were that fundholding was disbanded but replaced by primary care groups (PCGs). These were led by GPs and nurses with significant influence over commissioning of services undertaken by health authorities. They were also provided with information to be able to compare and influence local colleagues' performance in terms of prescribing and referral rates. By his second term in power, Blair renounced the policy to reduce competition, and instead he pursued policies to strengthen the market and increase the provision of services by private providers.

It is interesting to read in his autobiography, *A Journey*,[12] that Blair recognized that driving improvements in public services, including the NHS, through 'targets and piece-meal top-down reform, even with significant extra funding' was not delivering the changes he had hoped for. He 'wondered … whether it had been right to dismantle wholesale GP commissioning in the NHS.'

As PCGs grew and merged, taking over the statutory responsibilities for commissioning from health authorities and becoming trusts in their own right (primary care trusts, PCTs), GPs lost their influence on commissioning. So in order to regain their engagement, practice-based commissioning (PBC) was proposed in guidance published by the Department of Health (DoH) in December 2004.[13]

Practice-based commissioning

Following the guidance, PBC groups, primarily run by GPs, were set up across the country. While these groups took on variable levels of responsibility for commissioning of services with differing degrees of engagement from GPs, PCTs retained the statutory responsibility for commissioning. Groups were monitored and results of the monitoring have been published.[14]

Underpinning the argument that GPs should be at the forefront of commissioning, some well-documented successes were achieved by PBC groups, as shown by the following three examples:

- In Cumbria, in order to address a severe financial deficit, the PBCs set up a range of community-based services. Working in six consortia of GP practices, covering a total population of 500 000 people, they capitalized on community hospitals, and utilized GPs with specialist interests and consultants working in the community to reduce the workload of the two local acute trusts by reducing patient admissions and achieving earlier discharges, thereby achieving significant savings.
- The Torbay Integrated Care project, running since 2005, was aimed at those aged 65 and over – some 33 000 people – living in the area. Once again, it lowered admission rates, lengths of stay, overnight bed occupancy rates for urgent care, and increased same-day discharges. It has improved care for patients in the community by better integration of social care and healthcare and reduced secondary care dependency.
- Colchester PBC Group commissioned a wide range of integrated cost-effective, community-based services by building strong working relationships between PCT provider services, social services, secondary care, and private and voluntary sectors. The commissioners achieved the NHS Alliance Oak Award, 2009, for their achievements and innovation.

Performance management of general practice – the 2004 contract

It is also notable that just before the introduction of PBC, the government, through the NHS employers, negotiated with the General Practitioners Committee (GPC) of the British Medical Association (BMA) and agreed a new national General Medical Services (GMS) contract for GPs. Introduced in 2004 (known for many years afterwards as the 'new GMS contract', a name which, at the time of writing, remained in place), it was designed to enable better control of workload by GP practices but also to enable PCTs to tailor services to local needs: it heralded performance management of general practice for the first time.

The GMS contract is made up of four main components:

- *Essential services* – the only component of the contract that is obligatory for all GMS practices to undertake.

- *Additional services* – including services like contraceptive services and childhood surveillance that can be opted out of by practices.
- *Enhanced services* – these are optional services, some of which are nationally developed and offered to all practices (directed enhanced services, DES); others of which are developed nationally but PCTs choose whether to offer them to practices in their areas (national enhanced services, NES); and others that are negotiated locally between practices and PCTs (local enhanced services, LES).
- *Quality and Outcomes Framework (QOF)* – this is a points-based system for providing specific care to certain groups of patients with chronic diseases. By achieving certain high levels of care, shown by achieving outcome targets for disease management (e.g. achieving target blood pressure levels in hypertensive patients; acceptable blood sugar levels in diabetics (monitored by measuring HbA1C levels) and ensuring preventative measures are given to patients, such as flu vaccinations), points are awarded to a maximum level. Higher points are achieved for the more difficult targets to hit. Worth over £130 per point for the average-sized practice (dependent upon weighted list size), income streams from the QOF are dependent upon achievement. If the total number of points is achieved then QOF income represents nearly one-third of practice income. It could be argued that this represents, by far, the largest proportion of performance-related income in any public service. Research has shown significant improvements in outcomes for patients since 2004 in the disease areas covered by QOF.

One significant difference between the current contractual arrangements and those before 2004 is that the contract is between the practice (known as a 'provider') and the PCT, and not with individual GPs, as was the case before 2004. This means that patients are registered with a practice (not an individual doctor) and the provider has much more freedom in terms of the staffing levels necessary and how the services are delivered.

Most of the remaining GP practices not working under the national GMS contract work under a contract negotiated locally with the PCT. This contract is known as a personal medical services (PMS) contract, and was introduced in 1998. It has many of the elements of the GMS contract, including QOF, but has other areas specifically tailored to local need.

Equity and excellence: liberating the NHS

Within 2 months of the Conservative–Liberal Democrat coalition taking power after the general election of 2010, the Secretary of State for Health, Andrew Lansley, published a white paper entitled *Equity and Excellence: Liberating the NHS*[15] (followed by a number of subsequent publications embellishing parts of the white paper), which set out the aims and aspirations for the NHS in England and proposed wide-ranging reforms of the whole NHS management structure. It proposed the removal of the 10 strategic health authorities (SHAs) and the 151 PCTs to be replaced by a single national NHS Commissioning Board and GP commissioning consortia made up of local GP practices. Recognizing the benefits achieved under fundholding and, more recently, by PBC, the white paper proposed that the statutory responsibilities for ensuring appropriate services are purchased for local people from a variety of providers, should be placed firmly upon the shoulders of GPs (along with the statutory, financial and governance responsibilities). Under the proposals, commissioning of primary care would not be undertaken by consortia but by the NHS Commissioning Board.

The proposals have been described as the most momentous changes to the NHS in England since its introduction in 1948 (probably costing, in the end, at least £2 billion). Even Sir David Nicholson, the NHS Chief Executive at the time, described the reform as the largest health system management change in the world – so large 'that you can actually see it from space'. Meanwhile, the *British Medical Journal* described it as 'Dr Lansley's Monster', suggesting it was 'too soon to let it out of the lab'.[16]

In addition to the abolition of SHAs and PCTs to be replaced by the NHS Commissioning Board and GP consortia, the key aims set out in the white paper were as follows:

- Patients should be at the centre of decision-making – 'No decision about me without me'.
- All practices would have to be engaged at some level in the commissioning processes.
- There were to be no restrictions on size and geographical area covered by consortia.
- Competition between providers would prevail and be strengthened, enhancing the role of the private sector and what at the time was known as 'any willing provider' in healthcare provision.
- Competition would enhance patient choice.
- Monitor, one of two regulatory bodies, would promote and ensure competition.
- The second regulatory body, the Care Quality Commission (CQC), would be responsible for licensing all healthcare providers and monitoring the quality of services.
- The setting up of local bodies of service users and carers, called HealthWatch, would advise commissioning consortia.
- There would be a 45 per cent reduction in expenditure on management.
- Health and well-being boards (HWBs) would be set up by local authorities to hold commissioners to account within their areas.

The Health and Social Care Bill 2011 was brought before parliament in January 2011 but came under such severe criticism from MPs on both sides of the House, as well as from other commentators, such as the Royal Colleges and the BMA, that there was a review of the proposals and a further period of consultation by an independent advisory panel, led by Professor Steve Field, called the 'Future Forum' between April and June 2011. Known as the 'listening exercise', a summary of the report is available on the DoH's website.[17]

Summary of changes to the Health and Social Care Bill 2011 following recommendations by the Future Forum

As this chapter is being written, the Health and Social Care Bill is still on its passage through parliament before becoming law and we await further amendments (therefore, this part is mainly written in the present and future tenses). Even the nomenclature has changed – commissioning groups, for example, are no longer called 'GP commissioning consortia' and are now known as 'clinical commissioning groups' (CCGs), because of the wider involvement of nurses, hospital consultants and other professionals. However, unless there is a complete U-turn and the Bill is abandoned, it is unlikely that the principles, as summarized here, will be significantly changed in the final Act.

Key principles

Vitally, the Secretary of State for Public Health retains the responsibility for promoting the NHS and is accountable for securing the provision of healthcare services, as has been the case since the NHS Act of 1946, to be achieved by holding the NHS Commissioning Board to account.

With strengthened emphasis on governance arrangements, the amendments go some way towards addressing concerns expressed about possible emerging conflicts of interest. Two examples are potential conflicts arising as a result of GPs commissioning services from organizations in which they have financial interests, and proposed 'quality premium' payments being seen to be paid to consortia and passed on to GPs for reducing referrals to the secondary sector, thereby undermining that vital trust placed in doctors by their patients.

While the aim is still to have CCGs set up and ready to take over the statutory responsibilities of PCTs by April 2013, they will have to be authorized, and therefore capable and willing, to do so. This will slow down the timetable slightly, which currently looks like the Grand National with just as many potentially lethal hurdles to be jumped.

1. Patient, service user and carer involvement with public accountability

The rights of patients, as set out in the NHS Constitution,[18] are embedded within the Bill. Therefore, patient, public and carer involvement runs throughout the proposals – 'no decision about me without me':

- CCGs are to have two lay representatives on their governing board, overseeing patient, public and carer involvement and ensuring transparent governance.
- Local HealthWatch (originally known as Local Involvement Networks, LINks) must include representation from different user groups.
- HWBs have a duty to involve service users and the public.
- Monitor will have duties to ensure public and patient involvement at all levels.
- Patient choice of provider remains paramount.

2. Clinical Commissioning Groups

- The CCGs will gain statutory responsibility for the commissioning of services for patients and take on full budgetary responsibility.
- As well as two lay representatives, CCG governing boards must contain a range of doctors, nurses and other health professionals, including consultants (with no conflicts of interest, i.e. not from local acute trusts).
- CCGs will have to seek the approval of HWBs as part of the establishment process.
- Generally their boundaries must be co-terminous with local authority boundaries unless a clear acceptable rationale can be demonstrated to the NHS Commissioning Board that this is not appropriate.

3. Emphasis on 'integration of care' and quality over competition

- There is a determination towards better integration of care, with the emphasis on wider clinical involvement through multi-professional CCG boards, through the formation of 'clinical senates' (offering clinical expertise to CCG boards) and through CCG and local authority boundaries being co-terminous. This will enable a more strategic approach to children's services, including safeguarding children, as well as health and social services for vulnerable adults.
- Public health specialists, strengthened clinical networks and experts in adult and child social care will be fully involved in commissioning.
- HWBs will have a role in promoting joint commissioning.
- While the promotion of competition for provision of all public services remains a cornerstone policy within the response to the Future Forum recommendations, the emphasis upon competition is now on quality and improvement of patient services, not to drive the market economy.
- The regulator, Monitor, will protect and promote patients' interests and support integration of services rather than promote competition and privatization for the sake of it.

- Tariffs for integrated care pathways will be developed and single health and social care budgets promoted.
- 'Any willing provider' becomes 'any qualified provider' (AQC) with CQC ensuring licensed providers maintain high-quality services.

4. Transparency, openness through strong governance

- Governance rules have been significantly tightened up. One of the lay members on the governing board is to oversee the key elements of governance to ensure transparency and accountability and to ensure adverse conflicts of interest are averted.
- The boards are to hold open, minuted meetings and the CCG is to publish details of contracts with provider organizations.
- CCGs will not only have to achieve authorization from the NHS Commissioning Board, but will remain accountable to it.

5. HWBs and health improvement

- Local authorities are to have greater influence over commissioning of healthcare through HWBs, which are currently being set up. They will take on responsibilities for health improvement, promotion of strategic working between health and social care and alignment of commissioning in these areas. They must engage with patients and service users.
- HWBs will have powers to scrutinize major commissioning decisions and refer them to the NHS Commissioning Board if deemed necessary. Meanwhile, local authorities will still be able to challenge service reconfiguration through existing, statutory scrutiny functions.
- CCGs will be expected to align commission plans with the intentions of the HWBs.
- Local authorities will hold the responsibility for public health functions.
- Meanwhile Public Health England will be set up as an independent but executive agency within the DoH, advising on health protection and emergency planning.

Conclusion

In response to solving the financial difficulties of the NHS and attempting to improve outcomes and reduce inequalities in healthcare, successive governments have continued to develop policies which promote market-style competition and encourage those closest to patients, namely GPs and other professional colleagues, to take responsibility for commissioning of services from a plurality of NHS, private and voluntary providers.

The latest massive reorganization in England (which is still unfolding at the time of writing), described by Haines as looking 'like a (highly complex) solution in search of a problem',[19] is on the back of the worst global economic crisis since 1945, with the NHS facing financial constraints the like of which have not been seen since the 1950s, and requiring £20 billion in productivity improvements overall.

Whether one approves or not of fundamental reforms to the NHS on a scale of this size, what is absolutely clear is that there has never been a greater need for robust clinical leadership to deliver the reforms in a way that achieves improvements in services for patients and ensures they are not forgotten during the inevitable chaos that will ensue. The focus must not just be on new management structures – a further 'shifting of the deckchairs on the Titanic' – but must remain on improved outcomes for patients.

Summary

❏ Among a host of pressures for change in the NHS, this chapter describes the two key drivers that have led to major management reorganizations since 1990: the drive for improved quality, and the drive for better efficiency and cost-effectiveness in a system that costs more to the Treasury than it receives from income tax.

❏ The quality driver poses a serious dilemma to doctors in management roles, who find themselves caught between clinical colleagues, who want the very best available care for individual patients, irrespective of cost ('maximally effective care'), and organizational managers, who want the best outcomes for the maximum number of patients within a tight cost envelope ('optimally effective care').

❏ The media has reported on countless situations where quality of care in the NHS has been woefully inadequate, placing untold pressure on politicians to respond, but high-quality care is very costly.

❏ The financial dilemmas faced by the NHS have existed since 1948 but have become particularly acute during a global recession. This chapter highlights why successive Secretaries of State for Health have believed that those closest to the patient, namely clinicians (and in particular GPs), are considered to be essential in making commissioning decisions to help achieve maximum efficiency in the NHS.

❏ These two compelling drivers have resulted in the latest reorganization of the NHS in England, which has seen an £80 billion commissioning budget handed over to GPs and other clinicians working in CCGs. Meanwhile, local authorities are forming HWBs to influence the commissioning decisions made by CCGs. The aim is to improve efficiency and increase community-based care by developing care pathways and integrating services (particularly for those with long-standing chronic illness) and achieving better outcomes for patients.

References

1. Donabedian A (2003). *An Introduction to Quality Assurance in Health Care*. New York: Oxford University Press.

2. Appleby J, Devlin NJ (2004). Measuring success in the NHS: using patient-assessed health outcomes to manage the performance of health care providers. London: King's Fund/Dr Foster.

3. Appleby J (2009). *PROMs: Counting What Matters Most to Patients*. London: The King's Fund. Available from: http://www.kingsfund.org.uk

4. Harker R (Social and General Statistics) (2011). *NHS Funding and Expenditure* SN/SG/724. Available from: http://www.nhshistory.com/parlymoneypapter.pdf. Accessed: March 2012.

5. Appleby J (2011). What's happening to NHS spending across the UK? *Br Med J* 342, d2982.

6. The Treasury (2010). *Spending Review 2010*. London: TSO. Available from: http://www.hm-treasury.gov.uk

7. Timmins N (2010). Where do the cuts leave the NHS? *Br Med J* 341, c6024.

8. General Medical Council. *Good Medical Practice*. Available from: http://www.gmc-uk.org

9. Department of Health. *Working for Patients.* White paper. London: HMSO.

10. Dixon J (1998). 1 The Context. In: Le Grand J, Mays N, Mulligan J-A (eds). *Learning from the NHS Internal Market; A review of the Evidence.* London: King's Fund.

11. Goodwin N (1998). 4 GP fundholding. In: Le Grand J, Mays N, Mulligan J-A (eds). *Learning from the NHS Internal Market; A Review of the Evidence.* London: King's Fund.

12. Blair T (2010). *A Journey.* London: Hutchinson.

13. Department of Health (2004). *Practice Based Commissioning: Promoting Clinical Engagement.* London: DoH. Available from: http://www.dh.gov.uk/

14. Department of Health (2010). *Practice Based Commissioning Group and Independent Leads Survey: Wave 3.* London: DoH. Available from: http://www.dh.gov.uk/

15. Department of Health (2010). *Equity and Excellence: Liberating the NHS.* London: DoH. Available from: http://www.dh.gov.uk/

16. Delamothe T, Godlee F (2011). Dr Lansley's Monster – Too soon to let it out of the lab. *Br Med J* 342, 237–8.

17. Field S (chairman) (2011). *NHS Future Forum; Summary Report on Proposed Changes to the NHS.* Available from: http://www.dh.gov.uk/

18. Department of Health (2010). *The Handbook to the NHS Constitution.* London: DoH.

19. Haines A (2011). NHS rethink: charade or cause for new hope? *Br Med J* 342, d3995.

Chapter 2

Quality and safety

Elizabeth J Haxby

- Introduction
- Roles and responsibilities of the medical manager
- Staying informed as a medical manager
- Clinical risk management
- Developing quality improvement capacity and capability
- Engaging clinicians
- Summary
- References

Introduction

The NHS was established to provide healthcare for those who need it, free at the point of delivery and funded by taxation. No formal quality agenda existed until 1983 when the Griffiths report noted a lack of accountability for quality at the local level and subsequently clinical staff were drawn into management teams with responsibility for service quality. *The New NHS, Modern, Dependable,*[1] published in 1997, was the first government white paper to address issues of quality and effectiveness and announced the establishment of two organizations:

- the National Institute for Clinical Excellence (NICE) (now the National Institute for Health and Clinical Excellence) to develop and publish national evidence-based guidelines applicable across the NHS
- the Commission for Healthcare Improvement (the Care Quality Commission since 2009) to ensure the NHS maintained high-quality, safe healthcare.

In 1998 *A First Class Service: Quality in the NHS*[2] set out a strategy to create a 'modern health service that delivers high quality care for all'. The core concept of clinical governance was introduced to ensure high standards were achieved and the NHS would be 'more open and truly accountable to the public':[3]

> *Clinical governance is a framework through which NHS organisations are accountable for continually improving the quality of their services and safeguarding high standards of care by creating an environment in which excellence in clinical care will flourish.*

The following year, 1999, saw the publication of *Clinical Governance in the New NHS,*[4] which provided guidance on implementation and required the development of systems to oversee the integration of clinical governance principles into healthcare. Alongside this, *Supporting Doctors, Protecting Patients* provided proposals for professional regulation.[5]

Three significant events have resulted in major changes to professional regulation and healthcare risk management systems and practice:

- 1999 – *The Royal Liverpool Children's Enquiry* investigated retention and disposal of human organs and tissue removed postmortem.[6] Recommendations related to improving the consent process, better communication with parents and ensuring robust systems for postmortem activity were in place.

- 2001 – *The Bristol Royal Infirmary Inquiry* into paediatric cardiac surgery services highlighted failures due to poor leadership, lack of teamwork and an environment which lacked transparency and openness.[7] Recommendations identified the need for a change in culture to ensure lessons are learned and suggested fundamental changes to the monitoring of healthcare outcomes.
- 2006 – *Good Doctors, Safer Patients* was published following the Shipman Inquiry with the aim of promoting and assuring good medical practice through appraisal and revalidation of doctors.[8]

These events highlighted that patients are often harmed by the healthcare system and that many incidents and some deaths could be avoided through implementation of consistent, reliable, evidence-based healthcare along with an understanding of human factors such as leadership, teamwork and communication. *An Organisation with a Memory* was the output of an expert working group brought together by the CMO to discuss errors and harm in the NHS and how it could learn from what had gone wrong and implement safer systems of care.[9] Data from epidemiological studies across the world support the contention that approximately 1 in 10 in-patients in NHS hospitals will suffer some sort of adverse event contributing to harm or death. Following this report the National Reporting and Learning System (NRLS) was established to monitor all incidents reported within the NHS, identify themes and publish safety alerts so that steps could be taken within NHS organizations to ensure patient safety, such as keeping concentrated potassium solutions in locked cupboards to prevent inadvertent administration.

In 2008 following consultation with over 2000 healthcare professionals Lord Darzi published *High Quality Care for All; NHS Next Stage Review Final Report*,[10] in which he recommended improvements to the NHS to ensure high-quality care, including greater patient choice with guaranteed access to the most clinically effective and cost-effective drugs and treatments. He stated: 'To ensure quality is at the heart of the NHS there needs to be an emphasis on patient safety and published data on the quality of care.' New assessment processes were to be implemented, focusing on:

- quality of care
- safety
- patient experience.

Each healthcare organization is required to publish an annual 'quality account' with a range of indicators agreed locally with commissioners and nationally with the Care Quality Commission.[11] All NHS and social care providers are required to be registered with the regulator in order to provide services and must demonstrate compliance with designated standards. In addition to this, commissioners now make a proportion of providers' income conditional on quality of service provision and innovation through the Commissioning for Quality and Innovation Framework (CQUIN), which requires a demonstration that national, regional and local goals, which are changed annually, have been met before payment is made.[12] The introduction of 'never events',[13] events that may result in patient harm or death and for which commissioners would withhold funding, has intensified the focus on ensuring that robust systems and processes are in place to ensure safe care for all patients whatever their interaction with healthcare services and whenever it occurs (see Box 2.1).

The NHS is currently undergoing radical change and reform following the publication of *Equity and Excellence; Liberating the NHS*,[14] which sets out how the NHS will:

- put patients at the heart of the system
- focus on continuously improving things that really matter to patients – the outcome of their healthcare
- empower and liberate clinicians to innovate, with freedom to focus on improving healthcare services.

> **Box 2.1** List of never events[13]
>
> 1 Wrong site surgery
> 2 Wrong implant/prosthesis
> 3 Retained foreign object post-operation
> 4 Wrongly prepared high-risk injectable medication
> 5 Maladministration of potassium-containing solutions
> 6 Wrong route administration of chemotherapy
> 7 Wrong route administration of oral/enteral treatment
> 8 Intravenous administration of epidural medication
> 9 Maladministration of insulin
> 10 Overdose of midazolam during conscious sedation
> 11 Opioid overdose of an opioid-naïve patient
> 12 Inappropriate administration of daily oral methotrexate
> 13 Suicide using non-collapsible rails
> 14 Escape of a transferred prisoner
> 15 Falls from unrestricted windows
> 16 Entrapment in bedrails
> 17 Transfusion of ABO-incompatible blood components
> 18 Transplantation of ABO or HLA-incompatible organs
> 19 Misplaced naso- or oro-gastric tubes
> 20 Wrong gas administered
> 21 Failure to monitor and respond to oxygen saturation
> 22 Air embolism
> 23 Misidentification of patients
> 24 Severe scalding of patients
> 25 Maternal death due to postpartum haemorrhage after elective Caesarean section

Allocation of healthcare funding and commissioning will sit with GP commissioning groups, which will decide what services to purchase from providers. The pressure on providers to demonstrate delivery of high-quality and cost-effective care has never been greater. Managed appropriately, this should mean more choice, better access and safer care for patients for whom quality means listening to their concerns and involving them in decisions about their care and treatment, all of which contributes to the achievement of a better outcome.

The role of the medical manager in quality and safety

There are five key attributes that medical managers must develop and acquire in their quality and safety leadership role:

- They must have complete clarity about their role and responsibilities within the organization.
- They must be informed and knowledgeable about quality and safety issues – local, national and international.
- They must be involved in all aspects of clinical risk management in its broadest sense.
- They must develop capacity and capability to manage and supervise quality improvement initiatives at both a personal and an organizational level.
- They must engage clinicians and other healthcare professionals within their organization.

These will be considered in turn in the following sections.

Roles and responsibilities of the medical manager

There are many roles that clinicians can hold in relation to quality and safety within their practice and organizations. From a professional standpoint the General Medical Council (GMC) clearly sets out expectations that doctors are required to meet in their day-to-day interactions with patients and their duties to employers,[15] including taking part in systems of quality assurance and quality improvement. In addition the GMC has published guidance for medical managers[16] emphasizing the knowledge, skills, attitudes and competence required, including understanding of the following:

- the main clinical and other issues relevant to those they manage, including the nature of clinical and other risks
- the roles and policies of local agencies involved in healthcare
- the needs of patients, carers and colleagues and the culture of the organizations in which they work
- the structure and lines of accountability in the organization in which they work.

All of these are vital when taking on a managerial role with responsibility for quality and safety. Quality and safety may become part of the medical manager's remit if they are a clinical or divisional director, but it is increasingly common for clinicians to take on roles specific to patient safety, quality improvement or transformation. In many cases this will be as an associate medical director or similar.

It is essential to understand the organizational structure and, in particular, the committee structure through which the local and national quality and safety agenda will be implemented and monitored. In addition, it is important to establish who is responsible for patient safety and quality of care at board level; there should be a nominated executive and a non-executive director with direct accountability for patient safety. Each organization will have a set of strategic aims, the achievement of which sets the direction for all activity within it. For quality and safety to be seen as a priority, both must be included as one of the strategic aims with a clear plan setting out how they will be delivered and how assurance will be provided that care is safe and of a high quality. Direct clinician engagement in the development of a quality and safety plan or strategy is fundamental to success. Such a plan should clearly articulate what the national and local priorities are, how they will be delivered and monitored and who is responsible for implementation and within what timescale. Regular review at an appropriate committee with summary reports to the board should be routine.

Chairing and attending meetings of committees and groups with a remit for safety and quality will undoubtedly feature somewhere in the job description and this requires skill, political awareness and good time management. It is important to ensure there is suitable administrative support and that any terms of reference are reviewed and renewed on a regular basis to ensure the group is achieving what is required. Membership of the committee should reflect the nature of the work, and appropriate representation of relevant staff groups and patients, where possible, is important. Reporting lines must be clear, and if minutes or reports are to be submitted up to a higher level, it goes without saying that they must be accurate, relevant and succinct, highlighting the key points to be communicated. While everyone subscribes to the importance of quality and safety, evidence supporting a particular view or approach should be sought and referred to when necessary.

> **Key points**
>
> **Roles and responsibilities**
> - Clarify the level of responsibility for quality and safety within your role.
> - Contribute to the development of the quality and safety strategy in your organization.
> - Link up with the corporate team which deals with performance and clinical governance and identify the committee structure and pathway for quality- and safety-related initiatives, policies and monitoring.
> - Ensure any committees you attend or chair have clear terms of reference and lines of reporting.
> - Engage with executive and non-executive directors who are accountable for safety and quality at board level.

Staying informed as a medical manager

It is a feature of many medical managerial posts that most learning takes place whilst doing the job. Some managerial skills will have been acquired through attendance at management courses or, in some cases, via the acquisition of an MBA or equivalent. However, the medical manager with a responsibility for quality and safety must be well informed and knowledgeable about the subject. There are numerous books and increasing numbers of courses, but, more important than these, medical managers must familiarize themselves with relevant Department of Health (DoH) publications such as *An Organisation with a Memory*[9] and *Safety First*.[17] An understanding of the quality and safety standards and requirements of organizations such as the Care Quality Commission, Monitor and the NHS Litigation Authority (NHSLA), to name but a few, will help to identify common themes and links, something that is invaluable when seeking an overview of the national quality agenda.

Publications and reports flood into healthcare organizations daily and include National Confidential Enquiry into Patient Outcome and Death (NCEPOD) reports, Central Alerting System (CAS) alerts, device advisories from the Medicines and Healthcare products Regulatory Agency (MHRA), Royal College guidelines, NICE guidance and notices from the chief medical officer. Depending on your role, it may fall within your remit to deal with, disseminate or take action on some or all of these. This should be done as systematically as possible using pre-defined pathways throughout the organization which are directed to the relevant individuals or teams.

The new approach to commissioning means there will be a lot more face-to-face interaction between purchasers and providers, traditionally a corporate activity. Medical managers with a quality and safety remit or clinicians briefed by them must be aware of and involved in discussions about CQUIN indicators and quality accounts, as well as any service reviews and inspections that pertain to clinical care. This is to ensure that unrealistic goals and time-frames are avoided and issues of importance to clinical teams are addressed and included as appropriate. Non-medical managers are keen to demonstrate compliance with all external standards and occasionally will be keen not to disclose evidence of less than optimal performance, when in fact this may be the very issue that needs to be highlighted and addressed.

While the general principles of patient safety are fairly simple to grasp, developing leadership skills, getting to grips with teamworking and human factors can be more challenging. Courses, meetings and seminars are available at both national and international levels and a number of organizations offer tailored training for individuals and groups which can be very beneficial. Specialist fellowships also exist. Being informed about quality and safety will improve managers' credibility and arm them with the knowledge required to drive forward the improvement agenda in their area. It is likely that as a lead managers will be relied upon to advise about training and development of other staff – medical and non-medical – and this requires a thoughtful approach linking in with established professional programmes.

Medical managers will be involved in a range of activities in which quality and safety feature, many of which are covered in other chapters, e.g. appraisal and revalidation, dealing with difficult colleagues and implementing evidence-based healthcare. The next section focuses on clinical risk management and patient safety. Effective systems for managing safety will bring clarity and direction to, and inform, subsequent quality improvement initiatives.

Clinical risk management

Clinical risk management is a fundamental part of any patient safety and quality strategy. There are five key elements:

- risk awareness
- risk identification
- risk assessment
- risk control
- risk review.

Risk awareness

Healthcare is complex with increasing numbers of interventions in older patients with multiple co-morbidities. An expanding array of medicines, more sophisticated imaging and advances in technology may mean that more treatments and therapies are available but they also add risk to the healthcare environment. An understanding of risk-prone situations and an ability to predict hazards and risks are vital in preventing safety incidents. An open and fair culture helps to promote safety, whereas a blame culture will encourage staff to hide their mistakes and not report when things go wrong.

Risk identification

Incident reporting

A range of terms, including adverse clinical events, medical errors and critical incidents, has been used to describe episodes when care has not gone as planned and a patient either has been at risk of harm or has actually been harmed as a result. The current accepted term is 'patient safety incident', which is defined as 'any unintended or unexpected incident which could have or did lead to harm to one or more persons'. This is a very broad definition and to assist reporters it may be helpful to provide 'trigger lists' of specific events which should be reported.

All incidents reported within NHS healthcare organizations are uploaded to the NRLS on a regular basis. Current estimates indicate that the NRLS receives upwards of one million incident reports per year – many are 'no harm' events but a significant number are events in which a patient was harmed or died as a result. The most commonly reported events are medication incidents, falls and complications of treatment. Each organization should have an incident reporting policy and a robust system for the reporting and management of events so that actions can be recorded and tracked. Training should be provided for staff in what and how to report, and clear lines of reporting should be established such that less severe events are investigated and managed within the relevant department or unit, while more serious incidents which contribute to a patient's death require a formalized approach which should be clearly set out in a serious incident policy.

A rise in major incidents or the occurrence of multiple low-harm events occurring in a particular unit or team should prompt a root causes analysis (RCA). This is aimed at establishing exactly what happened and why, the contributory factors (see Box 2.2) and what action or intervention could prevent recurrence, i.e. how the root cause could be dealt with effectively. A number of tools are available to assist the RCA process, but training and expertise are required to produce a useful result. The subsequent action plan should be overseen by a suitable group or committee to ensure that changes are implemented. Regular reports on incident numbers, type and severity should be communicated throughout the organization, along with details of any lessons learned and changes to practice.

Box 2.2 National Patient Safety Agency patient safety incident contributory factors (www.npsa.nhs.uk)

- Patient factors
    - Clinical condition
    - Social factors
    - Physical factors
    - Psychological/mental factors
    - Interpersonal relationships
- Individual (staff) factors
    - Physical issues
    - Psychological issues
    - Personality
    - Social/domestic issues
- Task factors
    - Guidelines/procedures
    - Protocols
    - Decision aids
    - Task design
- Communication factors
    - Verbal
    - Non-verbal
    - Written
    - Electronic
- Team factors
    - Role
    - Congruence
    - Leadership
    - Support
    - Cultural factors
- Education and training factors
    - Competence
    - Appropriateness

- Availability
- Accessibility
- Supervision
- Equipment and resources factors
  - Equipment supplies
  - Visual display
  - Integrity
  - Positioning
  - Usability
- Working condition factors
  - Environment
  - Design of physical environment
  - Administrative
  - Staffing
  - Time/workload
- Organizational/strategic factors
  - Organizational structure
  - Policy, standards, goals
  - Externally imported risks
  - Safety culture
  - Priorities

Feedback sessions are helpful to demonstrate that reports lead to change and also to inform staff about what has gone wrong in other areas. The emphasis on local reporting and management must be maintained to promote ownership of both problems and solutions.

Acute trigger tool

There is good evidence that voluntary incident reporting systems only 'pick up' approximately 5–10 per cent of all patient safety incidents. The acute trigger tool, which is the UK adaptation of the Institute for Healthcare Improvement (IHI) Global Trigger Tool,[18] is a tool for screening patient case notes on a regular basis. Using a paper-based proforma for a retrospective case note review, it adopts a system of triggers to identify possible harm events in randomly selected sets of case records. It focuses on harm events as opposed to adverse events and does not seek to determine preventability. Once a harm event is identified, the severity is assessed using a validated tool (the National Coordinating Council for Medication Error Reporting and Prevention index). This information can then be measured over time (producing a harm rate per 100 bed-days) and used to identify areas for further exploration and improvement within the hospital. Where particular issues are identified, e.g. hospital-acquired pneumonia, a group should be established to explore this in depth and address any remediable issues.

Mortality and morbidity meetings

All in-patient deaths should be reviewed in a suitable forum. Mortality meetings tend to be better established in the acute sector, particularly in surgical specialities, but should become routine for all multidisciplinary teams. They are an opportunity to identify areas of clinical risk and agree actions to address them with those directly involved in care delivery. However, managerial involvement, both medical and non-medical, is vital if service redesign or specific resources form part of an action plan. Discussions should be documented, along with a register of attendance, and identified risks should be entered in the relevant risk register (see the section 'Risk review' later in the chapter) for monitoring and management.

Complaints and claims

These are a rich source of information about areas of system failure and risk, and key lessons should be regularly reported across the organization. Rigid timescales apply to the management of and response to complaints and claims, which often require clinical expertise to ensure appropriate communication with complainants. Medical managers must be actively involved in shaping written responses and in direct meetings with families to ensure honest and open disclosure about what happened and what is being done to prevent further episodes.

Clinical audit

Effective clinical audit can reveal system defects and lack of compliance with relevant standards. In general, audit is poorly performed in NHS organizations due to failure to complete the audit cycle and demonstrate active changes to practice when weaknesses have been identified. Each unit/area should have an audit strategy which includes audits looking at national, organizational and local standards. The results should be reviewed at an appropriate group or committee, and action plans should be rigorously monitored.

Safety walkrounds

Quality and safety should be promoted across the organization, and executive patient safety leadership walkrounds (EPSW) are an opportunity for executives to meet with frontline staff in all departments, on a regular basis, to discuss safety issues particular to that environment, provide support in dealing with specific problems and also acknowledge the important role that staff providing direct patient care have in ensuring safety. Issues highlighted at an EPSW should be tracked and followed up to ensure agreed changes have occurred. This activity helps to link executives to units/teams and brings a sense of direct responsibility for the safety of that service.

NCEPOD/NICE including new interventional procedures

External reports often identify key areas of risk (e.g. NCEPOD and out-of-hours surgery) or set the standards for particular services or treatments, e.g. NICE technology appraisals, guidance and clinical guidelines. These will generally be regarded as 'best practice' and regulators and external reviewers will expect there to be a systematic process for the assessment of these publications, appropriate implementation or, where there is disagreement with the guidance, evidence that it has been considered and justification for the lack of compliance. Commissioners will question any treatment that is delivered outside of NICE recommendations and so clinicians must be aware of and up to date with any guidance that pertains to their practice. Managing the introduction of new interventional procedures is a very important patient safety issue and is covered elsewhere in this book.

Patient safety alerts/equipment advisories

Patient safety alerts/equipment advisories are sent directly via a single point: the Central Alerting System (CAS) liaison officer, who is an identified individual in each healthcare organization. The alerts come from the MHRA, the National Patient Safety Agency (NPSA), NHS estates and the like, and highlight safety concerns about devices, medicines, clinical practices, etc. Each alert must be assessed for relevance and acted upon as appropriate. This may require recall of equipment, notification of patients with particular devices (e.g. pacemakers), development of guidelines and protocols or training and competence assessment of staff. In each case, an action plan is required and the alert should be placed on the risk register until the risk has been removed or mitigated. Statements of compliance with alerts are held on a central website and organizational compliance with alerts is published regularly and is accessible to the public.

Risk assessment

Clinicians are very familiar with risk assessment of patients in their area of expertise, e.g. airway assessment for anaesthetists or suicide risk assessments in mental health. However, in many specialities, such risk assessment is rarely formally documented in a standardized way and remains within the realm of 'clinical expertise'. In relation to healthcare delivery, risk assessment needs a more formal approach in order to demonstrate that risks are identified, their severity is known and recorded, and treatment plans are in place to manage them. There are numerous matrices available to provide numerical scores for risks; usually a combination of likelihood and severity is used to produce a rating for each risk, which is then entered in a risk register. The rating allows ranking of risks, which informs business planning and investment so that appropriate treatments and controls can be developed. Although many risks are identified in retrospect, after an untoward event has occurred, each organization should have a programme of proactive risk assessment activity – that is to say, every area should undertake risk assessments across its area of activity, clinical, financial and reputational. In some specialist units, such as imaging, staff are well versed in risk assessment due to the stringent health and safety and Ionising Radiation (Medical Exposure) regulations, which require this. However, many areas will not have experience in risk assessment and so a programme of education, training and support will be necessary. A common risk assessment matrix is shown in Figure 2.1.[19] High rated/ranked risks should be regularly reported to the board so that they can prioritize and direct activity and funds appropriately.

Risk control

The purpose of risk identification and assessment is to ensure that appropriate controls and treatments are put in place to mitigate risks. Modern healthcare is a highly complex activity with multiple interactions between people and technologies on a daily basis. Removal of risk is rarely an option, but on occasion it is possible; for example, if multiple strengths of the same drug are in use and mis-selection is a risk with potentially adverse consequences then stocking only one strength will remove the risk of mis-selection for that particular drug. In general, the aim is to mitigate risks and reduce them to a tolerable level. Depending on the nature of the risk, there are a number of general strategies to controlling risk, some of which are more effective than others:

- Human action controls – checking drug dosages before administration, undertaking a team briefing before starting an operating list, using checklists to ensure all appropriate actions have been completed prior to transferring a patient.
- Administrative controls – policies, procedures and protocols, e.g. transfusion, consent, prescribing, standardization of care delivery through integrated care pathways.

Death	= 5	5	10	15	20	25
Severe	= 4	4	8	12	16	20
Moderate	= 3	3	6	9	12	15
Low	= 2	2	4	6	8	10
No harm	= 1	1	2	3	4	5
Severity		Rare = 1	Unlikely = 2	Possible = 3	Likely = 4	Certain = 5
		Likelihood				

Likelihood rating	Description
Almost certain	Will undoubtedly recur, possibly frequently
Likely	Will probably happen but is not a persistent issue
Possible	May occur occasionally
Unlikely	Do not expect it to happen but it is possible
Rare	Can't believe that this will ever happen

Severity	Description
Death	May result in death
Severe	May result in permanent harm
Moderate	May result in moderate increase in treatment and may cause significant but not permanent harm
Low	May require extra observation or minor treatment and cause minimal harm
No harm	Has the potential to cause harm

Figure 2.1 Risk assessment matrix (5 × 5). (Keele University/National Patient Safety Agency; based on risk matrix in *A Risk Matrix for Risk Managers*.[19])

- Physical controls – insulation on hot pipes, lead aprons in imaging departments, locked cupboards for controlled drugs/concentrated potassium.
- Natural controls (time, placement, location) – isolation of infected patients, separation in time of intravenous and intrathecal drug administration.

Before agreeing and implementing controls, it is important to find out if the control will work or if it will introduce a new level of risk. Regular review including audit of controls will help to identify if any system changes or new practices are having the required impact.

Risk review

All identified risks – clinical, financial and organizational – should be assessed and recorded in a central repository called a risk register. Each division, directorate or clinical area holds a local risk register which feeds into the main trust risk register. The risk register contains information on levels of risk, types of control, who is responsible and time-frames for action. New risks, which may be identified from various sources, including internal issues (e.g. incidents) and external reports, alerts or requirements, must be entered in the register in a systematic way. The risk register informs the board of the risk profile of the organization and should inform decision-making for business and financial planning so that investments in resources and services are directed at reducing risk and the board can assure itself that risks are under control.

Risks must be regularly reviewed to up- or downgrade them depending on the effectiveness of the controls or on new hazards which have been identified. Regulatory reviews are often orientated towards assessing compliance with established standards, but also towards how well an organization manages clinical, operational and financial risk and adopts best practice.

Key points

Clinical risk management

- Be familiar with relevant literature on patient safety and quality improvement and ensure you receive all relevant documents from external organizations.
- Be cognizant of the risk management process and how to identify and control sources of risk.
- Have an overview of all quality- and safety-related activities in your organization and understand the requirements of commissioners and regulators.

Developing quality improvement capacity and capability

Quality indicators

Every service, department or patient pathway should have a number of indicators which relate to the quality of that activity. For interventions such as surgery this is fairly simple, and indicators usually include mortality, selected morbidity/complications, length of stay, theatre utilization rates, etc. For non-interventional specialities such as heart failure or respiratory medicine, indicators may be more process-related, e.g. compliance rates with relevant NICE guidance, or outpatient department waiting times. In mental health a matrix of indicators is often used, covering measures of clinical effectiveness, patient experience and social functioning, while in general practice indicators might be related to referral rates for particular diagnoses.

The key to finding quality indicators is that they are useful to the team to which they relate, they are relatively easy to measure and changes will prompt a response to address whatever problem has been identified. Increasingly, commissioners are establishing quality indicators for services they purchase to facilitate benchmarking between providers. Indicators will also exist at an organizational level and are set externally, such as methicillin-resistant *Staphylococcus aureus* (MRSA) rates, 2-week cancer wait compliance and procedure cancellations. The suite of indicators used should reflect the breadth of operational activity and be regularly assessed for utility.

National indicators are commonly used to benchmark services and identify poorly performing organizations. Persistent poor performance will trigger an improvement notice or an inspection. Indicators should be reported to the board and disseminated across the organization so that everyone can see how they are performing.

Quality improvement

The medical manager may be more involved in planning quality and safety initiatives than in implementation. However, knowledge and skills are required to undertake formal quality improvement work. To identify what aspects of a service need to be improved, a clear understanding of what is going wrong or what is suboptimal is required. This information will be provided through an effective risk identification programme from both internal sources (e.g. patient safety incidents) and external sources (e.g. safety alerts, NCEPOD reports). Healthcare staff are keen to improve their services, provided:

- there are clear goals
- their views are acknowledged
- they are provided with training and support
- their needs are incorporated into the solution.

Quality improvement science is a relatively new discipline in its own right, but the basic principles feature in a number of familiar philosophies (e.g. lean, six-sigma, total quality management). They all require the application of basic principles:

- What are we trying to accomplish?
- How will we know if a change is an improvement?
- What changes can be made that will result in an improvement?

Clinicians find quality improvement techniques hard to grapple with due to the ingrained requirement for a randomized controlled trial to prove the efficacy of any intervention or treatment and their predilection for large audits which take many months and often only tell you what you already knew, i.e. that you are not meeting a particular standard. Using quality improvement techniques to make rapid change can be extremely rewarding and can persuade late adopters that things can be done differently. Often quality improvement involves asking the question, 'How can we do this here?' rather than 'How should this be done?' For instance, there is sufficient evidence to support the introduction of care bundles in a number of areas, particularly the perioperative period (surgical site infection care bundle) and critical care (ventilator-associated pneumonia care bundle).[20]

Taking the surgical site infection care bundle as an example (see Box 2.3), consistent and reliable delivery of all elements of the bundle have been shown to reduce surgical site infection rates, so the issue is not whether to introduce it but how to do so in a particular organization. Finding the right people and place to start is crucial, and if you aim to make it easy to do the right thing through multiple small tests of change then sustainable spread will follow. The key to success is to establish process (e.g. completion of the bundle) and outcome measures (e.g. surgical site infection rates) and to measure frequently, providing visual feedback to the staff involved so that they can assess their progress.

Box 2.3 Surgical site infection prevention care bundle

- Clip not shave
- 2% chlorhexidine skin preparation
- Antibiotics within 60 min of incision
- Maintain normothermia
- Maintain blood sugar in diabetics between 4 and 12 mmol/L

Staff involved in quality improvement activity will require training and support. Sharing experience and learning with other similar organizations can be beneficial, as can the setting up of local quality networks which have proved very successful in some parts of the UK.

Key points

Developing quality improvement

- Be involved in developing local quality indicators and negotiating indicators with commissioners
- Take part in service reviews, regulatory inspections and external assessments
- Build quality and safety training into your professional development programme and work out what you can contribute to building capacity and capability within your organization by training others

---

Engaging clinicians

Medical staff are intensely interested in and feel responsible for the quality of care they personally deliver, and focus their attention on that which they feel they can control. On occasion their priorities may not be completely aligned to those of the organization that employs them. For example, managers may wish to standardize a care pathway with the aim of delivering cost-effective care for a large group of patients, while clinicians want to deliver what they consider to be the best care for the group of patients they treat in their own particular way. This apparent conflict can result in tension such that clinicians feel that quality and safety are activities that are done to them rather than by them. However, there is no doubt that the most successful quality and safety initiatives and improvements are those that are led or driven by clinicians. In order to improve the quality and safety of healthcare for all patients, clinicians and managers must engage, listen and share by pooling resources and energy to meet their common goal – high-quality, safe care. In 2007 the IHI published a guide called *Engaging Physicians in a Shared Quality Agenda*,[21] which set out a framework comprising six elements, as follows:

- Discover common purpose – good outcomes for patients
- Reframe values and beliefs – develop a partnership and promote system and individual responsibility for quality and safety
- Segment the engagement plan – identify champions, educate and inform leaders, facilitate training and skill acquisition, work with cynics and laggards
- Use engaging improvement methods – standardize appropriately, use data intelligently, make it easy to do the right thing
- Show courage – support and encourage those trying to improve quality and safety
- Adopt an engaging style – involve clinicians from the start and make their involvement visible, value and respect their time, build trust and communicate candidly and frequently.

Thinking carefully about each of these elements when developing the quality and safety strategy will enhance the likelihood of success by ensuring clinicians feel:

- valued
- they have a voice
- their endeavours will be recognized.

Effective communication is key to maintaining confidence that change is for the right reasons and patients will benefit.

Summary

❏ The delivery of high-quality, cost-effective, safe healthcare is the priority for the NHS.

❏ All healthcare organizations should have a clinical governance strategy and a quality improvement programme developed by clinicians and approved by the board.

❏ Effective implementation of initiatives to improve the reliability and safety of healthcare is dependent on having clear aims, effective medical leadership and active engagement by clinical staff.

❏ Medical managers have a key role in improving quality and safety across the NHS, although most of their energy will be focused on engaging clinicians and establishing a culture of learning.

❏ Medical managers with responsibility for delivering the quality agenda must provide consistent and clear messages across the organization.

❏ It is important to demonstrate commitment by contributing to organizational systems and processes as well as being informed about the wider quality agenda.

❏ Establishing education and training programmes as well as internal and external networks to share progress and learning will help to spread sustainable change.

References

1. Department of Health (1997). *The New NHS: Modern, Dependable*. London: DoH. Available from: http://www.dh.gov.uk/

2. Department of Health (1998). *A First Class Service: Quality in the NHS*. London: DoH. Available from: http://www.dh.gov.uk/

3. Scally G, Donaldson LJ (1998). Clinical governance and the drive for quality improvement in the new NHS in England. *British Medical Journal* 317, 4.

4. Department of Health (1999) *Clinical Governance in the New NHS*. Available from: http://www.dh.gov.uk/

5. Department of Health (1999). *Supporting Doctors, Protecting Patients*. Available from: http://www.dh.gov.uk/

6. Redfern M (chairman), Keeling J, Powell E (2001). *The Royal Liverpool Children's Enquiry*. London: The Stationery Office. Available from: http://www.rlcinquiry.org.uk/download/index.htm. Accessed March 2012.

7. Bristol Royal Infirmary Inquiry (2001). *The Bristol Royal Infirmary Inquiry*. London: The Stationery Office. Available from: http://www.bristol-inquiry.org.uk/. Accessed: March 2012.

8. Department of Health (2006). *Good Doctors, Safer Patients*. London: DoH. Available from: http://www.dh.gov.uk/

9. Department of Health (2000). *An Organisation with a Memory*. London: DoH. Available from: http://www.dh.gov.uk/

10. Department of Health (2008). *High Quality Care for All; NHS Next Stage Review Final Report*. Available from: http://www.dh.gov.uk/

11. Department of Health (2012). *Quality Accounts.* Available from: http://www.dh.gov.uk/

12. Department of Health (2008). *Using the Commissioning for Quality and Innovation (CQUIN) Payment Framework.* Available from: http://www.institute.nhs.uk/commissioning/pct_portal/cquin.html http://www.dh.gov.uk/

13. Department of Health (2011). The 'never events' list for 2011/12. London: DoH. Available from: http://www.dh.gov.uk/

14. Department of Health (2010). *Equity and Excellence; Liberating the NHS.* White paper. London: DoH. Available from: http://www.dh.gov.uk/

15. General Medical Council (2006). *Good Medical Practice.* London: GMC. Available from: http://www.gmc-uk.org/

16. General Medical Council (2006). *Leadership and Management for all Doctors.* London: GMC. Available from: http://www.gmc-uk.org/

17. Department of Health (2006). *Safety First: A Report for Patients, Clinicians and Healthcare Managers.* London: DoH. Available from: http://www.dh.gov.uk/

18. Institute for Healthcare Improvement (IHI). IHI Global Trigger Tool for Measuring Adverse Events. Cambridge, MA: IHI. Available from: http://www.ihi.org/knowledge/Pages/

19. National Patient Safety Agency (2008). *A Risk Matrix for Risk Managers.* National Patient Safety Agency. Available from: http://www.nrls.npsa.nhs.uk/

20. Department of Health (2007). *Saving Lives: Reducing Infection, Delivering Clean and Safe Care 2007.* Available from: http://www.dh.gov.uk/

21. Reinertsen JL, Gosfield AG, Rupp W, Whittington JW (2007). *Engaging Physicians in a Shared Quality Agenda.* IHI Innovation series white paper. Cambridge, MA: Institute for Healthcare Improvement. Available from: http://www.ihi.org/knowledge/Pages

Chapter 3

Leadership styles and skills

James Matheson and Jacky Hayden

- Introduction
- The rise of clinical leadership
- Qualities of a leader
- Leadership styles
- Leadership skills
- Overcoming barriers to clinical leadership
- Summary
- References

Introduction

This chapter looks at leadership in today's NHS and the skills and knowledge required for leaders in the health service's exciting future. We examine what is understood by leadership qualities, both historically and scientifically, through a review of the literature, and their application to NHS roles. We discuss a selection of the many proposed leadership styles advocated for greater efficiency and better results and review their merits. We also look at the leadership skills required for work and, in the final section, 'Overcoming barriers to clinical leadership', we look at the real-life considerations, barriers and hazards to applying those skills in daily practice and discuss how to overcome them.

The rise of clinical leadership

The UK's National Health Service (NHS) was founded in 1948 with the guiding principles of providing healthcare to meet the needs of all, provided free at the point of delivery and based on clinical needs rather than the ability of the patient to pay. To meet this ambitious goal, the NHS has grown into an enormous organization, employing over 1.7 million people – the NHS website proudly claims that, throughout the whole world, only China's People's Liberation Army, the Indian Railways and Wal-Mart employ more. It is also diverse, fielding 400 000 nurses, 120 000 hospital doctors, 40 000 general practitioners as well as cleaners, porters, pharmacists, ambulance staff and many more, all critical to success in delivering quality healthcare and coming from all corners of the world.[1] And the NHS has been successful – spectacularly so – in improving life expectancy in the UK from 64 years for men and 68 for women in 1947[2] to 80 and 82 years, respectively, in 2007.[3]

Such an organizational colossus requires resources of some magnitude and even the 2009 NHS budget of over £100 billion failed to cover costs of staffing, drugs and equipment, infrastructure maintenance and training, education, research and development for the future. The demands on these resources are huge, with the NHS dealing with one million people every 36 hours – a staggering 463 people per minute.[1] Resource management and prioritization have always been of critical importance to achieving the NHS aims and never more so than now, as spiralling drug and equipment costs have raised financial pressures in a time of marked economic downturn. How the NHS manages its resources and directs its staff to achieve better quality care in the face of these challenges has become a major focus of strategic thinking, and much of the attention has fallen on the concept of clinical leadership.

In 1983 the Griffiths report sought to remedy 'the lack of a clearly-defined general management function throughout the NHS'[4] by introducing a structured general management framework to replace the previous arrangements. Prior to 1983 the NHS had been led by doctors, nurses and administrators taking responsibility for their individual areas of concern. Since this introduction a division has evolved between NHS clinicians providing patient care and management staff controlling the resources which provide the patient services. In some areas this division has become perceived as a dichotomy and has even developed into an enmity between two groups whose cooperation is essential to provide vital services for patients.

In his 2008 report *High Quality Care for All: NHS Next Stage Review*,[5] Lord Darzi sought to close this gap in the interests of improving the quality of care delivered by the NHS. He stated that, 'Clinicians are **expected** to offer leadership and, where they have appropriate skills, take senior leadership and management posts in research, education and service delivery'. The message was widely well received and was transformed into a call to action by many, including the General Medical Council:[6]

> It is not enough for a clinician to act as a practitioner in their own discipline. They must act as partners to their colleagues, accepting a shared accountability for the service provided to patients. They are also expected to offer leadership, and to work with others to change systems when it is necessary for the benefit of patients.

In 2008 the NHS Institute for Innovation and Improvement published the results of its collaboration with the Academy of Medical Royal Colleges, the collected UK medical and surgical college bodies, in *The Medical Leadership Competency Framework* (MLCF; see Fig. 3.1).[7] The framework was the culmination of a consultative process with patients and service providers, an extensive review of the evidence base and literature in healthcare leadership and an analysis of existing leadership frameworks, and provides the means by which leadership is introduced to clinicians from their student days, through clinical training and continuing into years of service.

Figure 3.1 The Medical Leadership Competency Framework.[7]

The framework specifies five principal domains of leadership – demonstrating personal qualities, working with others, managing services, improving services and setting direction – and details how each of these domains should be developed throughout a clinical career. It is a constituent part of the latest *NHS Leadership Framework*[8] and is now being incorporated into undergraduate education and postgraduate training programmes across the specialities.

In 2009, the National Leadership Council was established as a subcommittee of the NHS Management Board, to champion this new priority for leadership within the NHS, supporting the development of leaders and leadership in the organization and challenging where such development is lacking. The Council's priorities are reflected in its workstreams of developing clinical leadership, NHS board development, supporting top leaders, inclusion of all in leadership roles, and identifying and nurturing emerging leaders for future generations.

Leadership is certainly a high priority in the NHS's drive to improve quality in patient care and its nature is subject to much debate. Myriad definitions can be found of leadership (and, more specifically, clinical leadership) with heated arguments on what is included and what is left out. For practical purposes, in delivering NHS care, the definition below is a sound start:[9]

> The essence of clinical leadership is to motivate, to inspire, to promote the values of the NHS, to empower and to create a consistent focus on the needs of the patients being served. Leadership is necessary not just to maintain high standards of care but to transform services to achieve even higher levels of excellence.

Clinical leadership is emerging as a duty of clinicians at all levels and is an exciting opportunity for all who desire delivery of quality patient care. The aim of this chapter is to provide an overview of how that can be achieved.

Qualities of a leader

Think about what we mean by a leader. The word itself is emotive and when we think of it, a particular figure or stereotype springs immediately and unconsciously to mind. Sometimes that figure will be a well-known leader with a large media profile – a political leader or a celebrity CEO – whose successes in their fields are evident but who may be far removed from any leaders we work with in the NHS and who perhaps demonstrate qualities we would rather not see in the people to whom we report and in whom we entrust patient care.

The stereotyped 'qualities of a leader' and the caricatures conjured up by the term 'leader' are often very different from the qualities seen in successful leaders in the NHS. Among the top 20 images yielded by a Google search of the term 'leader', 19 were man-made stylized images of leadership and only one was a human being (Prime Minister David Cameron, in this picture emulating American President Barack Obama). The notion of the leader is often different from the reality. What, then, are the true qualities of a leader?

Unsurprisingly, this question has been extensively explored. Throughout history, stories have been recorded of those whose achievements in uniting nations, waging wars and defeating seemingly insurmountable challenges have rendered them worthy of the title 'great'. The term 'born leader' is often applied to such people and the notion of leaders being born with a pre-determined set of personality traits persists among some people to this day. Such leaders often demonstrate the 'alpha male' set of qualities: physical strength, fearlessness, extroversion and indomitable self-belief born of a less equitable age, where physical dangers were the greatest challenges. In our work, the physical dangers are generally fewer, but the challenges are often just as great.

Psychologists have, for many years, studied what makes up a person's character and have long sought to break down personality into its constituent parts. In the early 1960s Tupes and Christal[10] described the 'Big 5' personality traits – openness, conscientiousness, extroversion, agreeableness and neuroticism – as being the elements which, to greater or lesser extents, defined our personalities. Their theory gained popularity in the 1980s and has remained a mainstay of personality research since.

Openness to experience is said to encompass those people with an intellectual curiosity, who are receptive to the variety of life. Conscientiousness describes the attributes of the diligent, motivated by a strong sense of duty. Extroversion is a characteristic of those who enjoy the company of people and assert themselves within social groups and who generate and develop ideas through discussion. Agreeableness refers to the ability to get along with others and generally requires the ability to cooperate and demonstrate compassion and empathy to achieve this. Neuroticism, generally regarded as a negative personality trait, defines a susceptibility to stress, anger or low mood, but may include an ability to anticipate pitfalls.

Judge *et al.*[11] conducted a meta-analysis of these traits in leaders. They found significant, albeit weak, correlations with leadership success in the traits of extroversion, conscientiousness and openness to experience. Agreeableness scored very low and neuroticism demonstrated a marked negative correlation. Their leaders, it would seem, are open, conscientious extroverts, who are not always agreeable but certainly not prone to neurotic self-doubt.

For leaders within the NHS, certain personal qualities such as integrity are expected and are even described as competencies within the MLCF (NHS Institute for Innovation and Improvement,[7] p. 23):

Competent doctors:

- uphold personal and professional ethics and values, taking into account the values of the organization and respecting the culture, beliefs and abilities of individuals
- communicate effectively with individuals, appreciating their social, cultural, religious and ethnic backgrounds and their age, gender and abilities
- value, respect and promote equality and diversity
- take appropriate action if ethics and values are compromised.

This would rate the personality traits of conscientiousness and openness highly within the NHS framework.

These qualities were further explored in *The NHS Leadership Qualities Framework* (LQF).[12] The LQF website describes five personal qualities for the NHS leader:

- self-belief – described as the inner confidence to succeed and overcome obstacles to service improvement
- personal integrity – defined as a commitment to openness, honesty, inclusiveness and high standards
- self-management – managing your emotions in challenging circumstances
- drive for improvement – in terms of enhancing health service performance
- self-awareness – has to do with understanding one's own limitations and strengths.

The LQF's concept of leadership qualities differs from those based on 'the born leader' or personality trait theory in that it promotes a set of values that can be learned through a '5 Es' development plan, rather than being congenital characteristics one is lucky enough to be blessed with:

- *examine* – identifying your leadership development needs
- gaining *experience* in on-the-job activities
- receiving *exposure* to those from whom you may learn
- accessing relevant *education*
- and, finally, *evaluate* – assessing the effectiveness of what you have done.

The LQF is being superseded by *The NHS Leadership Framework*[8] (Fig. 3.2) but at the time of writing its website remains operational.

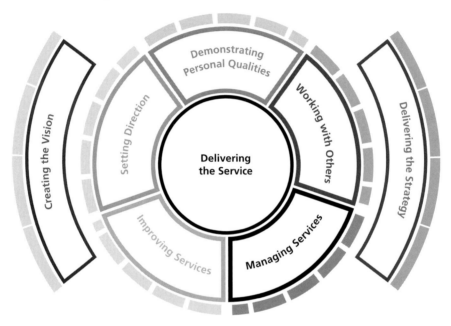

Figure 3.2 The NHS Leadership Framework.[8]

There is a desire in today's NHS to encourage leadership at all levels. For such an initiative to succeed, all team members need to be able to recognize in themselves their leadership qualities and be shown how to develop them and put them to use in improving health services. *The NHS Leadership Framework* provides a practical tool to that end.

Key points

Leadership qualities

- Research shows a correlation between successful business leadership and the character traits of extroversion, conscientiousness and openness to experience.
- Within the NHS, integrity and dedication to ethical practice are highlighted but, increasingly in the literature, leadership is promoted as a set of behaviours which can be adopted at all levels.

Leadership styles

Even more extensively explored than the characteristics of a leader is the question of what style of leadership is most likely to bring success. The idea of a leadership style as a set of behaviours that a person chooses to display further distances us from the notion that a leader is simply 'born' and reinforces the concept that successful leadership can be learned. We can all compare and contrast the behaviours of various people we know in leadership positions and see some striking differences. Some will speak as if their word is law, while others will make sure they take on board everyone's opinion before formulating a plan. Yet others will seem to take on a different leadership style each time we see them. The chances are that some of these behaviours will have been picked up from the extensive literature on leadership styles or from observing and emulating leaders around them. As whole papers, and even books, have been written on each theory, we can't hope to offer a comprehensive review within the confines of this chapter but, for illustrative and practical purposes, we will take a look at two of the principal theories of leadership styles and how to apply them.

Goleman leadership styles

Daniel Goleman, writing in the *Harvard Business Review*,[13] drew on the research of a consulting firm which had examined the leadership of 3871 executives. He described six styles of leadership:

- coercive
- authoritative
- affiliative
- democratic
- pacesetting
- coaching.

Goleman illustrates the *coercive* leadership style with an example of a CEO brought in to turn around a failing company who instigates a 'reign of terror', bullying and sacking his employees. He is eventually dismissed himself. Goleman suggests the coercive is the least successful style of leadership as it alienates the workforce, but adds that it may have its uses in extreme moments.

The *authoritative* leader, as described by Goleman, is a visionary who sees a clear goal for the organization and drives the team towards it. He or she motivates people by showing them how their work is important to achieve the organizational aims and gives feedback, positive or negative, according to how successful they are in reaching the team's goal. The leader's own enthusiasm is constant. This, says Goleman, is the most successful leadership style and can be applied in almost every situation. In some scenarios, however, such as when the team members are more experienced than the leader, the style may not be the most appropriate.

Affiliative leaders believe that people come first and adapt their style accordingly, giving employees the freedom to do their jobs in the manner they think most effective. The affiliative style gives much positive feedback and is very successful in building a sense of belonging within the team. Goleman suggests this style be used to build team cohesion and boost morale, but cautions that it should not be used alone as it may allow poor performance to go uncorrected and give the impression of a lack of firm direction in times of difficulty.

The *democratic* leader seeks the opinions of all team members and takes them into account before reaching a decision. The strengths of this approach are that all team members feel involved and that their opinions are valued. The weaknesses are that consensus can be hard to reach and the discussion may involve endless meetings, with little achieved. The style may be successful when all the team members are competent and knowledgeable, but Goleman warns against it when this is not the case.

Pacesetting leaders lead by example. They set extremely high standards for the organization and exemplify them themselves. At first glance the approach seems positive but Goleman cautions against using it other than sparingly, as team members' morale plummets as they seek to match an unrealistic personal comparison rather than striving to meet an organizational goal.

Coaching leaders help their employees to identify their areas of strength and weakness and support them in formulating plans to develop or address these so that they can achieve their work goals and career aspirations. They give clear instructions and good feedback and are expert at delegating tasks so as to challenge their team members. Goleman says that, although the coaching style has markedly positive effects on performance and the working environment, it is not often used as it requires substantial time to be committed in communication, teaching and training. It also requires that the recipient be open to the style and falls down when an employee or the team is stuck in set ways.

Goleman does not advocate one style of leadership as suiting all people at all times. Rather he suggests selecting from the styles in much the same way as a golfer chooses a club, to best suit the situation at hand. This approach would also make sense in the healthcare setting when, for example, the democratic style of leadership that would make perfect sense at a multidisciplinary team meeting to discuss a complex patient discharge might prove disastrous if applied to a surgical emergency on the operating table.

The One Minute Manager

In the business world, a series of books entitled *The One Minute Manager* proved a dramatic success. In *Leadership and the One Minute Manager*, Blanchard *et al.*[14] relate the discussions of an entrepreneur as she seeks to learn about leadership styles from the 'one minute manager'. Again, different styles of leadership are advocated but here, instead of different styles for different situations, different styles are proposed for different people according to their levels of competence and experience. 'There is nothing so unequal as the equal treatment of unequals', says the *One Minute Manager*, quoting Aristotle (p. 33).

The *One Minute Manager* describes four styles of leadership, to whom they are applied and when:

- Directing – this is telling people exactly what to do, how and when to do it and then making sure it is done just as directed.
- Coaching – this is a style where the leader continues to direct, setting tasks and ensuring they are completed, but also explains why the task is being done, seeks input from the team member and supports them in doing their work.
- Supporting – in this style, the leader shares some responsibility for decision-making with the team and supports team members in accomplishing their tasks.
- Delegating – the delegating leader gives responsibility for decision-making and task accomplishment over to team members.

In considering how to apply these styles, the *One Minute Manager* describes four stages of development (D1–D4) through a worker's career:

- D1 is where someone, starting a new job or role, is enthusiastic with high commitment but little knowledge and skill, hence low competence.
- D2 is where employees, after some time in post, have learned a little useful knowledge and skill and so are of low to some competence – but they are beginning to appreciate how much more there is to learn and are losing enthusiasm and therefore of low commitment.
- D3 workers have attained moderate to high competence but have perhaps lost interest in their work or lack confidence in their own abilities, leaving them with variable commitment.
- The D4 employee has moved through this phase and demonstrates both high competence and high commitment.

The *One Minute Manager* believes that each development level has a matching best leadership style. For D1s, a directing style where the leader structures, organizes, teaches and supports the employee is most appropriate. By D2 a coaching style where the leader both directs and supports comes into play. A supporting style is applied to D3s, as the leader listens, praises and facilitates. Finally, to those who have achieved the D4 level of development, the leader can delegate, turning over day-to-day decision-making to the employee. The styles and how they are applied are summarized in Figure 3.3.

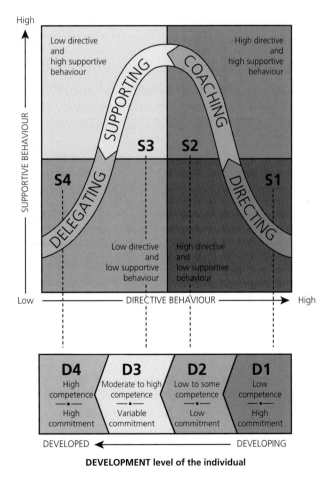

Figure 3.3 The *One Minute Manager's* situational leadership model. (*Source*: www.12 manage.com)

Once more, it is easy to find some correlation with NHS practice and one might be able to recognize people at different stages of the *One Minute Manager*'s development scale among colleagues and recognize some of the leadership styles from the workplace. The *One Minute Manager* emphasizes that the transition in leadership styles is a gradual process, keeping step with the employee's development. In the busy NHS, newly qualified staff are frequently delegated hugely challenging responsibilities and left to deal with them with little perceived support. To avoid such circumstances and the failures in patient care they can bring about, there is much to be learned from the notion of tailoring one's leadership style to the needs of the people in the team.

In applying leadership styles, the leader must also consider the leadership processes present in or appropriate to their organization. In the NHS a 'transactional' leadership process is often evident where good performance is elicited through offering rewards such as clinical excellence awards, and, perhaps more commonly, poor performance is deterred through fear of punishment such as a stern 'talking to' if a job is not completed. Many of the NHS reports and initiatives referred to in this chapter, however, take a different, 'transformational' approach, in which an inspirational, improved state is envisaged for the organization and the leader seeks to achieve that state by motivating followers within the organization to work towards and achieve it.[15]

Key points

Leadership styles

- Many styles of leadership are described within an extensive literature on the subject of how to improve the efficiency of organizations and enhance the productivity of teams.
- The leadership styles discussed in this section offer a variety of leadership behaviours and there is agreement that no one style fits all people and all situations.
- To be an effective leader, one must learn to recognize where and when to apply the different styles and then recognize the correct moment for change.

Leadership skills

Discussion of whether leadership can be learned has filled many books but one concise answer can be found in the *Advanced Life Support* handbook (p. 6):[16]

> Team leadership can be considered a process; thereby it can become available to everyone with training and not restricted to those with leadership traits.

Many institutions, from business leadership colleges to military academies, are built on the foundation that leadership can be taught and learned and the Academy of Medical Royal Colleges agrees:[7]

> The development of leadership competence needs to be an integral part of a doctor's training and learning. The MLCF is intended as an aid and driver for this and to enable a doctor in the NHS to be: A Practitioner; A Partner; A Leader. (p. 6)

The MLCF has now been incorporated, along with *The Clinical Leadership Competency Framework*, into *The NHS Leadership Framework*, which details what skills the competent clinical leader should possess, opportunities for learning or developing them and examples from practice. The framework's domains are listed in Box 3.1 (see also Fig. 3.2).

Box 3.1 The domains of *The NHS Leadership Framework*[8]

1. Demonstrating personal qualities

1.1 Developing self-awareness
1.2 Managing yourself
1.3 Continuing personal development
1.4 Acting with integrity

2. Working with others

2.1 Developing networks
2.2 Building and maintaining relationships
2.3 Encouraging contribution
2.4 Working within teams

3. Managing services

3.1 Planning
3.2 Managing resources
3.3 Managing people
3.4 Managing performance

4. Improving services

4.1 Ensuring patient safety
4.2 Critically evaluating
4.3 Encouraging improvement and innovation
4.4 Facilitating transformation

5. Setting direction

5.1 Identifying the contexts for change
5.2 Applying knowledge and evidence
5.3 Making decisions
5.4 Evaluating impact

6. Creating the vision

6.1 Developing the vision for the organization
6.2 Influencing the vision of the wider healthcare system
6.3 Communicating the vision
6.4 Embodying the vision

7. Delivering the strategy

7.1 Framing the strategy
7.2 Developing the strategy
7.3 Implementing the strategy
7.4 Embedding the strategy

The NHS Leadership Framework can be found on the NHS leadership website (www.nhsleadership. org.uk) and, in conjunction with the links and resources provided online, can provide a roadmap to the development of successful clinical leadership. An example of how a clinician might use these resources is given in Case study 3.1.

Case study 3.1

Dr AB is a core medical trainee with a desire to improve patient safety and a tentative interest in clinical leadership. She decides to use a peer assessment tool review to highlight areas for her leadership development. (From October 2011 the Leadership Framework 360° feedback tool has been available online, allowing for a confidential insight from peers and managers to demonstrate where leadership strengths and development needs might lie.)

At the review, Dr AB's educational supervisor directs her to *The NHS Leadership Framework* and, in particular, to 'Improving Services' to see how she might take forward her interest in patient safety. Within her supervisor's *Guidance to Integrating the Clinical Leadership Competency Framework into Education and Training*[17] she finds the required competencies listed:

- Obtain and act on patient, carer and user feedback and experiences.
- Assess and analyse processes using up-to-date improvement methodologies.
- Identify healthcare improvements and create solutions through collaborative working.
- Appraise options and plan and take action to implement and evaluate improvements.

The guidance also lists the knowledge she needs to demonstrate to meet the competencies described. It directs her to improve her knowledge of clinical governance and its role in improving services and to become familiar with the processes and principles of evaluation, audit and clinical guidelines and she begins to read around these subjects. She makes use of LeAD, the e-learning resource available on the e-Learning for Healthcare website (www.e-lfh.org.uk) with online modules to help users develop the competencies from *The NHS Leadership Framework* and books from the library to develop her knowledge.

On the ward round Dr AB finds that one of her patients has been prescribed a hefty dose of warfarin which has raised his international normalized ratio (INR) to dangerous levels and delayed his discharge. There is a hospital policy on warfarin prescribing but this has not been followed and, indeed, cannot be found on the ward. A clinical incident is registered and Dr AB identifies the opportunity for a patient safety intervention.

Now familiar with evaluation processes, Dr AB decides to audit warfarin prescribing in the hospital. She contacts the hospital's Clinical Audit Office, who support her with the design of the audit, and recruits a Foundation Doctor to assist in carrying out the task. Discussions with the junior reveal worrying inconsistencies in the way medical students are taught to prescribe warfarin, with some receiving no teaching at all. Dr AB decides to survey the hospital doctors on their training in this area.

Dr AB analyzes the data and finds that much of the warfarin prescribing in the hospital does not match the guidelines, resulting in poor INR control, which has repeatedly proven dangerous. Many of the doctors prescribing warfarin have had no training and several were unaware of the existence of the full guidelines. Many wards had incomplete or no guidelines available. In doing this, Dr AB realizes she has demonstrated several of the skills listed in the framework:[17]

- Analyze and identify the factors affecting the delivery of a service.
- Apply appropriate methods of evaluation.
- Undertake and contribute to clinical audit.

Dr AB presents her results at the hospital's clinical audit meeting, highlighting the danger to patients as well as extended hospital stays, which increase costs, and contrasting the hospital's performance with figures from a neighbouring trust. She proposes they adopt a multifaceted intervention to improve the situation involving directing doctors to an online training resource, educating doctors in training at the hospital in warfarin prescribing and ensuring adequate availability of the hospital's guidelines on the ward.

Dr AB has demonstrated the remaining skills from the framework: synthesizing data from other audits and using it to contribute to her own audit meeting.

The measures are enthusiastically adopted at first and an initial repeat audit shows an improvement in practice, which gives great satisfaction to Dr AB that she has contributed to improved patient safety, for now. To ensure that practice does not deteriorate in the future she entrusts a repeat audit in 1 year's time to her junior assistant.

At her next review meeting Dr AB and her supervisor discuss the audit process and the supervisor notes that she has been actively demonstrating the attitudes and behaviours required for this leadership competency, particularly in displaying a 'positive attitude to engaging in quality improvement'. Dr AB now has the evidence that she has achieved the leadership competencies they had initially discussed but that, along the way, she achieved much more from the framework, including working with others, setting direction and managing services. Her supervisor records a very positive statement in her portfolio.

Dr AB concludes that her leadership development has helped improve patient safety, improved the performance of her organization and enhanced her career progression. She decides to take it further. Dr AB's supervisor advises her to get in contact with the Emerging Clinical Leaders Network (eCLN), a group set up to encourage and support involvement in clinical leadership, and she attends the next meeting.

At the meeting she is encouraged to build upon her early success and is introduced to new opportunities to develop her leadership skills. She joins a buddying system which puts her in touch with a manager at her hospital in the hope that they may breach the clinical/managerial divide and take forward her new ideas for service improvement. Dr AB learns of a leadership training programme initiated by her Deanery and the Leadership Academy, which provides a year of group teaching and individual coaching in leadership skills for Foundation Doctors (http://www.leadership.londondeanery.ac.uk/) and encourages her enthusiastic FY1 to apply. For her own part she begins seriously considering application for a 'Darzi' Fellowship in Clinical Leadership, reading in the programme's recent evaluation that 'A group of leaders has been equipped with knowledge and understanding of the NHS, complex organizations and themselves, and personal, interpersonal, quality improvement and change skills to support and sometimes lead service change, improvement and leadership capacity building projects'[18] and contemplating whether, in a few years' time, that group of leaders might include her.

Key points

Leadership skills

- The NHS Institute for Innovation and Improvement and Academy of Medical Royal Colleges have detailed a series of leadership competencies and how they might be developed and demonstrated in *The NHS Leadership Framework*.
- Through this framework and supporting resources available online, and through organizations and specific training posts, clinical leadership can be learned and employed.

Overcoming barriers to clinical leadership

It is, of course, one thing to read about clinical leadership in a textbook and quite another to apply it in the real world. This section covers some of the barriers to successful leadership in the NHS and suggests how to navigate them.

Surveys[19,20] into what deters clinicians from involvement in clinical leadership frequently turn up similar findings, which can be grouped under three broad headings:

- A lack of leadership development opportunities:
  - Doctors are not selected on their leadership abilities.
  - Leadership has not been part of the medical school curriculum.
  - Leadership has not been part of clinical training.
  - Leadership training is disconnected from hospital work.
  - Clinical leadership opportunities are perceived as limited.
  - A shortage of appropriate role models.
  - Few opportunities for practice and feedback.
- Financial or career disincentives:
  - Leadership activities are seen as extra hours with no financial reward.
  - Leadership work can distance a clinician from potential financial and career rewards such as clinical excellence awards, private practice and research.
  - The cost of leadership training may be an added financial burden to the trainee.
  - There has been little career structure or opportunity for career progression associated with clinical leadership in the past.
- Fundamental perceptions:
  - The perception that clinical leadership is dissociated from patient care.
  - The belief that there is no need for a clinician to be involved with managerial work for a complete career.
  - Perceived hostility between management and clinicians and the fear that a clinical leadership role may be seen as 'joining the dark side'.

There is also another element to individuals' reluctance to become involved in leadership, which is less well documented in surveys but commonly emerges in discussion. This reluctance is a combination of the modest wish not to be seen as arrogantly extolling one's leadership virtues over the heads of one's peers and the fear of a hostile reception from said peers if one does. Within our culture there remains a suspicion of self-promotion and an iconoclastic satisfaction in pillorying those who put themselves on a pedestal, especially if they fail. This perception that, if you stick your neck out, you may get your head chopped off is sometimes also reinforced from outside.

One difficult aspect of leadership is accountability when things go awry. Even when the leader in question is not directly responsible for a problem, it is likely he or she will be held accountable if they were in charge at the time.

In 2010 concerns over patient safety at Stafford Hospital led to an inquiry by the then Healthcare Commission (HCC). The results were widely reported in the media as scandalous and leadership at the Mid-Staffordshire NHS Trust was heavily criticized:[21]

> The HCC made a number of criticisms of the leadership of the trust which ran the hospital, saying there was a 'longstanding lack of medical and general leadership' and that nurses' leadership had also been poor.

The HCC report listed a series of shortcomings which, it estimated, led to around 400 excess deaths at the hospital over 3 years and, while the senior manager had received reports describing him as 'a first class chief executive' over this time, an indication of the general perception is given by the headline of this *BBC News* article, 'Stafford Hospital deaths: Ex-boss "largely responsible".[21] Such headlines are far from rare, as the following examples show: 'NHS bugs "due to poor leadership",[22] 'C. difficile bosses should quit',[23] and 'Poor leadership and chasing targets "hampers patient care".[24]

Many of the identified barriers to involvement in clinical leadership are systemic within the NHS and so their removal must involve as many people within the system as possible. Much has been done in terms of increasing the leadership development opportunities available since Lord Darzi's reports, with leadership now included in medical student education, in some speciality training curricula and with leadership courses and fellowships available to some doctors in training. Many clinicians, however, remain ignorant of the opportunities and resources available, and uninformed or unconvinced of the benefits of making clinical leadership a part of their work in providing quality care for patients.

To overcome this barrier, a working culture where the encouragement of clinical leadership is the norm must prevail. From the most junior level upwards, clinicians must be empowered to take a role in improving patient services and to have their power to improve patient care demonstrated to them. Examples of success in clinical leadership should be conveyed to all staff through newsletters and other communications and include suitable recognition of the individuals responsible. Leadership activities should be provided close to home and linked directly to hospital work so that they may be seen as part of the job, rather than something which takes doctors away from their duties and away from their patients. The financial disincentives for clinical leadership may be removed by providing additional study leave and subsidies for leadership development events so that those who wish to attend do not have to use their annual leave and end up poorer for the decision.

Much can also be done to bridge the perceived divide between managers and clinicians in order to remove any stigma attached to clinical leadership roles. In some areas, hostility has developed between the roles due to ideas that clinicians are focused only on patient care and remain deliberately ignorant of the need to manage resources in order to provide that care, and that managers don't care about patients, just the money. Leadership texts often discuss the differences between leaders and managers, almost always to the detriment of managers, while missing the point that successful leaders almost always have to manage and successful managers almost always have to lead. Buddying schemes, partnering clinicians with managers to learn about each other's jobs, are sound developments but simpler methods such as encouraging clinicians to attend key management meetings and involving managers in clinical environments will have a similar effect. In one innovative scheme, medical trainees and management trainees learn together through joint project work and seminars. Most important is informing the realization that both roles are vital to the success of the organization that has as its goal the provision of quality patient care.

A fear of the consequences of leadership is harder to combat. An environment where leadership is encouraged, seen and rewarded at all levels will reduce reluctance to become involved. Ultimately leaders must be accountable for their team's actions, which may include some failures as well as successes. The best strategy to reduce the consequences of failure lies in the promotion of excellence, and the organization that nurtures and develops its leaders and cherishes their achievements will be an organization that is best placed to succeed.

Key points

Barriers to leadership
- Within the NHS there are many perceived barriers to involvement in leadership, including cultural concerns, financial disincentives and the fear of accountability.
- These may be overcome through closer teamworking, linking leadership roles with career progression and promoting excellence in practice.

Summary

❏ Excellence in clinical leadership is a key factor in providing quality patient care.

❏ The resources to develop clinical leaders and the opportunities for them to flourish are coming into place.

❏ In order to effectively utilize this potential force for improvement, all of us working in the NHS must contribute to an environment where leadership is encouraged, nurtured and celebrated.

References

1. NHS UK (2011). *About the NHS*. Available from: http://www.nhs.uk/

2. Office for National Statistics (2002). *Life expectancy at birth, UK*. Available from: www.ons.gov.uk

3. Leon DA (2011). Trends in European life expectancy: a salutary view. *Int J Epidemiol* 40, 271–7.

4. Department of Health and Social Security (1983). *Griffiths Report: NHS Management Inquiry Report*. London: DHSS. Available from: http://www.sochealth.co.uk/history/griffiths.htm. Accessed: March 2012.

5. Department of Health (2008). *High Quality Care for All: NHS Next Stage Review Final Report*. London: DoH. Available from: http://www.dh.gov.uk/

6. General Medical Council (2009). *Tomorrow's Doctors: Outcomes and Standards for Undergraduate Medical Education*. London: GMC. Available from: http://www.gmc-uk.org/

7. NHS Institute for Innovation and Improvement and Academy of Medical Royal Colleges (2010). *Medical Leadership Competency Framework. Enhancing Engagement in Medical Leadership*, 3rd edn. Coventry: NHS Institute for Innovation and Improvement.

8. NHS Institute for Innovation and Improvement and Academy of Medical Royal Colleges (2011). *The NHS Leadership Framework*. Coventry: NHS Institute for Innovation and Improvement. Available from: http://www.leadershipqualitiesframework.institute.nhs.uk/

9. Department of Health (2007). *Our NHS, Our Future: NHS Next Stage Review Interim Report*. London: DoH.

10. Tupes EC, Christal RE (1961). Recurrent personality factors based on trait ratings. Technical report ASD-TR-61-97. Lackland Air Force Base, TX, USA: Personnel Laboratory, Air Force Systems Command.

11. Judge TA, Bono JE, Ilies R, Gerhardt MW (2002). Personality and leadership: a qualitative and quantitative review. *J Appl Psychol* 87, 765–80.

12. NHS Institute for Innovation and Improvement (2005). *NHS Leadership Qualities Framework.* London: NHS Institute for Innovation and Improvement. Available from: http://www.nhsleadershipqualities.nhs.uk/

13. Goleman D. (2000) Leadership that gets results. *Harvard Business Review* March–April: 78–90.

14. Blanchard K, Zigarmi P, Zigarmi D (2004). *Leadership and the One Minute Manager.* London: HarperCollins.

15. Bass BM (1985). *Leadership and Performance Beyond Expectation.* New York: Free Press.

16. Resuscitation Council (UK) (2011). *Advanced Life Support,* 6th edn. London: Resuscitation Council (UK).

17. NHS Institute for Innovation and Improvement and Academy of Medical Royal Colleges (2011). *Guidance to Integrating the Clinical Leadership Competency Framework into Education and Training.* Coventry: NHS Institute for Innovation and Improvement.

18. Stoll L, Foster-Turner J, Glenn M (2010). *Mind Shift: An Evaluation of the NHS London 'Darzi' Fellowships in Clinical Leadership Programme.* London: London Deanery. Available from: http://www.london.nhs.uk/

19. Mountford J, Webb C (2008). *Clinical Leadership: Unlocking High Performance in Healthcare.* London: McKinsey & Company. Available from: http://www.knowledge.scot.nhs.uk/

20. Stanwick T, McKimm J, eds (2011). *ABC of Clinical Leadership.* Oxford: Blackwell.

21. *BBC News* (2010). Stafford Hospital deaths: Ex-boss 'largely responsible'. Available from: http://www.bbc.co.uk/news/uk-england-stoke-staffordshire-11426817. Accessed: March 2012.

22. *BBC News* (2007). NHS bugs 'due to poor leadership'. Available from: http://news.bbc.co.uk/1/hi/health/7061890.stm. Accessed: March 2012.

23. *BBC News* (2007). C. difficile bosses should quit. [Cited: 2011 July 25]. Available from: http://news.bbc.co.uk/1/hi/england/kent/7044552.stm. Accessed: March 2012.

24. *The Times* (2008). Poor leadership and chasing targets 'hampers patient care'. London.

Chapter 4

Information technology, innovation and healthcare

Hameen Markar and Nadeem Mazi-Kotwal

Introduction

Over the last few years, there have been significant developments in data storage and delivery. Innovations in information technology (IT), the ever-increasing power of microprocessors and improved connection to the internet with a wide range of devices have not only transformed the way we read news, watch videos, listen to music and seek information, but have also influenced storage and sharing of information.

While the general trend is one of increasing reliance on electronic gadgets and digital documents, there is an obvious over-reliance on paper in healthcare systems around the globe. The reluctance of healthcare professionals to use information systems is a worldwide issue with health services being traditionally slow to adapt to such changes.[1]

Although IT has played a crucial role in many recent social and political revolutions, bringing down regimes that were decades old,[2,3] they remain to be adopted with a sense of enthusiasm in the NHS. Information technology, if used appropriately, is likely to bring down costs and generate savings while facilitating communication and coordination within and between organizations. In healthcare it can also reduce risks and improve the quality of care.[4,5]

Using technologies to increase efficiency and productivity is a very appealing concept to policymakers. Unfortunately, it has remained difficult to harness their powers for day-to-day frontline clinical work for a variety of reasons, including a degree of reluctance and resistance to change from medical staff. The considerable initial setup costs and the necessity for staff to retrain and develop new skills are potential barriers.[6]

One might assume that in commercial health markets, the changes would have been more readily adapted due to a business model of work. This do not appear to hold true and the health sector has been quite sluggish in evolving to meet the needs of the current markets. Although there has been a lot of reliance on IT for communication and back-office work, its use in day-to-day clinical practice has been poor. The GP surgeries in the UK are perhaps an exception. The uptake has not been helped by the high-profile failures of projects such as the NHS Executive's Healthcare Information Supporting Systems (HISS) initiative or the ambitious £12.4 billion 'Connecting for Health'[7] national programme for IT. The concerns about data security, especially with issues surrounding confidentiality, have further hampered uptake of these initiatives.

In the future, healthcare systems in most countries will be expected to deliver better quality of care for a greater proportion of people with higher morbidity, with fewer staff, fewer resources and smaller budgets. These have led to serious questions being raised about the cost-effectiveness of such projects.[8,9]

This chapter attempts to analyse the various arguments surrounding these issues and the contribution that IT and other related innovations can make to improving the existing healthcare system. We will also discuss some strategies that can be employed to utilize these innovations and increase productivity, in the context of the following areas:

- personal organization
- clinical practice
- organizational functioning
- ethical issues.

IT and innovations in personal organization

Communication

One of the most widely used applications of IT is email and calendar software, such as Microsoft's Outlook or Mozilla's Thunderbird. The NHS Network (NHS net) has evolved gradually and has been consistently handling about a million emails a day.

The ability to send a message out cheaply and easily to thousands of recipients within a fraction of a second is a huge development from the days of postal contact. The emails are sent out in a format that is easily readable and the ability to store emails, sort emails by various attributes like sender, recipient and date sent, is enormously helpful in facilitating coordination and communication.

On the other hand, if one is not well organized, emails can virtually take over one's life. Strategies will therefore have to be developed to deal with the ever-increasing number of emails. Although emails sent within the NHS network are thought to be generally safe, security and confidentiality remain major concerns in the NHS. Another drawback is that emails can be impersonal, as the overall range of expressions is limited to text alone. It is easy to put together a message and send it off with a few keystrokes, but once sent that message cannot be retrieved. Therefore, emails must be read carefully before the 'send' button is pushed, particularly as they can be stored for as long as the recipient wants and also forwarded to others. One must be careful not to 'reply to all' unnecessarily. This can be annoying and often causes additional work besides wasting other people's time. Email etiquette needs special consideration particularly with the use of handheld devices.[10]

Key points

Communication

- Set aside time daily to go through and reply to emails.
- Set up filters and folders to organize emails.
- Be aware of email etiquette.
- Be aware of patient confidentiality issues.
- Always carry out a spellcheck and read before you send.
- Do not send emails in anger – review in draft form after a cooling down period.

Organizing the diary

Calendar applications such as Outlook Calendar are equally helpful tools that allow you not only to create appointments and manage a list of pending actions but also to assist in organizing meetings, view schedules of the group invited, set up reminders for tasks pending and so on. It is beyond the scope of this chapter to go into the technical details of how this can be accomplished. The help option in most computers will be a good starting point.

Handheld computers and mobile phones

Another area of rapidly evolving innovation is handheld computers and mobile phones. With portable access to the internet, they can be of huge benefit. For example, such devices can store a range of medical textbooks and formularies which are available for purchase and download. Some journals, such as the *British Medical Journal,* have started to design a template specifically for use with such devices. Younger doctors, who are more likely to use these devices, have found them extremely useful tools to store and retrieve large amounts of medical and scientific information and data, thus enhancing significantly the delivery of safe, effective clinical care.[11] Handheld devices are also used in various other settings, such as passing on handover notes to colleagues, recording and submitting research and clinical audit data.

IT and innovations in clinical practice

Checklists and protocols

There is a strong drive in the healthcare industry to simulate the aviation industry's adoption of checklists to simplify complex procedures and minimize errors of omission. A significant proportion of errors in healthcare settings are due to ineptitude and a lack of discipline. Gone are the days when doctors were given the benefit of the doubt where errors were concerned. Failures are no longer attributed to a lack of knowledge and the assumption now is that healthcare workers knew what should be done but didn't do what they should.[12]

A checklist specifically outlines the various steps to be taken to complete a procedure correctly. In this way it helps to prevent critical steps from being inadvertently omitted. The use of checklists will require a well-functioning team and it is an attempt to solve what is essentially a cultural problem with a technical solution. Where used appropriately, they have been highly effective in improving outcomes, especially in reducing infection rates after surgery and in intensive care units.[13] Checklists are also widely used in assessment of suicide risk in mental health services.

In fact, checklists are now used widely across various specialities in the health service. They are particularly useful in surgery before a major operation, helping to avoid disasters such as operating on the wrong side. Setting up local protocols and checklists supported by well-trained staff has significantly improved standards of care and minimized errors in recent years. The World Health Organization recommends that its published checklist should be followed as part of surgical procedures and encourages organizations to adapt it for local use.[14]

Automated pharmacy alerts

Information technology can be used to provide automated alerts within healthcare systems. Such alerts can prevent the prescribing of inappropriate drugs and incorrect doses by integrating with existing healthcare systems to check patients' medical records for information such as age, sex, weight, drug allergies, current prescriptions and drug interactions. The prescriber is automatically alerted if any pharmaceutical concerns arise, thereby decreasing adverse incidents and drug errors. Such alerts are also used to prompt the need for certain blood tests, e.g. white cell count with the use of clozapine.

Automated alerts can be used with good effect to:

- prevent the prescription of a sensitive drug
- monitor drug interactions
- monitor significant side-effects
- monitor dosage
- monitor certain blood tests and results, e.g. serum lithium levels
- prompt for periodic review.

Patient health portals

Patient health portals allow individuals to maintain a personal health record securely on the internet. A personal health record is an online application that allows users to store their health information in a secure and standard format. This information can be shared with healthcare providers. It allows users to store all their health-related information in one place and means they can access it at any time and anywhere as long as there is internet access.

In addition to storing information, patient health portals also allow users to monitor and update their records. With greater connectivity in the future, it may be possible to obtain investigation results and other health-related information, such as blood pressure and blood sugar levels, directly from the system and monitor these over a period of time.

Personal health portals are different from electronic health records (discussed later in this chapter) in that the user owns and is responsible for the former, while the latter are maintained by the healthcare provider. This distinction is something that may well become more blurred in the future.

Many companies are developing patient health portals and providing users with the ability to create personal health records. The most prominent among these are the Microsoft HealthVault and Google Health, and in the UK the NHS is offering a similar service called NHS Healthspace.[15] It is hoped that Healthspace will in future be synchronized with NHS databases. The NHS is also rolling out, in a phased manner, summary care records,[16] holding basic information for each registered NHS user, and a Healthspace Communicator which will allow users to access clinical information via email from their healthcare service providers.

The further organic development of this would be a degree of standardization that allows the patients' portals to integrate seamlessly with primary and secondary care records into a single health record with varying levels of read and write access for the patient and service providers.

Telemedicine

Telemedicine is a rapidly developing interface between medicine and IT. It provides a connection between two remote locations and allows the exchange of medical information among clinicians by audiovisual means.

Telemedicine is being embraced enthusiastically by primary care practitioners in remote areas to obtain advice from hospital specialists. It allows for rapid assessments, diagnosis and initiation of the appropriate treatment. This is particularly useful in isolated rural areas with fewer specialists and would be of obvious benefit in developing countries.[17,18]

Specialities such as dermatology,[19] radiology and pathology do not always need face-to-face patient contact, and telemedicine can help by facilitating the transfer of medical images for reports and opinions. Similarly, video-conferencing is also being widely used in situations that don't require physical examinations, such as in the assessment of mental illnesses and the delivery of psychological therapies.[20]

Telemedicine also has educational uses and is being increasingly used in clinical teaching courses and conferences. Video-conferencing is also gaining in popularity among non-medical managers in the NHS for various managerial meetings and conferences.

Key points

Telemedicine

- Connects remote locations.
- Allows the exchange of medical/clinical information.
- Facilitates second opinions and/or specialist advice.
- Can be useful in psychological assessments and therapies.
- Useful for teaching and conferences.

Robotic surgery

Although relatively new in the surgical field, the scope for robot-assisted surgery (with a surgeon in the vicinity operating with remotes) is likely to advance and evolve in the future. It may not be long before some operations are independently performed by robots.

In robot-assisted surgery, the surgeon is presented with a magnified image of the operating area and is able to operate with good control of surgical instruments. It has also been possible to connect two machines in remote sites via IT and for a surgeon to operate remotely.

Robotic surgery is most commonly used for prostatic operations, and, though expensive, its use is likely to spread to other operations in the future. Robotic surgery has all the advantages of keyhole surgery (e.g. smaller incisions and decreased blood loss) and, in addition, offers good access and the involvement of highly skilled surgeons from a distance. However, as yet there is no clear evidence that the outcomes are any better than those of conventional surgery.[21]

IT and innovations in organizational functioning

Electronic health records

Electronic health records (EHRs) refer to the electronic versions of patients' medical history and progress that are maintained by health service providers and are updated periodically at each intervention and review. It is envisaged that these will eventually replace paper files, leading to 'paperless' case records containing all relevant demographic details, medical history, and laboratory and other investigative data. The EHR can be strengthened further by interfaces which provide evidence-based information and alert clinicians to potential errors such as incorrect doses, sensitivity to medication and possible drug interactions.

Electronic health records have several benefits. The information is typewritten, thus eliminating legibility issues due to poor handwriting, and it can be easily accessed by relevant health professionals. EHRs also prevent duplication of clinical information and investigations. Easy storage of information, quick access, the ability to search and retrieve specific details readily and the possible links with evidence-based information programmes all make EHR an attractive option.

Despite these and many other benefits, there is a need for more robust research to support the efficacy of EHRs, both clinically and financially.[22] There are concerns that these systems might reduce clinicians to 'expensive typists', eating up valuable time that could be better spent on clinical activity. Unfortunately the uptake has been poor and the initial costs may be an influencing factor.[23] Ongoing concerns about the security of such potentially sensitive and confidential medical data and a fear of 'loss of data' are also proving to be barriers to widespread use. However, as long as appropriate security systems and advanced encryption technology are in place, the arguments for EHRs being safer than paper records merit serious consideration.

Some organizations are looking at developing a 'joint ownership' of EHRs with patients and allowing patients access to specific parts of their health record. With many players on the market offering EHR software platforms, there is a need for a standardized format for storing the information. This will make it easier to share information between organizations that use separate software systems.

Digital dictation

Digital dictation refers to the recording of speech as a digital audio file for later transcribing. Use of digital recorders has gradually begun to replace the traditional cassette tape recorders across most healthcare providers. Letters can be dictated either directly on to a computer or on to a portable recorder. There has been a rapid improvement in software programs handling these files and they can be encrypted and sent securely by email or stored in designated folders for later use.

There are several advantages in moving away from cassette tape recorders, not the least of which is the occasional blank or missing tape. The audio quality of a digital recorder is often much clearer, making it easier to transcribe. Most modern portable digital recorders now have more advanced options that are available as standard. For example, the 'record-append' and 'record-insert' functions allow text to be added in the appropriate place without having to re-dictate the subsequent details, unlike a cassette recorder which only has a record-overwrite function. A digital file is also easier to store and send electronically. Similarly, the typist or the clinician can rewind or fast-forward to the desired location almost instantaneously.

There is no doubt that digital dictation increases efficiency and reduces the turnaround time for such work. It reduces delays in the files reaching the typist, allows the transcriber to see exactly how much recording time is left to be transcribed (which was not possible with analogue tapes) and allows priorities to be flagged up. It can also be used to share and distribute workload and, with further modification, might alert staff to the absence of dictated notes following a clinic.

Speech recognition

Speech recognition software goes one further than a digital recorder and transcribes direct speech or a digital audio recording of speech automatically using complex speech algorithms and the processing power of modern computers. Such software has come a long way since the 1950s when programs were only able to recognize single spoken digits. There has been continuous improvement since then, albeit in small increments. The efficiency of speech recognition software improves as it builds up a profile of speakers, as they spend more time 'training' it to recognize their particular speech patterns. To be very effective, however, the speaker needs to dictate clearly at a slow, steady speed, which can be difficult.

It is easy to see how good speech recognition would be useful in any situation where one would otherwise have to type, with the spoken words transcribed in just a few moments. But because of the current lack of accuracy and the need therefore to spend time correcting mistakes subsequently, it is not yet very popular with clinicians. However, there has been a gradual acceptance and adoption of speech recognition systems that fetch digital audio files and transcribe them into a draft text document, which is then reviewed by secretarial staff for further corrections before final approval by the clinician.

The narrative nature of a medical dictation, the differences in pronunciation and the awkward pauses that arise while a clinician is thinking about what to say all make it difficult for automated software to accurately convert speech into text. Therefore, in spite of major advances, speech recognition software has not been adopted with much enthusiasm outside the limited home environment, mainly because of its relative immaturity and inaccuracy. The political ramifications of possible job losses arising from its adoption might also have limited its use to date.

Data security

There are two key concerns in the area of data security: protecting information stored on computer hard drives and peripheral devices, and preventing unauthorised access to online communication. The security of the former can be greatly increased with the use of encryption, while online communication can be made more secure with the use of 'https' protocol.[24]

Encryption transforms data using sophisticated mathematical algorithms to make it unreadable, at least to those who do not have the appropriate key/password with which to unscramble or 'decrypt' the data. There are several encryption algorithms, but the recommended one is the 256-bit Advanced Encryption Standard. Encryption addresses the security issues surrounding lost data, as data in files, folders, entire drives of laptops/computers, portable USB drives and email attachments can be carried, transferred or emailed safely. Of course, this relies on the key/password itself remaining secure, which is a security issue in itself.

With regard to online security, the 'https' protocol, which is sometimes seen at the start of website addresses instead of the usual 'http', provides security by transmitting http information through an additional encrypted system. This goes a long way to eliminating the possibility of eavesdropping that is relatively simple with the http protocol.

Mobile working

Improvements in communication technologies and devices have made it much easier to access information – and therefore to work – remotely. Staff are no longer bound to an office desk and computer and can now use a number of devices to connect to office systems at any time and from almost anywhere.

All of this has been possible due to the advances in wireless connectivity (WiFi, 3G, 4G) and to the availability of more powerful portable devices. Mobile phone technologies such as 3G and 4G have provided a high-speed, mobile connection to the internet. The ability to have secure remote access to an organization's network and emails via a virtual private network has resulted in much more flexible working and increased productivity.

Business intelligence

Business intelligence generally refers to an IT-based solution that automates the extraction and analysis of business data. There is no doubt that to increase efficiency within an organization, a good business intelligence system is essential, helping to increase the appropriate utilization of resources and identify ways of saving time and resources.

Business intelligence brings together information from various sources within an organization and provides factual reports and insight into the finances, human resources, clinical activity and performance, among other things. It ensures that crucial facts and figures are available in a timely manner and helps managers to make informed decisions.

Compared with traditional legacy methods of manually collecting the data and formulating a required report in days, such a system would be able to provide reports within minutes, freeing up staff for other work.

Some areas in which a business intelligence system would be applicable in the healthcare context are waiting list analysis, patient pathway tracking, costing of outpatients by speciality, costing of patient treatment by diagnosis, length of in-patient treatment by diagnosis, procurements, stocking levels, resource utilization and payment-by-result analysis.

Performance management and incentives

With robust performance management and appropriate incentives in place, significant gains can be achieved by identifying areas of best practice and concerns, focusing on continuous improvement and improved outcomes.[25]

Two good examples of innovations by organizations to improve the quality of healthcare are key performance indicators (KPIs) and the Quality and Outcomes Framework (QOF). KPIs provide a standardized framework to define and measure the progress of organizations over a period of time. Standardized KPIs also help organizations to compare their performance with their peers and on a national level.

The QOF was introduced as a voluntary scheme for GP practices, who are awarded points for achievements against specific indicators.[26] These points are converted into financial rewards, providing a strong incentive for individual practices to strive towards achieving the desired targets. It is postulated that when these improved clinical achievements become standard and routine clinical practice, the financial incentives will no longer be needed. A common criticism of such incentive schemes is that while they can improve a particular area of clinical practice, there is little evidence to suggest that they are cost-effective and there is every possibility that the practice will cease to use the scheme when the incentive is withdrawn. Furthermore, unfunded work that is not incentivized can be left on the back burner in organizations focused on commercial incentives.[27] Such incentive schemes may not promote health or improve the health differences that drove the incentive schemes in the first place.[28]

Ethical issues

The cardinal ethical principles of any innovation can be grouped broadly into four categories:[29]

- respect for autonomy – respect for the decision-making capacities of an autonomous individual
- no maleficence – not to cause harm to others
- beneficence – preventing harm and providing benefits
- justice – just distribution of benefits, costs, risks and so on.

In addition, a key main ethical consideration in relation to innovations in IT and healthcare is the necessity to protect and promote confidentiality at all times. The presence of large amounts of sensitive data in one site raises concerns about theft or loss of data. Innovations such as the setting up of a centralized NHS database as part of the Connecting for Health initiative have stressed heavily the need for the NHS Network to be as secure as possible, but it is still vulnerable to unknown loopholes.

With the increasing reliance on technology and computer systems, especially in general practice, it can be argued that the use of computers during consultations, with the resulting decrease in eye contact between the doctor and the patient, adversely affects the professional doctor–patient relationship. Innovations of a technical nature, such as checklists and protocols, can make the service provider appear impersonal and distant and could even de-skill an individual in the art of clinical assessment.

There is currently no clear evidence to suggest that the considerable initial setup costs associated with most IT innovations are cost-effective. In fact, the lower demands on non-clinical administrative time resulting from such innovations could be offset by an increased demand on doctors' time. The use of medical and nursing time for administrative and secretarial work, for example, such as submitting data electronically could, in fact, be more costly. But this has to be weighed up against the advantages associated with, for example, a clinician having rapid access to notes, allowing them to make more informed decisions.

Conclusion

Information technology is advancing at a rapid pace. The lack of adequate resources and increasing demands on the healthcare services have compelled policymakers to look to innovations, IT and different models of service delivery as means of improving the service quality and efficiency and reducing costs. In the future, healthcare systems globally will be required to improve productivity and quality with little or no additional resources or finance. This is particularly relevant in the current economic climate, and it is not difficult to envisage the collapse, or at best a significant deterioration, of standards in the NHS in future, in the absence of innovative technological advances.

Thus far, the healthcare sector has lagged behind other industries in adopting new technologies. Developing and implementing innovative ideas are attractive options bearing in mind the benefits they can bring, but implementing such technologies in a live system that is actively caring for the health of individuals can be potentially dangerous and requires careful assessment, particularly of the risks.

Introducing innovations requires a strong belief in the changes, a dedicated team and decisive leadership. The lack of strong evidence in respect of the cost-effectiveness of healthcare innovations and difficulties in performing a robust economic analysis are two of the many issues that are currently hampering more rapid change.

Summary

❏ Innovations will play a substantive role in shaping the healthcare system in the future.

❏ Developing and implementing innovations are appealing to policymakers for the benefits they might bring.

❏ Implementing innovations requires firm belief, dedication and effective leadership.

❏ It is easier to introduce innovations in back-office function than it is in frontline clinical duties.

References

1. Berwick DM (2003). Disseminating innovations in health care. *J Am Med Assoc* 289, 1969–75.

2. Harb Z (2011). Arab revolutions and the social media effect. *M/C Journal 14.*

3. Kyriakopoulou K (2011). Authoritarian states and internet social media: instruments of democratisation or instruments of control. *Human Affairs* 21, 18–26.

4. McCullough JS, Casey M, Moscovice I, Prasad S (2010). The effect of health information technology on quality in US hospitals. *Health Aff* 29, 647–54.

5. Schiff GD, Bates DW (2010). Can electronic clinical documentation help prevent diagnostic errors? *N Engl J Med* 362, 1066–9.

6. Heathfield H, Pitty D, Hanka R (1998). Evaluating information technology in health care: barriers and challenges. *Br Med J* 316, 1959–61.

7. Department of Health Informatics Directorate. Connecting for Health. Available from: http://www.connectingforhealth.nhs.uk/

8. Lock C (1996). What value do computers provide to NHS hospitals?. *Br Med J* 312, 1407.

9. Coye MJ, Kell J (2006). How hospitals confront new technology. *Health Affairs* 25, 163–73.

10. Stac L. *12 Tips for Better E-Mail Etiquette.* Available from: http://office.microsoft.com/

11. Al-Ubaydli M (2004). Handheld computers. *Br Med J* 328, 1181–4.

12. Gawande A (2010). *The Checklist Manifesto.* Profile Books.

13. Haynes AB, Weiser TG, Berry WR, *et al.* (2009) A surgical safety checklist to reduce morbidity and mortality in a global population. *N Engl J Med* 360, 491–9.

14. *World Health Organization* (2009). *Safe Surgery Saves Lives.* WHO. Available from: http://www.who.int/

15. NHS HealthSpace. https://www.healthspace.nhs.uk

16. Summary Care Record. https://www.healthspace.nhs.uk/visitor/visitor_carerecord.aspx

17. Wootton R (2008). Telemedicine support for the developing world. *J Telemed Telecare* 14, 109–14.

18. Fraser HSF, McGrath St JD (2000). Information technology and telemedicine in Sub-Saharan Africa: economical solutions are available to support health care in remote areas. *Br Med J* 321, 465.

19. Finch TL, Mair FS, May CR (2007). Teledermatology in the UK: lessons in service innovation. *Br J Dermatol* 156, 521–7.

20. Wootton R (2001). Recent advances: telemedicine. *Br Med J* 323, 557.

21. Lanfranco AR, Castellanos AE, Desai JP, Meyers WC (2004). Robotic surgery – a current perspective. *Ann Surg* 239(1), 14–21.

22. Poissant L, Pereira J, Tamblyn R, Kawasumi Y. The impact of electronic health records on time efficiency of physicians and nurses: a systematic review. *J Am Med Inform Assoc* 2005 12(5), 505–16.

23. Blumenthal D, Tavenner M (2010). The 'meaningful use' regulation for electronic health records. *N Engl J Med* 363, 501–50.

24. American Medical Association (2010). HIPAA Security Rule: Frequently asked questions regarding encryption of personal health information. American Medical Association. Available from: http://www.ama-assn.org/

25. The NHS Institute for Innovation and Improvement (2008). *Performance Management.* Available from: http://www.institute.nhs.uk/

26. NHS. *Quality And Outcomes Framework.* The Health and Social Care Information Centre. Available from: http://www.qof.ic.nhs.uk/

27. Doran T, Kontopantelis E, Valderas JM, Campbell S, Roland M, Salisbury C, Reeves D (2011). Effect of financial incentives on incentivised and non-incentivised clinical activities: longitudinal analysis of data from the UK Quality and Outcomes Framework. *Br Med J* 342, d3590.

28. Gulland A (2011). GP incentive scheme has had little effect on health inequalities in England. *Br Med J* 342, d2536.

29. Gillon R (1994). Medical ethics: four principles plus attention to scope. *Br Med J* 309, 184.

Chapter 5

Healthcare commissioning and contracting

John Hague and Matt Fossey

Introduction

The advances in modern medicine lead to tremendous financial pressure, requiring judgements on what care should be paid for that would challenge even the wisdom of Solomon. No system in the world is immune from these pressures, as the possibilities in medicine have now comprehensively outstripped the ability of any but the very wealthiest to pay for them.

Over a period of time equal to the length of a single medical career, we have progressed from the position where a patient with a myocardial infarction would be routinely cared for at home, as hospital admission did not confer any realizable benefit, to one where patients are being helicoptered to regional centres for immediate surgery. Although the modern Western answer may well confer prognostic and other benefits in the long term, it is, by anyone's reckoning, fearsomely expensive.

Again, within the same career, we have seen diagnostic imaging progress from a situation in which most small hospitals could provide most investigations at very reasonable cost, to one in which a vast number of very expensive machines are available to provide imaging at a unit cost that has a significant impact on health budgets. The challenge is further augmented by advances in therapeutics, where custom-made immunological treatments offer a realistic chance of cure from cancers that represent a certain death sentence to those who cannot afford the treatment – the problem being that the majority of the health systems worldwide cannot afford the technology.

Within medicine there is increased competition between specialities. There is a growing body of evidence that properly addressing the mental state of a patient with a long-term physical condition confers significant benefit in terms of their physical state, with the cost of care being significantly reduced. Yet it remains a challenge to commission any increase in spending on mental health services – for who would vote for a service from another branch of medicine that would have the result of reducing expenditure in one's own? Which politician is brave enough to prioritize a mental health service over a scanner?

Every commissioning system needs to be able to handle risk, be it clinical or financial, and recent history in most countries can point to examples of failures of both. In Mid-Staffordshire in England, in the late 2000s, concerns about standards in the acute trust led to an inquiry, which concluded that 'patients were routinely neglected by a Trust that was preoccupied with cost cutting, targets, and processes, and lost sight of its fundamental responsibility to provide safe care'.[1] To summarize, a preoccupation with meeting financial targets was associated with increased clinical risk. The trick in effective commissioning is to balance and mitigate both risks, both in the initial commissioning of the service and during performance management of the contract.

In the USA there have been significant developments and lessons, with some commissioning groups of doctors ceasing to trade for financial reasons, and significant political opposition to 'socialized medicine'. Combined with this has been the development of large professionally led health maintenance organizations (HMOs), such as Kaiser Permanente. These often emphasize patient education and community provision as a means of driving down cost, and accumulation of knowledge about management of data flows and clinical and financial risk, albeit with many systems still relying on paper medical records. We have a lot to learn from these systems. France has, according to the World Health Organization (WHO), 'the best health system in the world',[2] having a reputation for high standards of care and facilities, yet this comes at a cost that is no longer viewed as sustainable, with more tests, longer hospital stays and more spending on pharmaceuticals than most other countries.

Across the world, commissioners responsible for purchasing healthcare have to balance infinite financial risk against the risk of poor outcomes. The goal is to deliver a service that is as perfect as possible, at a cost that is as small as possible, while simultaneously not making the population feel they have a poor health service, and allowing those who work within the service some pride in doing a good job, while at the same time not having to ask health staff to work so hard that they 'burn out'.

The history of commissioning in England

Commissioning is a relatively new term in UK healthcare. Until the 1980s it was usual for healthcare to be provided by local health authorities with little attention paid to exactly how the service was provided, and with no 'purchaser–provider split' in most cases. There was no idea at all of the price of healthcare, how many patients were made better or the unit cost of individual procedures. To a large extent, this reflects the lack of information systems available at the time, along with a different political background where, for some years, the NHS was not controversial as today.

The beginnings of the purchaser–provider split began with the policies of the Thatcher government in the early 1990s. In the early days there was little clinical involvement in the decisions. This was changed with the introduction of GP fundholding, in which individual practices, responsible for the primary care of between 2000 and 20 000 patients, were given budgets to buy their patients' community and secondary care as well. Not all practices joined the scheme, so health authorities continued to commission care on their behalf. Broadly the scheme was a success, with practices being able to buy care that met their patients' needs in a more local, timely and economic way than had been possible before. Health authorities oversaw the GP fundholders and were in turn overseen by regional health authorities. The end result of this process was that some areas of the country boasted superb, innovative healthcare, while other areas lagged behind. This became known as 'the postcode lottery', as the quality of secondary care delivered to patients often depended on which GP they were registered with.

A change in national government led to a decade-long period of multiple reorganizations of the NHS, driven centrally by prescriptive plans such as national service frameworks (NSFs) setting out exactly how care should look in most areas of disease. These NSFs were in turn administered by 'local implementation teams' (LITs). Clinical advice to health authorities was provided by small primary care groups, each with their own board and multi-professional 'professional executive committee' (PEC). These organizations were quickly found to be too small to successfully influence large providers, and were amalgamated to produce just over 300 primary care trusts (PCTs), in an exercise called 'shifting the balance of power', in 2002, which also saw the amalgamation of the 95 health authorities to form 28 overseeing strategic health authorities (SHAs), with PCTs gradually amalgamating to just over 150 larger organizations. In 2006 the SHAs were reduced to 10 in number. An outside observer could be forgiven for wondering whether, with each reorganization following so quickly on the heels of the previous one, and with commissioners having to concentrate on internal organizational change, there was any time left to do any actual commissioning.

Clinical engagement was originally provided through the LITs and PECs, with practice-based commissioning (PBC) being introduced in 2004.[3] This had the stated aim of:

- introducing a greater variety of services, from a greater number of providers in settings that are closer to home and more convenient to patients
- increased support of clinician-to-clinician dialogue about improving and developing care processes
- early and continuing involvement of practitioners in service development
- an additional set of levers to aid demand management.

There was variable uptake of PBC, both on the side of PCTs and GPs – in some areas it prospered, and in others led to a deterioration of relationships, with innovative GPs feeling that their good ideas were being blocked by PCTs. It was recognized that the quality of healthcare commissioning needed to be raised, leading to the introduction of a programme called 'world class commissioning' in 2007. Of this, the Department of Health said:[4]

> World class commissioning will be the key vehicle for delivering a world leading NHS, equipped to tackle the challenges of the 21st century. People are living longer, their lifestyles and health aspirations are changing, and the nature of public health and disease is evolving. By developing a more strategic, long-term and community focused approach to commissioning services, where commissioners and health and care professionals work together to deliver improved local health outcomes, world class commissioning will enable the NHS to meet the changing needs of the population and deliver a service which is clinically driven, patient-centred and responsive to local needs.

As with many of the changes discussed above, there was variable take-up of world class commissioning, with many areas paying lip service, but carrying on as before.

A further change of administration has introduced another development by abolishing PCTs, radically reducing the number of SHAs and giving the majority of commissioning power to what were initially called GP-led commissioning consortia (GPCC) and subsequently renamed clinical commissioning groups (CCGs), following a legislative 'pause' when the initial proposals proved too radical to be accepted. Overseeing all of these is the NHS Commissioning Board.

Clinical engagement

An example of well-organized clinical leadership in commissioning is provided by the Improving Access to Psychological Therapies (IAPT) programme. It was recognized from the start of this programme that clinical engagement was essential to achieving the aims of delivering 3600 new psychological therapists across half the country within a 3-year time-frame, especially when the training did not exist and neither did the two types of workers envisaged. Clinical engagement in the commissioning began at a national level with representatives from general practice, psychiatry and various talking treatment modalities on both the governing board of the programme and the expert reference group. A national primary care leader had one GP leader per SHA reporting to him, and the SHA leads, in turn, had one GP leader per PCT reporting to them. The SHA leads and national leader formed a network that met regularly at national level, with the PCT leads meeting at regional level and being responsible for clinical engagement in commissioning IAPT services at a PCT level. Each GP leader would only be 'commissioning' for a few hours a week, with the majority of the administration being handled by professional administrators with a civil service or clinical background. This split of responsibilities worked well, with medical leaders providing the inputs that they were best suited to, while others provided the administrative support that ensured the success of the programme. An early finding of the IAPT programme was that many medical leaders felt inadequate to the task in hand. To combat this, leadership training was organized at a regional level, along with 'coaching' of the leaders.

Areas of the country that were able to embrace these principles developed vibrant networks of clinical leaders who were engaged with their community, respected by their clinical peers, had good relationships with their commissioning colleagues and had a group of well trained peers to turn to for advice. It is no surprise that often the same areas developed high-quality clinical services in many areas and that these have continued to prosper.

The commissioning and contracting process

This section gives a very brief overview of the components of the commissioning cycle. It is not intended to be a guide to commissioning. As a consequence of the anticipated restructuring of the NHS, there is a wealth of good-quality information available for new commissioners. In particular, commissioners should be familiar with the ongoing work of the King's Fund in this area,[5] and online information is available from the now defunct National Mental Health Development Unit,[6] the NHS Information Centre[7] and NHS Primary Care Commissioning,[8] among others. A general guide to practical commissioning has been produced by the Joint Commissioning Panel for Mental Health[9] and specific examples of care pathway work are also available.[10]

This chapter has already looked at some of the challenges facing the NHS as it moves into a phase of transition between the existing commissioning arrangements and the future structures described within the *Liberating the NHS* white paper[11] and the government's responses following the recent listening exercise and the *NHS Future Forum* report.[12]

A review by Smith *et al.*[13] concluded that there are a number of clear advantages in commissioning services from a primary care perspective, but this needs to fall within the continuum of other commissioning models, from the personalization of care budgets through to a national commissioning framework. These approaches are at the core of the government's reform agenda. Good quality primary care-focused commissioning, driven by determined, well motivated and experienced managers and clinicians, can help to change long-standing working practices and cultural inertia within NHS systems.[14]

In countries that have sought to introduce a purchaser–provider split, through either private insurance schemes (e.g. the USA) or regulated health insurance markets (such as that implemented in the Netherlands and Belgium), the core principles remain consistent: understand the need, plan how this will be met, implement it and review the outcomes. Failure to do this runs the risk of commissioners merely becoming the passive payers of bills rather than dynamic and active healthcare leaders, a risk highlighted by analysis of commissioning within the Dutch system.[15]

Across a range of systems and healthcare models throughout the world, the commissioning cycle, in one guise or another, remains relatively constant. While the complexity of this in diagrammatic form varies from one publication to the next, or is adapted to reflect changes in regulatory systems, such as the Department of Health's world class commissioning competencies, commissioners must attempt to stay true to the core principles that underpin effective commissioning and explain how these core elements can expand to promote the effective commissioning of services and delivery of improved outcomes for the population they are seeking to serve. Although much literature, theory and opinion has been used to describe the commissioning process, it is in essence a simple cycle which involves identifying need, planning a response to meet the need, implementing plans and then reviewing the impact (see Fig. 5.1).

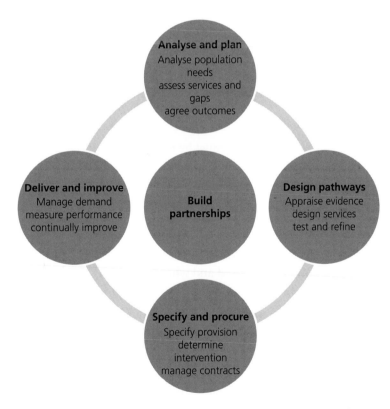

Figure 5.1 The clinical commissioning cycle. (Reproduced by kind permission of the Joint Commissioning Panel for Mental Health.)

Step 1: Analyse and plan

It is necessary to establish the importance of healthcare from patient, population, service and financial points of view in order to determine what is required. Good commissioning decisions should be based, first and foremost, on an excellent understanding of the population coupled with a sound evidence and knowledge base. Commissioning should not be about simply looking at what is already in place and determining whether this capacity is sufficient to meet current demand. An appreciation of the emerging demographic trends, population history of healthcare resource utilization and emergence of new treatments and services is key to this stage of the commissioning cycle.

Primary care trusts and local authorities already have a statutory obligation to carry out a joint strategic needs assessment (JSNA).[16] This obligation is strengthened through *Equality and Excellence, Liberating the NHS*.[11] CCGs and local authorities will be required to demonstrate, through the local health and well-being board structure, how their plans meet the priorities set out in the JSNA.

The JSNA should bring together the full range of local partner agencies to tell a strategic story about the needs of the population, both current and projected, and be used to plan for the development and delivery of future services. This can be particularly useful in the planning of services for large population groups or to identify particular changes in an area's demographic profile.

Of course, needs assessments do not need to be population-wide and commissioners will often wish to look at services or needs that are related to much more focused and targeted groups. This can be based on demographic profile, disease group or another common factor and can be carried out to meet specific priorities or issues that have a more local resonance, including, for example, introducing more alcohol practitioners in an area of high alcohol-induced morbidity or introducing psychological therapies into long-term condition care pathways.

In carrying out a needs analysis, it is also essential that commissioners consider what is not currently in place and where there are gaps in provision, what the risks are and how these might be mitigated within available resources.

Central to any plans, even in the early stages, must be the quantum of the resources that are available to commissioners. This should include an analysis of total financial resource, including opportunity cost from existing services, and an analysis of the impact cost of the initiative that they seek to implement.

Step 2: Design pathways

It is important to determine what information or data are available about the quality, effectiveness and cost of current services, how they are used and what kind of services are needed by patients and the public, in order to inform how best to design pathways of care.

Having completed the needs assessment, commissioners should now design or 'specify' the service they wish to commission. In contractual terms this will ultimately form part of the agreement between the commissioner and the eventual service provider and will form the basis upon which the service can be performance-managed.

The scale of this task can vary greatly and will obviously depend largely on the size and complexity of the service being commissioned.

Step 3: Specify and procure

It is imperative to determine what a good healthcare service looks like based on the local and national evidence. Specifying the service is, however, an essential component of commissioning and contracting and is often carried out in partnership with other agencies, including providers, to ensure the most effective agreements are reached about how the service will operate. However, caution should be applied if commissioners intend to procure a service through a competitive process, so as not to compromise a tender by giving an unfair advantage to one or more providers who may have been involved in drawing up the specification. Commissioners would wish to consider how they want to implement their planned service or initiative and take into account specific requirements regarding the procurement of services, taking legal advice as appropriate. At this stage the close involvement of the director of finance is vital to ensure that the proposal is affordable and has adequate resources allocated.

Step 4: Deliver and improve

This stage considers the services provided and how we can continually improve these to ensure they are safe, of the highest quality, clinically effective, provide a good patient experience and offer value for money, as well as performing to the contract and delivering national and local quality standards. At each stage of the commissioning cycle, commissioners need to work closely with patients and the public, health and social care commissioners, the voluntary sector and other stakeholders, including providers, to learn and adapt, given the interdependencies.

Although needs have already been considered in stage 1 of the process, the abilities of providers to meet needs and develop and improve services accordingly are key.

Building robust evaluation into service specifications, and then using this information to improve future service delivery, remains the most difficult aspect of the commissioning cycle. Recent examples of nationally prescribed good practice can be found in the development of the IAPT programme and its associated data set.[17] However, it is inevitable that in an environment of growing localism, national mandates such as these will become rarer, and commissioners will look to the NHS Commissioning Board for more support/guidance in this area.

It is also inevitable that evaluation of performance will highlight inadequacies in service specification. In the IAPT programme, initial plans were based around an estimate of performance, later refined into a complex workforce capacity tool. Both of these estimates were based on the very best evidence available at the time. Analysis of the huge amount of data produced by the IAPT programme has shown that actual performance differs from these estimates, leading to future estimates being refined. It is important that systems are mature enough to be able to adapt to changes required from evaluation.

Given the importance of the Nicholson challenge,[18] in which the NHS needs to make year-on-year efficiency savings of 4 per cent for 4 years from 2012 (this equates to an overall saving of some £20 billion), commissioners may also wish to consider the different ways in which services are evaluated, paying particular attention to cost-effectiveness and the broader question of quality-added life-years (QALYs).[19,20]

The changing commissioning landscape

The 2010 government spending review announced that between 2011–12 and 2014–15, the NHS will be subject to an unparalleled pressure to realize efficiencies and cost-effectiveness within the healthcare system. A total of £20 billion in efficiencies have to be found annually, with no inflationary uplift in the NHS budget.[18] Although this will inevitably put pressure on commissioning decision-making, it also provides an environment in which new and innovative commissioning can emerge. Remember that necessity is the mother of invention.

The principal mechanism by which the Department of Health is helping to drive local efficiency gains is the QIPP (Quality, Innovation, Performance and Prevention) programme.[21] Although there is currently no national QIPP workstream for mental health, some SHAs have begun to describe how QIPP could be applied to mental health pathways.

One of the criticisms that could be directed at the current QIPP workstreams is that mental health co-morbidity and its impact on the management of physical illness is not well considered. However, the economic case for providing robust liaison services in acute care has now been demonstrated, with a cost to benefit ratio of 4:1,[22] and this will hopefully stimulate commissioners and managers to consider the importance of treating patients holistically and how this benefits not only QIPP, but also the whole Nicholson challenge.[18] This can only be achieved through an integrated approach to commissioning healthcare.

It is important that readers are aware of the changing commissioning landscape and, in particular, the role of the NHS Commissioning Board. The Joint Commissioning Panel for Mental Health (JCPMH) has described the changing commissioning landscape in great detail.[9] In essence the NHS Commissioning Board will have two primary functions: a limited commissioning function and holding clinical commissioning groups to account.

Commissioners need to be mindful of the development of payment by results (PbR) for mental health[23] and how this will impact on the change in the commissioning landscape. The development of a PbR framework for mental health is important to attribute payments against level of patient need (as determined by allocation to an appropriate cluster). However, the PbR mechanism for mental health is secondary care-focused. This may be appropriate for financial arrangements, but compartmentalizes the patient journey, potentially providing challenges for vertical commissioning arrangements.

There is an increasing public and political expectation placed upon the NHS to provide quality services while at the same time remaining cost-effective. While the National Institute for Health and Clinical Excellence (NICE) remains the arbiter of clinical practice, there are other mechanisms that can drive the development of high-quality services,[24] including, *inter alia*, commissioning for quality and innovation frameworks (CQUINs) and patient-reported outcome measures (PROMs).[25] The CQUINs can also be used to further stimulate the development of new approaches to providing integrated physical and mental healthcare, through target-driven incentives.[26]

A commissioning opportunity – mental health and physical health co-morbidity

The Department of Health estimates that there are 15 million people living with a long-term condition (LTC) in England, and that these people are the main drivers of cost and activity in the NHS, as they account for around 70 per cent of overall health and care spend. People with LTCs are disproportionately higher users of the health services – representing 50 per cent of GP appointments, 60 per cent of outpatient and A&E attendances and 70 per cent of in-patient bed-days.[27] However, these figures can only be compounded if patients have co-morbid mental health problems. Physical illness increases the risk of mental health problems. NICE[28] has reported that compared with the general population, people with LTCs such as diabetes, hypertension and coronary artery disease have double the rate of depression and those with chronic obstructive pulmonary disease and cerebrovascular disease have triple the rate. People with two or more physical LTCs are seven times more likely to have depression.

Commissioning across mental and physical healthcare pathways (what is often referred to as horizontal commissioning) needs to be seen within the broader context of public health and the social care landscape. There is an emerging body of research evidence showing that better management of co-morbid mental health conditions can lead to better outcomes.[29]

NHS Diabetes, an LTC-specific organization, has recently published extensive guidance for clinicians on the importance of mental and emotional health in the management of diabetes,[30,31] and these outcomes cannot be realized without the associated robust commissioning that builds psychological interventions into the diabetes care pathways.[10]

Commissioning services that meet the mental health needs of people with physical conditions in primary and secondary care can both reduce the impact of and prevent development of mental illness in these higher-risk groups. This approach would involve a vertically integrated commissioning model. Some studies also show that appropriate management of mental health conditions leads to better physical health outcomes and compliance with treatment regimens.[29]

Commissioning appropriate care pathways, at the critical interface between physical and mental health, has the potential to begin to address the system efficiencies demanded by current government policy while meeting the holistic needs of the patient. In effect, a multidimensional commissioning approach needs to be adopted that spans the barriers between primary and acute care, and encompasses the needs of the individual through the commissioning of services outside of the sometimes reductionist health paradigm.

Conclusion

As the NHS implements its new structures, it is important that the commissioning of services is not undertaken in isolation, but seeks to integrate the overall health and well-being of individuals and the local community into efficient service structures. It is conceivable that there will be a shift in commissioning emphasis towards health promotion and the prevention of illness. Given the necessity of finding system efficiencies, there should also be a focus on evidence-based, value-for-money and cost-effective interventions that sit across the whole life course. Commissioning of services should also offer greater choice through the development of the personalization agenda and enhanced working arrangements with the voluntary and private sectors.

Having clinicians' involvement in commissioning is going to be vital to ensure delivery of these aims. Those clinicians who are involved need to be well trained in medical leadership, the theory of commissioning and clinical governance, provided with sufficient time to perform the tasks required of them, and be backed up by an able administrative team of experienced commissioners. Finally they need support from board-level sponsors to ensure that their commissioning decisions are implemented with a minimum of delay.

Summary

❏ Commissioning involves specifying and purchasing defined services to meet potentially infinite clinical need, which will grow every year, with finite resources.

❏ Every commissioning system must handle both the clinical and financial risks inherent in this tension.

❏ Close involvement of clinicians in commissioning can help to mitigate these risks.

❏ Clinicians involved in these roles need dedicated time and administrative support, and need to be trained for the role.

❏ The commissioning cycle must include measurement of performance, coupled with continuous improvement, achieved through adapting to changes revealed by evaluation as necessary.

❏ Commissioning needs to integrate all health services, providing well-being from cradle to grave, and ranging from prevention (which will become more important during the financial crisis) to mental and physical health.

❏ Commissioning services that cross these traditional boundaries can provide better value, delivering improved clinical outcomes at lower cost.

References

1. Department of Health (2010). *Robert Francis Inquiry report into Mid_Staffordshire NHS Foundation Trust*. London: Department of Health.

2. Aire S (2011). French healthcare: the high cost of excellence. *Br Med J* 342,1524.

3. Department of Health (2004). *Practice Based Commissioning: Promoting Clinical Engagement*. London: Department of Health.

4. Department of Health (2007). *World Class Commissioning, Adding Life to Years and Years to Life*. London: Department of Health.

5. Imison C, Naylor C, Goodwin N, Buck D, Curry N, Addicott R, Zollinger-Read P (2011). Transforming Our Health Care System: Ten Priorities for Commissioners. London: The King's Fund.

6. National Mental Health Development Unit (2011). Available from: http://www.nmhdu.org.uk/.

7. NHS Information Centre (2011). Available from: http://www.ic.nhs.uk/commissioning.

8. NHS Primary Care Commissioning (2011). *Personal Learning for Commissioning*. Available from: http://www.pcc.nhs.uk/commissioning-cycle-pdev. Accessed: March 2012.

9. Bennett A, Appleton S, Jackson C (2011). *Practical Mental Health Commissioning: A Framework for Local Authority and NHS Commissioners of Mental Health and Wellbeing Services*. Available from: http://www.jcpmh.info

10. NHS Diabetes (2011). *Commissioning Mental Health and Diabetes Services*. London: NHS Diabetes.

11. Department of Health (2010). *Equality and Excellence: Liberating the NHS*. London: Department of Health. Available from: http://www.dh.gov.uk/

12. Department of Health (2011). *Government Response to the NHS Future Forum Report*. London: Department of Health. Available from: http://www.dh.gov.uk/

13. Smith J, Mays N, Dixon J, Goodwin N, Lewis R, McClelland S, McLeod H, Wyke S (2004). *A Review of the Effectiveness of Primary Care-led Commissioning in the UK NHS*. London: The Health Foundation.

14. Ham C (2007). *Commissioning in the English NHS: the Case for Integration*. London: Nuffield Trust for Research and Policy Studies in Health Services.

15. Figueras J, Robinson R, Jakubowski, eds (2005). *Purchasing to Improve Health Systems Performance*. Maidenhead: Open University Press.

16. Local Government and Public Involvement in Health Act (2007).

17. National IAPT Programme Team (2011). The IAPT Data Handbook: Guidance on Recording and Monitoring Outcomes to Support Local Evidence-based Practice. Available from: http://www.workingforwellness.org.uk/

18. The Treasury (2010). *Spending Review 2010*. London: TSO. Available from: http://www.hm-treasury.gov.uk/

19. Phillips C (2009). What is a QALY? London: Hayward Medical Communications.

20. EuroQol Group (2011). *EQ-5D: a Standardised Instrument for Use as a Measure of Health Outcomes*. Available from: http://www.euroqol.org/

21. Department of Health (2011). *Quality, Innovation, Performance and Prevention (QIPP) Workstreams*. London: Department of Health. Available from: http://www.dh.gov.uk/

22. Parsonage M, Fossey M (2011). *Economic Evaluation of a Liaison Psychiatry Service*. London: Centre for Mental Health.

23. Department of Health (2011). *2012–13 Mental Health PbR Guidance*. Gateway reference 16645. London: Department of Health.

24. Carr V, Sangiorgi D, Cooper R, Buscher M, Junginger S, eds (2010). Creating Sustainable Frameworks for Service Redesign at Practice Level in the NHS. Better Healthcare Through Better Infrastructure. *3rd Annual Conference of the Health and Care Infrastructure Research and Innovation Centre*; 22–24 September 2010; Edinburgh, Scotland.

25. Department of Health (2011). *PROMs in England: A Methodology for Identifying Potential Outliers*. London: Department of Health.

26. Department of Health (2010). *Using the Commissioning for Quality and Innovation (CQUIN) Payment Framework – Guidance on National Goals for 2011/12*. London: Department of Health.

27. Department of Health (2011). *QIPP workstreams: Long Term Conditions*. London: Department of Health. Available from: http://www.dh.gov.uk/

28. National Institute for Health and Clinical Excellence (NICE) (2009). *Depression in Adults with a Chronic Physical Health Problem: Treatment and Management*. London: NICE.

29. Naylor C, Bell A (2010). *Mental Health and the Productivity Challenge, Improving Quality and Value for Money*. London: King's Fund.

30. Richards L (2011). *Emotional and Psychological Support in Diabetes*. London: NHS Diabetes.

31. Diabetes UK (2008). *Minding the Gap: the Provision of Psychological Support and Care for People with Diabetes in the UK*. London: Diabetes UK.

Chapter 6

Measuring healthcare outcomes

Julian Flowers and Raja Badrakalimuthu

Introduction

Measuring the outcome of healthcare is not new but it is increasingly important. There are three main drivers:

- *Concerns about quality of care* – beginning with the Bristol Royal Infirmary Inquiry and the Shipman affair, but continuing more recently with the Mid-Staffordshire Inquiry.
- *Financial constraints* – universally, the funding to pay for healthcare is being outstripped by demand, and doubly so since the recession, with real-terms reduction or flat cash settlements for the NHS. This is shifting the focus away from paying for activity and towards productivity, paying for outcomes and 'value' – benefit or outcome of care per unit cost. Commissioners of care are increasingly looking towards outcome-based commissioning.
- *Politics* – allied to financial constraints there are a number of other issues, such as (perceived) public interest in outcomes, that are drivers for change and for a move towards public sector data transparency in order to hold public services to account (and to make the data available to generate new markets).

Taken together these factors have increased the demand for outcome measures and outcome measurement, and medical managers will be in the thick of it.

In this chapter we outline a practical framework for measuring healthcare outcomes, discuss the need to consider different perspectives in outcome measurement, emphasize the need for a population approach and give some examples.

Outcome measurement

The outcome of medical therapy has always been of interest – it is said that the medical profession only started doing more good than harm (in terms of lives saved) in the early part of the twentieth century. In ancient Egypt, untoward outcomes were punished by fiscal and financial penalties depending on the severity of the mishap.[1] Outcome measurement by hospitals in the 1800s was largely limited to collecting mortality statistics, with no regard for the results of the operations and interventions that were performed. Florence Nightingale (1820–1910) wrote, in her important 1863 treatise *Notes on Hospitals*: 'If the function of a hospital were to kill the sick, statistical comparison of this nature would be admissible.'[2]

Ernest Codman (1869–1940) was the first clinician to systematically follow up all patients to record the 'end result' of the surgical care they received in his hospital in Boston and his work laid the basis for future studies on the outcome of medical care.[3] He was keen on following patients up and publishing what happened to them. Nowadays we are more familiar with the work of Donabedian, who introduced the concept of structure, process and outcomes to evaluate medical care. He proposed a three-tier flowchart to evaluate medical intervention:[4]

- Structure – the characteristics of a healthcare setting, such as the inputs (e.g. beds, staff, equipment).
- Process – what is done to the patient.
- Outcomes – the health of the patient after intervention.

Why measure outcomes?

There are many reasons for measuring healthcare outcomes (see Box 6.1). Clinicians and services want to do the best for their patients. Commissioners and public health practitioners are interested in ensuring that need is met, that services are value for money and that health services continue to contribute towards overall health improvement. Policymakers and the public are increasingly interested in transparency and open publication of outcomes in the belief that it will drive up quality, improve choice and increase accountability. In other words, healthcare outcomes are everyone's business.

Box 6.1 Uses of outcome measures

- Healthcare policy evaluation
- Transparency
- Quality improvement
- Patient choice
- Political accountability
- Healthcare evaluation
- Economic evaluation
- Resource allocation
- Clinical decisions on individual patient
- Clinical governance: auditing performance against set standards
- Population health and needs assessment

As part of the outcome measures for accountability, the NHS is introducing an outcomes framework (NHS Outcomes Framework), which is a development of the quality framework (see Box 6.2). The NHS Outcomes Framework has four domains comprising 51 indicators, which measure outcomes. A complete data set is not available for all the indicators.

> **Box** 6.2 NHS Outcomes Framework
>
> - Effective care
>   - Reducing avoidable mortality
>   - Improved outcome for long-term conditions
>   - Improved recovery from acute illness
> - Positive experience of care
> - Safe care
> - For each domain there will be:
>   - Overarching indicators
>   - Improvement areas

Definitions

The Institute of Medicine defines healthcare quality as 'the degree to which health services for individuals and populations increases the likelihood of desired health outcomes that are consistent with current professional knowledge'.[5] In other words, a healthcare outcome is the extent to which a treatment, intervention or service achieved what it was intended to achieve – it compares what actually happened with what was expected to happen. A healthcare outcome can be thought of as the following equation:

$$\text{Healthcare outcome} = \frac{\text{Observed result of care}}{\text{Expected result of care}}$$

A number of things follow from this definition

- We need to know what happens to our patients – *observed result of care.*
- We need to know what are the objectives or potential outcomes of care – *which outcomes should we measure?*
- We need to know what the treatment or service is capable of achieving, i.e. its efficacy and effectiveness – *what is the expected result of care?*
- We need to know what patients want or hope to achieve – *whose perspective?*
- We therefore need to know what 'good' looks like and the extent to which we have achieved treatment goals – *what should we expect to achieve?*

This inevitably means we need a range of information and knowledge. Our knowledge of what treatments can or should achieve comes from a variety of sources, including:

- experience and observational studies
- what patients tell us
- clinical trials
- comparative effectiveness studies.

Types of outcome

No clinician goes to work to do a bad job or not to do the best for their patients. Healthcare systems each aim to provide cost-effective, high-quality services to patients and their carers, to promote optimal health and development and to reduce the personal, family and societal burden of morbidity affecting economic productivity of the community. Approaches to quantifying healthcare interventions have included measuring adverse events,[6] studying gains in life expectancy[7] or measuring the cost of a service in relation to health benefits.

Types of outcome measures include:

- physical/clinical (e.g. mortality)
- performance/function (self-care)
- economic (cost/benefit)
- humanistic (quality of life).

A comprehensive approach to outcome measurement is considered to include clinical outcomes, functional health status, cost and patient satisfaction. In this section we review different types of outcome measures.

Population health outcomes

The ultimate objective of the NHS is to improve healthy life expectancy. This is a combination of how long people live and the quality of their lives – either free from disability or in self-reported good health. Life expectancy is measured from mortality data, and mortality rates and life expectancy are routinely calculated by the Office for National Statistics (ONS) and the National Centre for Health Outcomes Development (NCHOD, www.nchod.nhs.uk). Information on healthy or disability-free life expectancy is more difficult to obtain, because we don't routinely collect data on disability or self-reported health. Life expectancy in England increases by about three months every year and the proportion of life lived in good health or without disability is also increasing (Fig. 6.1).

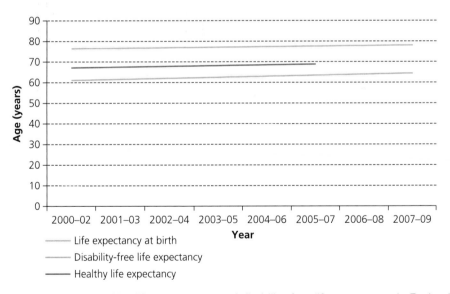

Figure 6.1 Life expectancy, healthy life expectancy and disability-free life expectancy in England. (*Source:* Office for National Statistics.[8])

Mortality data as outcome has a number of advantages:

- It is a 'hard' outcome that most people are interested in.
- It is measured accurately and completely (although there is variation in the coding of cause of death).
- Data is readily available and free.

Measure-based outcomes – event-based and time-based

Event-based outcomes, as the name suggests, are those which tell us whether some desired or undesired outcome has occurred, usually within a given time period, e.g. stroke, readmission, return to work or death. These are often presented as rates or proportions.

Time-based outcomes include a measure of follow-up or time to events. The denominator for these types of measures is usually patient time. Indicators using this approach include survival rates and years of life lost measures like quality-adjusted life-years (QALYs), disability-adjusted life-years (DALYs) and standardized rates of years of life lost (SYLLs).

A substantial proportion of modern clinical practice is preventive care. Although this has many names – e.g. prophylaxis, anticipatory care, chronic disease management – essentially we are moving from responding to symptoms or crises towards predicting and trying to prevent future events in patients or trying to slow disease progression. There is a strong evidence base to support this.

One of the problems this creates for outcomes measurement is that success is often measured by *absence* of outcome and cannot be assessed at an individual patient level (unless they have very frequent events or are at very high risk of an event). The fact that a patient hasn't suffered the event in question does not mean that treatment has been successful. Success can only really be assessed at a population level by a reduction in event rate.

Clinical outcomes

Taking diabetes care as an example, the ultimate objective of the service is to reduce mortality and complications of diabetes and improve the quality of life for people with diabetes. Clinical outcomes will relate to diabetic control (pattern of blood glucose and haemoglobin A1c [HbA1c]), absence of blindness and microvascular complications and so on. Service outcome measures might be:

- mortality rate in diabetes (deaths in patients with diabetes)
- mortality rate from diabetes (deaths from diabetes per 1000 of population)
- dialysis rate/rate of renal failure
- rates of blindness/retinopathy.

However, with the exception of mortality rates these are prevalence measures and cannot be reduced unless the incidence of complications is reduced, so the outcome measure of interest should be a reduction in the incidence of complications. Measuring this poses a number of difficulties relating to:

- relevant information systems
- data linkage, e.g. from clinical data to mortality data
- defining the onset of complication
- duration of follow-up.

For these reasons a population approach, including population registers, and annual review are essential for chronic disease management. This allows relevant data to be collected and outcome measures to be calculated.

Functional and patient outcomes – PROMs and PREMs

There is increasing interest not only in the clinical effects of care but also in the extent to which patients feel and function better as a result of treatment. Patient-reported outcome measures (PROMs) are increasingly being developed and used, based on (largely) well-validated instruments previously used mainly in research settings.[9] These measures tend to incorporate a range of outcome measures such as function, symptoms, well-being and mobility.

From April 2009 the Department of Health has required the routine measurement of PROMs for all NHS patients in England before and after receiving surgery, via its PROMs programme.[10] The initial data collection is for four elective procedures: hip and knee replacements, varicose veins and hernia repair. Three instruments are used: the EuroQol instrument EQ-5D (www.euroqol.org), a visual analogue scale and a disease-specific instrument (Oxford hip and knee scores and Aberdeen varicose vein scores).

Although the use of PROMs in clinical practice is well developed in some areas of clinical practice, in others it is still in its infancy. Nevertheless, aggregate data available so far suggests that there are variations and inequalities in thresholds for surgery (more deprived populations have higher PROM scores preoperatively), can demonstrate the benefits of treatment (e.g. there are large increases in EQ-5D scores following hip replacement) and points the way to future outcome measures. One concern about the use of PROM information is that the data is subjective. PROMs data should therefore be seen as complementing clinical and other information about patients and should be part of a report with other outcomes.

Alongside patient reporting of outcome, there is considerable effort in collecting data on patient-reported experience of their care in hospital or other healthcare settings (giving patient-reported experience measures, or PREMs). There are also increasing numbers of web-based services allowing patients and users to rate services and clinicians.

Measuring healthcare outcome: indicators and metrics

Choosing indicators or outcome measures

There are a number of suggested criteria for selecting indicators. Box 6.3 lists criteria for outcome measures, adapted from the Instrument Review Criteria of the Medical Outcomes Trust Scientific Advisory Committee.[11]

Box 6.3 Criteria for outcome measures

- Reliability and reproducibility
- Validity of measurement
- Responsiveness or sensitivity to change
- Ease of interpretability
- Flexibility and administrative usefulness
- Language and/or cultural adaptations

Another widely used source is the *Good Indicators Guide*,[12] which suggests the following criteria for filtering potential outcome measures:

- Does the indicator/measure address the key issues? Is it both important and relevant?
- Validity of measurement – does the indicator measure what it purports to measure (both on the face of it and in its construction)?
- Can the outcome be measured conceptually and can the data be collected (at reasonable cost and effort)?

- Ease of interpretability – is there variation; can a high or low value be interpreted; how will the results be communicated?
- Implications – what will you do with the result? Will people change their behaviour? Will there be unintended consequences (e.g. 'gaming', where the data is manipulated towards achieving a specific outcome or incentive)? How will the data be used – for performance or for improvement and feedback?

Anatomy of an outcome measure

Any outcome measure will have a number of essential components (see the *Good Indicators Guide*[12]), as follows:

- a rationale for choosing the outcome measure and what the outcome indicates
- a population at risk/of interest – e.g. people aged 15–45 years with diabetes
- a case definition for the numerator
- a unit of analysis – e.g. primary care trust, NHS trust, diabetic service
- an outcome numerator – e.g. the number of people with grade 1 or worse retinopathy
- a denominator – e.g. the population at risk
- a time-frame – e.g. between January and December 2010
- the value of the measure – e.g. proportion, rate
- a measure of uncertainty – e.g. confidence intervals or control limits
- frequency of measurement – e.g. monthly or weekly.

So, for example, the reporting rate to the National Reporting and Learning Service is often used as a measure of patient safety. This measures how well trusts report safety incidents to the National Patient Safety Agency. A high rate is currently thought to be good, indicating an open culture of reporting. The measure itself is a rate of reported counts of events per time period divided by total bed-days $\times$ 1000 (i.e. events per 100 bed-days). It is reported by NHS trusts on a quarterly basis.

Evaluation – the application and use of healthcare outcome measures

There are generally three questions that need to be answered:

- How are we doing? Are our outcomes what we should expect for a population like ours?
- Are we improving – are our outcomes improving?
- Are we improving relative to expectation, e.g. at the same rate as the national average?

Statistical methods using statistical process control methods are increasingly used for analyzing outcomes and performance.

How do you compare?

In order to understand current performance you need to make external comparison. This could be against an agreed professional standard, a literature-based reported achievement or direct comparison with data from peers, or the national or peer average.

One increasingly popular method for data-based comparison is the use of funnel plots (see Fig. 6.2).[13,14] These plot the value of an outcome measure of interest against sample size for the areas or units being compared, showing outliers and the degree of variation at a glance. Funnel plots can be calculated for a range of measures, and spreadsheet templates for many can be obtained from the Association of Public Health Observatories website.[15]

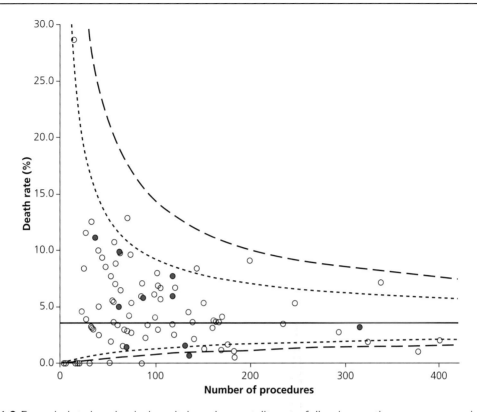

Figure 6.2 Funnel plot showing in-hospital crude mortality rate following aortic aneurysm repair for NHS trusts in England in 2009/10. The average rate is 4 per cent (solid straight line). The 'funnels' show the expected variation due to chance given the number of procedures. The narrow dotted line encompasses points within two standard deviations (SD) of the mean and the dashed line 3 SDs. Most points lie within the funnel, indicating that the variation is largely due to chance. All these trusts have a mortality rate consistent with the national average. There a few outlying trusts – five with rates >2 SD from the mean and several with low or zero mortality rates. There is a wide variation in the number of procedures per trust and a suggestion of a weak volume mortality relationship with lower mortality in larger trusts. (*Source*: HES.)

Are you improving?

This involves tracking your own performance over time. Change or improvement can be assessed using s-charts or run charts. Here the outcome measure is plotted over time against the long-term average value for the whole time period of interest.

Usually, in a stable system, data points will fluctuate up and down around the average in an unpredictable way. There are, however, a number of patterns in the data which are unlikely to be due to chance and are 'signals' or special cause variations. These variations may indicate a systematic issue worthy of investigation and include:

- eight or more points in a row either side of the mean
- eight or more points increasing or decreasing
- obvious regular patterns in the data
- extreme values.

An example tracking hospital mortality rates is shown in Figure 6.3.

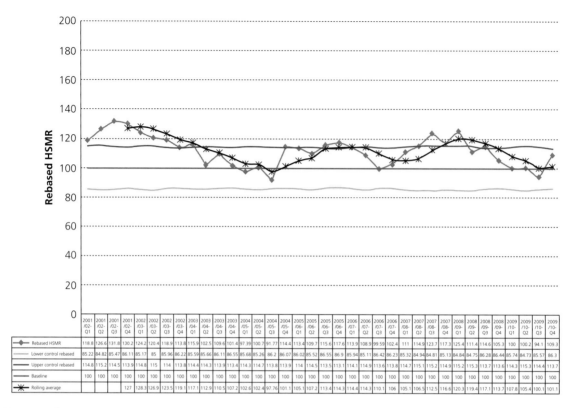

	2001 /02- Q1	2001 /02- Q2	2001 /02- Q3	2001 /02- Q4	2002 /03- Q1	2002 /03- Q2	2002 /03- Q3	2002 /03- Q4	2003 /04- Q1	2003 /04- Q2	2003 /04- Q3	2003 /04- Q4	2004 /05- Q1	2004 /05- Q2	2004 /05- Q3	2004 /05- Q4	2005 /06- Q1	2005 /06- Q2	2005 /06- Q3	2005 /06- Q4	2006 /07- Q1	2006 /07- Q2	2006 /07- Q3	2006 /07- Q4	2007 /08- Q1	2007 /08- Q2	2007 /08- Q3	2007 /08- Q4	2008 /09- Q1	2008 /09- Q2	2008 /09- Q3	2008 /09- Q4	2009 /10- Q1	2009 /10- Q2	2009 /10- Q3	2009 /10- Q4
Rebased HSMR	118.8	126.6	131.8	130.2	124.2	120.4	118.9	113.8	115.9	102.5	109.6	101.4	97.39	100.7	91.77	114.4	113.4	109.7	115.6	117.6	113.9	108.9	99.59	102.4	111	114.9	123.7	117.3	125.4	111.4	114.6	105.3	100	100.2	94.1	109.3
Lower control rebased	85.22	84.82	85.47	86.11	85.17	85	85.96	86.22	85.59	85.66	86.11	86.55	85.68	85.26	86.2	86.07	86.02	85.52	86.55	86.9	85.94	85.11	86.42	86.23	85.32	84.94	84.81	85.13	84.84	84.75	86.28	86.44	85.74	84.73	85.57	86.3
Upper control rebased	114.8	115.2	114.5	113.9	114.8	115	114	113.8	114.4	114.3	113.9	113.4	114.3	114.7	113.8	113.9	114	114.5	113.5	113.1	114.1	114.9	113.6	113.8	114.7	115.1	115.2	114.9	115.2	115.3	113.7	113.6	114.3	115.3	114.4	113.7
Baseline	100	100	100	100	100	100	100	100	100	100	100	100	100	100	100	100	100	100	100	100	100	100	100	100	100	100	100	100	100	100	100	100	100	100	100	100
Rolling average			127	128.3	126.9	123.5	119.1	117.1	112.9	110.5	107.2	102.6	102.4	97.76	101.1	105.1	107.2	113.4	114.3	114.4	114.3	110.1	106	105.1	106.5	112.5	116.6	120.3	119.4	117.1	113.7	107.8	105.4	100.1	101.1	

Figure 6.3 A control chart for hospital standardized mortality ratios (HSMRs). A typical trust should have an HSMR fluctuating around 100 (or below) and not exceeding the upper control limit (the upper solid line). In the example here, there are runs of consecutive data points exceeding the mean (100), and on several occasions the HSMR exceeds the upper control limit. This trust has had a persistently high HSMR. (Data reproduced with permission of Quality Intelligence East © QIE, 2011.)

The 'rules' for interpreting and creating run or control charts are beyond the scope of this chapter, but interested readers are directed to Carey and Lloyd[16] or the Association of Public Health Observatory briefings.[17,18]

Challenges and issues in measuring healthcare outcomes

Data quality

One of the major issues with measuring outcome is the lack of relevant data or the quality of data that is collected. The NHS collects a vast amount of data derived from returns or directly from clinical systems or audits. Increasingly there are national audits, but probably the single most important source of outcome data are Hospital Episode Statistics (HES). The Secondary Uses Services (SUS) dataset is the standard NHS database for performance and finance.[19] This data is collected directly from NHS trusts on a monthly or weekly basis and can be used to estimate mortality, length of stay, readmission rates and many other potential outcomes. It is increasingly being linked to other datasets such as PROMs and ONS mortality data.

HES data is used to generate hospital standardized mortality ratios and will be used as the source for the new NHS mortality index – the Summary Hospital-level Mortality Indicator (SHMI).[20] The HES data contains information on millions of in-patient episodes and A&E and outpatient attendances and has virtually complete population coverage so it can provide a wealth of comparative data. There is a similar database for mental healthcare known as the Mental Health Minimum Dataset (MHMDS).

These datasets are widely used by policymakers, public health, commissioners and researchers, but rarely by clinicians. The reasons for this have recently been reviewed by the Academy of Medical Royal Colleges (AMRC) and a key finding is that there is a 'vicious circle of data quality' – clinicians perceive the data as being of poor quality because they are insufficiently exposed and engaged, but they need to engage with the datasets to improve data quality. There is increasing evidence that HES data is at least as good as some clinical audit data and is more comprehensive than most.[21,22] Professional bodies are increasingly using and exploring the clinical value of HES for quality improvement and revalidation.

Unlike primary care data, HES data is relatively clinically limited, collecting data on diagnoses and procedures but little else. A key recommendation of the AMRC report is that the 'data quality is the responsibility of the consultant'. To facilitate this, clinicians need feedback in the data and means to enhance its quality.

Analyzed or raw HES data is available from a number of free sources:

- the NHS Information Centre (www.hesonline.nhs.uk)
- NHS comparators (www.nhscomparators.nhs.uk)
- quality and public health observatories – who can undertake bespoke analysis, provide data and have considerable expertise in using HES (www.apho.org.uk www.qualityobservatory.nhs.uk).

There are also a number of commercial sources (e.g. CHKS, Dr Foster Intelligence and Lightfoot Solutions), who buy the HES data from the Information Centre to develop 'added value' products.

It takes time…

For many outcomes it takes time to know whether or not they will develop, and demonstrating improvement or deterioration in health and care outcomes cannot be done instantaneously. As mentioned earlier, it takes at least seven or eight time periods to be confident that a change has taken place unless improvement is dramatic. The shorter the monitoring time period, the fewer the events and the less likely that it will be possible to detect change from period to period.

Alternatively one can use 'intermediate' outcomes, where there is evidence to link the clinical or intermediate outcome with the overall outcome, or more short-term outcomes like PROMs which are more focused on well-being and symptoms.

In the diabetes services, for example, HbA1c levels can be used as an outcome measure for both individual patients and the service. Using intermediate outcomes is legitimate if there is a clear causal link between the true outcome of interest and the intermediate measure. In the Quality and Outcomes Framework in general practice, GPs are rewarded for the proportion of the registered population with HbA1c < 7. There is clear evidence linking HbA1c with outcome in diabetes – there are links with mortality and diabetic complications.

Outcome or process?

Given the lack of outcome data, outcome measures and the relative infrequency of outcome events, some argue that process should be measured instead.[23] After all process is what we can directly influence and set standards and targets for. For example, rather than measuring mortality following primary angioplasty for ST-elevation myocardial infarction, it might be better to measure the proportion of patients who receive revascularization within target times. This is reasonable given that there is a strong evidential link between time to treatment and mortality, it can be measured contemporaneously, it is statistically more powerful and it can be influenced directly. In practice it is useful to have both process measures and outcome measures.

It is important to evaluate the process of care by which the particular outcome is measured. Outcomes management encompasses three components:[24]

- outcomes measurement – the systematic quantifying of outcome indicators at a single point in time
- outcomes monitoring – repeated measurement of outcomes indicators over time
- outcomes management – making use of information gained from monitoring care to improve clinical decision-making and delivery of healthcare.

To risk-adjust or not to risk-adjust

Comparing outcomes between organizations or units always causes anxiety and debate. Organizations want comparisons to be 'fair' – they usually want outcome measures to exclude or be adjusted for things beyond their control, such as age, sex, demographic factors, co-morbidity or case mix. Nevertheless, adjustment is in itself controversial – much of the debate around hospital mortality rates centres on the adjustments made and whether they introduce more bias than not adjusting at all.[25]

Adjustment works well when there is a professionally agreed evidence-based system for adjustment, and there is consistent, accurate and complete collection of variables needed for the adjustment process. Cardiac surgeons have led the way and publish outcome measures per unit and per surgeon for mortality from coronary artery bypass graft and valve surgery.[26] The question is often asked why this can't be done for other areas, and to some extent it is: 30-day mortality rates are available for a range of conditions and procedures, and clinical audits like ICNARC and MTOS create risk-adjusted comparative data but often there is no agreed method for case-mix adjustment, outcomes like mortality are not appropriate and relevant data is not collected.

Limitations of outcome measures in mental health

Types of outcome measures in mental health

Standardized symptom-based measures underpin psychiatric research, as mental health services involve the care of persons with chronic and functionally disabling disorders for which standard measures such as mortality have limited application. They include standardized instruments that quantify the frequency and intensity of symptoms (such as the Hamilton Depression Rating Scale)[27] and patient-based instruments, which measure the impact of mental health disorders on individuals and their day-to-day lives.

Global measures of outcome such as the Global Assessment of Functioning Scale[28] include some overall assessment by clinicians of both functioning and severity of psychiatric symptom intensity, which are applicable across patients irrespective of diagnosis.

As mental disorders are generally strongly associated with social dysfunction, instruments such as the Social Adjustment Scale[29] and the Index of Activities of Daily Living[30] have regularly been used as outcome measures of social functioning. Quality of life and health-related quality of life have been developed specifically for use among people with mental disorders and measure more than just psychopathological symptoms or single domains of health-related quality of life such as the Quality of Life Inventory (QOLI).[31]

The Health of the Nation Outcome Scales (HoNOS) was created by Royal College of Psychiatrists[32] as part of the development of a mental health minimum dataset. Clinicians have felt it to be psychometrically unsound and difficult to use despite claims that it was a useful adjunct to history-taking and a useful focus of discussion within multidisciplinary team meetings. Gilbody et al.[33] have suggested that the enduring benefit of this measure might therefore be as an adjunct to improve the process by which care is given – by improving professional communication – rather than as a measure of outcome, where it is widely held to be a flawed instrument.

Usefulness and limitations of outcome measures in mental health

There has been some scepticism over the use of outcome measures in mental health[27] – some suggested benefits are outlined in Box 6.4. Gilbody et al.[34] undertook a survey of the current use of outcome measures by UK psychiatrists in their practice and found that the majority of clinicians do not use them at all in their day-to-day practice except for screening cognitive impairment. They also reported that there is very limited evidence for the effect of outcome measurements on the management of patients in psychiatric settings, apart from the effect of routine outcome measurement on the detection and management of minor psychiatric disorders in general practice and in the general hospital.

Box 6.4 Usefulness of outcomes in mental health in improving patient care

- Identifying problems which might not otherwise be recognized by clinicians or those responsible for care
- Outcome measures might be used to monitor the course of patients' progress over time, to make decisions about treatment and to assess subsequent therapeutic impact
- Clinicians find data from outcome measures useful in formulating a more comprehensive assessment of patients
- Patients have the opportunity to provide information that is comprehensively assessed, thus aiding effective patient–doctor communication

---

Role of medical managers in outcome measurement and monitoring

Medical managers will play an increasing role in helping to improve the quality and value of the services they are responsible for in a number of ways:

- helping to shape outcome measures for their individual services, including benchmarking against peers or comparator services, and helping to develop appropriate outcome measures and indicators
- working with colleagues to improve the quality of data that is used for outcome measurement – in particular, engaging in improving the quality of HES and MHMDS data, which will be increasingly

used to develop comparative national information for trusts and services. This includes reconciliation between clinical databases and clinical audit data and the HES data[35]

- advising their organization on the publication of quality metrics and outcome measures in quality accounts
- board reporting and helping managers and boards to understand outcome measures
- participation in clinical audit
- developing systems for capturing and measuring outcome data.

For outcomes to be relevant to a service provider, such as a mental health trust, they must focus on potential areas for quality improvement that are appropriate to the provider's local needs. These will change over time as more information becomes available about what constitutes good performance. Outcomes have to help trust board members understand a system, compare it and improve on it, and will thus have to fit the following criteria:

- They must be clearly defined.
- They must genuinely measure improvement (rather than natural variation).
- They must reflect good data quality.
- They should be comparable now or in the future (and drawn from assured menus of indicators, if possible).

Good commissioning of a service depends on the most appropriate outcome measures populated with the best available data. A poorly designed or poorly chosen outcome measure with reliable data or a well-designed or well-chosen outcome measure with unreliable and/or untimely data is of very little value. Agreeing and articulating the objectives of a system can often be the most valuable part of the process of developing outcomes. Reaching a consensus about objectives has to start with a constructive conversation involving all the key partners in the team, system or organization. Box 6.5 provides an example list of outcomes that will be useful to trusts to gain an understanding of the service provision across the domains of patient safety, experience and clinical effectiveness, as well as staff experience of working for a service.

Box 6.5 A 'Balanced scorecard' of outcome indicators for a mental health service

Patient safety

- Rate of incidents reported per 1000 bed-days where there is a degree of harm reported as moderate, severe or death
- Rate of incidents reported per 1000 bed-days where the incident is classified as aggressive behaviour
- Proportion of bed-days on adult psychiatric wards occupied by patients aged 17 or under on admission, under the care of a psychiatric specialist
- Proportion of patients detained under the Mental Health Act 1983 who were absent without leave during the last quarter

Clinical effectiveness

- Proportion of admissions to the trust's acute wards that were gate-kept by the Crisis Resolution and Home-based Treatment Team (CRHT)
- Proportion of patients who experienced delayed transfer of care

- Proportion of patients with settled accommodation (number of patients with settled accommodation to number of patients on case load)
- Proportion of patients in employment (number of patients in employment to number of patients on case load)
- Proportion of patients who are contacted by CRHT within the four-hour waiting time (number of patients contacted within the four-hour waiting period to total number of referrals received by the CRHT)
- Proportion of in-patient wards within the trust with Accreditation for Inpatient Mental Health Services (AIMS)

Staff experience

- Proportion of staff feeling satisfied with the quality of work and patient care they are able to deliver

Patient experience

- Score regarding the patient's experience of feeling safe during their most recent stay
- Score regarding the patient's experience of being listened to carefully by the psychiatrist(s)
- Score regarding the patient's experience of being involved as much as they wanted to be in decisions about their care and treatment
- Score regarding the patient's experience of having had enough care taken of any physical health problems they had
- Score regarding the patient's experience of having their rights explained to them in a way that they could understand when they were detained (sectioned)
- Score regarding the patient's experience of having the number of someone from their local NHS Mental Health Service who they could phone out of office hours when facing a crisis

Where to get data, help and advice

There is a wide range of published advice on outcome measures and their measurement, and a number of organizations that can help with data, measurement and benchmarking both within and outside the NHS. Key sources of advice include the following:

- quality observatories – these are regional bodies established by strategic health authorities to support the monitoring, benchmarking and measurement of quality locally. They provide help and support for quality accounts and profile organizational quality of care as well as providing bespoke clinical intelligence (www.qualityobservatory.nhs.uk)[36]
- NHS Institute www.institute.nhs.uk provides a range of tools for measurement, quality improvement and monitoring and educational packages.
- the *Good Indicators Guide*[12] – published by the NHS Institute, it gives practical guidance on indicator development and monitoring
- public health observatories – provide access to a range of population health data, measurement and monitoring tools and health outcome dashboards (www.apho.org.uk)
- the NHS Information Centre – a key NHS data and statistics provider (www.ic.nhs.uk).

There are also commercial providers, such as CHKS and Dr Foster Intelligence, which are used by many NHS trusts for benchmarking information and outcome data.

Summary

❏ Measuring healthcare outcomes will be increasingly important in the future as interest in the quality, safety, clinical variation and value of health services grows.

❏ There is a move away from considering the quantity of healthcare to looking at its quality and value – this requires an understanding and measurement of healthcare outcomes.

❏ Measuring outcomes needs a population as well as a clinical approach.

❏ The government has developed an outcome framework for which it intends to hold the NHS to account.

❏ There are many types of and perspectives on outcomes, e.g. population vs patient, clinical vs functional, desirable vs non-desirable.

❏ All good outcome measures have a set of criteria or characteristics, e.g. a numerator which defines the outcome of interest, a denominator (the population at risk), a measure of uncertainty, and one or more comparators.

❏ Medical managers need to understand the potential range of patient, clinical, functional and population outcomes for their patients and services and where that information comes from.

❏ Outcome measurement requires comparison, which includes benchmarking against colleagues, other healthcare organizations or other healthcare systems as well as tracking outcomes over time.

❏ Medical managers have a particular responsibility to help their colleagues improve data quality. This may involve local data and outcome feedback.

References

1. Schwartz JS, Lurie N (1990). Assessment of medical outcomes. New opportunities for achieving a long sought-after objective. *Int J Technol Assess Health Care* 6, 333–9.

2. Iezzoni LI (1996). 100 apples divided by 15 red herrings: a cautionary tale from the mid-19th century on comparing hospital mortality rates. *Ann Intern Med* 124(12), 1079–85.

3. Neuhauser D (1990). Ernest Amory Codman, M.D., and end results of medical care. *Int J Technol Assess Health Care* 6(2), 307–25.

4. Iezzoni LI (1997). Assessing quality using administrative data. *Ann Intern Med* 127(8 Pt 2), 666–74.

5. Lohr KN (1990). Medicare: a strategy for quality assurance. *J Qual Assur* 13(1), 10–13.

6. Detsky AS, Redelmeier DA (1998). Measuring health outcomes–putting gains into perspective. *N Engl J Med* 339(6), 402–4.

7. Wright JC, Weinstein MC (1998). Gains in life expectancy from medical interventions–standardizing data on outcomes. *N Engl J Med* 339(6), 380–386.

8. Office for National Statistics (2012). *Health Expectancies in the United Kingdom 2002–2002 to 2007–2009*. Available from: http://www.ons.gov.uk/

9. Browne J, Jamieson L, Lawsey J, Van Der Meulen J, Black N, Cairns J, *et al*. (2007). *Patient Reported Outcome Measures (PROMs) in Elective Surgery*. Report to the Department of Health. Available from: http://www.lshtm.ac.uk

10. The Information Centre For Health And Social Care (2012). *Provisional Monthly Patient Reported Outcome Measures (PROMs) in England, – April 2011 to October 2011: Pre-and Post-operative Data*. London: NHS Information Centre.

11. Weaver M, Patrick DL, Markson LE, Martin D, Frederic I, Berger M (1997). Issues in the measurement of satisfaction with treatment. *Am J Managed Care* 3(4), 579–94.

12. Pencheon D (2008). *The Good Indicators Guide: Understanding How to Use and Choose Indicators*. Available from: http://www.apho.org.uk/

13. Spiegelhalter DJ (2005). Funnel plots for comparing institutional performance. *Stat Med* 24(8), 1185–202.

14. Spiegelhalter D (2002). Funnel plots for institutional comparison. *Qual Safety Health Care* 11(4):390–391.

15. Association of Public Health Observatories. Tools & Resources. Available from: http://www.apho.org.uk/

16. Carey RG, Lloyd RC (2001). *Measuring Quality Improvement in Healthcare: A Guide to Statistical Process Control Applications*. Milwaukee, WI: American Society for Quality.

17. Association of Public Health Observatories (APHO) (2011). *Dying to Know: How to Interpret and Investigate Hospital Mortality Measures*. York: APHO.

18. Association of Public Health Observatories (APHO) (2008). *Technical Briefing 2: Using statistical Process Control Methods in Public Health Intelligence*. York: APHO.

19. Department of Health (2011). The Operating Framework 2011/12. London: DoH.

20. The Information Centre For Health And Social Care (2011). *Summary Hospital-level Mortality Indicator*. Available from: http://www.ic.nhs.uk/

21. Aylin P, Bottle A, Elliott P, Jarman B (2007). Surgical mortality: Hospital episode statistics v central cardiac audit database. *Br Med J* 335, 1468–5833.

22. Jarman B, Bottle A, Aylin P, Taylor R (2002). Mortality rates. Dead confusing. *Health Serv J* 112.

23. Mant J, Hicks N (1995). Detecting differences in quality of care: the sensitivity of measures of process and outcome in treating acute myocardial infarction. *Br Med J* 311(7008), 793–6.

24. Maloney K, Chaiken B (1999). An overview of outcomes research and measurement. *J Healthcare Qual* 21(6), 4–10.

25. Mohammed MA, Deeks JJ, Girling A, Rudge G, Carmalt M, Stevens AJ *et al* (2009). Evidence of methodological bias in hospital standardised mortality ratios: retrospective database study of English hospitals. *Br Med J* 338, b780. Available from: http://www.bmj.com/cgi/doi/10.1136/bmj.b780

26. Care Quality Commission (2010). *Heart surgery in the United Kingdom*. Newcastle upon Tyne: CQC. Available from: http://heartsurgery.cqc.org.uk/

27. Hamilton M (1967). Development of a rating scale for primary depressive illness. *Br J Social Clin Psychol* 6(4), 278–96.

28. Endicott J, Spitzer RL, Fleiss JL, Cohen J (1976). The Global Assessment Scale. *Archiv Gen Psychiatr* 33, 766–71.

29. Weissman MM, Bothwell S (1976). Assessment of social adjustment by patient self-report. *Archiv Gen Psychiatr* 133(9), 1111–15.

30. Katz S, Ford AB, Moskowitz RW, et al (1963). Studies of illness in the aged. The Index of the ADL: a standardized measure of biological and psychosocial function. *J Am Med Assoc* 185: 914–9.

31. Lehman AF (1983). The well-being of chronic mental patients. *Archiv Gen Psychiatr* 40(4), 369–73.

32. Wing JK, Beevor AS, Curtis RH, Park SB, Hadden S, Burns A (1998). Health of the Nation Outcome Scales (HoNOS). Research and development. *Br J Psychiatr* 172, 11–18.

33. Gilbody SM, House AO, Sheldon TA (2003). Outcomes measurement in psychiatry: a critical review of outcomes measurement in psychiatric research and practice. Available from: http://www.york.ac.uk/inst/crd/crdreports.htm

34. Gilbody SM, House AO, Sheldon TA (2002). Psychiatrists in the UK do not use outcomes measures. National survey. [Internet]. *Br J Psychiatr* 180(2), 101–3.

35. Spencer S (2011). *Hospital Episode Statistics (HES): Improving the Quality and Value of Hospital Data.* Leeds: NHS Information Centre.

36. Department of Health (2010). Quality Accounts toolkit 2010/11 Advisory guidance for providers of NHS services producing Quality Accounts for the year 2010/11. London: DoH. Available from: http://www.dh.gov.uk/

Chapter 7

Change and project management

Hameen Markar

Introduction

This chapter deals with two related issues – change management and project management. When projects are developed and managed, it often leads to significant change within an organization. This change also needs to be managed, and thus management of change and management of projects are closely linked to one another. The first part of this chapter is mainly on change management and the second part deals with the broad principles of project management.

Management of change

All business organizations undergo continual changes. Such changes usually involve organizational development and take place at different points in the organization's history. Some changes are brought about by internal factors such as change of management or leadership, acquisitions and takeovers, while others are brought about by external factors, such as increased competitiveness and wider economic issues. At the forefront of changes are managers and leaders, who not only have to implement the change but also have to ensure that staff and other stakeholders are engaged and supportive of them. Changes are meant to develop and improve the functioning of the entire organization – or at least a part of it – but they can have a significant impact on individuals or groups of staff, employment conditions and morale. In the National Health Service (NHS) and even in business organizations, changes are not always clearly defined, are sometimes driven by financial considerations and often fail to achieve their main aims. A *Harvard Business Review* survey showed that over 70 per cent of the objectives are not achieved in most change processes.[1]

Before the implementation of any programme of change, there are some questions that need careful consideration: What is the current state of the organization? Why is the change necessary? How will the change affect the organization and its staff? What are the aims and objectives of the proposed change? On many occasions, business (and perhaps also medical) leaders fail to lead through lack of vision, lack of conviction, lack of skills or plain fear of failure.[2] There is currently a burgeoning literature on change management. However, most, if not all, of these publications are related to the business industry and there is very little on managing change in a public sector organization such as the NHS. Although the principles of change management are similar in both the private and public sectors, there are certain issues that are peculiar to the NHS. The different needs of the patient and of the organization, the diverse professional views of doctors, nurses and other frontline clinicians, and the strong opinions of stakeholders such as the GPs, allied health groups, private health organizations and voluntary bodies make change management in the health sector considerably more complex.

Medical managers have the unenviable task of promoting such change to a highly intelligent and knowledgeable professional group that has strong credibility with the general public. In the following we deal with the basic concepts of change, types and models of change, change methods in the NHS, the differences between managing change in a commercial environment and the NHS, the role of the medical manager in the change process and problems of managing change in the NHS. It is hoped that both medical and non-medical managers in the NHS will find this chapter of practical value in their day-to-day working environment.

What is change management?

What is change? This refers to a transformation from one situation, A, to another situation, B. Therefore, another useful definition of change management is 'the coordination of a structured period of transition from situation A to situation B in order to achieve lasting change within an organization':[3]

SITUATION A → SITUATION B

The arrow in the above equation denotes the change or implementation process. This looks quite simple but such a change will have an impact on two things. First, there is the organizational or mechanical process that relates to strategic, operational, structural and financial perspectives of change; and, second, the personal or psychological process that will affect employees, their jobs, responsibilities and morale. Effective change management involves careful handling of both these aspects to ensure a smooth transition from one position to another that will enable employees and other stakeholders to accept and embrace the changes (Fig. 7.1). Therefore, change management has two main focal points: management of the business or mechanical processes and management of the psychological processes. The former is referred to as the mechanical approach and the latter as the psychological approach to change.[4]

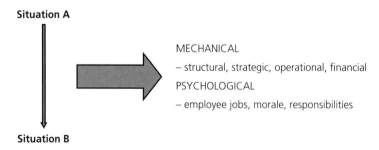

Figure 7.1 Mechanical and psychological approaches to change.

Successful change management requires effective handling of both mechanical and psychological processes. If the focus is mainly on the mechanical approach, it is likely to encounter resistance from employees and stakeholders.[4] Similarly, a change process that takes a predominantly psychological approach will have a happy and contented workforce but with significant deficiencies in the operational and business components. Jeff Hiatt and Tim Creasey discuss this in their change management tutorial series, suggesting that 'engineering (mechanical) and psychology fields are contributing to a convergence of thought that is crucial for successful design and implementation of business change'.[4]

Types and models of change

There are several theories and models of change, particularly in the commercial world, and they include:

- episodic or continuous change[5]
- planned or emergent change[6]
- developmental, transitional or transformational change.[7]

An episodic change is occasional and involves a radical change from one position to another. There is usually no connection between the two positions, and this type of change can cause significant disruption. Continuous change, on the other hand, is an incremental change that evolves over a period of time. Such change can be slowly accommodated by the system, is less likely to cause major disruption and is characterized by changing and adapting new ideas as the process evolves. When a change involves moving from one situation to another in a stepwise and structured manner, it is called a planned change; by contrast, an emergent change is spontaneous, evolves as an adaptive response to other changes in the environment[6] and is not necessarily linked to service development.

Within the health service most changes are planned, or at least they should be, as they are usually large-scale changes and are often related to service development. Thus, the many changes in community care in mental health are planned changes that have been introduced over a period of time in a gradual, step-by-step and structured manner. A planned change is usually carried out on the basis of good evidence that such a change will lead to significant improvement in outcome measures.

An emergent change, on the other hand, evolves as a direct consequence of other changes in the environment and emphasizes the need to be responsive and adaptive.[6] An example of an emergent change is that of nurse practitioners taking on tasks that previously would have been done by doctors, such as the prescribing of certain drugs. Some would argue that such changes are not necessarily associated with improvement of clinical services and are driven largely by the need to make efficiency savings.

Ackerman[7] takes a different view of change and talks about developmental, transitional and transformational change. A developmental change refers to a gradual process of change that evolves over a period of time. Such changes are common in business organizations as well as the NHS and include, for example, the establishment of electronic record-keeping in general practices. A transitional change is one in which a new state is produced from the old state through a process of transition. This involves the management of an interim transitional situation over a period of time, until the new state is implemented and firmly established. Revalidation and recertification of doctors by the General Medical Council (GMC) is an example of a transitional change.

Transformational change, according to Ackerman, is the emergence of a new situation from the remnants of an old, chaotic, failed situation. This is a radical change that can result in an entirely 'new' organization with a different structure, culture and strategy. Some of the changes proposed in the NHS white paper *Equity and Excellence: Liberating the NHS*[8] are, some would argue, of transformational proportions.

Models of change

Just as there are various theories of change, so there are different models of change. It is outside the scope of this chapter to review all the different models that are currently practised; however, there are two models that are worth mentioning: Lewin's three-step[9] and Kotter's eight-step[10] models.

Lewin's three-step change involves:

1. Unfreezing the current situation
2. Motivating staff to move towards the new situation
3. Re-freezing the new situation – a process of consolidating and stabilizing the new position.

Lewin's model is centred on the psychological and emotional components of change. It does not deal sufficiently with the mechanical issues.

John Kotter's 'eight steps to successful change' is widely acknowledged and practised in business circles. Kotter's eight steps, described in his highly acclaimed book *Leading Change*,[10] have been summarized as follows:

1. Increase urgency
2. Build the guiding team
3. Establish vision and strategy
4. Communication
5. Empowerment
6. Short-term wins
7. Encourage and persist – don't let up
8. Consolidate the change.

Both these models are very popular in change management and can be applied with some modification to changes in the health service. There are several other theories and models that can be adopted in practice, but a detailed review of this subject is outside the remit of this chapter.

Key points

Types and models of change

- A change process has both mechanical and psychological components.
- Successful change management requires careful handling of both components.
- Several types of change exist – episodic/continuous, planned/emergent, transitional/ transformational or developmental.
- There are many models of change; two particularly popular ones are Lewin's three-step model and Kotter's eight steps to successful change.

Change methods in the NHS

The selection of an appropriate change method will depend largely on the type of change envisaged. The proposed change can be structural, functional or cultural, or a combination of all three. Michael Beer and Nitin Nohria, professors at Harvard Business School, suggested that all changes are driven by either developmental or economic needs and coined the terms Theory E and Theory O.[11] Theory E is when the change is driven by economic considerations and is usually the result of financial difficulties. Some of the changes proposed in the health service in response to the current recession will fall into this category. In Theory E, the changes are driven from the top by the management executive, and staff and stakeholder views are given less consideration. This system works well, at least in the short term, in organizations with a strong hierarchical management structure. In Theory O, the change is driven by developmental needs and requires considerable staff support and commitment. Therefore, it is applicable to those organizations that have a non-hierarchical, flat management structure. It involves wide consultation with employees and other stakeholders and relies heavily on staff commitment and cooperation.[12]

Neither approach is guaranteed to succeed.[12] While Theory E may produce the desired financial results in the short term, it can lead to a depleted, poorly skilled and highly demoralized workforce. On the other hand, Theory O is a long-term, multi-year proposition, and most organizations cannot work to an unlimited timescale.[12]

Therefore, organizations prefer a combination of the two processes applied in varying measure based on specific organizational needs.

Business vs NHS change management

How does all this translate to change management in the NHS? In the business world, changes are brought on primarily by the need to remain competitive in an open, sometimes hostile marketplace. Does this also apply to the NHS? Is the NHS a business organization driven to some extent by financial motives?

Most management and clinical staff would agree that the NHS is really a semi-business organization. Although funded by central government with services delivered free to the public, many of the recent changes in the NHS, including some of the proposals in the current white paper, suggest a strong, competitive business bias. The acquisitions of failing trusts, the reorganization of community health services and the proposed changes to commissioning, including involvement of the third sector, lend support to this notion.

Like most other business organizations, the NHS also continues to go through various changes. Some of these are clinically driven while others, more so in recent times, have a financial basis. However, unlike other business organizations, the identity and role of the customer in the NHS are not clearly defined. In any business, the customer pays for the service and has the right to choose and accept or reject it. However, in the NHS, customers who are the service users have little influence in choosing the service they want. Despite concerted efforts by successive governments, both primary and secondary care services are based largely on the locality (i.e. on the postcode) and purchased by primary care trusts (at the moment) and GP commissioners (in the future) with little or no service user involvement. For this reason, some would argue that the NHS can never be run on a truly business model and customer choice will always have its limitations. Moreover, unlike in business organizations, the NHS has several stakeholders (other than the service user and carer), such as the GP commissioners, the third sector, private healthcare organizations and, above all, a vocal, strong and intelligent workforce supported by their unions and professional bodies. In business, outcome measures can be more easily validated, e.g. annual profits or share dividends, but in NHS trusts, outcome measures can be wide-ranging and sometimes difficult to quantify.

In addition to these fundamental differences, there is one other key distinction. This is in relation to the management structure. In most business organizations the management structure is hierarchical with a top-down approach, whereas in NHS trusts, it is non-hierarchical and flat. Thus, financially driven changes are more likely to succeed with a strong top-down approach, whereas similar changes in NHS trusts with a flat management structure are likely to fail (see discussion on Theory E and Theory O in the previous section).

Medical and non-medical managers will do well to bear these key differences in mind when changes are introduced or managed in the NHS (Table 7.1).

Table 7.1 Differences between commercial and NHS organizations

Business organization	National Health Service
Financially driven	Clinically driven (or should be)
Customer-focused	Locality-based (postcode)
Quantifiable outcome measures	Difficult to quantify outcome measures
Few stakeholders	Multiple stakeholders
Hierarchical management structure – top-down approach	Flat management structure – consultative approach

Medical managers and change management

Despite all that I have said above, change is necessary in the NHS not only for clinical and service improvement, but also for financial reasons. Thus, all medical and non-medical managers should have a good understanding of the change management process. This becomes even more important in the light of the proposals in the white paper *Equity and Excellence: Liberating the NHS*,[8] which, if accepted and implemented, will radically change provision of health services in the UK. This has been recognized as one of the biggest and perhaps most ambitious change management programmes in the world. An editorial in the *British Medical Journal*[13] points out that 'like all other structural reorganizations in the NHS, this one aims to improve health outcomes. What's lacking is any coherent account of how these reforms will produce the desired effects.'

Medical managers must recognize their crucial role in managing and effecting change in the coming years. They have to understand and accept change, communicate appropriately with staff and other stakeholders, get the support and cooperation of frontline clinical staff and, above all, ensure that patient safety is not compromised. Most of the changes have an impact on all aspects of NHS care – clinical, teaching, training and research – and therefore medical managers with their understanding and knowledge of all these areas have a responsibility to play a leading role in the change process. No service initiative or change will succeed without the support and cooperation of doctors and other clinicians who are primarily responsible for delivering these changes. Dealing with a medical workforce that is vocal, intelligent, often opinionated, sometimes dogmatic and even resistant to change needs considerable tact, diplomacy and change management skills.

A good understanding of change management is therefore essential for all medical managers in the NHS.

Key points

Change methods in the NHS

- Change is inevitable and continuous in the NHS.
- Successful change requires the support and cooperation of frontline clinical staff.
- Change will impact on all aspects of the service – clinical, teaching, training and research.
- Successful change requires all medical managers to have a good understanding of the change process.

What are the main problems in managing change in the NHS?

As mentioned earlier, most NHS organizations have a flat, non-hierarchical management structure. Furthermore, changes in the NHS are usually driven by developmental needs and require strong staff and other stakeholder commitment. And unlike private business companies, the NHS bodies are accountable to the public who have, quite rightly, a major voice in its development. For all these reasons, changes in the NHS must follow the Theory O which can take months to implement and years to consolidate and produce measurable results.

There are several problems that are peculiar to the NHS in relation to managing change. Change processes are either prescriptive or consultative. The former is driven from the top with little or no staff involvement (Theory E). The latter (Theory O) involves considerable staff participation and agreement. In the NHS, the proposed change is often prescriptive with clear directives from the top, but the process of implementing the change locally can be consultative. Herein lie the difficulties that confront medical managers in the implementation phase when clinical staff do not agree with the central proposal. In the future, changes are more likely to be driven by economic considerations and will be increasingly prescriptive in nature. Delivering such change in a non-hierarchical organization with a flat management structure will present significant challenges to medical managers. These difficulties are further compounded by the rapid pace with which changes are introduced in the health service. Bearing in mind that most of these changes follow Theory O, which requires time to implement and consolidate, it would be difficult for managers to demonstrate any appreciable benefits within a short period. This in turn can have a negative and demoralizing effect on staff.

Project management

Over the past few years, project management in the NHS has received a lot of attention, particularly following several failures in a number of IT projects such as the West Midlands regional supplies organization. A direct consequence of these failures has been the adoption of a formal project management system and most NHS organizations are beginning to use PRINCE2 (**projects in controlled environments**) methodology. Rittel and Webber[14] refer to 'tame and wicked' problems in relation to projects. Tame problems have a clear focus and possible solutions are understandable and unambiguous, while wicked problems are complex and the solutions remain ambiguous. John Edmonton has observed that PRINCE2 may be suitable for 'tame' and not for 'wicked' problems, which are the focus of most organizational change activities in healthcare.[15] The PRINCE2 method for project management is seen by many as a rigid, tight system with specific goals, deadlines, tasks and targets. Edmonton[15] has opined that such a system is unlikely to succeed in the NHS and has suggested a less rigid and more open-minded alternative collaborative approach.

Regardless of the method adopted, management of a project, whether in the NHS or in the business sector, involves managing change, which to a large extent involves managing people. This is in addition to managing and implementing the project. Most projects will have a project manager who will be responsible for project delivery. The project manager will head the project team and coordinate and manage all team activities. It is the project team that will plan, schedule and deliver. As a medical manager, you may or may not be a member of the team. However, you will still have full responsibility for clinical and patient safety issues. If the project involves changes in medical education and/or training of junior doctors or research, the medical manager's participation becomes even more important. You will also be expected to have a good understanding of the financial and operational aspects of the project. Thus, your primary role in project management is to manage the change process with your medical colleagues and ensure that clinical effectiveness and patient safety are not compromised at any stage.

In managing the change process, one of the first things you will have to undertake is to convince senior medical colleagues that the change is not only necessary but will also be safe and clinically effective. Most changes and projects in the NHS are seen by many clinicians as cost-cutting exercises that are financially driven with no clinical basis. One of the main reasons for this scepticism and sometimes even resistance to change is a misunderstanding of the aims of the programme or project.[16] Clinicians often assume that projects are rushed through for business reasons and do not have any clinical benefits. Therefore, as a medical manager it is your responsibility to undertake a comprehensive review of the clinical issues involved, particularly in relation to efficacy and patient safety. This review should seek answers to questions such as the following:

- Is this change really necessary?
- What are the main objectives of the change and what are we trying to achieve?
- Are these changes being driven primarily by clinical or financial considerations? If the latter, how would it impact on the efficacy and safety of a clinical service?
- What are the potential benefits to the patient?
- What are the gains for the organization?

Once you have carefully evaluated these issues, you will be in a strong position to have meaningful and informed discussions on the project with your clinical colleagues. Remember, it is necessary for you to be convinced of the merits of a project – its clinical effectiveness and safety – before you try to persuade your colleagues to accept it. Following this review, if you reach the conclusion that there are some aspects of the project that may compromise clinical care or patient safety, it is your responsibility to bring this to the attention of the project team and higher management.

Doctors must always bear in mind that their primary responsibility is towards their patients. Medical managers may come across situations where there is conflict between patient and organizational interests and have to use all their clinical, diplomatic and negotiating skills to manage the conflict without compromising clinical care or patient safety at any time.

Having done the background review, the next step is communication and education. At this stage, the medical manager should establish a good, effective communication team comprising senior clinicians who have accepted the proposals. This communication team must set up lines of communication with all frontline clinical staff, non-medical managers and outside stakeholders, including GPs, the third sector and voluntary organizations. It is always useful to have senior frontline clinicians take the lead in communicating with GPs and outside stakeholders, because they have considerable credibility and are also well placed to discuss the clinical effects of change and how it will affect the service user.

Successful project management requires clear communication and discussion of complex issues with a diverse and sometimes hostile audience. The project team will have their own communication plan and deal with progress of the project and present regular reports to the board and executive team. A medically led communication team will deal with clinical matters relating to patient care directed mainly at frontline clinicians, service users, carers and local GPs. The medical manager must ensure that the two teams work together and avoid contradicting each other.

Implementation

Background review, education and communication are followed by implementation. Various aspects of implementation, such as estate facilities, financial matters and human resource issues, will be managed by a number of non-medical managers within the project team. This will be based on the chosen methodology for the project, such as PRINCE2. Although the medical managers' role is primarily related to clinical governance, effectiveness and patient safety, they must ensure that the facilities are suitable, resources have been identified for medical staff, appropriate job descriptions have been prepared and medical staff with the right skills and competencies are recruited. The medical manager and senior medical staff must also be involved in the development of operational policies, clinical guidelines, staff training and clinical supervision. The medical manager should delegate some of these key tasks to senior clinicians who have the appropriate skills and expertise.

It is during this phase of project management that resistance will emerge. Resistance manifests itself in different forms, ranging from passive expressions of discontent to open hostility and even sabotage.[17] A good manager should anticipate possible resistance and be prepared to deal with this, taking into account the type, source, nature and impact of the resistance. The support of health service staff, particularly doctors, is crucial to the implementation and sustainability of any project[16] and medical leaders must find ways of engaging clinical staff from the very beginning. A clear understanding of the project and effective use of a competent communication team will offset some of these difficulties at an early stage.

Consolidation

Implementation of a project is followed by consolidation. This involves the change being accepted by all concerned and firmly embedded in the day-to-day functions of the organization. This can take several months and depends to a large extent on successful outcome measures. Therefore, it is important for medical managers to have a clear understanding of the objectives and expected clinical outcomes, both favourable and unfavourable, of the project. Thus, for example, the expected positive outcomes of setting up an acute assessment unit in an emergency department are a reduction in A&E waiting times and a decrease in bed occupancy. On the other hand, such a service can also result in an increased length of stay in an acute ward, as only those patients with more serious illnesses are likely to get admitted. There is also a possibility of an increase in untoward incidents if patients who require admission and hospital treatment are discharged home or if the home treatment services are not adequately robust.

A good medical manager must not only be aware of these possible outcomes but also put measures in place to reduce the risks involved. This can include a comprehensive risk assessment and management training programme, weekly inter-departmental/team meetings, patient surveys, regular audits and reviews of activity data and qualitative surveys involving patients, carers and staff. Medical managers must harness the support and cooperation of clinical staff, both doctors and nurses, to do these reviews and audits. Senior clinicians must be given an opportunity to present such data to the executive team and the trust board, as well as to outside stakeholders such as the commissioners, local GPs, third sector and voluntary organizations. This is a dynamic process that requires constant input from managers at all levels.

Conclusion

In this chapter I have tried to deal with various aspects of managing change in the NHS. I have discussed the theories and models of change commonly used in commercial settings and how these apply to the NHS. The chapter discusses the differences between change management in the business world and the NHS, the main drivers for change in a health service organization and the role of the medical manager in project management. The most important message, and one that is well worth repeating, is this: senior medical staff must be involved with the change process from the very beginning. No change is likely to succeed if there is no engagement with frontline senior medical staff.

Summary
- ❏ Change is continuous in any organization and the NHS is no exception.
- ❏ Changes in business fail to achieve their aims and objectives in 70 per cent of cases.
- ❏ Changes are often financially driven and not clearly defined.
- ❏ Change management in the NHS requires consideration of several issues peculiar to the health industry.
- ❏ The differing needs of the patient and the organization, the views of frontline clinicians and other stakeholders and public opinion must all be taken into account.

References

1. Beer M, Nohria N (2000) Cracking the code of change. *Harvard Business Rev* 78, 133–41.
2. Nugent K (2010). *Change, Bring It On! A Simple, Workable Framework for Leading and Managing Successful Business Transformation*. Oxford: Infinite Ideas Ltd.
3. Website of Change Management Coach: http://www.change-management-coach.com/definition-of-change-management.html
4. Website of Change Management Coach: http://www.change-management.com/tutorial-definition-history.htm
5. Weick KE, Quinn RE (1999). Organisational change and development. *Ann Rev Psychol* 50, 361–86.

6. Website of the Happy Manager: http://www.the-happy-manager.com/theory-of-change-management.html/

7. Ackerman L (1997). Development, transition and transformation: the question of change in organisations. In: Hoy J, Van Eynde D (eds). *Organisation Development Classics*. San Francisco, CA: Jossey-Bass.

8. Department of Health (2010). *Equity and Excellence: Liberating the NHS*. London: Department of Health.

9. Lewin K (1947). Frontiers in group dynamics. In: Cartwright D, ed. *Field Theory in Social Science*. London: Social Science.

10. Kotter JP (1996). *Leading Change*. Boston, MA: Harvard Business School Press.

11. Beer M, Nohria N (2000). *Breaking the Code of Change*. Boston, MA: Harvard Business School Press.

12. Luecke R (2003). *Managing Change and Transition* (Harvard Business Essentials). Boston, MA: Harvard Business School Publishing Corporation.

13. Delamothe T, Godlee F (2011). Dr Lansley's Monster – Too soon to let it out of the lab. *Br Med J* 342, 237–8.

14. Rittel H, Webber M (1973). Dilemmas in a general theory of planning. *Policy Sci* 4, 155–63.

15. Edmonton J (2010). A new approach to project managing change. *Br J Healthcare Man* 16, 225–30.

16. Gollop R (2004). Influencing sceptical staff to become supporters of service improvement: a qualitative study of doctors' and managers' views. *Qual Saf Health Care* 13, 108–14.

17. Markar H, Iankov B (2010). Management of psychiatric services. In Puri B, Treasden I, eds. *Psychiatry: An Evidence-based Text*. London: Hodder Arnold.

Chapter 8

Evidence-based healthcare and medical management

Mark Agius and Anton Grech

- Introduction
- What is evidence-based medicine?
- The evidence base
- Evidence-based healthcare in clinical practice
- Conclusion
- Summary
- References

Introduction

In this chapter, we describe what evidence-based healthcare is, how it impacts on the role of the medical or clinical director, and what mechanisms medical managers should have in place to implement evidence-based medicine in a healthcare organization.

What is evidence-based medicine?

Sackett *et al.*[1] define evidence-based medicine as 'the conscientious, explicit, and judicious use of current best evidence in making decisions about the care of individual patients'. Practising evidence-based medicine means integrating the clinician's individual clinical expertise with the best available clinical evidence from systematic research. By individual clinical expertise, we mean the proficiency and judgment clinicians have acquired as a result of their clinical experience and clinical practice, which, of course, they constantly update with ongoing further training. Clinicians demonstrate this expertise through more effective and efficient diagnosis and in effectively understanding and implementing patients' concerns, rights and preferences when making clinical decisions about their care.[1]

The 'best available clinical evidence' includes all clinically relevant research, including research in basic sciences, and especially patient-centred clinical research into 'the accuracy and precision of clinical examination, diagnostic tests, identifying useful prognostic markers, as well as the efficacy and safety of treatments, be they therapeutic, rehabilitative or preventive'.[1] Good doctors use both their own clinical expertise and the best available evidence, as neither is sufficient on its own. Without clinical expertise, inappropriate evidence may be used unwisely. Even the best evidence may not be applicable to, or may be inappropriate for, an individual patient.[1] On the other hand, if there is no regard to current best evidence, practice easily risks becoming out of date, and thus can result in inappropriate patient care.[1] Hence, it is incumbent on clinicians to update their knowledge of the evidence base constantly, so as to ensure their practice continues to be appropriate. It is worth considering that many pieces of best evidence are in fact population outcomes; for instance, evidence might suggest that the use of a small dose of aspirin reduces the risk of myocardial infarction in the general population, but this may be entirely inappropriate in a patient suffering from duodenal ulceration. Hence the evidence must be 'tailored' to the individual patient. Clinical evidence may inform, but can never replace, the doctor's individual clinical expertise, since it is this expertise which determines whether the evidence does indeed apply to the individual patient and how it should be applied to the patient's care plan.[1]

Concern has been expressed that evidence-based medicine will be used by commissioners and managers to attempt to cut healthcare costs.[1] In reality, the application of best clinical evidence to medicine may actually have the opposite financial consequences, that is, an increase in costs, as Sackett *et al.*[1] suggest: 'Doctors practicing evidence-based medicine will identify and apply the most efficacious interventions to maximize the quality and quantity of life for individual patients; and this may raise rather than lower the cost of their care.' Such an increase in costs would be driven by and would lead to a rise in healthcare standards because the best evidence had been applied. Clearly, such an application of evidence-based medicine will have implications for costs within the health service. It will be necessary, therefore, to carefully assess the costs implied by the evidence-based improvement in practice, and the local and national implications of the need to afford the improvement in healthcare required by the evidence.

There is now an expectation among the general population, and therefore also among legal and medico-legal circles, that all medical services, primary or secondary, should deliver effective care which can be recognized as 'evidence-based'. This is because of the easy availability, via the internet, books and other media, of guidelines which purport to be evidence-based. Hence it becomes very important that medical directors and other medical managers should be able to ensure that the treatment provided by the services under their care is based on good evidence.

The need to use evidence-based medicine arises in individual organizations in several ways. It may be necessary to assess the care provided for individual cases when assessing whether appropriate treatment was provided (as in the case of investigating serious untoward incidents). It may be necessary to develop 'treatment pathways', which are both evidence-based and auditable, in order to ensure that the patients who are dealt with by the organization are appropriately treated and recover. It will be necessary to ensure that treatment guidelines are kept appropriate and up to date. Whole new services may have to be developed, and the outcomes of the treatment provided by them will have to be validated by audit and outcome measurement in order to ensure that those services are properly designed, funded and provide the patients with the outcomes in health improvement which are expected. If they do not, then services may have to be redesigned. It is also true that, often, the development of complex treatment pathways will require negotiation to develop joint methods of working across primary and secondary care, and any negotiator will need to have a very good knowledge of the evidence in order to ensure that such joint working guidelines are accepted by all parties, many of which (such as GP principals) may not be under the organization's direct control.

Key points

What is evidence-based medicine?

- Evidence-based medicine is the conscientious, explicit and judicious use of current best evidence in making decisions about the care of individual patients.
- To practise evidence-based medicine is to integrate the clinician's individual clinical expertise and the best available clinical evidence from systematic research.
- Evidence-based medicine is not an attempt to cut healthcare costs; instead it requires that the best care that evidence will support is provided for the patients, and hence makes the case for adequate resources.

How is evidence-based medicine used in organizations?

- To assess whether appropriate treatment is being provided.
- To develop 'treatment pathways', which are both evidence based and auditable.
- To ensure that treatment guidelines are kept appropriate and up to date.
- To help develop new services and assess their impact.
- To enable negotiation to develop joint methods of working across primary and secondary care.

The evidence base

Although randomized trials and meta-analyses are considered evidence of high quality, evidence-based medicine is not restricted to such studies. The aim of evidence-based medicine is always to seek out the best existing evidence for a particular clinical question under consideration. It is possible that clinical trials and meta-analyses will not have been carried out in relation to the particular issue. It could be that the best available evidence is of another kind, e.g. epidemiological evidence, technological evaluations of new techniques, or basic science such as genetics or immunology. In reality decisions often have to be taken in the absence of double-blind controlled trials and meta-analyses, simply because they have not been carried out or because they are actually inappropriate. Sometimes other professionals do not realize this.

The best available evidence refers to any published evidence which is relevant and includes the following:

- meta-analyses and systematic reviews
- a single-blinded controlled study
- descriptive studies
- expert consensus statements
- epidemiological evidence
- technological evaluations of new techniques
- basic science such as genetics or immunology.

It is also worth remembering the hierarchy of evidence: the highest graded evidence is a meta-analysis of several double-blind trials, as this weighs up evidence gained in as unbiased a way as possible from several sources; lower in rank is a single double-blind study; and expert consensus statements occupy the lowest rank of all (see Box 8.1). The fact that a meta-analysis does not exist in relation to the issue at hand does not mean there is no evidence available, but simply that the best available evidence is of a lower grade than a meta-analysis. It is this best available evidence which must be acted upon.

Box 8.1 'Hierarchy' or Categories of Evidence

- Category I – meta-analysis of randomized controlled trials (RCTs) or at least one RCT
- Category II – at least one controlled study without randomization or at least one other quasi-experimental study (or extrapolated from category I evidence)
- Category III – non-experimental descriptive studies
- Category IV – expert committee reports or opinions and/or clinical experience of respected authorities

It goes without saying that all pieces of evidence, i.e. each published paper, single trial or meta-analysis, need to be critically scrutinized in order to understand and deal with the bias that may exist as a result of how a trial is designed and conducted, what biases the observers/participants of the trial may have had, and how effective trials are at proving or disproving a particular issue. What appears to be the best evidence on a particular subject may not, in fact, be the most appropriate, because the evidence is tainted by bias, or because the trial was not designed to answer the specific question it is now being used to answer. Thus, the skill of critical appraisal by which a clinician evaluates evidence as presented in various publications is of vital importance to the practitioner of evidence-based medicine.

When assessing therapy, it becomes important to evaluate the available trial evidence critically. As the randomized trial, and especially a systematic review or a meta-analysis of several randomized trials, is considered much more likely to inform us and less likely to mislead us, it has become the 'gold standard' to evaluate effectiveness of a treatment.[1]

Evidence-based healthcare in clinical practice

What tools, then, should medical managers have access to in order to ensure the effective practice of evidence-based medicine in their organization? The tools that are necessary are, fortunately, also tools which are necessary to management in general, and one could argue that every business which intends to succeed should have these. Indeed, in the UK, general practice has been using these tools for years, but in many areas, secondary care is only slowly catching up.

The tools that should be at every medical manager's disposal are:

- access to evidence-based guidelines
- the facility to do effective literature search
- a database of patients, diagnoses and treatments
- an effective system for regular audit
- a system for the measurement of treatment outcomes
- a capacity to integrate a range of clinical data within and across departments in each trust and to derive inferences from these.

We will now discuss each of these tools in succession.

Access to evidence-based guidelines

The use of guidelines has become an inevitable part of patient care in recent times. It is difficult for every doctor and health professional to be constantly aware of every piece of evidence about the treatment of every condition and to have the time to collate and appraise each piece of evidence. Hence the need to have someone else to do this and make it easily available. In the UK, this is done by the National Institute of Health and Clinical Excellence (NICE), but there are many other guidelines available from various medical associations and societies in different specialities around the world.

These guidelines vary in quality, from important pieces of work such as systematic reviews of the evidence regarding various conditions (e.g. the NICE guidelines, which also publish the detailed evidence on which they are based) to consensus statements from a group of experts. This is why the authority of such guidelines needs to be critically assessed.

Guidelines are context-specific, but their presence on the internet makes it possible for them to be read and applied in places for which they are not intended. Thus, NICE guidelines are to be used in the context of the UK National Health Service, with all its known difficulties and constraints, but in fact, the very high reputation of NICE means the guidelines are sometimes quoted and applied in countries with very different health services. Where this is the case, even NICE guidelines should be read and used with a degree of caution.

A good way to illustrate this is with an example. There is, in Slovakia, as in the UK, pressure to reduce numbers of psychiatric beds. However, community psychiatry has not been implemented in Slovakia as yet, while the NICE guidelines on the management of schizophrenia, in recommending assertive working and family interventions, assume that community psychiatry is available. The NICE guidelines are therefore inappropriate in the Slovakian context in relation to reducing bed numbers, because the community teams presupposed by the NICE guidelines do not exist (see Fig. 8.1).

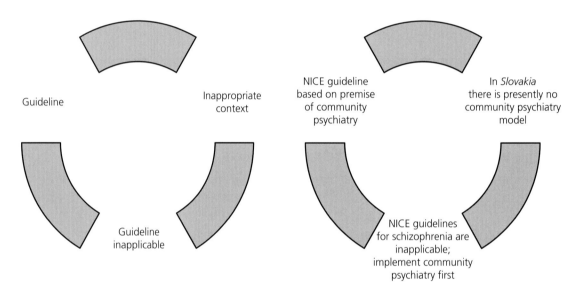

Figure 8.1 An attempt to apply guidelines outside their context can be ill-advised, as illustrated here with the National Institute of Health and Clinical Excellence (NICE) guidelines and Slovakia, where, at the time of writing, there is no community psychiatry model.

Sometimes guidelines can be used as a justification for an effective treatment that has no licence; an example is the recent recommendation by NICE that sertraline should be used as first-line treatment for generalized anxiety disorder, despite the fact that sertraline is not licensed for this condition.[2] In this way, an authoritative guideline may change the medico-legal status of a particular therapy by endorsing it.

On the other hand, even NICE guidelines may come to conclusions which, because of the underlying evidence, can be challenged. For example, the change in the NICE guidelines on schizophrenia[3] from always prescribing an atypical antipsychotic to prescribing either a typical or an atypical antipsychotic, whichever the doctor and the patient choose, was based on the CATIE[4] and CUtLASS[5] studies. Both these studies were carried out on patients with chronic schizophrenia, rather than in the first episodes of psychosis, and important observer bias has been pointed out in CUtLASS.[5] As this evidence base on which the change to the guidelines was made is open to challenge, the guidelines themselves can be challenged (see Fig. 8.2).

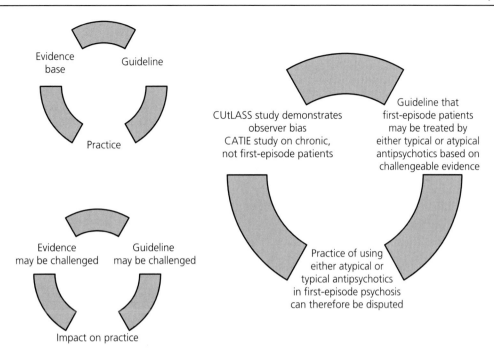

Figure 8.2 Problems with the evidence base can leave guidelines open to challenge, as illustrated by the change in the National Institute of Health and Clinical Excellence (NICE) guidelines on schizophrenia.

Guidelines do go out of date as new evidence and therapies emerge, so they need to be constantly reviewed and updated.[6] A few years ago, one of the authors complained that the NICE guidance on depression did not include augmentation of antidepressants with atypical antipsychotics, despite there being evidence in favour of this, and that the guidelines regarding generalized anxiety disorder did not refer to the use of pregabalin.[7] Both these issues have been dealt with in updated versions of the guidelines.

There is also evidence that doctors do not necessarily follow guidelines if they are sent 'from on high', without their involvement in the guideline development process. This was the case with the World Health Organization (WHO) guidelines for mental health in primary care.[8]

There is now published evidence that the implementation of guidelines is an important task in the development of evidence-based medicine. Studies have demonstrated that there are a number of difficult issues to be faced when implementing guidelines across a health organization, including prejudices to be overcome, e.g. feelings that 'this is not how we do it here', 'I know what works for my patients', 'this is cookbook medicine' and 'the aim is not good patient care but cutting costs'. It has been demonstrated that an education programme using focus groups and followed by audit is more effective than just delivering the guidelines cold and expecting them to be followed because they have been made 'mandatory'.[9-11]

Nevertheless, guidelines continue to be a key means of delivering the best care to patients. One important task, in view of the above discussion, is to empower a group of local clinicians to develop a local guideline, based on the evidence from the national guidelines, across both primary and secondary care and which is owned by clinicians in both fields. Once developed, this could be presented to all local clinicians at an educational event, and constitute a simple care pathway, approved by both primary and secondary care, which all parties can sign up to. This was implemented to very good effect in the 1980s by a local group, the 'Luton Young Physicians Group', who developed excellent care pathways for all manner of conditions, ranging from managing asthma and diabetes to referring patients for gastroscopy and managing peptic ulceration.

There is one final cautionary word about guidelines: there cannot be a guideline for every situation. For instance, it is well known that most guidelines recommend monotherapy with antipsychotics for schizophrenia, but psychiatrists often find it is only by using poly-pharmacy, with a number of unlicensed combinations of medication for which there is no evidence, that some psychotic symptoms can be treated. Hence, it should not be surprising that audits to ascertain adherence to guidelines will never produce 100 per cent positive results. Many factors cause non-adherence to guidelines in individual patients, and we would suggest that a 75 per cent adherence be viewed as a very successful outcome.

The following should be noted in respect of non-adherence to guidelines:

- Should guidelines not be adhered to, an auditing process should require that individual clinicians state why they were unable to apply the guidelines in particular cases.
- Investigation of such patients will identify groups that are particularly difficult to treat. These may include co-morbidities, which may require special guidelines.
- There should be a realistic benchmark (75 per cent) for adherence to a guideline.
- A benchmark allows for non-adherence to guidelines, such as the one on monotherapy in schizophrenia mentioned above. One must bear in mind that in certain EU countries, such as Slovakia, there is public health pressure to adhere to monotherapy in treating schizophrenia, while in other European countries, such as Croatia, health insurance companies will not reimburse treatments unless they comply with specific guidelines, and there may be difficulty if a treatment does not fall within these guidelines.

An interesting example surrounding the issue of co-morbidity was recently published by the present authors' team. On investigating why certain patients with obsessive compulsive disorder (OCD) required much more care from the team than was expected, it was found that this group comprised patients whose OCD was co-morbid with bipolar disorder. There are no NICE guidelines for such a combination of illnesses.[12]

Key points

Guidlines

- Guidelines may be based on systematic reviews or expert consensus statements.
- They are context-specific.
- Local guidelines need to be developed from more general guidelines.
- They can sometimes justify an unlicensed treatment.
- They may come to conclusions that can be challenged.
- They often go out of date.
- They need to be implemented with care, using focus groups and educational sessions – and implementation should be followed by audit.
- 100 per cent adherence is unlikely, given the variability among patients.

The facility to do effective literature search

As has been noted, guidelines, no matter how evidence-based, rapidly go out of date as new evidence emerges. There is a risk in trusts attempting to follow guidelines slavishly that medical managers may rapidly find themselves being outflanked by their more academic colleagues, if they do not keep up with the latest evidence. Hence a medical director should be able to, as issues present themselves, search the literature for the latest evidence and adapt trust guidelines and standards appropriately.

By and large the best way to do this is via PubMed, which is free and accessible on the internet, and on which a search for articles on a particular subject, including summaries of the articles, can be acquired in minutes. It should be routine practice to carry out literature searches at regular intervals on various subjects and to update guidelines accordingly.

Many provider trusts have a framework around clinical effectiveness, including NICE coordination and clinical audit. There is usually a baseline assessment when a NICE guideline or technology appraisal is published, followed by a financial assessment of the funding gap, which should then lead to a discussion with commissioners. Once implemented, there are audit loops to monitor compliance. However, this involves considerable time and effort and it is usual for a medical director to have an assistant such as the clinical director for clinical governance, to assist with such matters. It is also important that medical directors do not allow themselves to be bounced into decision-making before they have had an opportunity to review the evidence, even though other members of the board may, for political or financial reasons, be pressing for a quick decision. Some journals are not available on PubMed, and Google Scholar is fast becoming an alternative source of information on the literature.

With regard to this question of accessing the literature, a word needs to be said about the Cochrane Collaboration. This is a very useful source of information in the form of high-quality systematic reviews of topics, and hence an excellent source of category I information. However, its very high quality can be a problem in some areas where extremely high-quality studies are not necessarily that important. The problem is that Cochrane only includes very high-quality studies (category I) in its systematic reviews, excluding those that are not up to its exacting standards. The result is that, in an area such as the development of new services, it is possible that studies that are not acceptable to Cochrane will contain valuable information about the expected outcomes of such services – if you were to consult Cochrane alone, these would be missed.

An example of this is the development of early intervention services for psychosis. At least four studies[13–16] have compared the work of such services with treatment as usual, but only one (Thorup et al.[13]) of the four is a study that meets the Cochrane criteria. The information on the other three is therefore not available from this source. This means that, whereas other professionals may believe that Cochrane is the only source of evidence-based information, the medical director must review all other available evidence in order to get as broad a view of the subject as possible. It should be pointed out that this issue is a particular problem for Cochrane when there are insufficient studies of a high enough quality to meet the Cochrane criteria, and early intervention is a very good example of this.

Database of patients, diagnoses and treatments

Knowledge of the evidence base is insufficient by itself to put into effect evidence-based medicine. It is necessary to be able to assess the resources required, to negotiate with commissioners and to deploy the resources properly. In order to do this, what is necessary is simple epidemiology.

It is notable that general practitioners have been using epidemiology for years. John Fry had been hugely influential in working out the expected numbers of patients with each condition on an average GP's list.[17]

Before the advent of computers, GPs used to be enjoined to keep a card index of diagnoses, and since then they have been able to keep a database on their trust computers of all the details of the patients in their practice. It is extremely interesting for ordinary GPs to compare the figures given by Fry for 'average GP list sizes' with their own data. Any major deviation from the average signifies either incomplete epidemiological information or an important factor which is influencing a particular locality.[17]

Secondary care has been less effective at computerization. In mental health trusts, all diagnoses and *International Statistical Classification of Diseases and Related Health Problems-10* (ICD-10) codes are collected and sent by computer to the Department of Health for the collection of statistics, but it is difficult to show that this information is used for the planning of services. And yet such information is of the utmost importance in the development of services.

Thus, for example, in the development of a new service for schizophrenia, the appropriate way in which a secondary trust, primary care and the local commissioners should begin to plan the service is to pool the information from all local GPs' lists along with the information known to the trust. This should inform the medical director of the incidence and prevalence rates of this condition in a particular locality. This information can then be used in the development of a business case and the allocation of resources. In this way, planning will not be based on guesswork, but on a rational estimate on what evidence-based resources will be required to provide the service.

It is also worth noting that the use of epidemiology does not stop at the assessment of the resources required by a service; it can also be used to help with their deployment. An assessment of the location of cases with psychosis in Luton, in the UK, showed that there were substantially more cases in the Dallow and Biscot wards than elsewhere, these wards also having substantially higher deprivation indices than the rest of the town.[18] This fact should inform the design of the community mental health teams, with more staff being allocated to work in these areas.

These wards provide a further challenge for the local GPs. There is a very large South Asian population, and it is therefore likely that there will be a high incidence of diabetes and hypertension, and hence cardiac and kidney disease, in these wards. Any increase in the number of cases of these diseases will be noted, as discussed earlier,[17] in the databases of the local GPs' computer systems. This is an example of epidemiological evidence directly affecting the way treatment is delivered, as the local GPs have the challenge of promoting health in all these areas in a population with a specific cultural background and services therefore need to be designed to help particular ethnic minorities.

There is little evidence, however, that resources such as databases with epidemiological data are used in this way by trusts. As a consequence, under-resourcing of services in many areas, in particular mental health services, persists.

However, it is clear that such use of epidemiology is essential to the rational provision of health services. Furthermore, GPs have always used data from their databases to prove they have achieved various targets, such as immunizations and cervical cytology. Clearly, it would be extremely sensible if each unit or team in the trust held its own database, not just of diagnoses, but also of treatments, such as medications, psychological interventions and outcome measures. It is extremely important for a team to be able to measure its performance against evidence-based standards.

> **Key points**
>
> **Databases**
> - Databases are a very useful source of epidemiological data and every GP practice has one on its computer.
> - Secondary care trusts have been much slower to develop databases.
> - They are helpful in carrying out audit, and it is proposed that each unit in a trust should hold a database that can be used for internal audit by the unit staff and can feed into a central trust database.
> - When new services are planned, the GP databases should be shared with the secondary service and the commissioners so that services are adequately resourced to work in an evidence-based way.

An effective system for regular audit

Once resources have been allocated to a particular project, and the service has been set up, it becomes extremely important to be able to audit how services are being delivered. As we have argued, it is of great value to team morale that the team members themselves are able to record their progress with individuals and to be able to measure their performance against evidence-based standards. Hence it is of real importance that each team in the organization maintains a database of their patients and uses it to carry out an audit of that database against a number of evidence-based process measures and outcomes. It is on the basis of this audit that it can be shown that evidence-based medicine is being practised.

Audit consists of setting standards (hence using evidence-based medicine), measuring against those standards how a system is performing, identifying the weaknesses, making recommendations and finally re-auditing in order to see how these recommendations have improved services.

Audit is therefore the simplest way in which evidence-based healthcare can be put to work in an organization. However, in the past, audit has sometimes been seen as an end in itself. The audit department would do a certain number of audits throughout the year and this would be presented to commissioners as evidence that audit was going on in an organization. In other words, audit was seen as something of an aim in itself, rather than a tool to improve standards in an organization. Also, sample audits which are anonymized will not help to identify patients whose care could be called into question by the audit results.

However, the access to databases, as described in the previous section, should make audit a very important tool in the hands of a medical manager. Audits of the workload of every team in the organization can be carried out against evidence-based standards, and 'outliers' (i.e. teams performing at a different standard from the others) can be identified. Because all patients will be on the database, it will be possible to identify which patients are not receiving care up to the audit standards, and hence remedial action can be carried out to immediately improve standards, or ascertain that they are being followed.

One important aspect of this is how to decide what to measure in order to assess that a particular standard is being followed. Sometimes a medical manager may have to use a surrogate measure since it is not possible to measure something directly. This may take some ingenuity. When one of the present authors was a GP, he would routinely audit the outcomes of his treatment of hypertension, asthma, hypercholesterolaemia and diabetes. To do this he decided to audit blood pressure readings, peak flow readings, cholesterol measurement and HbA1c measurement, respectively. These would be recorded regularly at three-month intervals and would give a reasonable idea about how the patients were progressing as a group and also how they were progressing individually.[19,20]

Recently it became necessary to audit the outcomes of the treatment of depression in a community mental health team. It was not possible to audit ratings on a scale, as rating scales were not available for all the patients. Instead, data on discharge rates for depression for the team and reduction in suicide rates were used successfully to carry out the audit.[21]

Key points

Audit

- Audit requires a database.
- It should be carried out against evidence-based standards.
- All patients with the condition should be audited, rather than just a sample of patients.
- Audit should be used to facilitate discussion about why certain patients are not receiving treatment according to evidence-based guidelines.
- Indirect measures may sometimes be used in an audit.

A system for the measurement of treatment outcomes

Ultimately, the reason for evidence-based medicine is to provide optimal treatment for patients. In order to be able to assess this, it becomes necessary to measure outcomes. Outcome measurement may simply be to answer the question, 'How many patients recover?', but there can be other important outcomes too (see Box 8.2). In mental health, it is necessary to measure the reduction of symptoms, which is done through the use of rating scales; however, this is not done frequently in day-to-day clinical practice, although it is always carried out in research. Recovery from mental health problems is becoming an important clinical outcome, and includes the capability of patients with chronic mental health problems to manage their own illness. The Recovery Star is used to assess such patient empowerment. Ultimately, the final tests of recovery are functional outcomes, such as how many patients are able to return to work and how many achieve full social inclusion. Collation of all these outcome measures will show that the evidence-based practice that has been instituted is providing effective patient care.

Box 8.2 Types of Outcome Measures (Particularly but not Solely Used in Mental Health)

- Symptomatic measures – symptom rating scales
- Administrative measures – e.g. HoNOS PbR (the Health of the Nation Outcome Scales Payment by Results) puts patients into clusters for administrative purposes and may be used to compare units
- Recovery measures, e.g. Recovery Star – measures patient empowerment
- Functional outcomes – measure whether people return to normal functioning, e.g. return to work or education

---

The choice of outcome measures therefore depends on what we are attempting to measure. Are we simply measuring whether symptoms have abated? If so, rating scales for symptoms are what we need to use. Such scales may include the Brief Psychiatric Rating Scale (BPRS) to measure psychosis symptoms and the Hamilton Depression Scale to measure depression. Recently, the Department of Health issued an 'outcome compendium', which is a collection of rating scales to measure symptomatic outcomes for the use of the NHS in England.[22] Such symptomatic outcomes are analogous in physical health to measuring blood pressure, peak flow and HbA1c to assess outcomes in hypertension, asthma and diabetes, respectively.

If, for reasons of administration, we want to measure how one unit is functioning in comparison with another, we can use tools such as the Health of the Nation Outcome Scales (HoNOS), which is too simplified to measure detailed symptoms, but does give a good measure of how one ward may be doing in relation to another. Tools such as HoNOS and its derivative, HoNOS Payment by Results (HoNOS PbR), can be used to measure administrative outcomes.[23] Recovery outcomes, including empowerment of the patient, are also important to measure and the Recovery Star is an important tool for this.

Finally, we have argued very strongly for the use of 'functional outcomes', such as 'How many patients have returned to work and education?', 'How many patients have been discharged?' or 'How many are no longer suicidal?'[15,24] Functional outcomes are very real assessments of the quality of a patient's life. They overlap, but do not replace, symptomatic outcomes and recovery outcomes. It appears that all these four types of outcome measurements are important in that they measure different things. Together they provide an excellent measure of how evidence-based healthcare helps to maximize patient outcomes.

A capacity to integrate data

To provide successful leadership, a medical manager needs to have the capacity to integrate, for each trust and each individual unit, the information provided by the guidelines and the more up-to-date literature searches with the data on patients and therapies provided by the database and audits, and to derive inferences from these.

In order to achieve this, a whole integrated clinical governance department needs to be put in place (see Fig. 8.3). The manager must consider the guidelines and the literature searches carried out on a specific topic and, together with a small group of other interested clinicians and managers, develop local guidelines for the trust. Guidelines must then be rolled out to the individual teams, wards and other units, in such a way that they can be understood and adopted by consensus. This may require meetings and focus groups in each unit, and there will be much work to enable clinicians to take ownership of the guidelines. The results of audit need to be fed back to the teams, and thus the work of the teams can be measured against standard outcome measures. Finally, the guidelines need to be updated as necessary. It must be understood that all of this activity, which is key to clinical governance, needs to take place in a coordinated way. What should not happen is that there is an audit department, a NICE committee, an IT department, and so on, all working independently and each unaware of the data available to the other groups. It is the responsibility of the medical manager to lead the coordination of these various groups.

Within general practice, these departments do not exist. Instead, and perhaps very effectively, in a good practice which knows its patient population, the functions of the audit department and the NICE committee are taken over by the GP partners and the IT system of the practice. Now that

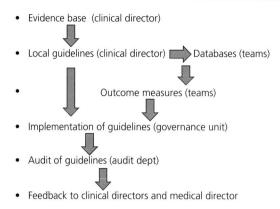

- Evidence base (clinical director)
- Local guidelines (clinical director) ➡ Databases (teams)
- Outcome measures (teams)
- Implementation of guidelines (governance unit)
- Audit of guidelines (audit dept)
- Feedback to clinical directors and medical director

Figure 8.3 Integration in evidence-based medicine.

GPs are forming into commissioning groups, it becomes important that each practice is able to contribute to the information gathering of the group, via the data held in their IT system, and to contribute by involvement of partners to the commissioning strategy of the groups.

Conclusion

In order to develop evidence-based medicine in an organization, we have described a series of measures. We have described how to develop local guidelines which are evidence-based, being based on systematic reviews such as NICE guidelines which are constantly updated with the latest evidence. We have referred to the use of epidemiological data from primary and secondary care to design services and how to combine them with the evidence-based guidelines in order to achieve proper resourcing of services. We have described how services can, as a consequence of the epidemiology, be deployed in the right way.

The chapter has also reviewed how local databases in teams or, indeed, in general practices can be used to measure local results and process measures, and how outcomes in organizations can be audited. We have described how appropriate outcome measures, also developed on the basis of evidence, can be measured for every service.

However, the final requirement for instituting evidence-based practice in an organization is that all these functions should be collated in order to ensure that the organization is producing appropriate outcomes and is therefore fit for purpose. The medical director is the key person who is most in a position to ensure this.

It is, in fact, quite possible to have organizations where each of these 'tools' is in place but the outcomes are not collated. There may be a team set up to measure the adherence to NICE guidelines. This team may be separate from the audit department, which in turn has no method of influencing the development of local guidelines. Teams may not be able to measure their own outcomes, because they have not been encouraged to set up a local database. Even the epidemiological data on diagnoses may simply be sent on to the Department of Health without being used to aid in planning local services.

All of this could be happening because local managers are seeing the various requests from commissioners and the Department of Health as targets in themselves, which are then not connected to provide a bigger picture. The medical director is in a unique position to change this and say to a board: 'If the Department of Health is asking us to report on an issue, and the guidelines say this line is to be taken, while our local epidemiology shows that we have X cases a year, then our services need to be configured in this particular way, so that we can achieve these measurable outcomes.' Such an attitude, which utilizes all the resources of an organization and which focuses them to produce a particular result, is the effect of the proper introduction of evidence-based medicine into an organization.

Summary

The application of evidence-based medicine to a service involves the following:

❏ The medical manager identifies the evidence base for a particular subject from a literature search on the subject and the identification of appropriate national guidelines on that subject.
❏ From this basis, local guidelines adapted to the local team's circumstances are evolved and agreed.
❏ Then outcome measures which will indicate an optimum service are chosen and implemented.
❏ Data is collected in a database held by each clinical team.
❏ The database is used to audit the decided outcome measures.
❏ Feedback of the outcome (and process) measures is returned to the medical managers who will make adjustments and then re-audit.

References

1. Sackett D, Rosenberg WMC, Muir Gray JA, Brian Haynes R, Scott Richardson W (1996). Evidence based medicine; what it is and what it isn't. *Br Med J* 312, 71.

2. National Institute for Health and Clinical Excellence (NICE) (2011). *NICE Clinical Guideline 113 – Generalised Anxiety Disorder and Panic Disorder (With or Without Agoraphobia) in Adults.* Available from: http://www.nice.org.uk/

3. National Institute for Health and Clinical Excellence (NICE) (2009). *Schizophrenia: Core Interventions in the Treatment and Management of Schizophrenia in Adults in Primary and Secondary Care.* Available from: http://www.nice.org.uk/

4. Lieberman JA, Stroup TS, McEvoy JP, Swartz MS, Rosenheck RA, Perkins DO, Keefe RS, Davis SM, Davis CE, Lebowitz BD, Severe J, Hsiao JK (2005). Clinical Antipsychotic Trials of Intervention Effectiveness (CATIE) Effectiveness of antipsychotic drugs in patients with chronic schizophrenia. *N Engl J Med* 353: 1209–23.

5. Jones PB, Barnes TR, Davies L, Dunn G, Lloyd H, Hayhurst KP, Murray RM, Markwick A, Lewis SW (2006). Randomized controlled trial of the effect on quality of life of second- vs first-generation antipsychotic drugs in schizophrenia: Cost Utility of the Latest Antipsychotic Drugs in Schizophrenia Study (CUtLASS 1). *Arch Gen Psychiatry* 63, 1079–87.

6. Agius M (2010). Guidelines in psychiatry. *Psychiatr Danub* 22, 42–5.

7. Agius M, Chapman S, Trokudes D, Taylor C, Klepacka K, Bugler R, Buckle M, Zaman R (2009). Nice Mental Health Guidelines. http://www.bmj.com/

8. Croudace T, Evans J, Harrison G, Sharp DJ, Wilkinson E, McCann G, Spence M, Crilly C, Brindle L (2003). Impact of the ICD-10 Primary Health Care (PHC) diagnostic and management guidelines for mental disorders on detection and outcome in primary care. Cluster randomised controlled trial. *Br J Psychiatr* 182, 20–30.

9. Forsner T, Wistedt AA, Brommels M, Forsell Y (2008). An approach to measure compliance to clinical guidelines in psychiatric care. *BMC Psychiatry* 25, 64.

10. Forsner T, Hansson J, Brommels M, Wistedt AA, Forsell Y (2010). Implementing clinical guidelines in psychiatry: a qualitative study of perceived facilitators and barriers. *BMC Psychiatry* 20, 8.

11. Forsner T, Wistedt AA, Brommels M, Janszky I, de LeonAP, Forsell Y (2010). Supported local implementation of clinical guidelines in psychiatry: a two-year follow-up. *Implement Sci* 26, 4.

12. Darby L, Agius M, Zaman R (2011). Co-Morbidity of Bipolar Affective Disorder and Obsessive Compulsive Disorder in a Bedford Community Psychiatry Team. Psychiatria Danubina vol 23 supplement 1. P130–133.

13. Thorup A, Petersen L, Jeppesen P, Ohlenschlaeger J, Christensen T, Krarup G, Jørgensen P, Nordentoft M. Integrated treatment ameliorates negative symptoms in first episode psychosis– results from the Danish OPUS trial. Schizophr Res. 2005 Nov 1; 79(1): 95–105.

14. Craig TK, Garety P, Power P, Rahaman N, Colbert S, Fornells-Ambrojo M, Dunn G. The Lambeth Early Onset (LEO) Team: randomised controlled trial of the effectiveness of specialised care for early psychosis. *Br Med J.* 2004 Nov 6;329(7474): 1067

15. Agius M, Shah S, Ramkisson R, Murphy S, Zaman R. [2007]. Three year outcomes of an Early Intervention For Psychosis Service as compared with treatment as usual for first psychotic episodes in a standard Community Mental Health Team-Final Results. *Psychiatr Danub* 19, 130–8.

16. Zaytseva Y, Gurovich IY, Shmukler A (2010). Effectiveness of the integrated long-term program of management of patients after first psychotic episode in 5-year follow-up. *Psychiatr Danub* 22, S92–4.

17. Fry JD, Young RW (1992). *The Health Care Data Source Book: Finding the Right Information and Making the Most of It.* Chicago, IL: American Hospital Publishing.

18. Agius M, Ward C (2009). The epidemiology of psychosis in Luton. *Psychiatr Danub* 21, 508–13.

19. Agius M (1989). Screening for cardiovascular risks. *Mims Magazine* June, 81–5.

20. Agius M (1989). A clinic to control hypertension. *Mims Magazine* May, 85–92.

21. Agius M, Gardner J, Liu K, Zaman R (2010). An audit to compare discharge rates and suicidality between antidepressant monotherapies prescribed for unipolar depression. *Psychiatr Danub* 22, 350–3.

22. National Institute for Mental Health in England (2008). *Outcomes Compendium.* Available from: www.dh.gov.uk/

23. Agius M (2010). Outcome measures in psychiatry. *Psychiatr Danub* 22, 38–41.

24. Agius M, Shah S, Ramkisson R, Murphy S, Zaman R (2009). Developing outcome measures for serious mental illness; using early intervention as an example. *Psychiatr Danub* 21, 36–42.

Chapter 9

The role of the board and its directors, including the executive medical director

Geraldine O'Sullivan

- Introduction
- Overview of NHS boards
- Role of the medical director
- Attributes and skills
- Summary
- References

Introduction

This chapter will describe a typical NHS board of a foundation trust and the role of the executive medical director within it. Many chapters in this book refer to the role of the medical director and this chapter describes it in detail. It is also worth noting that the role of the medical director in private healthcare organizations as described by Empey and Peskett in Chapter 20 is different in its scope from the role in NHS organizations.

Overview of NHS boards

To understand the corporate role of the medical director, it is important to know about NHS boards and their responsibilities. This chapter will give an overview of NHS boards, their responsibilities and composition, as well as providing an understanding of corporate governance, which lies at the heart of effective, well-managed organizations. NHS boards are modelled on private sector boards and the lessons from corporate failings in the private sector have been applied to NHS boards. The chapter will also describe the role of directors and outline the role of the medical director in detail.

The role of boards of foundation trusts and corporate governance

The role of a board of directors in the business world is to ensure the long-term success of the company in the interests of its shareholders and wider stakeholders.[1] The model of private sector boards was introduced to the NHS in the early 1990s with the commencement of NHS trusts. The Department of Health[2] set out its proposal to create NHS foundation trusts as independent legal entities in 2002 – i.e. public benefit corporations with strong governance arrangements which are accountable to local people, who can become members and governors. Each NHS foundation trust has a duty to consult and involve a board of governors (comprising patients, staff, members of the public and partner organizations) in the strategic planning of the organization. Foundation trusts are set free from central government control and are no longer performance-managed by health authorities. They have financial freedoms and can raise capital from both the public and private sectors within predetermined borrowing limits. They can retain financial surpluses to invest in improving NHS services. They are overseen by Monitor (the independent economic regulator of NHS foundation trusts) and quality is regulated by the Care Quality Commission.

Given the stringent authorization process underpinning foundation trusts, corporate governance has been strengthened in NHS boards with the recognition that a foundation trust board needs people with the right level of skills and expertise to provide strategic drive to lead the organization and to ensure optimal use of the greater freedoms offered by this status. The accountability of foundation trusts to the community has been strengthened through its membership and its board of governors.

The creation of foundation trusts has led to a need for a much more strategic outlook from NHS trusts and has coincided with a number of other changes that have challenged NHS organizations and exposed the need for strong leadership. These include much more rigorous performance management, the need for organizations to work as part of a larger health and social care system, a much faster pace at which the health system works and the requirement for a large range of technical skills.[3]

Corporate governance is essentially the way an organization is run, and it applies to all companies and boards. In essence, it has to do with the accountability of an organization and how it assures itself that the business is being well run. There have been a number of reports over the last 20 years, usually written in the wake of scandals, that now set the benchmark for good boardroom practice across the private and public sectors and set out what is required for good corporate governance in companies in general. These cover accountability, integrity, transparency and risk management. There are important lessons for NHS boards that are particularly pertinent bearing in mind the new freedoms and responsibilities that have been devolved to them as foundation trusts. The NHS has had its own scandals, including Bristol, Alder Hey and, more recently, Mid-Staffordshire, related to poor governance. For NHS trusts, the basis for sound corporate governance includes attendance to clinical governance, risk management in its widest sense (not just clinical risk), controls assurance and financial governance. An NHS trust board will focus on these prime responsibilities.

Good governance of NHS foundation trusts

Many papers have been written about good governance in the NHS,[4–7] and there is general agreement that the tasks of NHS boards stem from the primary role of ensuring the long-term success of the organization in the interests of patients and the wider community.

The governance of foundation trusts is built around the corporate board, which sets the direction of the organization, provides its leadership and is responsible for ensuring its long-term success. The directors share collective responsibility for the direction and control of the organization.[6] Each director has a role in ensuring the probity of the organization's activities and contributing to the achievements of the organization's objectives in the best interest of patients and the wider public.[6]

A corporate board typically consists of:

- chair
- non-executive directors
- executive directors, including chief executive officer
- company secretary (though not strictly an official board member).

Typically, there are an equal number of non-executive directors (NEDs) and executive directors (EDs) with an additional non-executive chair leading the board, who is responsible for the composition of the board. The equal number of NEDs and EDs should ensure that one group does not dominate decision-making, and typically an NHS board will have up to six non-executive directors and six executive directors.

As board directors, all have the same status,[6] with EDs and NEDs sitting on a single board, under the leadership of the chair; this is described as a unitary board. The board will set strategy, taking account of the views of its governors, members and wider stakeholders. Even though the company secretary is not an official member of the board, the company secretary works closely with the chair and has an important role to ensure compliance with regulators' imperatives/requirements and therefore oversees the board agenda to ensure these items are timetabled on to board agendas.

The dual roles of chair and chief executive officer are vital to setting the trust's culture and values.[5] The chair is responsible for leading the board and ensuring a good working relationship between the executives and non-executives so that no individual or small group of directors dominates the board's decision-making.[8] In NHS trusts, the chair is also responsible for liaison with governors, including chairing the board of governors. The foundation trust chair therefore plays a crucial role in linking the board of governors to the board of directors.[6]

The chief executive officer (CEO) is responsible for the day-to-day management of the organization and for operationalizing the decisions and strategy of the board.[7] The relationship between the chair and CEO is crucial to the success of the organization and it is important that the relationship is balanced, with neither one being too dominant. If the relationship is poor or too close, it can have negative consequences.

The CEO will have a number of executive officers to assist in the management of the organization. Typically, the CEO will have a director who is an expert on financial issues, and NHS boards have a statutory obligation to have a doctor and a nurse as executive directors on the board, who usually share responsibility for quality and safety.

Non-executive directors are responsible for providing independent scrutiny and constructive challenge of their executive colleagues.[7] NEDs are often chosen for their diverse expertise and usually the chair will recruit NEDs with a range of expertise and skills, thereby enhancing the diversity of the board.[5,8] Executive directors bring detailed knowledge of the organization's operations and management systems and of the health and social care sector, as well as specialist clinical and managerial expertise, while NEDs are strategic, challenging and more detached.

The EDs are responsible for implementing the strategy. NEDs monitor this, questioning and probing the executive team on its performance, based on good information which is reviewed regularly at board meetings. The different roles of the NEDs and EDs are set out in Box 9.1, but ultimately there is collective responsibility.

Box 9.1 The roles and responsibilities of directors

Non-executive directors

- Strategic
- Challenging
- Diverse skills
- Independent scrutiny

Executive directors

- Implementation of strategy
- Operational management
- Specialist expertise in health sector
- Visible leadership

There is a consensus that in general the best boards are those where all directors, whether executive or non-executive, contribute to the work of the board and do not restrict their input to their particular function/interest.[7,8] In practice, a successful board is one that works as a team and, although NEDs and EDs have different roles, as board members they share the same corporate responsibilities. In foundation trusts all directors share responsibility for the finances as well as the quality and safety of services. There is often a delicate balance to be made between achieving financial targets and maintaining quality and safety of services.

Assurance and risk

One of the important roles of the board is to identify and manage risks that threaten the success of the organization and its services. Boards are therefore responsible for ensuring that risks are recognized and that steps are taken by executives and management to mitigate them.[8] The board will therefore lead the organization effectively within a framework of prudent controls that allows risks to be recognized and managed. Board members will ensure that they can deliver the strategy by making sure the right people and resources are in place. They will also shape and set the organization's values, ensuring its obligations to patients, the local community and Secretary of State are understood and met.

Non-executives need to be reassured that the systems of internal control, including clinical governance and financial management, are properly established and that appropriate systems of risk management are in place. This is particularly important as the board develops new strategies to modernize the way the organization works and provides or procures services for patients.[6]

By focusing on strategy, scrutiny of performance and the tasks associated with clinical governance, risk and financial management, the governance of the organization will be far more secure and enriched.

Subcommittees of the board that aid accountability

The board will have a number of subcommittees in order to ensure accountability which will usually be chaired by a NED. There are three main subcommittees in NHS trusts: the audit, remuneration and quality committees.

The audit committee

Every NHS organization has an audit committee reporting to the board with responsibility for effective internal control. Traditionally, audit committees have primarily concerned themselves with scrutiny and review of financial systems, financial information and matters of compliance with the law. However, other internal controls are equally important, particularly risk management. Under controls assurance the audit committee should be concerned about all controls. It is responsible for the relationship with the internal auditors who will carry out audits of the organization's systems and is a means of providing objective assurance on the adequacy of the organization's internal controls.[5, 8]

The remuneration committee

The remuneration committee oversees the pay of EDs and ensures that no director is responsible for determining his or her own salary and that remuneration is commensurate with the role.[8]

The quality committee

There is no statutory requirement to have a quality committee but many care organizations now have one that reports to the board on quality issues.[5] The quality committee provides an additional opportunity for members of the board to probe and scrutinize the organization's performance against indicators of quality. It can support the board in placing quality at the heart of what it does.

Key points

NHS boards – overview

- NHS boards are made up of non-executive and executive directors, led by the chair.
- Even though non-executive and executive directors have different roles, the NHS board is a unitary board.
- The directors are collectively responsible for the success of the organization.
- Good corporate governance centres around accountability, openness and strong internal controls.
- The NHS board is accountable to the local community and the Secretary of State.
- The board sets strategy along with values and culture.

Role of the medical director

When NHS trusts were introduced in 1991, the statutory role of medical director was created. It is generally acknowledged that the role of the medical director has changed and expanded since then. Over the past 10 years there has been increasing recognition of the importance of this role in improving quality and safety in healthcare delivery. Alongside the statutory responsibility of being a board member, the medical director has a fundamental leadership role.[9]

Both the British Association of Medical Managers (BAMM)[10] and the NHS Confederation[11] have carried out surveys of the roles of medical directors. When the first review was done by BAMM in the mid-1990s, a lot of variation was found in the responsibilities of medical directors.[10] At that time it seems that the medical director on the board had no specific functional role, unlike, for example, the finance director, who had a clear responsibility for overseeing the financial accounts of the trust. When the NHS Confederation repeated a similar survey in 2009,[11] it found that even though there were differences in the way the medical director roles were designed within trusts, in general the responsibilities had much in common, as discussed in the following sections.

The medical director's responsibility and accountability are, of course, to the board (for the overarching corporate responsibility) and to the CEO (for the functional responsibilities). With the other EDs, the medical director shares responsibility for driving change and quality improvement within the organization. The consensus view is that the medical director has two main roles: a corporate role and a functional role.

Corporate role

With the development of foundation trusts there has been a lot of emphasis on developing high-quality boards in the NHS, with strong governance leading to much greater clarity about the roles of its directors both collectively and individually. As a result, the corporate role of the medical director has become clearer (see Box 9.2). The medical director is a full member of the board and therefore has a collective responsibility along with all directors to ensure the ongoing success of the organization, so that optimal high-quality, safe care is delivered to patients.

Box 9.2 Corporate role of the medical director

- Board director
- Influences strategy, culture and organizational values
- Monitors organizational performance
- Brings a clinical perspective to board decisions

The medical director has a shared responsibility with other directors for setting strategy and culture, ensuring the financial viability of the organization, monitoring operational performance, and overseeing quality and safety within a framework of accountability. However, medical directors' particular set of experience and skills enables them to bring a clinical perspective to key decisions made by the board.[11] Medical directors are uniquely placed to integrate their clinical position on the board with other activities, from overarching governance to patient safety to strategy. The strategy is the board's blueprint for the overall direction that the organization will be taking in terms of sustainability, growth and managing competition, and sets the parameters within which the EDs move the organization forward. The medical director influences the strategy and brings a clinical perspective to inform and shape the content. Quality should be driving strategy and the medical director is pivotal in embedding this in the organization's strategy. The role is strategic and the medical director plays a part in looking to the future direction of clinical services. Because of their clinical knowledge and awareness of the impact of demographic changes and other trends in healthcare, medical directors are often well positioned to understand the competitive field, opportunities for growth and, indeed, imminent threats to the organization.

The board and executive team will have developed a balanced scorecard set out in a dashboard to monitor the organization's performance. This gives a quick overview of the organization's 'health' in all the essential areas, which typically include finances, quality and safety, the customer (in its widest sense) and the workforce. It is essential that finance is not simply left to the finance director. All directors, including the medical director, should understand the financial aspects of the organization, including the annual income and expenditure, margins, budgets and cash flow, as well as having an understanding of Monitor's financial ratios, which are used to indicate the financial health of the organization. The financial aspects of capital projects also need to be understood.

The medical director, along with the director of nursing, has a responsibility to present the clinical view to the board. In particular, that responsibility involves keeping the board informed about the potential clinical implications of financial decisions, and should see rigorous discussions taking place at board level about balancing financial and clinical risks and putting necessary mitigations in place. The medical director provides a crucial link between clinical services and the board through their networks, ongoing clinical expertise and links with clinical directors.[9]

Functional role

The three key areas of clinical governance, the quality agenda and professional leadership form the basis of the functional responsibilities of the medical director. These are summarised in Box 9.3 and discussed in detail in the following sections.

Box 9.3 Functional responsibilities of a medical director

- Clinical governance
- Overseeing quality and safety including quality accounts
- Leading the medical workforce
    - Recruitment
    - Developing talent
    - Medical workforce planning
    - Management structure
    - Medical education and training
    - Appraisal and revalidation
- Other responsibilities
    - Research and development
    - Caldicott Guardian
    - Maintain an external perspective

Clinical governance

Typically, the medical director will set the framework for clinical governance in the organization, usually alongside the director of nursing, which brings together the overall picture of quality in the organization (see Box 9.4).

Box 9.4 Clinical governance: the overall framework around quality and safety of clinical care

Clinical risk management

- Incident management system including recording, investigation and learning from adverse events

Patient and customer experience

- Patient satisfaction including complaints, feedback, patient information

Clinical effectiveness

- Implementation of National Institute for Health and Clinical Excellence (NICE) and evidence-based practice, care pathways and clinical outcomes
- Clinical audit and the audit cycle
- Implementing national guidance around patient safety and quality

Professional development, management and training

- Ensuring the workforce is competent and capable to deliver clinical care
- The medical director will focus particularly on the medical workforce

---

Quality and safety

Clinical governance involves the creation of a framework around quality and safety of clinical care within the organization and putting robust systems and processes in place to ensure the safe delivery of care. These include a system for monitoring of quality and safety, so that any lapses are picked up early and reported to the board. Action can then be taken to address unsafe practices and deficiencies in care so that they are rectified quickly, lessons are learned and the learning is disseminated. Over the last few years, the emphasis on quality and safety has increased, perhaps as a result of scandals that arose because boards were more concerned with the financial aspects of the organization.

Quality accounts have been developed and in many organizations the medical director leads on these. Typically, the quality accounts consist of between 12 and 25 key quality indicators that are realistic but difficult to attain and which the organization aims to improve on during the annual cycle. They are developed annually in collaboration with key stakeholders and typically include specific indicators and targets around the triumvirate of patient safety, customer experience and clinical effectiveness. These are approved by the board and reviewed regularly at board meetings in the course of the year. In terms of their importance and monitoring by the board, they are the quality equivalent of the organization's financial accounts. Similar to the financial accounts, quality accounts are published annually in the organization's quality report.

Leading and managing the medical workforce

The NHS is changing, with the emphasis moving away from the centrality of the 'professional expert' to the patient as expert. Leading the cultural shift and articulating this to clinicians form part of the sensitive but important role of the medical director. In addition to a general leadership role within the organization, the medical director has a specific responsibility to lead and direct the medical workforce.

Medical workforce planning and recruitment

Medical workforce planning is an important task of the medical director, so that the staffing remains appropriate and relevant to the challenge of delivering the required service. This is especially true when the service may be changing in response to innovations and societal shifts, such as those associated with social and economic demands. In planning the medical workforce, any gaps in expertise/talent should be identified. A strong process around recruitment is important and medical staff appointments have to be made in the context of the strategic, long-term direction of the trust. It is essential that doctors with the right training and skills are appointed to the right posts for the right reasons.[9]

As part of the recruitment process, it is important to check that the appointees' values fit with those of the organization. A good recruitment process can avoid problems whereby aspirations of a particular doctor do not match the values of the organization. Therefore, overseeing the recruitment process of medical staff, in order to avoid subsequent problems, is an important task for the medical director.

Following recruitment, it is important to promote the involvement of newly appointed consultants in the wider organization from the outset, so that they feel committed to its success. This will encourage consultants to operate beyond their basic clinical role, allowing them to develop and channel their talents and become strong clinical leaders to their teams and possibly the wider organization.

Developing a strong medical leadership and management structure

A crucial role of the medical director is to spot talent and develop future medical leaders for the organization. The strong medical and clinical leadership that results provides a good support structure and the firm foundations for medical engagement that have been shown to be key in ensuring an organization's success.[12] It also provides support for the corporate and functional roles of the medical director. Without this, the medical director can be drawn into problems and crises that arise in the day-to-day delivery of healthcare. It is important that medical directors are able to avoid spending time on direct operational issues that could lead to neglect of the key corporate and functional roles they need to focus on. A strong medical management structure allows appropriate delegation.[11]

Medical directors need to have an overview of the medical workforce and ensure that the consultants are fit and willing to take on the challenge of leadership. A developmental programme for medical managers will ensure they have the skills to lead and manage clinical services, and that they have a sufficient understanding of finances, performance management, project management and leadership. This programme will need to be repeated at 3- to 5-yearly intervals with opportunities for mentoring and coaching of medical managers in the interim. This enables the development of a talent pool of clinical leaders and provides a strong framework to assist succession planning. It will also promote a framework of strong medical and clinical involvement in operational management and service delivery.

The medical director may not directly manage the clinical directors, but the latter group will be professionally accountable to the medical director. Whatever the line management arrangements, it is important that there are regular meetings between the medical director and medical managers in the organization to ensure good communication. It is also useful for the medical director to maintain an informal network among colleagues to avoid isolation. This is important not only from a personal perspective but also to be aware of service issues across the organization and to gauge the morale of the workforce

Managing the medical workforce

The medical management structure provides the basis for engagement with doctors through good communication and involvement of clinicians. It also enables corporate strategy and policy to shape and determine service delivery and allows two-way communication: assessing the mood on the ground and creating alignment between the organization and doctors.[11]

Through the medical management structure, the medical director should ensure that the job planning process and appraisal system for all consultants and medical staff are fit for purpose. Specifically, the medical director needs to see that job planning is carried out annually, is consistent in approach across the organization and that trust resources are used optimally, i.e. they are value for money. It is essential that job plans and objectives for clinicians are aligned with the organization's annual plan and its general strategic direction. Each year the job planning round should be a means of shaping and directing the work done by consultants.

It is important to try to manage disengaged colleagues where possible by aligning the individual's aspirations with the goals of the organization. This is not always possible but it is worth trying. From time to time, there will be difficult and antagonistic individuals who need to be managed. A strong framework of job planning and appraisal with a clear code of conduct for doctors, which draws on the General Medical Council's *Good Medical Practice: Duties of a Doctor*[13] and the organization's reasonable expectations of its workforce, will provide the basis for managing the medical workforce as a whole.

Even with strong recruitment and operational management processes, problems can occasionally arise. It is therefore important that the medical director has processes in place to monitor the quality of clinical work using a variety of means, such as monitoring of incidents, clinical audit, patient and carer feedback, peer review and anonymized 360-degree feedback. When problems are identified they should be addressed early so that no harm comes to patients. However, there must also be a fair, thorough set of procedures to follow, including an impartial investigation to gather the evidence so that appropriate action can be taken.

Furthermore, the medical director must put effective mechanisms in place to improve a clinician's performance if it is not up to scratch, at the same time making sure that the well-being and safety of patients are not compromised by a poorly performing doctor.[14] The medical director will have a local procedure in place based on the national framework for managing doctors in difficulty (see Chapter 14 for more on this).

Revalidation for doctors and medical director as responsible officer

Appraisal and revalidation are discussed in detail in Chapter 16. Again, each organization will have a local policy for appraisal and it is essential that there is a robust process within the organization to enable the medical director to carry out the role of responsible officer for revalidation.

In summary, it is the medical director's responsibility to ensure as far as possible that the doctors in their organization are fit and safe to carry out their clinical roles – fit at time of appointment, that they maintain those skills and have the correct attitude towards their patients. Alongside this, it is important that the medical director provides a supportive culture where colleagues with personal and/or health difficulties can be assured of receiving the support and professional help they may require. The medical director should also have an 'open door' policy so that colleagues who want to discuss personal difficulties can do so at an early stage. From time to time there will be sensitive issues to deal with and therefore fostering a supportive environment for colleagues who are distressed or ill is important, especially among a professional group that finds it difficult to acknowledge the need for help.

Medical education

The medical director also oversees the processes around medical education, ensuring that they are robust and that there is an appropriate balance between training and service commitments in the organization. The ongoing development of speciality doctors is also part of the medical director's responsibility and he or she may have an associate medical director for medical education who will have good networks both inside the organization and externally to deliver high-quality education. Typically, the medical director through the associate medical director will ensure that there is a good reliable framework for medical education in the organization. The associate medical director must translate national policy around medical education into local action and keep the executive informed of any potential impact of changes in medical education on service delivery. It is also important that there is a framework for the ongoing development of middle-grade doctors so that this important group of medical staff continues to learn and develop.

The medical director is also responsible for making sure the organization complies with workforce legislation relevant to doctors, such as the European Union's Working Time Directive, and implements recommendations following Royal College accreditation visits. Having a well-regarded training scheme for medical trainees has many benefits, including enhancing the organization's reputation and providing a cohort of medical consultants from which to recruit in the future.

Other responsibilities

Medical directors are often responsible for research and development (R&D). The importance of R&D varies enormously between organizations, from being a major contributor to innovation and reputation in big academic hospitals to being a relatively minor feature in other organizations. However, most organizations will have some clinicians who are engaging in research. Whatever the size of R&D activity, the medical director has to ensure that there is an R&D strategy approved by the board, an operational policy that clarifies the steps to be followed by staff when planning a research study and, most importantly, that research governance standards are clearly outlined in a policy document and are adhered to. These are the minimal requirements. Teaching hospitals with significant R&D activity will have a well-developed infrastructure in place to support and monitor R&D activity.

The medical director may be the Caldicott Guardian for the organization, responsible for protecting the confidentiality of patient and service-user information and enabling appropriate information-sharing, and may also hold other responsibilities depending on the number of EDs on the board.

It is important to have a strong external perspective and links. Staying abreast of national and international changes in healthcare delivery by reading journals, attending conferences and networking is important to facilitate an awareness of potential trends and changes in healthcare delivery. This external perspective also provides a comparator for many aspects of the organization's activities and standards which is useful. A key finding of the Mid Staffordshire inquiry was that an external perspective was lacking.[15] The medical director will often have many external links with other medical directors, general practitioners, deaneries and royal colleges. The medical director may also sit on regional committees.

Key points

Tips for the medical director

- Stay in touch with colleagues.
- Spot talent and develop succession plans.
- Put a strong medical management structure, both operational and professional, in place.
- Gradually shape culture.
- Model and articulate strong values.
- Develop a code of conduct.
- Maintain a strong external perspective and networks.

Attributes and skills

Personal qualities required for medical director role

As a director of a public body, the medical director must live up to the seven principles of public life outlined by the Committee on Standards in Public Life, sometimes referred to as the Nolan Committee.[16] These are:

- selflessness
- integrity
- objectivity

- accountability
- openness
- honesty
- leadership.

As medical directors have a key leadership role within their organization, they need to promote and model the behaviours they expect of their staff. These typically include integrity, honesty, energy, open communication style, good judgement and proportionality. In addition to these personal qualities the following attributes/skills are, in my view, useful in the role:

- strong values driven by desire to make a difference
- strategic vision
- good people management skills
- good interpersonal skills including the ability to influence
- self-awareness, reflection and emotional intelligence
- fairness
- resilience.

The role is very broad, so the ability to analyze and assimilate data and information fairly quickly is helpful. In addition, good communication skills are important, including the ability to bring clarity to complexity and to articulate what is expected of the people in the organization. Many of these skills can be innate but they can also be developed and improved during a career in medical management. There is no doubt that experience helps, as well as commitment to the role.

I am often surprised by the attitude of some colleagues that the medical director role is one that is done for just a few years and then handed on to another consultant. Like most challenging posts, experience and wisdom are important. The assumption that a senior clinician can easily step into this demanding and complex role is, in my view, erroneous. Even though senior clinicians are highly educated and skilled individuals in their own area of expertise, they do not necessarily have the business skills necessary to run an organization that needs strong leadership to successfully manage complex healthcare issues in a rapidly changing and evolving healthcare environment.

Skills required for the corporate role

The Institute of Directors states that directors need both independence of mind and the ability to collaborate with others to reach the right decisions.[8] At board level, medical directors need to form their own views, articulate them and enter into discussion and debate so that the board comes to the right collective decision. As a director, the medical director is accountable to the board and not to the CEO, who is the line manager, and must therefore exert independent judgement and opinion. The Institute of Directors outlines a research-based set of attributes among directors that leads to effective organizations.[8] All directors won't necessarily possess all these attributes, but, collectively, each board should have these attributes:

- strategic perception
- decision-making
- analysis and use of information
- good communication skills
- confident and influential interaction with others
- achievement of results.

Developmental aspects and support of the role

Before taking on the role of medical director, the person will generally have acquired a good understanding of operational issues as a clinical director, and of professional issues as an associate medical director. Boards of NHS organizations have become more sophisticated and akin to those of the business world, and essentially the medical director requires the skills expected of an executive director of a large business. It is advisable, therefore, to undertake training in the corporate aspects of the role and gain a fuller understanding about how boards of big organizations work.

Once in the role of medical director, self-management becomes important in order to deal with the day-to-day demands. Resilience and the ability to manage the stress that comes with occasional personal challenges from colleagues and others are also crucial. Ethical issues arise from time to time, particularly as competition within the healthcare system in the UK grows, with NHS organizations and boards becoming more focused on growth and expansion. Medical directors can face dilemmas as a result of the tension between the professional values of improving the patient experience and what corporate responsibilities demand in terms of competition. These have to recognized and managed, and ongoing mentorship or coaching is often helpful in this respect.

Medical directors need to be adequately supported on a day-to-day basis to carry out their role. The amount of support required will depend on the range of responsibilities, but with smaller trust boards and fewer EDs it is likely that, in addition to being responsible for the medical workforce and their professional issues, medical directors will have significant functional responsibilities, as outlined earlier in the chapter. The support of associate medical directors and perhaps a non-medical manager to lead on clinical governance will be required. Having a structure to support their functional responsibilities, as well as a robust operational medical management structure, frees up medical directors to take a meaningful strategic lead and can help them to avoid being dragged into daily operational problems.[11] They will typically have a team of associate medical directors, clinical directors and medical leads, all of whom should share an understanding of the organization's direction and goals.

One of the decisions that any new medical director has to take is whether or not to continue in clinical practice. There are advantages and disadvantages to maintaining some clinical practice. Those advocating the importance of retaining clinical responsibilities talk about having credibility with colleagues, being a genuine clinical voice on the board, staying in touch with the demands of the frontline and experiencing first hand the consequences of board decisions. On the negative side, it means that there is less time to devote to the corporate and functional responsibilities of the role. There is no right or wrong answer, but based on personal experience, continuing in clinical practice sets the medical director apart on the board as a genuine clinical voice who can speak authoritatively on issues to do with quality and safety. However, as a director of a large organization, it is unlikely that the medical director could realistically devote more than one day each week to clinical practice.

In summary, the medical director post of a healthcare organization is a position with executive director responsibility. Even though the role is demanding and is not for the faint-hearted, it is also a stimulating one within an ever rapidly evolving healthcare system. Furthermore, it is usually very rewarding on a personal level, as the medical director is well placed to improve the quality of healthcare provided to a large community of people.

Summary
- ❏ The NHS board is modelled on boards in the business world, with non-executive and executive directors operating as a unitary board.
- ❏ There are clear corporate governance arrangements with accountability to the community through the board of governors.
- ❏ The medical director has both corporate and functional roles.
- ❏ The role of medical director has a key leadership responsibility within the organization.
- ❏ Being a medical director is demanding, but rewarding.

References

1. Webster M (2007). *The Director's Handbook: Your Duties, Responsibilities and Liabilities.* London: Institute of Directors, Pinsent Masons.

2. Department of Health (2002). *A Guide to NHS Foundation Trusts.* London: Department of Health.

3. NHS Confederation (2009) *Reforming Leadership Development…Again.* London: NHS Confederation Publications.

4. Monitor (2010) *The NHS Foundation Trust Code of Governance.* Available from: http://www.monitor-nhsft.gov.uk/

5. NHS Leadership and National Leadership Council (2010). *The Healthy NHS Board. Principles of Good Governance.* Available from: http://www.leadershipacademy.nhs.uk/

6. NHS Confederation (2010). *The Foundations of Good Governance.* (Produced in partnership with Beachcroft.) London: NHS Confederation Publications.

7. Department of Health (2003). *Appointment Commission Governing the NHS: A Guide for NHS Boards.* London: Department of Health.

8. Institute of Directors (2007). *The Effective Director; Building Individual and Board Success.* London: Institute of Directors.

9. Simpson J (1997). Moving into management. *Br Med J* 314, S2–7080.

10. British Association of Medical Managers (BAMM) (1996). *The Roles and Responsibilities of the Medical Director.* Stockport: BAMM.

11. NHS Confederation (2009). *Future of Leadership Series: Developing NHS Leadership – the Role of the Trust Medical Director.* London: NHS Confederation Publications.

12. Ham C, Dickson H (2007). *Engaging Doctors in Leadership. What Can We Learn from International Experience and Research Evidence?* Coventry: NHS Institute for Innovation and Improvement.

13. General Medical Council (2006). *Good Medical Practice.* London: GMC.

14. British Association of Medical Managers (BAMM) (2001). *The Duties of the Medical Director.* Stockport: BAMM.

15. Francis R (2009). *Independent Inquiry into Care Provided by Mid Staffordshire NHS Foundation Trust.* Available from: http://www.wirral.nhs.uk/

16. Committee on Standards in Public Life (1995). *Standards in Public Life.* Available from: www.publicstandards.org.uk/

Chapter 10

The doctor as chief executive

Philip Sugarman

Introduction

This chapter is intended to offer medical practitioners a very practical insight into the demands of senior healthcare management roles, including that of chief executive. It should also assist a doctor in understanding the work of management colleagues. Chief executive jobs differ between larger and smaller organizations, and in the public, commercial and charitable sectors, but there is a core commonality.

The underlying assumption in this chapter is that readers have a good knowledge of certain clinical services, but that their career so far has not equipped them fully for senior management. This is a challenge that doctors have faced for many years, including those who take on administrative roles in hospitals and health boards, and those who become directors of clinics or physician executives in the varied healthcare cultures in, for example, Europe and America. The lack of a career path for doctors to become chief executives, in terms of learning and development, as well as pay and progression, remains very apparent in the UK National Health Service (NHS),[1] and doctors aspiring to such roles need to some extent to be self-taught, learning on the job. With the lack of a set career path, they must have the spontaneous drive and ambition to seek opportunities to gain experience, and to take on management and leadership responsibility.

Many readers will have attended courses and conferences, and read assorted papers on leadership, management, governance and similar themes, often specific to areas of healthcare.[2] Some of this content is also now appearing in medical training curricula in the UK, which is promising for the future. I attempt here not to summarize this knowledge base, nor to explicitly pursue a competency-based approach or other accepted framework of reference, nor even to list the available literature. Rather I suggest that personal accounts of leadership roles are particularly useful to certain audiences including doctors,[3] and therefore offer a brief personal account in straightforward language, which describes the challenges as frankly and as simply as possible. To some extent this sets the tone for how doctors should themselves approach a chief executive role, and is informed by what I have understood from a variety of mentors, peers and colleagues over the years, and by what I have observed and learnt first-hand. I particularly focus on people issues which I see as fundamental, before covering other key areas, including personal and career aspects.

Scope of chief executive's responsibility

People and culture

People are supremely important in any endeavour, but especially in the provision of healthcare. Most doctors will have built their people approach on personal and professional values, often being sympathetic, supportive and tolerant with nearly all patients, most nurses and the majority of medical colleagues. Many will, at times, not approve of colleagues whose work attitudes they perceive are not up to scratch. All this is certainly consistent with having high professional standards, but some colleagues, often the brightest, are highly critical thinkers by inclination, which is always a mixed blessing. A more strategic approach to people does not come naturally to everyone. It is essential to hold a strong guiding belief that people are central to the quality and effectiveness of healthcare, and to accept that the role of people, professions and culture in healthcare is immensely complex. Those who think in terms of systems may have some advantage in making sense of what are still very hierarchical structures in terms of status, team roles, power and pay in healthcare.

Medical careers do not provide education in employment law, contemporary human resources theory and practice, or a business view of people management. To some extent this can be remedied by short or long courses, including the relevant parts of a Master of Business Administration (MBA) course. Nevertheless in a career journey towards being chief executive, any doctor will have to learn about the realities of people management, including some bruising experiences, such as recruiting the wrong person in a key role and struggling with the consequences for a period of time, or managing occasional aggravating disputes or disciplinary processes. More importantly, they will need to evolve an effective way of positively managing team members to make sure the job gets done to a high standard, and this will always be a mix of practical goal-setting and review, and the more subtle processes of encouragement, inspiration and delegation. It is, of course, necessary to work with the formal processes of an employer, understanding the many human resources policies, and the particular training, team and personal development activities in vogue at the time. To ensure the highest level of effectiveness, the work of team members must be closely aligned to the wider strategy of the organization, rather than just a mixed list of worthwhile tasks, which may suit the employee's preferences. The skills to develop and project the organization's vision and strategy are a key part of the chief executive's role, as discussed later in this chapter.

Experienced chief executives, after years in a successful management career, emphasize the importance of keeping things simple, focusing on the strategic, often common-sense fundamentals. They typically give the view that if you have the right people, the right culture and strategy will emerge, and you can make a success of almost any challenge in a competitive and risky world. So on the people side, they talk informally about 'refreshing' their teams, by which they mean inspiring and re-energizing, as well as 'hiring and firing'. It is a long journey for many doctors to adapt from the people approach inherent in healthcare, to move beyond feelings of attachment and personal sympathy for long-standing staff, to clearly prioritize the interests of the patients and the mission of the organization to deliver great healthcare, where necessary, above the interests of employees (the current chief executive of the NHS describes this as being 'on the side of the angels'[4]).

What holds many senior managers back from a culture of openness, personal development, and challenging and refreshing their team is their own fear of change. The temptation is to recruit people in one's own image (often based on personality, style and professional knowledge as much as personal background or gender) and, unconsciously, to cling to them. The key to success is to really understand the principle of diversity – and the huge value in having members of the team who think differently, including people who are in some ways much cleverer than the chief executive. Leadership success is based on the enlightened self-interest of hiring a talented team, and then managing them effectively. The chief executive must particularly exemplify this approach in recruiting and leading their core team of executive directors, setting the tone for the organization.

Looking at hiring first, chief executives must ensure that their organization's recruitment and reward strategies and structures are fit for purpose – to attract and retain high-calibre people. It is important that a medical chief executive does not neglect this area because it is unfamiliar. Much of this (and much else about an organization) can often be simply gauged by just looking afresh at job adverts online. Of course, there may be restrictions and even inflexibility in the packages on offer, especially in the public sector, but the sheer quality of the recruitment process is an essential area for focus. The chief executive, the human resources team he/she employs, and the wider management team will need to know 'what good looks like', by which I mean they must be able to formulate what they are looking for in an ideal candidate, and to have a consistent approach which intelligently attracts and selects good candidates from among others. This is a skill in short supply, with extant research showing that panel interviews (including traditional consultant appointment committees) alone have little ability to predict future work performance. There is, however, longstanding evidence in support of assessment centres.[5]

As regards 'firing', the chief executive needs to take a positive, 'big picture' view. The reality of winners and losers is key to modern business and management culture at the top level, although this is rarely said openly. Quite simply in any team at any level there will be people who are visibly forging ahead, making great things happen, and others who are for whatever reasons falling behind the pace of change, holding others back, as well as a large group in the middle. A very attractive programme of reward, praise and appreciation must be in place, and in addition a culture of direct, clear feedback and development support, with all the proper procedures and resources. However, key signs which must be addressed include poor presentation and performance in meetings, complex team and interdepartmental problems, and the inability to agree to and deliver on goals. The task is to find a way to quickly boost or refresh the motivation and performance of individuals; indeed, it is a great pleasure to be able to develop someone's career and contribution, or at least put it back on track.

It is true, however, that failure should not be rewarded, and that a culture of 'jobs for life' is as unhealthy in healthcare management as anywhere else. For a few employees all measures will sadly not be effective in a reasonable time, and they will fall behind. It is the duty of the chief executive to ensure that, at the right time, someone else is given a chance. The route of exit, either to a more genuinely suitable role or sometimes to the job market, may be varied, but should not be protracted.

An organization that does not regularly create space for great new people and promote others into new roles at every level will never excel. Having said that, there is some evidence that healthcare organizations, in trying too hard to be 'business-like', can overdo this. If lengths of tenure for senior managers (including chief executives) become too short, such jobs will only appeal to those with few options, bringing recruitment problems (including candidate calibre and quality). Recent reports describe just this picture at the top of many NHS organizations,[6] as well as commercial organizations during times of stress. What many organizations and tough-minded chief executives fail to understand is that this saps morale unless there is a balance of positive rewards, strong team-building and the determined development of an open organizational culture. There needs to be a high level of training, coaching and mentoring activity, away days, 360-degree feedback and the like, to create a culture where people are open to change and personal development, creating a pool of home-grown talent, as succession planning for the future. Through championing these approaches, a medical chief executive can positively show how they 'believe in people'.

To achieve all this, the chief executive will need to have the right director responsible for human resources in place, with the necessary range of professional knowledge and skills, able to develop the chief executive's vision of people management.

Operational management: cost and quality

Doctors are trained to be observant on detail, and they naturally bring this trait into management. However, it is important to take a 'big picture' view on the range of business issues, not being distracted by operational decisions on expenditure and quality, except as a way of grasping a strategic overview of the endeavour.

The efficient use of finite resources for maximum health benefit is obviously right. The conflict between saving or making money and healthcare values can be very intense at a local level, when resources are short for a particular patient or service. In practice this means balancing the pursuit of value in services, e.g. the required quality outcome at the lowest cost. The difficulty comes in measuring quality and outcomes, and ensuring that short-term financial pressures do not lead to subsequent quality failures. This is the source of the proliferation of healthcare quality, safety and clinical governance initiatives at government, regulatory, commissioning and organizational levels. The chief executive's job is to support others such as the medical and nursing directors to work on the many formal indicators of quality which continue to be developed, from mortality data to patient-reported outcomes measures. However, it just as important to keep a clear strategic overview of what really matters for patients, and what are the true determinants of quality. These include the suitability of buildings and equipment, the quality and morale of staff, the clarity of the service model and the effectiveness of operational management. As a chief executive, it is essential to have confidence that the top clinicians and managers of each service really know how best to run that particular branch of healthcare. There is huge variation in what quality of patient care can be provided for a fixed cost, depending on the effectiveness of the managers and leaders of the service. So, in fact, many of the solutions on quality and finance come back to people management.

In developed countries, value is clumsily measured in currency terms, so money is as important in healthcare as anywhere else, and much effort goes into keeping track of it. A doctor is not an accountant, but a chief executive will employ many from this profession, including a finance director as a key colleague. An accountant's job is to bring transparency to prices, income, costs, profitability and financial planning, and a medical chief executive needs to hone skills to challenge accountants to plan and report matters clearly. This is a learning process like any other, which can benefit from relevant training, but a good finance function should provide clear answers to simple but intelligent questions, enable a healthy focus on the bottom line (rather than the numbers in the calculation), and support sound business decisions. Both managers and clinicians should be able to share in the success of the organization, and therefore have a motivation to pursue both long-term success and short-term efficiencies in their areas. It is natural to pursue profitable areas of care, to question and even eschew unprofitable ones, to set the highest sustainable prices and to drive down costs.

It may take a while for a medical chief executive to accept how all this competitive activity brings efficiency and frees up resources for more effective healthcare activity elsewhere – for example, through further investment when public spending savings are directed to best public health use, through improved profits attracting commercial capital into healthcare, and also through the use of charitable trading surpluses for further developments in line with a charity's mission. However, it is key to management in a competitive world to have an overview of these market forces at work, even in the sphere of healthcare.

Reputation and sales

I deliberately use these terms to encompass a spectrum of interactions with the world beyond the healthcare provider, include a range of networking activities by clinicians and managers, information flow via patients, purchasing commissioners, inspectors and academics, marketing and public relations materials and campaigns of various sorts, and the direct targeting of new business.

Doctors are well placed to understand the maxim 'reputation is everything in healthcare'. They will have a good grounding in how information spreads about the quality of care and expertise of a particular hospital, service or clinician. They will have less experience, and perhaps less interest, in the value that marketing communications and public relations can add. However, a chief executive will, in most modern healthcare providers, have a marketing and communications team of some sort, and must seek to ensure it functions effectively. The key trick is to build bridges between the cultures of healthcare and marketing. Clinicians have lots of good stories to tell about successes in care, regional and national recognition, new treatments and the like, and it is perfectly practical for these to be presented credibly and professionally for various audiences (internal and external), and disseminated widely to the benefit of the provider. Moreover this information should be martialled into marketing campaigns to support the brand and vision of the provider – how it wishes to be seen and what it plans to achieve. Similarly negative stories need to be managed with a credible 'counter-narrative', especially in an age when healthcare is under public scrutiny and potentially one-sided press attention.

As choice and competition become important in the UK market and elsewhere, independent providers of public and private healthcare increasingly have to develop sales strategies similar to those long established in other areas of commercial healthcare, such as medical devices and pharmaceuticals. It is likely that this will develop in state-run providers too. This requires all the elements of sales culture – a clear definition and branding of a range of services, a thorough analysis of the potential market and competition, a plan to impact potential buyers, and a professional sales team incentivized to meet sales targets. Much of this will be uncomfortable for doctors, who often have taken a low view of pharmaceutical sales representatives, for example. But this activity is essential in competitive cultures to allow great organizations to thrive. A targeted form of selling is seen in the response to tenders – making a winning bid – already a familiar part of the public healthcare landscape in the UK. Ultimately selling is about ensuring that those who may potentially benefit from the healthcare provider have those benefits communicated clearly to them at the point where they are about to make a decision. If successful, it becomes part of a journey for a patient or purchaser, which should hopefully end in a great outcome and the prospect of further use of the provider. This is how many good doctors naturally relate to their patients, and this is a good starting point for a medical chief executive. The ideal corporate culture in healthcare is to have all staff, especially senior clinicians, instinctively promoting the reputation of their services through sheer pride and enthusiasm, as an integral part of their professional networking. Obviously a medical chief executive must show leadership, being a role model for others in this area of activity, including through a variety of (one hopes) inspiring presentations and publications. It is also essential that one member of the executive team has clear-cut responsibility for sales and marketing activity, in addition to the medical director's responsibility for reputation for quality.

Patients and customers

Every chief executive needs to have a real grip of their customers' experience, and in healthcare this means patients, their carers and relatives, as well as business customers (such as NHS purchasing commissioners, referring clinicians and, in many jurisdictions, health insurers and so on). Doctors are in a strong position to have a good understanding of the patient's journey, having worked on the frontline in healthcare throughout their careers. However, they need to broaden their understanding by looking at healthcare not just from a doctor's point of view, but truly through a patient's experience, and they must keep this fresh by frequent interactions with patients and with services. It is particularly important to be observant in service visits, noticing how patients are being treated, if they are being kept waiting, how they are spoken to and what themes emerge repeatedly from complaints, incidents, patient surveys, audits and inspections, the opinions of staff and the like. Experiences of being patients themselves, and talking to friends and relatives who have been patients, are certainly important. Successful chief executives will be able to ground patient experience in their plans for cultural change in the organization, bearing in mind that staff in below-average quality services will not always realize that they are falling short of expectations.

Information for patients is certainly important, including timely explanations at various points, while information and billing have an impact on purchasing customers' experience of the service. Doctors may be tempted to think of healthcare as a technically definable product, consisting of a series of activities and interventions. While this is certainly helpful, what is equally important is the total care pathway and the true 'service' element, and how that service is offered, presented and explained at each step. In short, chief executives should be very focused on patients' and customers' subjective and personal experience of healthcare services from start to finish, in addition to objective measures of safety and effectiveness. They should think creatively about how services can be improved. Doctors are, of course, well placed to understand technical and service innovation in healthcare. Insights at this level can be the source of emergent strategy and sector leadership – areas core to the chief executive role.

Strategy: planning and risk

All organizations need to have a long-term planning function, and development programmes and change management processes which can implement strategy in a series of orderly steps. The medical chief executive will benefit from training in the business functions of market analysis and strategy definition (a central part of MBA courses), and programme and project management (typical short courses). While they will be knowledgeable about clinical governance, risk and audit, they may find the world of corporate governance, risk registers, internal and external corporate audit, healthcare market and financial risks perplexing. It is fair to say that, following the credit crunch, the entire framework of corporate risk management is under scrutiny. A personal view is that the best form of risk management is one that is integrated with forward strategy, i.e. the best form of defence is offence. A chief executive should have a frank understanding of where the organization is weak or exposed, and find ways of turning this around, bringing its strengths to bear. If they are up to speed with reality, then the output of strategic planning and risk management exercises should be of assistance in moving things on, but it should rarely be surprising.

Ultimately, in truly independent healthcare providers, the strategy should be led by the chief executive, whose personal strengths may well match the strategic needs of the organization at that time. For a doctor this could mean an appreciation of patient care and healthcare quality, of the trends towards specialization or community-based care, of the importance of modern equipment, or how to develop clinical leadership within services.

Communication

There is a clear opportunity for a doctor with a good facility for language to project a strong vision and exert real influence through 'thought leadership' and visibility, both internally and externally. However, success in this requires an appreciation of some important issues and a lot of hard work. In leading a large number of healthcare workers to implement strategic change in a healthcare provider, a chief executive will use a mixture of personal communication skills and an organized communications team, both key areas for development.

It can never be underestimated in the modern media age how important it is to craft a simple message, and repeat it using every possible channel. Communication includes face-to-face human interaction between managers and staff groups – such communication briefings must be mandated, supported and checked otherwise they will not be truly effective – and via a variety of digital means. We are now moving rapidly into a new media age, and chief executive as communicator-in-chief must have mastery of whatever means are necessary to get the message across. Many doctors will be strong on academic lecturing and even after-dinner speechmaking, but they are likely to be weaker on brief, clear, impactful 'comms' presentations, whether live or recorded. Writing professional papers is a useful communication skill, but very different from crafting soundbites and short pieces of staff communications and wider public relations. All these areas of activity will help the chief executive develop a mixture of the organization's strategy and their own perspective into a continuous stream of messaging necessary to steer the culture of a modern healthcare provider. Marketing communications are well covered in many MBAs, and media and presentational training is useful and widely available. There is, however, no substitute for planning, preparation and practice (i.e. rehearsals) for communication events. A great deal can be learnt and achieved by working closely with media-savvy colleagues who truly understand 'personal messaging'.

Personal strategy

Career choices

Partially or fully relinquishing clinical work for a career in management can bring a real degree of employment insecurity, sometimes matched by potential rewards, and certainly a change in professional identity.[1] Making this choice at an early- or late-career phase has very different effects. The healthcare manager or business leader who used to be a doctor many years ago, more prevalent in the independent sector, has less 'medical credibility' than the experienced medical director and clinician who has latterly taken a chief executive role. Keeping oneself medically accredited and up to date, and if so for how long, is a key decision. These career strategies are about managing personal risk, but more importantly choosing to do what one finds rewarding, particularly in terms of the potential to make a much bigger impact on healthcare.

It is essential from the start to see the link between organizational and career strategy. Aspiring chief executives must have a realistic grasp on what needs doing, how long it might take and what they might do for their next career stage. All this should help (at job interview) to clarify whether this is a case of the right person in the right place at the right time. Tenure in any job but particularly for a chief executive should have a natural flow – a beginning, a middle and an end. After a strong start in which one establishes a sense of direction and commences a strategy, somewhere in the middle can be found opportunities to make a big difference, to have something to be proud of and to demonstrate success (new services and buildings, expansion and awards, etc.). By the end, a team has been constructed which has the talent, skills and experience to take over – with several executives who have been led in their learning by the chief executive now good candidate chief executives themselves – so that truly great chief executives eventually do themselves out of a job. It is a mistake to hang on too long – it is better to fill the role and then gracefully hand over,[7] than be seen as past your sell-by date and perhaps be let go abruptly. A highly successful chief executive will be in demand and should be able to comfortably choose their next assignment at the right time for all parties.

Personal style

It seems natural that chief executives are often formidable, but probably only a minority are truly inspiring. There is a particular need early in role to hold one's ground in response to fears, demands and praise, which often push for a quick, impulsive decision. An inner confidence is helpful to fulfil this aspect of leadership, but there is no reason for this to be accompanied by grandiosity or dismissiveness (very common faults in people at the top of organizations). It is not difficult to smile and listen politely for a moment, even if you are rushed or have little idea which member of your staff you are talking to!

Important choices rest on personal integrity and leading by example. Some areas of probity are obvious, but social judgements about mixing with staff can be difficult. Too much anxiety about chatting or showing generosity (and then being talked about) can produce a remote figure. Just as common are those chief executives who allow themselves to misbehave in small or more significant ways. These issues are particularly important for the caring professions, but are common to a wide variety of roles.

Beyond such simple rules, it is a fact that one cannot change one's personality, so 'doing it your own way' is something to embrace as unavoidable. It is good to realize that, to relax in the role, one must enjoy the job one has chosen and make choices aimed at leading and inspiring the team. A great skill to acquire is to be able, at will, to boost the morale at service level – using the role to make dedicated people feel special. Overall, for a medical chief executive, a good aim is to be seen by the team around you, and more widely across the services, as accessible and friendly, but also highly professional and knowledgeable.

Visibility: set pieces

Much of the impact of any leadership role is made in set pieces, from major presentations in front of large numbers of people to regular appearances in front of key senior boardroom players and varied staff groups. There is no substitute to preparation for operational and board meetings, major staff briefings and external presentations, as well as service visits; this is true, to some extent, for more informal staff and patient encounters too. It is essentially a matter of customer service to perform well at these times, sharing a clearly articulated narrative which makes sense of the major challenges and available information. The assumed credibility of a doctor is certainly of assistance for a chief executive needing to win over an audience.

Often at the heart of very varied events, from one-to-one discussions with the chair of the board to very informal meetings, is a need for the chief executive to share a vision of the organization, and the strategy for achieving that vision. For chief executives with true mastery of their role, informal encounters not only will provide visibility around services and facilities, but will also be an opportunity to communicate vision and strategy to the people who really have to implement it. This is every bit as challenging, both intellectually and personally, as the practice of medicine, and many doctors will find it highly enjoyable and rewarding.

Readers will understand the importance of personal relationships between the chief executive and all the members of the board – both executive and non-executive. Many interactions are, of course, informal and others are built on formal reporting and governance. Ultimately, however, all these players, to fulfil their own roles, need the chief executive to visibly live and breathe in that role as central to the team, leading and embodying the vision, strategy and culture of the organization. The secret of a successful board, running a successful organization, is the leadership given by the chief executive, supported and managed by the chairman.

Thought leadership

This contemporary phrase nicely captures the cognitive aspect of a chief executive's role. It is essential to build up a mental map of the healthcare market and economy in which the organization sits, how its services currently function, and what the options are for change. This analysis of strategic opportunity must be articulated in key themes which can be picked up from any source and developed in any way – very much a personal mix of reading and conferencing, factual analysis, discussion and debate, and creativity. Some chief executives have the knack of extracting from the world 'ringing phrases' and using them to great effect, while others misfire with words that don't ring true. The challenge is to distance oneself from the overused phrases in a message-rich world, and find a way of articulating future thinking that is distinctive and memorable, without becoming so visionary that people don't buy it.

Strategic networking

I hope that readers with a medical background will see that the role of chief executive is very different from that of a clinician, but that many of the leadership themes are similar. Ultimately both the chief executive and the organization they lead sit in a complex world of individuals and groups, involved in both competition and cooperation of every kind. Interacting in this world, including with a host of external parties and in formal partnerships, involves a series of choices and opportunities to learn and influence. Navigating in this way the complex system we might call the 'healthcare space' is 'strategic networking'. What is essential is that the chief executive is proactive in this, always curious, learning and sharing ideas. It is right to be confident that hard work of this kind will lead to the emergence of solutions, which must then be communicated in an ever-changing yet coherent narrative.

Conclusion

The success of the chief executive's personal and organizational strategy is ultimately measured in terms of the impact they have on people's healthcare, and with luck this will be reflected fairly in their own reputation, as well as that of the organization. Doctors are well placed with their strong knowledge base to make exceptional chief executives, embracing a continuous journey of development, dedicated to the challenges and complexities of healthcare.

Summary

- ❏ Doctors must proactively seek opportunities to develop management skills.
- ❏ 'Hiring, inspiring and firing' are major personal challenges for most doctors.
- ❏ A real appreciation of patient service experience is crucial.
- ❏ Strategic planning and corporate risk management skills must be learnt.
- ❏ Organizational and career strategy should be synergistic.
- ❏ Personal communication skills are central to the role.
- ❏ Both set pieces and daily encounters require communication of vision and strategy.

References

1. Ham C, Clark J, Spurgeon P, Dickinson H, Armit K (2010). *Medical Chief Executives in the NHS: Facilitators and Barriers to their Career Progress.* Coventry: NHS Institute for Innovation and Improvement.
2. Sugarman P (2007). Governance and innovation in mental health. Editorial. *Psychiatric Bull* 31, 283–5.
3. Taylor B (2010). *Medical Leadership.* Toronto: University of Toronto Press.
4. Donelly L (2007). The SHA interviews, David Nicholson. *Health Service J* 1 January. Available from: http://www.hsj.co.uk/
5. Ungerson B (1974). Assessment centres – a review of research findings. *Personnel Rev* 3, 4–13.
6. Santry (2009). Startling senior executive turnover stifles NHS innovation. Available from: http://www.hsj.co.uk/
7. Sonnenfeld J (1988). *The Hero's Farewell. What Happens When CEOs Retire?* Oxford: Oxford University Press.

Chapter 11

Roles and challenges of a clinical director

Sajeeva Jayalath

- Introduction
- History
- The roles
- The challenges
- Conflicting issues
- Summary
- References

Introduction

The roles and challenges of a clinical director continue to evolve as the NHS changes its course of direction under political, financial and social demands. Each significant change in the NHS over the last 25 years has had an impact on the development of the clinical director's role. Despite this changing role, the importance of the clinical director position remains widely recognized and accepted, since it was introduced to the NHS in the 1980s.

History

The most influential contribution for the introduction of the role of clinical director was made by Roy Griffiths, deputy chairman and managing director of Sainsbury, in his famous report on the NHS in 1983.[1] Griffiths and his team found that there was no coherent system of management in the NHS at the local level and there was no structure within NHS organizations to evaluate performance, improve quality and work within a budget. He famously summarized his report as follows: 'If Florence Nightingale were carrying her lamp through the corridors of the NHS today she would almost certainly be searching for the people in charge.'[1,2]

During the 1980s, the government accepted Griffiths' recommendations and by 1985 general managers were appointed from inside and outside the NHS to hospitals and health units. Key concepts such as managing budgets, value for money, management training and education were introduced to all NHS organizations.

One of the crucial elements in the introduction of general management was the recognition of the importance of involving doctors, in particular senior doctors, in the day-to-day management of the NHS.[1,2] Although various models were adopted in the 1980s as a means of including doctors in management, none attracted more interest or support than the clinical director concept.

Interestingly, clinical directorates were first developed in 1972 at Johns Hopkins Hospital in Baltimore, USA, long before they were introduced to the NHS. The model suggested that clinical services should be organized into a series of directorates. Each directorate would have a clinical director or lead consultant, usually chosen by the other doctors within the directorate, to act on their behalf. The clinical director was expected to assume responsibility for providing leadership to the directorate and to represent the views of all the clinical specialities. The clinical director was also expected to initiate change, agree workloads and resource allocation with the unit general manager, and act as the budget holder for the directorate.[3]

In these early days, the relationship between the clinical directors and colleagues was not seen as one of line management. Rather, the clinical director was expected to negotiate and persuade colleagues.

By the 1990s, the role of the clinical director was being interpreted differently in various organizations. In an article published in *British Journal of Management* by Harrison and Miller in 1999,[3] the clinical director is described as a person who is responsible for and provides leadership to a team of consultant colleagues and junior medical staff within a directorate. Clinical directors would take responsibility for the directorate budget and business plans and get involved directly or indirectly in contract discussions with purchasers/fundholders.

Despite numerous attempts, it has not been possible to uniformly define the roles and responsibilities of a clinical director, which tend to vary from one organization to another. The roles and responsibilities Harrison and Miller described in the late 1990s still remain as the basic functions of a clinical director. However, the ever-increasing demands and responsibilities of NHS organizations have meant that the duties and expectations of a clinical director have also increased and diversified from clinical to operational, financial and even strategic tasks.

In most NHS organizations there is a hierarchical medical management system. The medical director is at the helm of medical management and is supported by the clinical directors. Some organizations may have a tier above or below the level of clinical directors, depending largely on the size of the organization. Box 11.1 lists the significant reports and government initiatives that contributed to the development of the role of clinical director.

Box 11.1 Significant events and government initiatives that contributed to the development of the role of clinical director

- 1983 – Griffiths Report
- 1998 – A First Class Service: Quality in the NHS – government consultation document which introduced clinical governance to the NHS
- 1999 – Introduction of National Institute for Clinical Excellence, now called the National Institute for Health and Clinical Excellence (NICE)
- 2001 – Appraisal for consultants working in the NHS; Department of Health
- 2002 – Introduction of foundation trusts and Monitor, the regulatory authority of NHS foundation trusts
- 2003 – Consultant contract
- 2007 – World class commissioning and clinical engagement
- 2008 – Our NHS Our Future: NHS Next Stage Review – Leading Local Change; Lord Darzi report
- 2008 – Service line management; Monitor
- 2009 – Licensing and revalidation; General Medical Council

The roles

The roles taken up by the clinical directors in a corporate modern-day NHS organization can be described under the following broad headings:

- supporting clinical governance (governance role)
- line management of doctors (supervisory role)
- supporting the running of the business of an NHS organization (operational role)
- supporting the development of the business of an NHS organization (strategic role)
- learning and development of skills and preparing for progression (personal development role).

Clinical governance

Clinical governance became an integral part of management in NHS organizations after the publication of the government consultation document, *A First Class Service: Quality in the NHS*, in 1998.[4] This document laid out the principles of clinical governance and paved the way for the establishment of the National Institute for Clinical Excellence, now called the National Institute for Health and Clinical Excellence (NICE). Clinical governance is defined as 'A framework through which NHS organisations are accountable for continuously improving the quality of their services and safeguarding high standards of care by creating an environment in which excellence in clinical care will flourish.'[4]

The famous seven pillars of clinical governance were described as:

- clinical effectiveness and research
- audit
- risk management
- education and training
- patient and public involvement and learning from complaints
- use of information technology
- staff and staff management.

Clinical directors play a very important role in the delivery of these tasks related to clinical governance. Some organizations have created separate clinical director posts with primary responsibility for clinical governance, while others have devolved the various functions of clinical governance to the generic clinical directors. Clinical directors will be involved, directly or indirectly, in supporting inculcation of the seven pillars of clinical governance.

Since the introduction of NICE, certain elements of clinical governance, such as clinical effectiveness, evidence-based practice and audits, have become standardized and therefore comparable between organizations. NICE guidelines provide a benchmark for the treatment of common medical conditions and most local audits are based on assessing practice against these NICE standards.

Most NHS trusts have a clinical governance committee which will implement and monitor NICE clinical standards, log audit and research activity, and work closely with the drug and therapeutics committee. The clinical directors will take a leading role in such committees.

Risk management, learning from experience, investigation of complaints and serious untoward incidents are other major components of clinical governance in which the clinical director will play a central role. The clinical director will also be responsible for the development of action plans based on the recommendations of investigations and the implementation of these plans to an agreed timescale.

Trusts participate in a number of national and local clinical audits every year. Clinical directors may get involved in coordinating and leading some of these audits. Invariably, the clinical directors will also be involved in developing recommendations, action and implementation protocols to improve practice standards following the audits.

Quality improvement is a key task for all medical managers in the NHS. Clinical directors will be responsible to their line manager (usually the medical director) in the delivery of various performance targets. Some of these are local targets set by the local commissioners, while others are national targets monitored by the Care Quality Commission. The clinical directors are expected to review these targets on a regular basis and have frequent discussions with their consultant colleagues to ensure that all targets are met within their directorates.

The management of 'quality' is inevitably a key role of a clinical director and takes considerable time and effort.

The key skills and knowledge clinical directors are expected to acquire to support their role in clinical governance are listed in Box 11.2.[5]

Box 11.2 The key skills and knowledge required to support the clinical governance role

- Identification, reporting and management of clinical risks
- Focus on prevention
- Training in root cause analysis
- Knowledge of complaints procedure
- Preparation of action plans
- Responding to major incidents
- Contingency planning
- Involving patients and carers
- Clinical audit and research

Line manager

The competency and quality of the doctors practising in the UK is monitored through a system of annual appraisals introduced in 2001.[6] With the introduction of the consultant contract in 2003, the annual appraisal was linked to the process of job planning for all medical staff.[7] While the appraisal is in relation to performance and professional development of the doctor, the job plans concentrate on the weekly timetable and the proportion of time a doctor should spend on direct clinical care (30 hours) and supporting professional activities (10 hours per week). Annual appraisals and job planning are compulsory for all doctors and the clinical director, as line manager, is held responsible for ensuring that these are carried out annually. Following the Shipman Inquiry, the procedure for annual appraisals was tightened further and linked to revalidation and re-certification with the appointment of responsible officers[8,9] (please see Chapter 16 for more detail on this). For the purposes of this chapter, it should be noted that although the medical director will be the responsible officer, the clinical directors will have to ensure that all medical staff in their directorates have completed an annual appraisal with approved job plans.

This enables the clinical directors not only to have a good understanding of the workload and competencies of the medical staff in their directorates but also to be involved in their personal and professional development.

The line management role is focused on individuals; this makes it different from the operational role of clinical directors which is focused on systems, although the two may overlap. In addition to appraisal and job planning, the role will involve managing doctors' training, development, performance and disciplinary matters. It also includes recording annual, study and sick leave of doctors, employment of locums and ensuring that doctors have secretarial support. A good clinical director will also be closely involved in activities such as the induction of newly appointed doctors, teaching and training of junior medical staff, continued professional development of all medical staff, monitoring of the duty rota, compliance with the European Working Time Directive and other related functions, although these are the primary responsibilities of the clinical tutor or the director of medical education.

Managing colleagues is one of the most challenging tasks for a clinical director. This becomes especially testing during a time of organizational change when effective management of available resources and cost-cutting have to be carefully balanced against clinical effectiveness and patient safety.

The key skills and knowledge that are necessary for a clinical director to be an effective line manager are listed in Box 11.3.[5]

Box 11.3 Key skills and knowledge to facilitate the role as a line manager

- Appraisal training
- Job planning
- Assessing and managing performance of colleagues
- Supervision
- Managing difficult colleagues
- Managing and leading change
- Teamworking and developing colleagues
- Counselling, coaching and mentoring
- Workforce planning
- Teaching, training, learning and development

Supporting the running of the business of the organization (operational role)

The clinical director has a key role in the day-to-day operational activities of the directorate. Most NHS trusts, and in particular foundation trusts, have greater autonomy in the organization and delivery of clinical services. Foundation trusts are also financially independent and have, to some extent, the freedom to retain any surplus and even borrow money from other sources.[10] These are monitored by independent regulatory bodies such as the Care Quality Commission and Monitor.

All NHS foundation trust organizations now have financial, quality and output performance targets that the organization is expected to achieve in order to retain business. The clinical director, as the link between management and frontline clinical services, has a significant role to play in achieving and maintaining these targets within the resources available. This can only be achieved with the support and cooperation of frontline clinicians and the clinical director therefore has a huge task in managing the medical staff to ensure that conflicts between organizational and clinical needs are ironed out and the business of the directorate continues.

When confronted with an operational problem, the clinical director should identify the problem, its consequences, possible causes and likely solutions, as illustrated in Case study 11.1.

Case study 11.1

Problem
- Shortage of acute admission beds

Consequences
- Clinical care is affected
- Admissions are delayed
- Patients are put at risk
- Inconvenience to patients and carers
- Targets are breached
- Contracts are jeopardized

Possible causes
- Inappropriate admissions
- Admitting staff are inexperienced and have a very low risk threshold
- Poor risk assessment processes
- Inadequate or ineffective community/home treatment services
- Ill-defined admission criteria
- Delayed discharges – consultant on annual leave and discharges managed by junior, inexperienced medical staff; poor communication between in-patient and community services; absence of care coordinator; social problems such as lack of accommodation; delayed investigations

Possible solutions
- Further training for clinical staff on risk issues, admission criteria
- Strengthen community/home treatment services
- Tighten admission/discharge criteria and other operational policies
- Ensure appropriate medical cover for consultant annual/sick leave
- Improve communication between in-patient and community teams – e.g. weekly multidisciplinary team/discharge meetings
- Strengthen covering arrangements in community teams
- Promote collaborative working practices with social services, local housing associations and other voluntary and statutory bodies
- Education and training of primary care workers, including GPs, to promote community treatment and management

Most clinical directors will be responsible for a budget allocated to the directorate. The budget will mainly include the salaries of the doctors in the directorate. It may or may not include money for locums. Clinical directors are expected to recruit and spend on locums within their budget. If the reserves in the budget do not allow for recruitment of a locum, finding medical capacity within the existing doctors and prioritizing the medical input to various services should be considered. Such arrangements can lead to other risks – both clinical and management. It is the responsibility of the clinical director to anticipate, evaluate and respond to such risks in an appropriate manner.

Clinical directors are increasingly involved in monitoring the performance, finance and contractual targets. Regular updates on compliance with targets are issued by the trust. Clinical directors may get invited to work with non-medical managers to develop action plans to resolve problems in areas where expected targets are not met. The action plans may include developing or changing operational protocols, changes to the working arrangements and performance of doctors.

Box 11.4 summarizes the skills and knowledge required by a clinical director to support the operational role.[5]

Box 11.4 Skills and knowledge required to support the operational role[5]

- Budget management and financial awareness
- Interpreting and monitoring performance, quality and financial targets
- Information sharing
- Consideration and assessment of service and clinical risks
- Performance management and development of colleagues
- Understanding of commissioning arrangements and how the organization works
- Use of legislative, policy and accountability framework
- Use of human resource policy and legislation
- Use of information management and technology

Supporting role in development of the business (strategic role)

Commissioning has been given prominence as a motivator for change in the modern NHS. It is likely that the principles of world class commissioning will remain, driving competition, innovation, value for money and quality of services. The world class commissioning document emphasized the importance of clinical engagement in strategic planning, service development and resource utilization.[11]

Clinical directors have a dual role of being practising clinicians and clinical leaders. The non-medical management of the organization, commissioners and the other stakeholders should value the clinical perspective provided by clinical directors. Sometimes there may be differences of opinion between managers, including commissioners, and GPs, user/carer organizations and other professional groups. It is often the clinical director's responsibility to discuss such differences and attempt to find a consensus view. Because of their frontline clinical responsibilities, clinical directors have considerable credibility with users, GPs and other frontline clinicians, and this must be used to good effect in planning and implementing change (see Chapter 7).

The introduction of the service line management model by Monitor is promising to provide clinical directors at ground level greater involvement in the strategic planning of their service units. Service lines are the units from which the trust's services are delivered, each with its own focus on particular medical conditions or procedures and its own specialist clinicians. Each unit also has clearly identified resources, including support services, staffing and finances.[12] For example, the cardiac service, pathology service or dementia service could be separate service units which are led by a clinical director together with a general manager. Each service unit will have the autonomy to function within a given budget and expected targets. The clinical directors in this model are expected to engage in a strategic and annual planning process for their designated unit.

The skills and knowledge desirable to support the strategic role is listed in Box 11.5.[5]

Box 11.5 Skills and knowledge required to support the strategic role

Communication

- Effective communication of information
- Negotiation
- Influencing
- Chairing meetings effectively
- Liaison and communicating with partners
- Listening
- Succinct presentations

Business skills

- Understanding the wider health environment
- Horizon scanning
- Develop business plans
- Undertake project management

Learning and developing skills and preparation for progression (personal development role)

None of the doctors who take up a clinical director role will have been specifically trained for that post. The opportunity to learn management skills for doctors is still limited. As described earlier, the roles that a modern clinical director is expected to perform require a large number of varied skills and knowledge.

Clinical directors should not only learn certain skills in relation to their various roles and responsibilities but also develop certain leadership attributes which are crucial for career progression. Therefore, the clinical director position is a great opportunity for personal development. One is not always born with leadership skills and these can be learnt and acquired over a period of time (see Chapter 3). Box 11.6 lists some of the core skills that I think are essential for good leadership.

> **Box 11.6** Key leadership skills/knowledge
>
> - Understanding one's leadership style
> - Understanding one's personality – reflective practice
> - Maintaining and developing professional competence
> - Time management and prioritizing
> - To be resilient
> - How to utilize courage or conviction
> - Respecting diversity
> - Managing stress

The challenges

The challenges of being a clinical director start from the day that a doctor decides to apply for or is called upon to take such a post. The questions most doctors will be asking themselves are:

- Why do I want to take up a managerial or leadership role?
- What do I gain?
- What can I contribute?
- What are the risks?
- Is this the right time?
- Do I have the appropriate knowledge and skills?

Clinical director posts are usually advertised internally in the trust. The post will have a job description and will be for a duration of two to five years. The job specification may vary widely depending on the organizational culture and needs.

Most doctors enter the medical management structure without any formal management training or experience. However, one would expect clinical directors to have a minimum of at least two years' experience as a consultant, so that they have a fair understanding of the trust's philosophy and its strategic direction. Experience in chairing committees, attending leadership training and shadowing a medical manager can all be useful in preparing a consultant to take on this role. However, most aspects of the job and, in particular, people management are learnt through experience and through a process of trial and error. There are several leadership training courses but nothing can replace good, hard practical experience at the coal face.

There are several advantages to being a clinical director. Equally, there are many disadvantages.[13] Perhaps one of the main attractions of the job is the influence it provides in shaping the future of the clinical services within the organization. It gives opportunities for the development of innovative service models that are not only clinically effective and safe but also financially viable. It allows for collaborative working with other partnership agencies and gives an insight into the difficult and contentious interface between organizational and patient needs. It enables one to develop one's knowledge and understanding of appraisals, job plans, contractual and other human resources responsibilities and budget management. Above all, it facilitates personal development and a greater understanding of human behaviour. These are only a few of the benefits of being a clinical director.

Like all management positions, however, being a clinical director is not without difficulties. These include excessive demand on one's time and personal life, reduction of clinical work, additional responsibility for the running of the service, management of difficult colleagues and implementation of clinical and management changes/decisions that are not always popular. A summary of the advantages and disadvantages of being a clinical director are listed in Box 11.7.

Box 11.7 The advantages and disadvantages of being a clinical director

Advantages

- Learning leadership and managerial skills through experience
- Broadening the understanding as to how the organization works
- Adding variety to once routine clinical work
- Broader opportunity of networking
- Broader opportunity of influencing
- Additional financial benefits
- Opportunity to implement new ideas and changes to practice

Disadvantages

- May have to cut down on time spent doing clinical and supporting professional activity
- Role can be very demanding on available time and resources
- Having to perform a role without prior formal training
- Having to take decisions which may not be popular with colleagues
- Having to manage conflicting interests between the organization and the profession
- Role, boundaries and responsibilities can be ill-defined
- Added responsibility

There are many challenges for a newly appointed clinical director and these are discussed below under the following categories:

- demand for knowledge and skills
- interpersonal interactions
- demands on time and responsibility
- organizational attitude and culture.

Demand for knowledge and skills

Gaps in managerial skills and knowledge will become obvious when a clinical director attends a management meeting for the first time. Such meetings often have a focus and language that are foreign to most doctors. There are large bundles of reports, business plans, policies and procedures, governance and statistical data that one has to read and be familiar with. These meetings often take doctors out of their comfort zone with a strong temptation to 'shut down' and wake up only when a clinical opinion is sought. The danger with this approach is that the clinical director ceases to be a fully participating member of the committee and is seen, instead, as an expert or specialist on clinical issues.

The challenge is to be patient and learn not only the 'management speak' but also 'management think'. We need to move away from our structured scientific way of thinking to a more general, lateral thinking mode. Most managers have no clinical experience and some of their views may therefore be seen as unworkable, unsafe and even ridiculous, but a good clinical director should always practise restraint and refrain from being patronizing or rude. Respect is a privilege that is gained by treating others with similar respect and understanding. One cannot expect respect purely by virtue of one's position or status.

Clinical directors must develop a good relationship with the directors of finance and human resources. Finance and human resource management are the two main areas where lack of knowledge can lead to endless difficulties and frustration. All managers are expected to deliver a safe service within the allocated budget and good financial management skills can be hugely beneficial in remaining within budget. Advice from human resources on recruitment, interview procedures, employment rules and regulations and, above all, disciplinary matters can be invaluable and must be sought if one is to avoid frustration and endless problems with unions and defence organizations.

Interpersonal interactions

This is one of the most difficult challenges for a newly appointed clinical director. The task becomes even more complex when the clinical director has to manage a difficult but very senior colleague or even a former clinical director. This can require a lot of patience, understanding and bundles of common sense. The challenge is not to allow professional differences to become personal ones. Professional and personal relationships must be kept separate at all times so that such conflicts do not affect decision-making. When resolving a problem, it is important to remain focused on the problem rather than on the individual. If the problem is inextricably linked to an individual's behaviour, then it might be helpful to define which specific behaviours or actions of the person are contributing to the problem. This would enable one to communicate the findings and support the individual along the lines of personal development.

Demands on time and responsibility

The email inbox of a clinical director is a very busy place indeed, and it expands as the clinical director dives deeper into the role. The deadlines for meeting managerial demands have the risk of eating into clinical time.

Striking a balance between managerial work, clinical activity and professional development is no easy task. There is, with additional work and responsibility, the risk of early 'burnout'. Clinical directors must know their own capacity for work and should be able to prioritize the workload in a sensible manner. They should learn to delegate where appropriate and say 'no' when necessary. Time management and being organized are valuable skills that one must try to develop at an early stage in the management career path (see Chapter 13).

Organizational attitude and culture

Finally, the culture and attitude of the organization can be a major challenge to a newly appointed clinical director. A hierarchical management model with a strong 'top-down' approach may not sit comfortably with the clinical director's management style. It is always a challenge to decide whether to go with the flow or express one's opinion in an objective, clear manner. The latter may run the risk of alienating senior non-medical managers, but clinical directors should always bear in mind their loyalty is to the service users and the organization and not to any particular individual or professional group. There is a big risk of picking up bad habits in management if exposed to an unhealthy culture and environment.

It will be helpful to draw boundaries, to be clear about one's principles and about what is negotiable and what is not. Patient safety and clinical care can never be compromised, irrespective of the consequences and this is one thing that all medical managers will do well to remember.

Conflicting issues

Throughout this chapter I have tried to highlight some of the important contradictions that a clinical director will have to face in medical management. Those aspiring to become medical managers should try to understand some of these conflicting issues (listed below) both from clinical and management viewpoints:

- professional interest vs organizational interest
- service interests vs business interests
- colleague vs manager
- clinical priorities vs financial priorities
- quality for individual vs best value for all
- independence vs regulation
- individual interests vs organizational interests
- individual/group performance vs organizational performance.

As individual practitioners, consultants have a responsibility to the professional bodies they belong to and to the organization they work for. This dual affiliation can also bring about conflict and this is often the reason for passionate debates at medical staff meetings.

Summary

❏ The role of the clinical director has evolved with the influence of key government initiatives and regulatory changes since the posts were introduced into the NHS in the 1980s.

❏ There is no uniformity as to how the role of the clinical director is defined in various NHS organizations.

❏ An attempt is made in this chapter to categorize the roles and demands of a clinical director in a modern-day corporate-style NHS organization.

❏ Most doctors acquire the skills and knowledge required to function as an effective clinical director through experience and reflective learning.

❏ There is a risk of 'burnout' if the required skills and knowledge are inappropriately used.

❏ The challenges for a clinical director are many, but with a right frame of attitude and approach, challenges can make the roles more interesting.

References

1. Department of Health and Social Security (1983). *Griffiths Report: NHS Management Inquiry Report*. London: DHSS. Available from: http://www.sochealth.co.uk/history/griffiths.htm. Accessed: March 2012.

2. Kennedy I (2001). *Learning from Bristol: The Report of the Public Inquiry into Children's Heart Surgery at Bristol Royal Infirmary 1984–1995. Final report*. Available from: http://www.bristol-inquiry.org.uk/

3. Harrison R, Miller S (1999). The contribution of clinical directors to the strategic capacity of the organisation. Br J Management 10, 23–39.

4. Department of Health (1998). A First Class Service: Quality in the NHS. Available from: http://www.dh.gov.uk/

5. The British Association of Medical Managers (BAMM) (2005). Self Assessment Standard Document. Stockport: BAMM.

6. Department of Health (2001). Appraisal for Consultants Working in the NHS: Guidance. Available from: http://www.dh.gov.uk/

7. Department of Health (2002). Consultant Contract Framework. Available from: http://www.dh.gov.uk/

8. Smith J (2002). The Shipman Inquiry. First Report. Available from: http://www.shipman-inquiry.org.uk/reports.asp

9. General Medical Council (2010). Revalidation – The Way Ahead. Available from: http://www.gmc-uk.org/

10. Department of Health (2002). *A Guide to NHS Foundation Trusts*. Available from: http://www.dh.gov.uk/

11. Department of Health (2009). *World Class Commissioning – An Introduction*. Available from: http://www.dh.gov.uk/

12. Monitor (2009). Toolkit 1: Working Towards Service-line Management: A How-to Guide. Available from: http://www.monitor-nhsft.gov.uk/

13. Thorne ML (1997). Being a clinical director: First among equals or just a go-between? *Health Serv Manage Res* 10, 205–15.

Chapter 12

Financial issues for doctors

Trish Donovan and Peter Graves

- Introduction
- Flow of funds
- Financial governance and control
- Financial planning, reporting and budget management
- Quality and efficiency
- Conclusion
- Summary
- References

Introduction

Following recent developments in NHS management and the current reform agenda that followed the review undertaken by Lord Darzi, *High Quality Care for All*,[1] there has been an increasing recognition that doctors need to be more involved in financial and commissioning functions and to have greater engagement in the overall financial and efficiency agenda. This includes budget management to ensure the best use of resources, to benefit those who use services. The history and rationale for this are set out in Chapter 1.

In the current economic climate, the NHS has entered a period that is more financially challenging than ever previously seen. The efficiency challenge over the coming years increasingly requires that doctors and other clinicians are engaged in service redesign and modernization to ensure that services are delivered as efficiently as possible, without compromising on service quality or safety. In England, the overall financial challenge is to make savings of £20 billion across the NHS over the 4 years from 2011/12.

The principles of QIPP – quality, innovation, productivity and prevention – are being implemented nationally as the approach to delivering the efficiency agenda, while improving quality through innovative working methods and increasingly focusing on prevention, recognizing the benefits of this approach in terms of both health and efficiency. QIPP initiatives are being developed across primary and secondary care, with less delineation between individual organizations and increased collaboration across the health economy.

This chapter considers the key points, provides an overview and sets out numerous definitions to enable a basic understanding of current NHS financial matters, including how money flows, the principles of budget management and the current financial regime and regulatory framework. Indicative current values are given, where appropriate, and sources of additional information are referenced for those who desire a more thorough understanding.

Flow of funds

Funding levels

The NHS represents a significant proportion of the UK economy, with the total expenditure amounting to around 8 per cent of gross domestic product (GDP).

The overall budget for the NHS for the 2011/12 financial year is £106 billion. Of this, the most significant element is primary care trust (PCT) revenue allocations, accounting for £89 billion, an increase of £2.6 billion or around 3 per cent on the previous year (at the time of writing, PCTs across England are amalgamating into 'cluster PCTs' or 'clusters' – where PCTs are referred to, this pertains to clusters) (see Fig. 12.1).

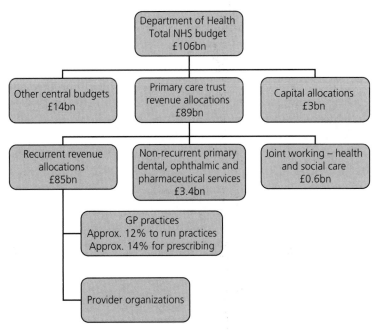

Figure 12.1 Summary of the flow of funds to the NHS.

Comprehensive spending review

As a government department, the Department of Health is given an expenditure budget, for a 3-year period, by HM Treasury, as part of the Comprehensive Spending Review (CSR) process. Budgets are set for:

- revenue – day-to-day operational running costs
- capital – non-consumable items with an expected life of more than a year and a value individually of greater than £5000, generally buildings, land and equipment.

In England, funding is currently routed via strategic health authorities (SHAs) and commissioning organizations (formerly PCTs), with the vast majority of funding being allocated to commissioning organizations, for onward processing. (Note that, in England, commissioning organizations, formerly PCTs, are currently subject to reform and this is described in more detail in Chapter 1.)

Commissioner (PCT) revenue allocations

The Department of Health currently allocates funding to commissioning organizations, based on the relative needs of their populations and in line with pace of change policy. This approach to the allocation of funds aims to enable the reduction of health inequalities, with commissioning organizations in a position to fund similar levels of services for populations in similar need.

Revenue allocations for the 2011/12 financial year amounted to £89 billion, accounting for around 80 per cent of the total NHS budget. This comprised:

- £85 billion in recurrent revenue allocations to PCTs, an increase of £1.9 billion over the previous year
- £3.4 billion for primary dental services, pharmaceutical services and general ophthalmic services non-recurrent allocations, an increase of £69 million
- an additional £648 million to support joint working between health and social care.

At the time of writing, commissioning organizations then nominally pass funds to practice-based commissioning groups on a weighted capitation basis known as an 'indicative budget', as they don't actually receive the funding, and the commissioning organization (currently the PCTs) retains the overall responsibility to achieve an end-of-year budgetary balance. Funding is then passed to provider organizations (NHS trusts, foundation trusts and independent/charitable sector organizations) on a contractual basis. Commissioning organizations have a statutory duty to operate within their funding limit.

The white paper, *Equity and Excellence: Liberating the NHS*,[2] published in July 2010, confirmed the establishment of an independent NHS Commissioning Board. Responsibility will transfer from the Department of Health to the newly established NHS Commissioning Board from 2013/14 for making revenue allocations to commissioning organizations, known as clinical commissioning groups (CCGs), and for providing commissioning guidance. At this time, the CCGs will receive the funding directly and take full responsibility for budgetary control.

In addition, the Department of Health is expected to establish a ring-fenced public health budget which will be allocated to local authorities (see Chapter 1).

The operating framework

The operating framework is currently published annually (usually in December) by the Department of Health. This planning document sets out both the service priorities and the financial rules for the coming year which informs the commissioning process.

Commissioning process/contracting income

NHS trusts and foundation trusts receive the majority of their funding via NHS commissioning contracts. The Department of Health has developed a model contract, which includes mandatory and locally agreed schedules. This is now used by the majority of NHS organizations, with contract terms of between 1 and 3 years being the norm, except in primary care. General practice, in particular, provides services under two main contracts:

- general medical services (GMS) contract, based on the NHS (General Medical Services Contracts) Regulations 2004,[3] which is negotiated nationally between the NHS Employers (on behalf of the government) and the General Practitioners Committee (GPC) of the British Medical Association (on behalf of GPs); this is a life-long contract

- personal medical services (PMS) contract, based on the NHS (Personal Medical Services Contracts) Regulations 2004,[4] which is negotiated locally between the practice and the commissioning organization (the PCT to date). Most of the features of the basic PMS contract reflect a GMS contract but it has additional elements and variations reflecting local needs. It usually runs for a 5-year term.

Provider organizations may also receive some income directly from SHAs or the Department of Health (e.g. for training), from other public sector organizations (e.g. local authorities) or via income-generating activities.

Payment by results and other activity contracts

Payment by results

Payment by results (PbR) is the main funding method for hospital services. This is a rules-based system designed to fund hospital-based activity. Implementation started in 2003/04 in acute and specialist hospital services. This process links payment to activity, with money following the patient and supporting the patient choice agenda.

The PbR system makes use of national tariffs to fund activity and standard classification of services into healthcare resource groups (HRGs), reflecting the volume and complexity of activity in the funding mechanism. Tariffs are revised annually. This method of funding replaced block contracts for acute services and continues to evolve with annual refinement of some elements as well as updated tariffs. In addition to the national tariff, a market forces factor is applied to allow for the fact that the cost of services varies in different parts of the country, based on market conditions (e.g. salary costs are generally higher in London as a result of London weighting/supplement).

The system which has been in place and continually evolving for acute hospital services since 2003 is currently under development for mental health and community services, for which activity remains funded largely on a block contract basis.

In moving to the PbR system, a code of conduct was developed by the Department of Health, which all NHS organizations operating PbR were required to adopt. This code was developed to ensure core principles were established, disputes were minimized and to provide a guide for resolution of any disputes.

As a funding system, this remains under development for the mental health and community sectors, although in 2011/12 there has been some progress towards the development of care clusters for mental health and it is anticipated that tariffs will be developed over the next couple of years.

While there is some movement towards cost- and volume-based contracts, in the absence of PbR most, but not all, contracts for mental health and community trusts remain on a block basis – meaning, simply, that a set amount of income is paid by commissioners for all of the services provided by the trust and no financial variations are routinely made for changes in activity volumes or acuity.

The Department of Health has published a number of documents on PbR on its website,[5] including *A Simple Guide to Payment by Results*,[6] which outlines the process and provides an overview of its development over recent years, and the *Code of Conduct for Payment by Results*.[7]

Block contracts

Block contracts are typically a relatively simple contractual arrangement whereby a fixed annual financial sum is paid by commissioners for all activities delivered by a provider. There may be an activity plan included, as well as significant monitoring metrics or performance indicators. However, funding does not routinely increase or decrease with variation in activity volumes. Service changes or developments are generally negotiated for significant changes and these would then result in a change in funding where appropriate.

Cost and volume contracts

Cost and volume contracts are, as the name indicates, arrangements whereby funding varies with changes in activity. These contracts generally have a tolerance level and involve the use of marginal funding rates above and below the tolerance, recognizing that the impact on a provider's cost base will not be at full cost for every unit of activity.

Key points

Flow of funds

- At around 8 per cent of GDP, NHS spending is a significant part of the UK economy.
- Budgets are split into capital (assets) and revenue (running costs).
- Hospital services are mainly funded by formal contract under the payment by results (PbR) mechanism.
- General practice services are mainly provided under PMS and GMS contracts.

Financial governance and control

NHS organizations need to ensure they have in place an effective system of control. This is generally reliant upon a range of systems, processes and procedures being in place to effectively ensure financial and other risks are minimized.

NHS bodies are required to appoint a director of finance as an executive member of the board, and this includes CCGs. The director of finance generally leads on matters of internal financial control, safeguarding of assets, financial stewardship, financial reporting, and so on.

The NHS financial year runs from 1 April to 31 March. Financial years are generally expressed in one of two ways, either '2011/12' or 'FY12' for the year 1 April 2011 to 31 March 2012.

As independent contractors, GP practices (and other independent primary care providers, such as dentists, pharmacists and opticians) are run in the same way as any other small business. A GP's income, for example, is based upon the profits made by the practice. Therefore, the risks are not the same as those faced by acute trusts and other NHS bodies. As such it is unnecessary for them to face the same level of financial scrutiny. For example, there are no rules or regulations pertaining to how much of the practice income is spent on staff or other expenses (except for complex regulations governing expenditure on buildings, rent and mortgage reimbursement); this is left to the discretion of the practice. Nevertheless, there are a number of tight mechanisms to validate practice claims for services provided and routine checks to validate Quality and Outcomes Framework (QOF) payments. Further, the commissioning organization can step in should patient services be shown to be suffering as a result of financial mismanagement.

Statutory break-even duty

NHS trusts have a statutory duty to achieve break-even, taking one year with another, meaning to maintain spending within available income. This performance is generally measured over a 3-year period.

Foundation trusts do not have the same statutory requirement to break even and are monitored via a financial risk rating as part of the compliance framework of the government's independent regulator of foundation trusts, Monitor. This is described below.

Primary care trust commissioning organizations have a statutory duty to work within their agreed annual allocations.

Annual accounts and report

Except for independent contractors, NHS organizations are required to produce an annual set of accounts in a predetermined format, to a set timescale, following the end of each financial year, as set out in the NHS Act 2006. Increasingly these accounts are becoming very similar to the accounts of commercial organizations. The NHS adopted the use of International Financial Reporting Standards (IFRS) in 2009, with the government having the final say on how these are interpreted and applied for the public sector, including the NHS.

NHS trusts are required to have their annual accounts formally adopted by the trust board and audited by independently appointed external auditors. The audited accounts are submitted to the Department of Health, which undertakes a consolidation exercise for the accounts of all NHS organizations. Each NHS organization must then also present its accounts at a public meeting before the end of September each year. This is generally done by the director of finance at the public annual general meeting, with the financial accounts, quality accounts and annual report presented as part of the review of the year.

The accounts include key statements and numerous notes plus supplementary tables of analysis. Examples of the two main statements – the statement of comprehensive income (previously called the income and expenditure statement) and the statement of financial position (previously called a balance sheet) – are given in Tables 12.1 and 12.2.

Table 12.1 Statement of comprehensive income

	2010/11	2009/10
	£000	£000
Revenue from patient care activities	95,000	90,000
Other operating revenue	15,000	14,000
Operating expenses	−107,500	−102,000
Operating surplus	2,500	2,000
Investment revenue	10	15
Gains on disposal of non-current assets held for sale	0	25
Finance costs	−2	−2

Continued

Table 12.1 Continued

	2010/11	2009/10
Surplus/deficit for the financial year	2,508	2,038
Public dividend capital dividends payable	−1,020	−1,000
Retained surplus for the year	1,488	1,038
Other comprehensive income		
Impairments and reversals	−5	−10
Gains on revaluations	50	100
Receipt of donated/government-granted assets	0	0
Net loss on other reserves	0	0
Net gains/(losses) on available for sale financial assets	0	0
Reclassification adjustments	0	0
Total comprehensive income for the year	**1,533**	**1,128**

Table 12.2 Statement of financial position

	2010/11	2009/10
	£000	£000
Non-current assets		
Property, plant and equipment	55,000	50,000
Intangible assets	10,000	9,000
Trade and other receivables	1,050	1,000
Total non-current assets	**66,050**	**60,000**
Current assets		
Inventories	500	500
Trade and other receivables	3,500	4,500
Cash and cash equivalents	5,000	4,000
Non-current assets held for sale	500	0
Total current assets	**9,500**	**9,000**
Total assets	**75,550**	**69,000**
Current liabilities		
Trade and other payables	−3,000	−4,000

Continued

Table 12.2 Continued

	2010/11	2009/10
Borrowings	−200	−250
Other financial liabilities	0	0
Provisions	−1,500	−1,700
Net current assets	**4,800**	**3,050**
Total assets less current liabilities	**70,850**	**63,050**
Non-current liabilities		
Borrowings −14,450 −14,738	−15,000	−16,000
Provisions −264 −884	−250	−200
Trade and other payables −227 −454	−300	−400
Other liabilities 0 −5,479	0	0
Total assets employed	**55,300**	**46,450**
Financed by taxpayers' equity:		
Public dividend capital 7,998 7,998	9,000	8,500
Retained earnings 5,418 5,106	8,300	5,950
Revaluation reserve 20,952 20,328	25,000	20,000
Donated asset reserve 63 70	5,000	5,000
Government grant reserve 29 29	3,000	2,000
Other reserves 716 −5,479	5,000	5,000
Total taxpayers' equity 35,176 28,052	**55,300**	**46,450**

Similarly, NHS foundation trusts also require their board of directors to formally adopt the annual accounts. These are also then presented to their board of governors for agreement and finally are submitted to Monitor, the independent regulator, and laid before parliament.

Independent contractors are not publicly accountable in the same way as NHS trusts and are not, therefore, statutorily obliged to produce accounts in this way.

Other management duties and financial targets

In addition to statutory responsibilities, NHS organizations have a number of management responsibilities and financial targets. These are outlined in the following sections.

Capital resource limit

This is a requirement to deliver a capital expenditure programme, for the financial year, within an agreed limit, the capital resource limit (CRL). The CRL is generally set with reference to the level of cash available for capital investment that has been 'internally generated' as well as any surplus generated by the organization that is also available for investment in assets. Internally generated funds arise as a result of non-cash accounting transactions, such as depreciation on assets. Trusts are permitted to undershoot their CRL but they are not permitted to overshoot it.

Any increase above internally generated funds requires agreement with the SHA and generally relates to major strategic capital investments.

External financing limit

NHS trusts are required to operate within an external financing limit (EFL), which is a limit on external cash borrowing. Foundation trusts are not subject to a CRL or an EFL and have more flexibility available to them in terms of commercial borrowing for capital investment. They are subject to Monitor's financial regime, which includes a prudential borrowing limit (PBL). This is a limit on the amount of borrowing the foundation trust is permitted and includes a short-term and a longer-term element.

Better Payment Practice Code

The Confederation of British Industries' Better Payment Practice Code (BPPC) provides a target for the payment of creditors, requiring NHS trusts to make payment to creditors within 30 days of receipt of goods or a valid invoice.

Although it is not a formal target, NHS organizations are also encouraged to make payment to small and medium-sized enterprises (SMEs) within 10 days wherever possible as a contribution to assisting cash flow in the local economy.

Monitor – the independent regulator of foundation trusts

As all NHS trusts are required to become foundation trusts over the next few years, an awareness of the independent regulator of foundation trusts, Monitor, and its functions is of increasing importance.

Monitor was established in 2004 and is directly accountable to parliament. Monitor currently assesses applicant foundation trusts, authorizes them where applications are successful and regulates them to ensure compliance with their terms of authorization, including how well they manage risk and ensuring they remain financially strong.

Monitor publishes a number of guidance documents on its website for both aspirant and current foundation trusts.[8]

Compliance framework

The compliance framework sets out the approach Monitor takes to assessing compliance of NHS foundation trusts with their terms of authorization. It is reviewed and updated annually and reflects the latest planning guidance and requirements of the operating framework. The latest version is available on the Monitor website.[9]

Financial risk rating

Part of the Monitor assessment process for aspirant foundation trusts and the compliance regime for existing foundation trusts is the calculation of a financial risk rating (FRR).

This is intended to be a forward-looking indicator of the financial risk associated with the organization, on a scale of 1–5, with 1 being the most risky and 5 the least. This is calculated quarterly for existing foundation trusts. A minimum rating of 3 is required for authorization as a foundation trust.

The FRR incorporates a number of individual calculations, including performance against financial plan, earnings before interest, taxes, depreciation and amortization (EBITDA), EBITDA margin and return on assets plus liquidity, with the overall rating representing a weighted average of the component calculations. This calculation is then subject to a number of overriding rules to determine the final FRR. If the FRR of a foundation trust falls below 3, indicating increasing financial risk, the trust will be subject to increased reporting requirements and intervention from Monitor.

Monitor's focus on the quality agenda has increased and the risk ratings indicating overall performance for foundation trusts, published quarterly, include both the FRR and the governance risk rating, indicating quality of service.

Financial rules and regulations

In this section the reference to NHS organizations does not include the independent contractor providers, some of whom may have 'NHS body' status.

Standing orders and standing financial instructions

Standing orders (SOs) and standing financial instructions (SFIs) set out the regulatory framework within which NHS organizations are to conduct business. All members of staff should be aware of the existence of these documents and their content as appropriate to their specific roles. Model SOs and SFIs[10] are periodically issued by the Department of Health and most organizations adopt a variation of these.

Standing orders set out the terms under which the board and its subcommittees operate. These include procedures on areas such as the composition of the board and its subcommittees, how meetings are run including voting rights, attendance, quorum and so on.

In addition to how meetings operate, SOs will set out details of the organization's scheme of delegation, decisions reserved for the board, register of interests, standards of business conduct and obligations of board members.

NHS organizations are required to have a set of SFIs. This is a set of rules that governs financial procedures in more detail than SOs. Foundation trusts are not required to have a set of SFIs. These documents are generally available on organizations' websites for all staff to access.

Scheme of reservation and delegation

NHS organizations publish a scheme of reservation and delegation setting out the powers that are reserved for the board (which may include items such as the approval of budgets or major contracts; receiving and adopting the annual accounts; and defining strategy) and those that are delegated to other officers in the organization (examples might include determining controls over data processing or approval of competitive tenders to a specified financial limit). Where relevant, the scheme will include financial limits so that powers/responsibilities are clear.

Foundation trusts have SOs both for the board of directors and for the board of governors and these are included within their constitution.

Internal audit

All NHS organizations are required to have in place an internal audit function, providing an independent opinion and assurance to the board, generally via the audit committee.

The role of internal audit includes working with management to assess areas of potential risk, highlighting areas of concern to the audit committee, reviewing the organization's system of internal control and providing assurance that controls are in place and operating effectively.

External audit

NHS organizations are required to have their accounts audited by independent external auditors. These are appointed by the Department of Health for NHS trusts and by the board of governors for foundation trusts.

Key points

Financial governance

- The system of internal financial control ensures risks are minimized.
- NHS organizations produce accounts annually and are subject to audit.
- NHS trusts have a statutory duty to achieve break-even on income and expenditure.

Financial planning, reporting and budget management

Most doctors will be expected to manage resources at some point, especially those who progress to more senior roles. However, even if not directly responsible for budget management, doctors are key influencers in terms of both generating and spending resources in NHS organizations. An understanding of the principles of budgetary control will therefore be useful.

It may also be helpful to understand the functions of the finance and other back-office teams and it is advisable to have key points of contact (whether within the organization or in a shared service/support organization) who can advise on financial, payroll and procurement policy and procedures in detail, should the need arise.

Financial planning

NHS organizations construct a forward financial plan, generally for a 3-year period. A more detailed financial plan and budget are then finalized in advance of the commencement of each financial year on 1 April, reflecting the latest planning information and contractual position.

At the time of writing, NHS trusts (commissioners and providers) are required to submit their financial plans to the SHA. By 2013, this will almost certainly be a role of the NHS Commissioning Board, to whom CCGs will have to submit their plans. CCG plans will also come under close scrutiny by statutory bodies currently being set up by local authorities, called health and well-being boards (HWBs). Foundation trusts submit their plans to Monitor, and most NHS provider trusts are expected to become foundation trusts over the next few years.

Reporting

Most organizations produce budget monitoring information based on a monthly reporting cycle. Information is produced at various levels for a variety of audiences, including overall summaries for reporting to the Department of Health/SHA (NHS trusts) or Monitor (foundation trusts), reports to the board and its subcommittees and detailed budget monitoring information for individual budget-holders. In all cases it is important that information provided is both accurate and timely.

A budget-holder report/statement will typically include income, pay and non-pay items and will generally indicate the annual budget, performance for the current month and a year-end forecast. A typical example is shown in Figure 12.2. These reports are often referred to as management accounts.

Budget report : Cost centre _____ : Budget manager : _____								Month : 03			
Annual budget £000	Item	Current month £000			Year to date £000			Full year forecast £000	Establishment		
		Budget	Actual	Variance	Budget	Actual	Variance	Variance	Budget	Actual	
100	Consultant	8	0	8	24	16	8	84	1.00	0.00	
60	Assoc specialist	5	0	5	15	15	0	0	1.00	1.00	
0	Locum medical staff	0	10	−10	0	10	−10	−100	0.00	1.00	
55	Nursing staff – Band 7	5	5	0	14	14	0	0	1.00	1.00	
20	Nursing assistant – Band 3	2	2	0	5	5	0	0	1.00	1.00	
0	Agency nursing	0	0	0	0	0	0	0	0.00	0.00	
35	Admin – Band 4	3	3	0	9	9	0	0	1.50	1.50	
207	Subtotal – pay	22	19	3	67	69	−2	−16	5.50	5.50	
200	Drugs	17	20	−3	50	45	5	0			
20	Office equipment	2	0	2	5	0	5	0			
10	Travel and subsistence	1	1	0	3	3	0	0			
230	Subtotal – non–pay	19	21	−2	58	48	10	0	0	0	
205	Total	41	40	1	124	116	8	−16	5.50	5.50	

In this example

– There are 5.5 staff budgeted, there is 1.0 vacant consultant post in the current month that is covered via locum usage. The locum cost exceeds the available budget by around £2000 per month and should this continue, the forecast year end position is:
– in non-pay, drugs costs exceed budget in the current month but remain within budget on a cumulative basis
– there is no spend so far on office equipment; this offsets the adverse in–month variances on other lines.

Figure 12.2 Sample budget report.

Budget management

Budget reports provide details of actual financial performance against the plan. The key to budget management is early corrective action where there are adverse variances. The information provided to budget managers should include sufficiently detailed variance analysis to facilitate understanding of the cause of any variance from the plan and to aid decision-making in terms of corrective action. Communication between budget managers and their finance lead is important so that all relevant information is quantified and reflected.

Budgets are delegated to managers within an NHS organization, in line with the organizational structure and their management responsibility. Increasingly provider organizations are developing a service line management approach (discussed later in this section) and this influences the budgetary responsibility and reporting process.

Establishment control

Typically most NHS trusts spend over 70 per cent of their resources on paying staff. Not surprisingly, therefore, this is a key area for budgetary focus. The funded level of establishment will be indicated on the routine budgetary information. There will be an internal authorization process associated with recruitment for temporary and/or permanent staff.

Flexible staffing is vital in the current environment, especially where funding varies with activity and acuity levels. However, there will be a tension between maintaining this flexibility and the costs associated with a temporary workforce. An agency premium for locum staff significantly increases the overall cost. There are a number of nationally agreed contracts for the provision of temporary/ locum staff and these should be utilized to get the best rates – failing to make use of available contracts can lead to paying significantly higher prices to the same temporary staffing provider.

Service line reporting and management

Increasingly, providers are producing information at service line level. Service lines may be specialities, sub-specialities or speciality groupings for which income and costs can be separately determined and managed. Some organizations are moving towards revised management structures that reflect service lines, so that their 'business' can be managed and reported in these groupings.

Service line reporting brings a number of key features, which assist providers in understanding the financial impact of various elements within the overall service portfolio. Service line reports facilitate the review of financial performance of different parts of the organization (service lines) at a fairly high level, typically by comparing the cost of those individual parts with the income that they generate.

As this approach is increasingly implemented, organizations are developing an understanding of costs and income at a service line level. Service lines may vary between organizations, as they are internally determined, but they are typically based on a hospital speciality, sub-speciality or grouping of specialities.

Use of this information has been increasing in recent years as organizations strive to understand the relative contribution of each service line. Similar to the methodology described in the following section for patient level costing (and often driven by the same IT system), costs and income for a service line are computed, indicating their relative contribution to the organization and whether a profit or loss is being made. This information can then contribute to informing decisions as to which areas the organization is best placed, in financial terms, to focus on.

Patient level costing

Increasingly being implemented, patient level costing, as the name suggests, is a costing methodology that aims to break down all costs to individual patient episodes. Through the development of IT systems, many items of expenditure can be directly attributed to individual patients (e.g. drugs or imaging) and other costs are apportioned and allocated on the best available basis, including, for example, space utilization for premises costs or clinical diary sheets or job plans for clinical pay costs.

By developing costing information at the individual patient level, it is possible to compare and benchmark costs and to develop an understanding of different practices and the impact these have on cost.

As organizations develop the information and capability to drill down into patient-level information, this helps to understand service line performance and will assist service line managers in improving productivity – for example, by identifying variations in clinical practice within a single type of patient.

This level of costing information is essential to commissioners and is constantly being analyzed in order to inform commissioning decisions. It is also being used as a performance tool to evaluate GP referrals and identify variation in referral patterns. Indeed, it is becoming progressively more controversial as financial pressures on commissioners are leading them to devise incentives which potentially reward low referrers.

Key points

Planning and reporting

- Financial plans are set for a 3- to 5-year period and updated annually; performance is then monitored monthly against the plan.
- Staffing is the most significant cost – generally exceeding 70 per cent.
- Flexible staffing is key in the current financial climate, enabling change and responsiveness to varying activity levels.
- Increasingly, services are being organized and managed by 'service line'.
- Costing is becoming more detailed, with most items now allocated at the individual patient level.

Quality and efficiency

There is an increasing recognition that quality and efficiency are linked and cannot be managed as separate agendas. The dilemma this can pose for doctors in management positions is explored in some detail in Chapter 1.

Cost improvement plans

Each year NHS organizations are required to develop and deliver cost improvement plans, releasing efficiency savings in order to deliver against their overall financial plan. As noted at the beginning of the chapter, the efficiency requirement over the next few years is greater than ever before seen in the history of the NHS. Historically most NHS organizations have delivered annual efficiencies in the region of 2 per cent. The requirement was significantly higher in 2011/12, with a number of organizations attempting to deliver a requirement in excess of 10 per cent.

Efficiency targets for commissioner organizations are derived as a result of a reduction in funding; for provider organizations they are derived from a combination of reductions in income from commissioners plus inflationary and other local cost pressures. The efficiency target is quantified as part of the financial planning process and is refined annually. Financially, the requirement is to identify and release recurrent (permanent) savings as opposed to non-recurrent measures that have to be either repeated or replaced each year.

NHS organizations are required to develop and monitor detailed savings plans on an individual scheme basis. More recently, these are also being risk-assessed in terms of their potential impact on patient safety and service quality, and regulators (the Department of Health via the SHA for NHS trusts and via Monitor for foundation trusts) require evidence that plans have been assessed and signed off by lead clinicians, including executive directors with lead responsibility for medicine and nursing.

QIPP

Quality, innovation, productivity and prevention (QIPP) is a term that has become widely used over the last couple of years to represent the programme management approach to the efficiency agenda facing the NHS, recognizing the increasing economic challenge.

It is now widely accepted that traditional methods of cost improvement are no longer sufficient to meet the level of savings required and that new ways of working are key to improvements in quality and also to releasing efficiency savings by way of service redesign, increased emphasis on health prevention and promotion. This will remain a serious challenge for CCGs, and in particular the doctors in lead management positions, for the foreseeable future as they try to achieve financial balance while at the same time pushing for clinical improvement and better outcomes for patients.

Conclusion

The NHS has entered the most challenging financial climate ever. The current efficiency challenge makes it increasingly important that clinicians are leading redesign and service modernization as key influencers. There are formal systems of financial governance, reporting and control and the more recent development of service line management and patient level costing information has facilitated a greater understanding of costs and cost drivers so that these can be influenced and controlled. This will ensure services are delivered as efficiently as possible without compromising on service quality or safety.

Summary

❏ The NHS has entered the most challenging financial climate ever, with around £20 billion efficiency savings to be delivered over the 4 years from 2011–12.

❏ Most NHS providers are targeting efficiency requirements of at least 4 per cent per annum.

❏ In addition to national efficiency requirements (4 per cent), QIPP initiatives are being implemented to drive up quality while reducing costs.

❏ The current efficiency challenge makes it increasingly important that clinicians are leading redesign and service modernization as key influencers.

❏ There are formal systems of financial governance, reporting and control in place.

❏ The recent development of service line management and patient level costing information has facilitated a greater understanding of costs and cost drivers so that these can be influenced and controlled.

❏ This approach will ensure services are delivered as efficiently as possible and that innovation is fostered without compromising on service quality or safety.

❏ While this is a very challenging financial climate, the NHS is on target to meet its overall financial plan for 2011–12.

References

1. Department of Health (2008). *High Quality Care for All: NHS Next Stage Review Final Report.* London: Department of Health. Available from: http://www.dh.gov.uk/

2. Department of Health (2010). *Equity and Excellence: Liberating the NHS.* London: Department of Health. Available from: http://www.dh.gov.uk/

3. NHS (2004). National Health Service (General Medical Services Contracts) Regulations 2004. Available from: http://www.legislation.gov.uk/

4. NHS (2004). The National Health Service (Personal Medical Services Agreements) Regulations 2004. Available from: http://www.legislation.gov.uk/

5. Department of Health. Website: http://www.dh.gov.uk/

6. Department of Health (2011). *A Simple Guide to Payment by Results.* Available from: http://www.dh.gov.uk/

7. Department of Health (2010). *Code of Conduct for Payment by Results: from 1 April 2010.* Available from: http://www.dh.gov.uk/

8. Monitor, Independent Regulator of NHS Foundation Trusts. Website: http://www.monitor-nhsft.gov.uk/

9. Monitor (2011). *Compliance Framework 2011/12.* Available from: www.monitor-nhsft.gov.uk/

10. Department of Health (2006). *NHS Trust Model Standing Orders, Reservation and Delegation of Powers and Standing Financial Instructions.* Available from: http://www.dh.gov.uk/

Chapter 13

Developing personal effectiveness: what does it take to become a good doctor?

Hameen Markar

- Introduction
- Managing and leading a multidisciplinary team
- Time management
- Communication
- Dealing with difficult colleagues
- Managing stress
- Maintaining confidentiality
- Tact, diplomacy and politics
- Conclusion
- Summary
- References

Introduction

This book is directed mainly at medical and non-medical managers in the healthcare services in the UK. It has a wealth of information on commissioning, safety and quality, board functions and project management and other related topics. The book also gives advice and guidance to medical staff including consultants who are not in management. Thus chapters such as information technology, doctors in difficulty, human resource issues and teaching and training will no doubt prove useful to all doctors, irrespective of their interest in medical management. However, there is another issue that is important to every doctor which is simply this: What does it take to become a good doctor? How could one improve one's personal effectiveness as a doctor?

As the GMC's booklet *Leadership and Management for All Doctors*[1] states: 'Being a good doctor means more than simply being a good clinician.' It is much more than merely keeping up to date with the latest advances and developments in one's speciality. No doubt such knowledge will help in the effective diagnosis and treatment of patients, but doctors deal with individuals and families, their problems, emotions and concerns on a daily basis and therefore have a more diverse role than merely diagnosing and treating. The GMC booklet goes on to outline the responsibilities of a doctor in relation to employment issues, teaching and training, planning and managing resources, helping to develop and improve services, and raising and acting on concerns involving patient care and safety. Thus the need for every doctor to have a sound understanding of leadership and management issues can no longer be ignored. Unlike managers who need no clinical skills (in most cases) to manage effectively, doctors, and in particular consultants, with no management skills will find it very difficult to accomplish their wide-ranging responsibilities both as clinicians and leaders.

All doctors, irrespective of their position in the organization, should have some basic management skills. These include effective time management, ability to provide leadership to multidisciplinary teams, managing difficult colleagues, including superiors, and managing stress and burnout. A repertoire of such aptitudes would enable doctors to develop their full potential and discharge their wide-ranging management, clinical, leadership and professional responsibilities successfully.

There is considerable evidence to show that most highly performing trusts have robust arrangements for good clinical engagement. To be meaningful, clinical engagement with frontline clinicians who have a good knowledge of management issues should be combined with a culture of openness and honesty. This would enable staff to speak out freely and raise concerns without fear of recrimination.

So being a good doctor means several things: staying up to date with clinical knowledge and skills, having a good understanding of management issues, having good management and leadership skills with a genuine desire to be self-critical, being able to learn from experience and reflect on one's practices, and being able to appreciate constructive criticism and work in partnership with others (see Fig. 13.1).

Figure 13.1 What does it take to be a good doctor?

This chapter will deal with common management problems that confront doctors on a daily basis and the knowledge and skills necessary to cope with such issues. These are basic management skills and include the following: managing and leading a multidisciplinary team, time management, effective communication, managing difficult colleagues, managing stress in the workplace, issues of confidentiality, and the chapter ends with a brief discussion on politics, tact and diplomacy.

Managing and leading a multidisciplinary team

The concept of multidisciplinary working is not new. Although the practice is much more common in certain specialities such as mental health, it is seen to some extent in all branches of medicine. It simply refers to a group of professionals from different backgrounds and skills working together towards a common goal, i.e. to provide a comprehensive package of care to patients and their carers. Most multidisciplinary teams (MDTs) have a manager who is responsible for the day-to-day management of the team. Although the role of the consultant is to provide clinical leadership to the team, this is closely associated with competent team management. Therefore, the relationship between the consultant, who is the clinical leader, and the team manager, who is responsible for the operational management of the team, is absolutely crucial and they sometimes have to work hard to develop a positive, mutually respectful professional relationship. This is the very foundation of a successful MDT and any weaknesses in this relationship will result in a dysfunctional team, which in turn will have an impact on clinical care and patient safety.

Consultants in a MDT have medical and, in some situations, legal responsibility for their patients and are often held accountable not only by the trust hierarchy but also by the legal system when things go wrong. Clinical errors can result from several causes such as poor management, team dysfunction, lack of training or low morale, and although concepts such as corporate and individual responsibilities are much discussed, it is often the consultant and not the team manager who will be held accountable. When there is disagreement between the consultant and the team manager (which is not uncommon), it should be resolved in private and on a one-to-one basis. If this fails, line managers may get involved, but other team members must be kept out of such matters. Failure to do this can cause splitting, team fragmentation and low morale.

In a well-functioning MDT, the relationship between the medical staff and non-medical members is also important. Consultants provide clinical leadership to the MDT and, in doing so, they should respect and recognize the diverse skills and experience of other team members. A purely medical view to solving clinical problems may not always seem right or even acceptable to other members of the team, and a good leader should have an open mind and take an inclusive approach to patient care. Professional rivalry and turf protection are common causes of dissent and unhappiness within teams. Some of the key features of successful and failed leadership in a mental health MDT are shown in Box 13.1.

> **Box 13.1** Key features of successful and failed leadership in multidisciplinary teams. (Modified with permission of Holloway and Chorlton[2])
>
> **Successful leadership**
>
> - Excellent clinical competency
> - Respect for staff, patients and carers
> - Effective communication – good listening skills
> - Availability
> - Taking responsibility – being held accountable

- Politeness
- Recognizing the skills and value of other staff
- Meeting time commitments
- Responding well to crises
- Always supportive of team members

Failed leadership

- Arrogance and high-handedness
- Rudeness to staff, patients and carers
- Unwilling to take responsibility
- Blaming others for mistakes
- Unavailability generally and in crisis situations
- Poor time-keeping
- Indecisiveness and clinical incompetence
- Undermining the team leader/manager
- Disrespectful towards other professional groups

Time management

I recommend to you to take care of minutes: for hours will take care of themselves.
(Lord Chesterfield, 1694–1773)

Management of time is one of the big problems of the modern business world. Despite a wide range of innovations and information technology, this continues to be a major issue in the NHS. Whether one is a clinician or a manager, a junior or a senior, good management of time and organization of one's day-to-day activities are important, not only to deliver one's professional responsibilities but also to maintain a healthy and rewarding personal lifestyle. Most NHS consultants and managers would admit to working excessively long hours, sometimes over 80 hours per week, and although this may be due to an excessive workload, it is often because the available time is not gainfully managed. Long working hours are associated with low productivity, ill health and poor performance[3] and are a common cause of high sickness rates in the NHS. The key to time management is being organized and this involves prioritization, planning, scheduling and delegating. In this respect, good secretarial assistance is invaluable. In the following I recommend some practical steps to good time management.

All clinicians have to fulfil certain clinical responsibilities on a daily basis: outpatient appointments, ward rounds, team meetings, junior supervision and patient-related correspondence with GPs and other agencies. These are contractual responsibilities that must take priority and could occupy the majority of the consultant's time each day. In addition, consultants are involved in a number of supporting professional activities, such as audits, research, junior supervision, teaching, training and appraisals, and then there are management and non-NHS work activities such as Royal College, Deanery and General Medical Council work. These 'secondary' non-clinical activities should be grouped into those which can be delegated and others that need your personal attention. The items in each group should then be prioritized as urgent and non-urgent. This is then followed by a process of planning and scheduling, where items are delegated and passed on to others or scheduled into your calendar based on their level of importance (Fig. 13.2).

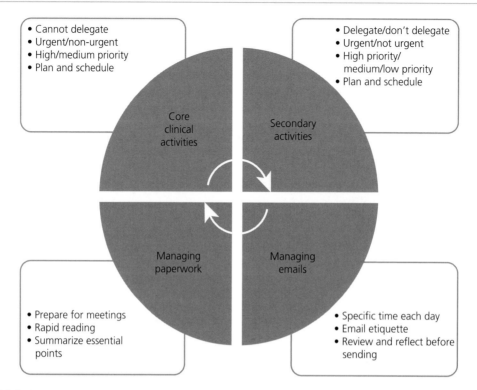

Figure 13.2 Time management activities.

Delegation is an important component of time management which is often under-used. Some consultants have difficulty in delegating, either because they have no confidence that the task will be carried out effectively or because they wish to maintain some control. Both these problems can be overcome if delegation is linked to regular reviews and progress reports. It is important to set aside adequate time for the different activities such as patient-related correspondence, writing reports, junior doctor supervision and appraisals, and in this respect, an electronic diary can be very useful.

Effective time management should also include some reflection of the day's work, which is best carried out at the end of each day. Learning lessons in this way can help with the modification and improvement of one's practice. It is also important to spend some time at the end of each day preparing for the following day's commitments. There is little point in attending meetings if one is not prepared and up to date with matters on the agenda. These reflection and preparation activities should take no more than 60–90 minutes each day.

There are some other points worth noting in relation to effective time management.

Managing emails (see also Chapter 4)

Set aside a specific time, say about 30–60 minutes, for dealing with emails on a daily basis. Do not 'reply to all' unless it is absolutely necessary. Delete emails which are general and do not require a response. If the reply can be short and specific, it is best to do so immediately. On the other hand, if it is likely to be long and requires some thought and discussion, it could be dictated as a draft and reviewed the following day before pressing the 'send' button. Follow email etiquette and avoid sending emails in irritation or anger.

Managing paperwork

This is a problem in most organizations, including the NHS. Very often there are huge amounts of material to be read, and a good management skill is the ability to read rapidly and summarize the salient points of a large and complex document in a few sentences. Attending a rapid-reading course could be useful. It is often possible to get a quick understanding of a long and complex document from the heading, introductory paragraph and conclusion. Diagrams, illustrations and summaries also give useful information that can be gathered quite quickly. There are a few documents that need careful review: policy documents, contractual papers, certain financial documents and letters, and correspondence to outside organizations such as the strategic health authority, Care Quality Commission or the General Medical Council. It is good practice to allocate a specific time to read through such documents and, if in doubt, get someone else who knows the subject to review and comment.

Managing meetings

All consultants have to chair meetings at some point in their career. Some also have to attend meetings and see other staff on a one-to-one basis. There are certain rules and etiquette that one should try to follow at such meetings: be polite and courteous, respectful of others, listen carefully to others' views, refrain from interrupting and avoid making personal remarks. This does not mean that one cannot be passionate or even fiery at times, but the arguments should be limited to the issues that are being discussed. If the meeting is with a subordinate on a one-to-one basis, ensure that you are well prepared and able to give adequate time for the meeting. If during such a meeting you find there is not enough time, it is always best to rearrange for another day.

Communication

Communication is at the heart of good management and clinical practice. The ability to communicate clearly and succinctly is without a doubt one of the main attributes of a good clinician. How useful is a sound clinical knowledge or good project management skills if these cannot be communicated to others in simple, unambiguous language? Poor, vague communication is not only a common cause of complaints but also the basis of misunderstandings and mistrust among doctors, patients and managers in the NHS.

The NHS Institute for Innovation and Improvement has recently introduced a structured communication guide for junior doctors called 'SBAR', which is an abbreviation for situation, background, assessment and recommendation.[4] This guide can be used to escalate a clinical problem or facilitate a handover and is mainly for clinical issues. It is a means of ensuring that essential clinical information is not excluded when clinical advice is being sought or patients are being handed over from one doctor to another during a change of shifts.

However, communication has a much wider context and can be verbal or written, direct or indirect, one-to-one or with several others, and within teams or between teams. Most consultants who are directly involved with patient care have to use many forms of communication, but for the purpose of this chapter we will concentrate on direct verbal contact.

What, then, is good, effective verbal communication? A good communicator is clear, concise and precise. Such people have the ability to summarize the essential points in a discussion with a couple of carefully constructed sentences. They are honest and open and hence command considerable credibility. They are courteous, sensitive and have a good understanding of their subject (see Fig. 13.3).

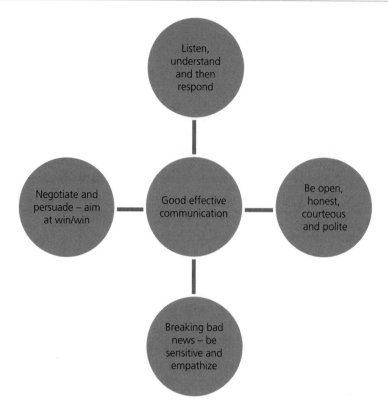

Figure 13.3 Good communication skills.

Perhaps the most important attribute of a good communicator, as Stephen Covey[5] points out in his popular book, *The 7 Habits of Highly Effective People*, is the ability to listen with the intent to understand. Most people listen, not with the intent to understand, but with the intent to reply. Many of us are thinking of counter-arguments and what to say in reply while the other person is talking and this is often the reason for interruptions. Covey refers to empathic communication, which is seeking first to understand and then to be understood. One can be a good listener, but unless this is combined with a genuine desire to understand what is being said, listening becomes meaningless. In a one-to-one conversation with patients, responding to their concerns without having understood the concerns can seriously undermine the doctor–patient relationship.

Breaking bad news is common in medical practice. While it is important to be open and honest in such situations, one must also show sensitivity and empathy. The latter refers to the ability to share the patient's or carer's feelings and emotions. This is more complex than simply being sensitive and requires a good knowledge of the person's social and cultural background.

Negotiation and persuasion are closely associated with good communication skills. Good negotiation involves some give and take with the aim being to achieve a win/win situation. Win/win is based on the idea that there is plenty for everybody and one person's success is not achieved at the expense of the success of another.[5] Although a win/win outcome is ideal, Covey admits that it is not always achievable and we should also learn to deal with win/lose outcomes. There is a lot in the literature on the importance of good communication and negotiation, but little has been written on 'persuasion'. To persuade, one must have a thorough knowledge of the subject, be honest and open, be clear of the aims/objectives and work towards a solution that brings some benefits to all concerned.

Dealing with difficult colleagues

While this is a common problem for medical managers, consultants who are not in management also have to deal with such situations from time to time. Consultants may have problems dealing with their line manager, who is often a medical colleague, other professional colleagues, junior medical staff and non-medical managers.

Sometimes people are seen as difficult because we fail to understand them. We must be careful not to label people as difficult simply because they do not agree with our views or are doing their job. There are two broad groups of difficult people: those who are difficult in certain situations (situation- or state-dependent) and others who are difficult in any situation (trait-dependent). The former are likely to be more amenable to discussions and persuasion, whereas the latter are entrenched in their ways and unlikely to respond in a positive manner to dialogue and debate. These two different groups of individuals have to be managed differently (see Fig. 13.4).

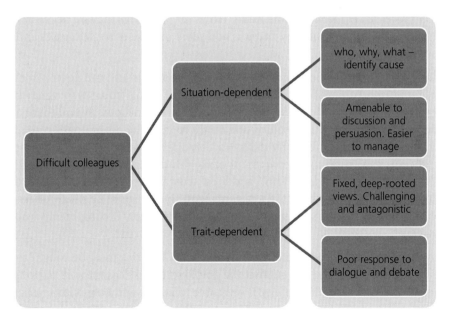

Figure 13.4 Managing situation- vs trait-dependent people.

In dealing with the first group, it is useful to ask yourself a number of questions. First, who is the difficult person? What is their position in the organization? Clearly, a difficult medical director or chief executive will have to be handled differently from a junior doctor.

Second, why is the person being difficult? Try to understand the likely reasons for the person's difficult behaviour which is situation-dependent: departmental policy decisions, demands from their superiors, financial constraints, excess workload, feeling threatened, poor morale and lack of trust and confidence. Family problems and ill health are also common issues that are often overlooked. The reasons for one's behaviour are not always clear-cut and may need careful investigation.

Third, think about the nature of the difficulty they present. This can take many forms: aggression and open hostility, refusal to cooperate, backstabbing/sniping, manipulating, micromanaging or pessimism. Each of these different types requires different management techniques. A high degree of emotional intelligence, i.e. the ability to recognize and control the emotions of others as well as your own, is a useful attribute to develop.

In dealing with such individuals, be open and honest, have one-to-one meetings if necessary, keep records of such meetings and be polite and non-confrontational but firm at all times. It might be necessary to challenge such individuals with facts and figures, research and audit evidence and aim towards a compromise solution. The chances of coming to an agreement are greater if a genuine attempt is made to understand and address at least some of their concerns.

The second, trait-dependent group of people are more difficult to deal with. Such individuals have deep-rooted personality traits that make them unduly suspicious, cynical, pessimistic and negative. They are difficult, uncompromising, have fixed views and are unlikely to respond positively to any discussions. Often they are quite challenging, sarcastic and antagonistic and sometimes even openly hostile and aggressive. Unlike with the first group, there is little point in having protracted discussions with such individuals, and trying to convince them with facts, figures and good research evidence can be futile. However, meetings may be necessary to explain the organizational position and strategy and it is advisable to have other witnesses and keep accurate records of these.

The attitudinal difficulties must be discussed at annual appraisals and the doctor in question must be offered an opportunity to attend training and educational courses that may be considered appropriate. If, despite such remedial action, problems persist and these are likely to impact on clinical care and patient safety, one ought to take the disciplinary route. Before embarking on such a route, ensure that you have a thorough knowledge of the appropriate policies and procedures such as the Department of Health document, *Maintaining High Professional Standards in the Modern NHS,*[6] and local trust policies on personal and professional misconduct and grievance procedures. Discussions with the National Clinical Assessment Authority (NCAA) should take place at an early stage, particularly if competency/capability matters are involved.

If a decision is made to exclude the doctor from work, NCAA advice must be sought at all stages. However, it must be borne in mind that the employing trust has the sole responsibility for disciplining all medical staff. The NCAA is only able to advise and help NHS trusts to handle cases quickly and fairly and to reduce the need for disciplinary action.[6] Medical managers and consultants must remember that if there is any possibility that public protection might be compromised by the actions of a doctor, serious consideration must be given to referring the matter to the General Medical Council.

Medical and non-medical managers can also have trait-dependent problems ingrained in their personalities. It is very difficult to deal with such managers, particularly when they are in a position of authority. Meetings with such individuals are sometimes necessary to resolve an issue and in these circumstances one must be polite and courteous, maintain a high degree of professionalism and keep written records. If difficulties persist, one should consider having an informal discussion with a senior colleague or raise the matter at the medical staff meetings.

The British Medical Association (BMA) and the defence organizations are also useful sources of advice. If all this fails and the difficulties continue, one may have to seriously consider taking a grievance against the manager as a last resort. However, one should always seek union or BMA advice before taking this route. If other colleagues have also had similar difficulties with the same manager, one should consider a collective group grievance rather than an individual one.

Managing stress

Stress and burnout are common phenomena in the NHS. However, in recent years there has been a significant increase in stress-related problems, resulting in a loss of productive working time, low morale, anxiety, depression, ill health and early retirement. It is being increasingly recognized that stress can cost organizations financially through absence, poor quality of care, complaints and litigation.[7]

Unlike in the past, doctors have become more familiar with the concept of stress and are now able to admit and discuss these matters more freely.[8] The causes of stress can be quite wide-ranging, from individual factors such as difficult family relationships to excessive workload, unrealistic targets and unsympathetic managers. In recent years, much has been done to combat stress among doctors in the workplace. Various organizations such as the BMA and the Royal Colleges have set up free advisory/counselling services, work hours for junior doctors have been reviewed and reduced[8] and comprehensive induction programmes for new starters have been introduced. These measures have focused mainly on stress related to workload and not so much on other factors at work, such as bullying, harassment, unrealistic targets, patient complaints, serious adverse clinical incidents and litigation (see Fig. 13.5). Medical managers, consultants and other medical staff receive little or no training in dealing with such matters.

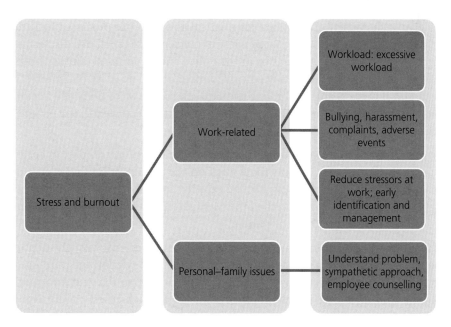

Figure 13.5 Measures for dealing with stress and burnout.

There are several publications on the management of stress in the workplace. Stress intervention techniques can be primary, secondary or tertiary[9] and involve reducing stressors and promoting a supportive environment, early identification and management of stress-related problems in individuals and teams, and the rehabilitation of individuals who have suffered stress. Despite various attempts by different organizations such as health service unions, the BMA and the Royal Colleges, there are very few NHS organizations that have a systematic, planned intervention technique for stress-related problems. As Firth-Cozens[7] pointed out nearly a decade ago, what we really need is a systematic, planned approach to the problem. This will be possible only when trusts recognize the huge cost to the organization not only financially but also in terms of manpower, recruitment, retention and reputation. In the current climate of service reorganizations and health reforms, this is a major problem which, if ignored, could result in serious consequences for the NHS.

Maintaining confidentiality

Patient information is generally held under legal and ethical obligations of confidentiality and should not be used or disclosed in a form that might identify patients without their consent.[10] Patients disclose highly sensitive, personal information to a doctor and it is the doctor's responsibility to ensure that such information remains confidential and is never disclosed, as far as possible, without consent. However, there are certain circumstances where disclosure of patient information without consent may be necessary. These can be broadly categorized under three headings.[10]

- disclosure related to providing healthcare
- disclosure related not to healthcare but for medical purposes such as research/audits
- disclosures unrelated to health or medical purposes.

In all three instances, information should be given only on a need-to-know basis. Disclosures to provide further healthcare can only be made with the patient's consent, unless the patient has no capacity to give such consent. Disclosure for medical and all other purposes requires consent unless public interest justifies such disclosure without consent. This includes disclosures required by law to courts such as Coroners' Courts or to the police and to certain statutory bodies with investigative powers such as the General Medical Council. The issue of 'public interest' is not always clear-cut and if there is any doubt, one should seek the views of one's defence organization. All discussions with the defence organization must be carefully recorded in the patient's notes for future reference.

Confidentiality and the related legal and ethical issues are much more complex in certain situations, such as with mentally ill patients. Doctors must work on the presumption that every adult patient, including those who have a mental illness, has the capacity to make decisions about their care.[11] If it is deemed that the patient lacks capacity, then the Mental Capacity Act (2005) should be used and decisions made in the best interests of the patient.

Similarly, children may not want information disclosed to their parents. In such situations, every effort must be made to persuade patients to allow disclosure. If they continue to refuse, and the doctor considers it essential to disclose certain information, then relevant information may be disclosed to the appropriate person without consent.[12] In all such cases, patients should be informed of the decision and the reasons for such disclosure should be accurately recorded in their clinical notes.

Doctors must bear in mind that the Human Rights Act 1998 allows individuals to litigate for breach of confidence. This is also considered as unprofessional practice by the General Medical Council and can result in disciplinary procedures.

Tact, diplomacy and politics

Most organizations can be viewed as political arenas and it can be argued that they have groups (professional) competing for limited resources.[13] NHS trusts are no different, with professional groups such as doctors having to use tact and diplomacy to manoeuvre the political landscape successfully. This requires a good understanding of the political issues facing the organization and the personal agendas of the key players, such as the chief executive, the director of finance, the chief operating officer and other members of the executive committee. Although these individuals are professionals and will be expected to deal with all issues in a professional manner, the human element can sometimes take over, in which case the personal agenda could override professionalism.

Having good political skills is the ability to understand one's emotions and, to some extent, identify and control other people's emotions as well – i.e. to demonstrate emotional intelligence.[14] This enables one to manage the impact of one's emotions on others and when linked with social awareness will help to build long-lasting meaningful relationships and social interactions – i.e. social intelligence.[15] This allows one to work and connect successfully with a range of others both within and outside the organization, which is often referred to as networking.

Networking skills are essential not only for partnership working and learning from others, which will help to provide an improved level of care and benefit the organization, but also at a personal level, to enhance one's reputation and credibility both at local and national levels. Building a network can be time-consuming and hard work but the benefits, when used appropriately, can be immense. Wedderburn Tate[16] asserts that networking is a key element in the process of continuous learning and good leaders understand the value of knowing who is doing what, when, where and with what result. This allows one to learn from the experience of others, avoid common mistakes and influence service development and change.

Conclusion

So what does it take to be a good doctor? How could one improve one's personal effectiveness? A doctor can usually take one of four career pathways: clinical, research/academic, teaching/ training or leadership/management. Most doctors choose to become clinicians, at least at the beginning of their careers, before developing a further interest, such as education and training or management, at a later date. Therefore, a thorough clinical knowledge is essential to become a good doctor. But a doctor's role is quite complex and involves many other tasks such as teaching and training, improving clinical services, ensuring clinical effectiveness and patient safety, research and audit. These responsibilities may vary in degree, depending on one's post, but all doctors should have some understanding of these diverse roles and functions. There are certain key skills and attributes that would help doctors to deal with them, and in this chapter I have discussed some of these: good communication, effective time management, working in MDTs, coping with stress and dealing with difficult colleagues.

It is unfortunate that such matters are not a part of the medical curricula. Medical undergraduates spend considerable time and energy learning the clinical and technical skills that are so important in the practice of medicine. While this is clearly necessary, I feel some attention should also be given to more generic topics such as those discussed in this chapter.

Summary

❑ Improving one's personal effectiveness as a doctor means developing one's ability to:

  ❑ manage and lead multidisciplinary teams

  ❑ manage time

  ❑ manage meetings

  ❑ communicate

  ❑ manage difficult colleagues

  ❑ manage stress

  ❑ be tactful and diplomatic.

❑ A good doctor requires the following:

  ❑ excellent clinical knowledge

  ❑ reflective practice

  ❑ the ability to be appropriately self-critical

  ❑ the ability to work in partnerships

  ❑ the ability to learn from experience

  ❑ the ability to give respect to gain respect

  ❑ good teaching/training skills

  ❑ good audit/research skills

  ❑ a desire to grant the highest priority to clinical care and patient safety.

References

1. General Medical Council (2012). *Leadership and Management for All Doctors*. Available from: http://www.gmc-uk.org/

2. Holloway F, Chorlton C (2007). Multidisciplinary teams. In: Bhugra D, Bell S, Burns A, eds. *Management for Psychiatrists*, 3rd edn. London: RCPsych Publications.

3. Kodz J et al. (2003) *Working Long Hours: A Review of the Evidence*, vol. 1. Main report. London: Department of Trade and Industry

4. NHS Institute for Innovation and Improvement (2010). *SBAR: Safer Care*. Available from: http://www.institute.nhs.uk/

5. Covey SR (1990). *The 7 Habits of Highly Effective People*. New York: Simon and Schuster.

6. Department of Health (2005). Maintaining High Professional Standards in the Modern NHS. London: Department of Health. Available from: http://www.dh.gov.uk/

7. Firth-Cozens J (2001). Interventions to improve patient wellbeing and patient care. *Soc ScI Med* 52, 215–22.

8. Firth-Cozens J (2003). Doctors, their wellbeing and their stress (editorial). *Br Med J* 326, 670–1.

9. Cooper C (1996). Stress in the workplace. *Br J Hosp Med* 55, 569–73.

10. Department of Health (2003). *Confidentiality: NHS Code of Practice.* Available from: http://www.dh.gov.uk

11. General Medical Council (2008). *Consent: Patients and Doctors Making Decisions Together.* Available from: http://www.gmc-uk.org/

12. General Medical Council (2004). *Confidentiality.* Available from: http://www.gmc-uk.org/

13. Perrewé, Nelson D (2004). The facilitative role of political skill. *Organizational Dyn* 33, 366–78.

14. Goleman D (1998). *Working with Emotional Intelligence.* London: Bloomsbury.

15. Goleman D (2006). *Social Intelligence.* New York: Bantam Dell.

16. Wedderburn Tate C (1999). *Leadership in Nursing.* London: Churchill Livingstone.

Chapter 14

Doctors in difficulty

Peter Old and Alastair Scotland

Introduction

About 227 000 doctors are licensed to practise by the General Medical Council (GMC). While only a very small proportion of practitioners get into difficulties, the impact of these difficulties can be great, both for individual patients and their families, and for the healthcare resources the consequent action consumes. The challenges faced by medical directors in managing practitioners in difficulty are among the most taxing, time-consuming and stressful aspects of their role.

This chapter sets out an approach to the management of doctors in difficulty based on a decade of experience of the National Clinical Assessment Service (NCAS) in dealing with over 6500 cases referred to it by medical directors and others.

The scale of the problem

In a study covering one NHS region, Donaldson[1] estimated that, over a 5-year period, concerns serious enough to warrant the consideration of disciplinary action were raised over about 6 per cent of all senior medical staff. The experience at NCAS over the 10 years of its existence is that for doctors in active clinical practice in the UK, the 'risk of referral' to NCAS is about one doctor in 200 per year. It should be stressed that this part of the discussion has its focus on concerns arising about practice, and not necessarily about shortcomings identified by any investigation, review of practice or performance assessment. That element will be considered later in this chapter. As a proxy measure of concerns arising about practice, we have used referral patterns to NCAS.

Within this overall risk of referral of about 0.5 per cent of the practitioner population each year, there is considerable variation between specialities. Obstetrics and gynaecology, psychiatry and general medical practice, for example, have a noticeably greater number of referrals than might be expected from the size of the workforce in these specialities, and anaesthetics and the general medical group of specialities have noticeably fewer (see Fig. 14.1).

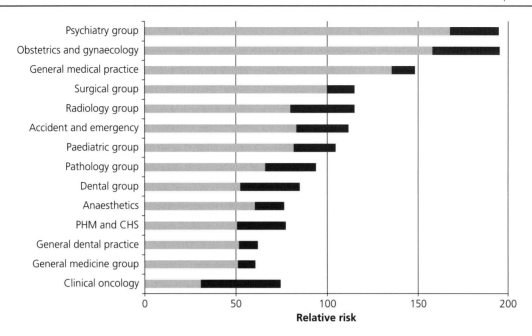

Figure 14.1 Relative risk of referral to the National Clinical Assessment Service (NCAS) by speciality, 2001–2011. Relative risk is given by speciality, comparing the observed referral rate with the workforce in that speciality as at 2007, and showing 95 per cent confidence intervals. PHM, public health medicine; CHS, community health service.

Aside from speciality, certain characteristics of doctors are associated with higher rates of referral, including practitioners' age, gender and place of qualification. These are discussed in the following sections. Figure 14.2 compares the influence of these various characteristics on the likelihood of referral, illustrating the importance of age.

Older practitioners

Among doctors in hospital and community practice, male doctors aged 60 and over are four times more likely to be referred to NCAS than male doctors aged under 40. Female doctors aged 60 and over are three times more likely to be referred to NCAS than those under 40. Among GPs, those aged 60 and over are seven times more likely to be referred to NCAS than those aged under 40.

The reasons for this pattern are not entirely clear but it may be revealing something not only about the educational needs of doctors as their careers progress, but also, and more fundamentally, about the expectations of practice from doctors over a senior career which may span more than three decades.

Gender

Male practitioners are two to three times more likely to be referred to NCAS and also more likely to be excluded or suspended from work, and this holds true for all ages. The reasons for this finding are not clear and it is therefore important we see more research in this area.

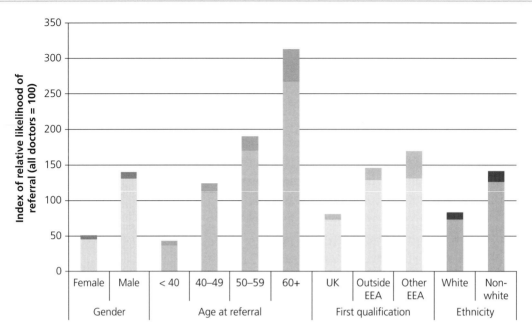

Figure 14.2 Comparison of likelihood of referral based on practitioner characteristics. Relative risk is given by speciality, comparing the observed referral rate with the workforce in that speciality as at 2007, and showing 95 per cent confidence intervals. EEA, European Economic Area.

Place of qualification

Doctors qualifying outside the UK are more likely to be referred to NCAS, and this is true whether the place of qualification is in the European Economic Area or elsewhere. While it is clear that factors relating purely to place of qualification and those relating to the ethnicity of the practitioner have an influence on these referral patterns, it is equally clear that their influence is far from simple and NCAS's work has suggested that the differences are more influenced by place of qualification and training factors at undergraduate level than by ethnicity.[2] Levels of concern among doctors qualifying in the UK do not differ between white and non-white groups. This suggests at the very least that there is a need for better induction and development of doctors joining the NHS from outside the UK.

Key points

Scale of the problem

- Dealing with doctors in difficulty can be very demanding.
- In most organizations, medical directors are unlikely to gain sufficient experience to be able to handle these relatively uncommon issues assuredly and with confidence.
- More attention needs to be given to proper induction, mentoring and support for doctors at all stages of their careers.

The nature of concerns about professional practice

If we explore practice concerns more fully and examine not only the nature of the presenting concerns but also what is identified at formal assessment, there are findings which are as striking as those revealed by referral patterns. NCAS records the nature of concerns about professional practice in all referrals made to it. Of 1472 consecutive cases referred to NCAS, 54 per cent were about clinical skills, but behavioural concerns were just as common (56 per cent), and 24 per cent involved health issues thought to be contributing to difficulties with practice. There was considerable overlap between those three principal areas (see Fig. 14.3).

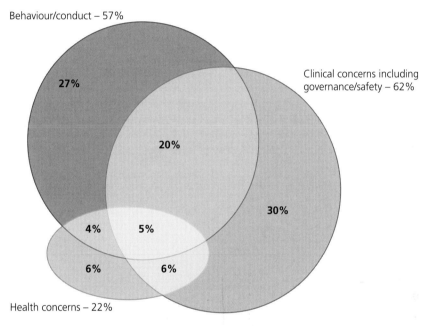

Figure 14.3 The nature of performance concerns in 2947 cases (December 2007–October 2010) referred to the National Clinical Assessment Service (NCAS).

One of the most striking findings from NCAS's work on referred practitioners is that there is a significant variance between the nature of the concerns presented at referral and what was revealed following an NCAS performance assessment – with behavioural issues (e.g. poor communication skills and poor leadership abilities) and issues relating to lack of workplace support providing significant contributions to the explanation of poor practitioner performance (see Figs 14.4 and 14.5).

Taken together, Figures 14.3–14.5 suggest that the ultimate cause of the concern about practice may not correlate with the proximal cause noted at the point of referral. It is noticeable that organizations appear to be particularly reluctant to identify their own contribution to the poor performance of practitioners they employ or contract with.

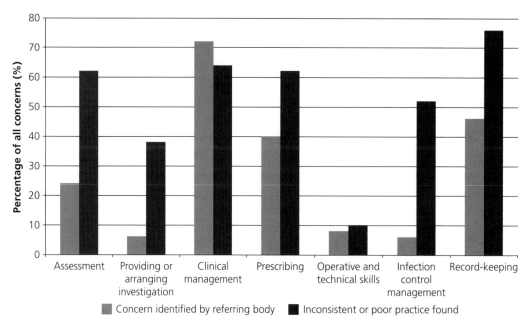

Figure 14.4 Comparison of initial concerns with assessment findings: quality of clinical care. The data refers to the 50 most recent National Clinical Assessment Service (NCAS) performance assessments as at June 2011.

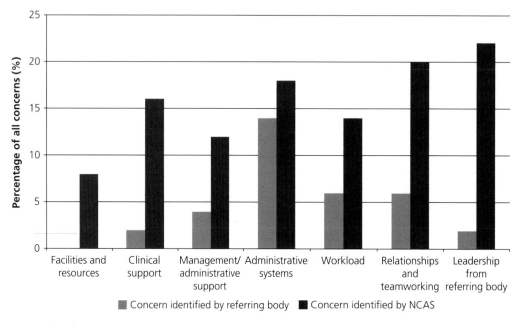

Figure 14.5 Comparison of initial concerns with assessment findings: context of practice. The data refers to the 50 most recent National Clinical Assessment Service (NCAS) performance assessments as at June 2011.

Early signs of difficulty

Concerns about a doctor's practice can come to light in many ways. Box 14.1 draws on the now widely quoted work of Paice and Orton,[3] summarizing the experience of staff working with doctors in postgraduate training. The signs would suggest the need for an approach to the doctor by a skilled senior professional, to identify any underlying factors and to set clear goals for improvement. This may prevent the problems becoming intractable, resulting in unfortunate consequences for patients, the doctor concerned and his or her colleagues.

Box 14.1 Early signs of the trainee in difficulty

- The 'disappearing act'
  - Not answering bleeps
  - Disappearing between clinic and ward
  - Lateness
  - Frequent sick leave
- Low work rate
  - Slowness in carrying out procedures, clerking patients, dictating letters, making decisions
  - Arriving early, leaving late and still not managing a reasonable workload
- 'Ward rage'
  - Bursts of temper
  - Shouting matches
  - Real or imagined slights
- Rigidity
  - Poor tolerance of ambiguity
  - Inability to compromise
  - Difficulty prioritizing
  - Inappropriate 'whistleblowing'
- 'Bypass syndrome' – junior colleagues or nurses find ways to avoid seeking the doctor's opinion or help
- Career problems
  - Difficulty with exams
  - Uncertainty about career choice
  - Disillusionment with medicine
- Insight failure
  - Rejection of constructive criticism
  - Defensiveness
  - Counter-challenge

While it is hoped that, increasingly, such concerns about doctors working in all grades will be identified through a review of performance against job plans, annual appraisal and the revalidation process, it remains overwhelmingly the case at present that action usually arises as a result of: concerns from colleagues; complaints from patients or relatives of patients; litigation following allegations of negligence; and information from the police or coroner. This situation presents significant challenges to the implementation of revalidation and other forms of competency assurance programme, as it will require a change in approach and attitude throughout the work of clinical governance in any healthcare system. Such a set of changes will have to be so pervasive as to amount to a change in the culture of clinical governance throughout the health system.

Regardless of how concerns come to light, there should be an initial consideration of the facts and a screening process to decide if further investigation is needed. All decisions, including decisions not to pursue the matter, should be recorded and the doctor made aware of the issues under consideration.

Key points

Nature of concerns

- 'What you think you are looking at may not be what you are seeing' – there may be more behind the presenting concern than at first appears.
- Consider the personal and organizational factors that may be contributing to the concerns.
- Despite attempts to identify performance concerns earlier and more proactively, most concerns about practitioners will continue to come to light through a reactive response to serious untoward incidents.

Gathering information

Before deciding on next steps, medical directors need to assemble an integrated overview of all the information available about the doctor in question. The principal aim of this is to gain an assurance about three key aspects of practice:

- Whether the practitioner is 'equipped for practice' – this is largely focused on the competence, training and overall clinical ability of the practitioner for the role to which he or she has been appointed. It is grounded on training, education and continuing professional development against standards of practice published by the relevant Royal College or faculty.
- Whether the practitioner is 'fit to practise' – this is largely focused on the standards and guidance of the professional regulator and is grounded in the professionalism and standing of the practitioner in relation to the GMC's *Good Medical Practice.*
- Whether the practitioner is 'fit for purpose' – this is focused on 'that practitioner in that post' and is concerned with whether the practitioner is meeting the requirements of the whole population of their patients for a service at their level of expected practice, e.g. as a consultant leading and delivering a service in the given speciality in that part of the country. It is therefore grounded in the management, delivery and integrity of the clinical service of which the practitioner is a part.

A key task for medical directors is to compile this information in a way that enables employing/contracting organizations to be assured, quickly and easily, that all information is being used to monitor performance and made available to support revalidation.

The currently available sources of information about the performance of practitioners working in the NHS are considerable and can be grouped broadly into three streams:

- benchmarking information, e.g. prescribing information, audit and outcome data, performance against clinical elements of directorate or practice business plans
- 'positive information' about the practitioner, e.g. information about career history, information from Royal Colleges and faculties, continuing professional development record, appraisal and other involvement in routine clinical governance work

- 'negative information' arising in or around the practice of the doctor, e.g. complaints, disciplinary history, incidents and incident reviews.

These streams, managed together, can contribute to the overall assurance that individual practitioners are competent; have gone through an approved training programme; are thought to be of good character; have no outstanding concerns about their practice, and are not the subject of any investigation into any outstanding concerns about their practice; have maintained their knowledge and skills and, therefore, are fit for purpose.

Deciding whether to investigate a concern

The purpose of an investigation is to determine whether or not a problem exists that requires action. Investigations themselves are often complex, time-consuming and potentially costly. They may have unintended consequences both for the doctor subject to the investigation and for the organization conducting it. Therefore, before committing to undertaking an investigation, medical directors should consider:

- whether all immediately necessary steps have been taken to protect the public by responding promptly and effectively to the concerns that have been raised
- whether all immediately necessary steps have been taken to protect staff, support the subject of the proposed investigation and protect any sources of evidence
- who else needs to be made aware of the investigation:
  - the doctor: the doctor needs to know about the investigation and be given the opportunity to comment before any decision, particularly a decision to proceed to a disciplinary hearing, is reached
  - the complainant: in many cases a complaint against the practitioner may be pursued in parallel with the local investigation. The complaints process will impose its own timescales and conditions, but in general complainants need to know that their concerns have been taken seriously and that appropriate action has been taken at the conclusion of the investigation
  - the chief executive and/or the board: organizations should have local policies in place governing how incidents are reported but remember that appeals arising from disciplinary processes may require the participation of board members who have not been involved in the initial stages
- whether the organization has clear and simply written guidance that explains the process it is about to embark on and its links to disciplinary procedures
- whether an investigation is really necessary – if the nature of the problem and any underlying issues are sufficiently clear from a preliminary review, then informal action may often be a more satisfactory method of resolving problems than a more formal route where the resources and time required outweigh the benefit gained
- the extent of investigation which is required. This is related to the above point: for example, an investigation may not be necessary if the facts of the case have been agreed and the doctor is willing to cooperate with any further action. It should be noted, however, that where a termination of employment or removal from a performers list is a potential outcome, the organization may still need to conduct a full investigation.

Detailed guidance on how to conduct a local performance investigation has been published elsewhere.[4] However, it is important to note here that the majority of investigations disclose either no problem or, at most, a problem that permits the doctor to remain in post. This reinforces the need for all investigations to be conducted in a way that recognizes that the organization may need to facilitate the doctor's return to unrestricted practice.

Key points

- Doctors who are deemed fit to practise may be unfit for the role and purpose for which they are employed.
- Investigations are often complex, time-consuming and potentially costly. Seek advice and take time to plan.
- Most doctors who are the subject of an investigation return to work.

Deciding on next steps

The NHS has found it very difficult to address concerns about the performance of doctors in a way that gives priority to protecting patients while at the same time recognizing that disciplinary solutions are rarely the fairest and most appropriate way of dealing with doctors who have genuine problems in their practice. Punishing all mistakes by disciplinary action creates a culture of blame and fear in which errors will be concealed and, ultimately, care becomes less safe.

While it is important that concerns about professional practice are tackled through training or remedial action wherever possible and appropriate, this should not lead to a reluctance in taking disciplinary action when it is warranted, whether from evidence of misconduct or of standards of practice that are so deficient that formal local or regulatory action is needed. However, given that such circumstances will be uncommon and that the stakes for both the doctor and the employing/ contracting organization are high, medical directors will want to take advice before embarking on a potentially costly and damaging course of action.

Suspension and exclusion from work

The term suspension is used in two entirely different circumstances – one relates to action taken against a doctor's registration, imposed by the General Medical Council, and the other relates to the temporary withdrawal of the doctor's name from the primary care organization's performers list. The term 'exclusion from work' is used in secondary care settings which are subject to the provisions of *Maintaining High Professional Standards in the Modern NHS* (MHPS).[5] This framework is discussed more fully later in this chapter.

Although the processes and regulations governing the suspension of GPs and the exclusion from work of doctors employed by NHS trusts differ, they both, in the end, mean that doctors are barred from duty, with significant costs for the NHS and serious consequences for doctors that cast a long shadow over their professional performance.

When an allegation is made against a member of staff which, if well founded, might lead to disciplinary action, suspension of the contract of employment or the contract for service is often considered. It is extremely important that any decision is taken only after carefully considering the reasons for doing so.

First, it should be borne in mind that suspension from employment on full pay is only in very rare circumstances part of a local disciplinary process, and in no circumstance does it constitute local disciplinary action. This is complicated by the fact that it is, by its nature, very public, in contrast to the disciplinary process itself, which may remain in strict confidence throughout. The most frequent reasons for suspending staff are:

- where the employer considers it is necessary to allow an acutely tense situation to settle – a 'cooling off' period – while the incident and/or allegations are investigated

- where the investigation of a case may be hindered by the presence of the person under investigation
- where the employer believes there is good reason for concern over patient safety which cannot be controlled by existing and practicable governance arrangements
- in the rare circumstance where dismissal for gross misconduct is being considered.

Alternatives to suspension and exclusion should be considered carefully before any decision is taken. For example, a primary care organization could ask doctors to withdraw voluntarily from performing part of their normal duties, and/or find them suitable alternative NHS work away from direct patient contact while investigations continue. Suspension should be used only if the primary care organization is persuaded that it is really necessary. It should be a 'rare event' and alternatives must always be considered.

Suspension from the performers list and exclusion from work are often described as neutral acts. The protection of a doctor's income during these episodes has been presented as a symbol of that neutrality, the purpose being to allow the unhindered investigation of serious allegations made against a doctor while also providing protection for patients, colleagues and, in some situations, the practitioners themselves.

However, suspension and exclusion are rarely perceived as neutral acts by doctors themselves. In essence, while they may be neutral in their intent, they are self-evidently not neutral in their effect. Indeed, commenting on the proposition that these are neutral acts, Lord Justice Sedley, giving judgment in a Court of Appeal case in 2007, said:[6]

> I venture to disagree, at least in relation to the employment of a qualified professional in a function which is as much a vocation as a job. Suspension changes the status quo from work to no work, and it inevitably casts a shadow over the employee's competence. Of course this does not mean that it cannot be done, but it is not a neutral act.

The cost of exclusions to the NHS and to the public has been well recognized for many years and led to the National Audit Office's report in 2003.[7] However, there has been much less scrutiny of suspension in primary care. In the year to September 2010 in England, an estimated total of 6500 working weeks were lost through the exclusion or suspension of doctors, at a cost to the NHS probably in excess of £20 million.[8]

Occasionally employers or primary care organizations will be faced with the situation where the GMC has suspended a doctor's registration as a decision of an Interim Order Panel (IOP). Such suspensions may last for up to 18 months. The IOP has a duty to act to protect members of the public and the wider public interest; it does not determine whether the allegations made against the doctor are true or false.

The question then follows that if a practitioner is unable to work following a decision of the GMC, is the employer or primary care contractor under a duty to continue paying the doctor? In primary care there is guidance from the Department of Health in England[9] containing the expectation that PCTs will mirror the GMC suspension and use suspension from the performers list as the means to justify payments to the practitioner. It remains to be seen if this position will hold more generally across both primary and secondary care as budgets become subject to intense scrutiny.

Formal disciplinary procedures

For doctors employed in the NHS in England (but excluding those working in primary care), the relevant national disciplinary framework is *Maintaining High Professional Standards in the Modern NHS* (MHPS).[5] It is mirrored by very similar provisions in Northern Ireland, Wales and Scotland, each of which has its own procedures, but in all jurisdictions, the MHPS can be considered as a guide to good practice in resolving concerns about professional practice. Foundation trusts in England are not required to use the MHPS framework, although, to our knowledge, all have chosen to do so.

Doctors working in primary care in England may be self-employed or employees of independent contractors or general medical practitioner partnerships. All remain subject to the Performers List Regulations (PLR).

Whatever the setting, local processes should have as their principal focus the resolution of any problems that have been identified. The aim, whenever possible, should be to preserve employment and not to end it. In this context, MHPS can be seen as a useful framework for managing concerns about the professional practice of doctors, and its principles apply in both primary and secondary care settings. It sets the objective as:[10]

> Wherever possible employers should aim to resolve issues of capability (including clinical competence and health) through ongoing assessment and support. Early identification of problems is essential to reduce the risk of serious harm to patients.

Potential outcomes of an investigation of concerns about professional practice are given as follows:

- there is a case of misconduct that should be put to a conduct panel
- there are concerns about the practitioner's health that should be considered by the NHS body's occupational health service
- there are concerns about the practitioner's performance that should be further explored by the National Clinical Assessment Service
- restrictions on practice or exclusion from work should be considered
- there are serious concerns that should be referred to the GMC
- there are intractable problems and the matter should be put before a capability panel
- no further action is needed.

The intention of both MHPS and the PLR was to move away from previous adversarial procedures whose principal feature was that they were led and overseen by the employer/contracting organization with many safeguards for the clinician but with no formal role for legal representatives. However, developments in the law[11] have eroded that principle, particularly in circumstances where what is at stake is not only the potential loss of a specific job but also the loss of a career.

Details of the procedures, the structure of panels and the processes to be followed are beyond the scope of this work but medical directors should seek advice at an early stage about how these matters are to be addressed.

Key points

Next steps

- Most problems about professional practice should be dealt with locally.
- Suspension and exclusion from work should be used only as a last resort. Alternatives should always be considered.
- Seek advice, at an early stage, before embarking on formal disciplinary procedures.

Support for doctors in difficulty

Many areas of a practitioner's life can be affected when he or she is in difficulty. There may be financial repercussions, and family and relationships may be affected. All of this can have a cumulative effect on the psychological well-being of a practitioner, leading to feelings of poor self-worth and loss of 'self'.

Doctors who find themselves in this position have been described as the 'second victim' of medical error:[12]

> In the absence of [support and] mechanisms for healing, physicians find dysfunctional ways to protect themselves. They often respond to their own mistakes with anger and projection of blame, and may act defensively or callously and blame or scold the patient or other members of the healthcare team. Distress escalates in the face of a malpractice suit. In the long run some physicians are deeply wounded, lose their nerve, burn out, or seek solace in alcohol or drugs.

It is important that practitioners register with a GP; those who are GPs themselves should do so with a different practice from the one where they work. There is evidence that although many doctors and dentists are registered with a GP, they tend not to consult their GP when they are unwell. As far as possible, practitioners in difficulty should be encouraged to access medical help through their GP. However, one reason for their reluctance to do so may be the fear of being referred to a specialist whom they know.

There are many different organizations providing support to doctors in difficulty, ranging from those offering practical skills-based training, counselling and coaching to those helping doctors who are dealing with mental health or addiction problems.

Doctors in difficulty – what NCAS offers

One of NCAS's core principles is to ensure that the focus of activity in professional governance is at the frontline of services as far as possible, providing specialist expertise to support local activity and involving national systems only where absolutely necessary. This carries two clear benefits:

- greater local capacity in predicting, preventing, identifying and handling performance concerns
- ensuring a proper balance of priorities in the use of scarce resources – skills, staff and financial.

The National Clinical Assessment Service will take a tiered approach to supporting revalidation by providing a variety of interventions based on different levels of input in the revalidation process and using its experience to advise on the most appropriate intervention. Within this approach, NCAS will provide help in the following areas.

Advice and support to medical directors/responsible officers

The National Clinical Assessment Service will provide advice and support to medical directors/responsible officers – and their equivalents in other health professions – on handling performance concerns emerging following appraisal, or during the process of considering an individual for recommendation for revalidation. Advice on handling performance concerns is currently a core area of work for NCAS and is free at the point of delivery. NCAS believes that revalidation will identify more individuals where there are concerns about their performance at an earlier stage. It will also contribute to regional groupings of responsible officers and medical directors and their equivalents if they are established.

Review of performance

A local review of specific areas of an individual's performance will also be provided by a panel of NCAS trained and accredited reviewers to help clarify an organization's concerns. NCAS is currently developing the method for such a review, which will be appropriate where a local organization needs more information about a practitioner's performance to help with the decision on the next steps to take. This will include a case note review and an interview with the practitioner.

Remediation and further training

The remediation and further training offered by NCAS range from general advice to bespoke local structured programmes. NCAS will support the local development of structured action plans where concerns have been identified during appraisals within the 5-year cycle for doctors or if the practitioner has difficulty in revalidating. The principles of structured action planning (including negotiating and securing funding for placements and supervision) that are currently used for NCAS cases are tried and tested. NCAS is planning to provide web-based tools, training for local staff and direct support to organizations/responsible officers in developing action plans.

Education programmes for medical directors/responsible officers

The National Clinical Assessment Service will provide education programmes for medical directors/responsible officers and their professional equivalents on tackling performance concerns locally. While continuing its existing programme of educational events, NCAS is developing a portfolio of initial training and ongoing professional development in areas of its expertise and experience, which will be available to medical directors preparing for their roles as responsible officers.

Areas covered will include:

- handling performance concerns
- undertaking investigations
- handling concerns about a practitioner's health
- handling concerns about a practitioner's behaviour.

All the services discussed in this section, NCAS believes, will contribute significantly to the successful implementation of professional revalidation, both keeping the development of maximum expertise at the frontline and ensuring a cost-effective approach.

Key points

Support for doctors in difficulty

- Being the subject of an investigation is stressful and potentially damaging. Doctors should be offered help and supported through the process.
- As well as local occupational health services, help and support are available through the doctor's own GP and other organizations (the NCAS publication *Handling Concerns about a Practitioner's Health* contains a list of resources).
- NCAS can provide support and training for medical directors and those taking on additional responsible officer roles.

Conclusion

It is rare for doctors in active practice to get into difficulties sufficient to need help outside of their team or organization, whether from NCAS or the regulator – year on year, this is the case for just over 1 per cent of doctors. It is also clear from the international literature that the difficulties experienced by this group are complex and do not lend themselves to straightforward processes. It is equally clear that the difficulties themselves have a big impact on public confidence in the health services. The experience of NCAS over its 10 years has consistently demonstrated that what lies behind concerns about professional practice is frequently more deep-seated and complex than at first sight: in essence, 'what you think you are looking at may not be what you are seeing'.

In any individual health organization or health economy, those responsible for professional governance will find themselves dealing only rarely with such established difficulties and will be under pressure to deal with them quickly, smoothly and assuredly. No one finding themselves dealing with such challenges, therefore, should be afraid to seek help.

Any successful approach to dealing with concerns about practice has some key elements at its heart. Tackling concerns with a view to resolving them must be built on the practitioner in context: the team, the organization and the relationship between these and the practitioner's working and personal life. The most successful resolution of concerns will therefore be built on a workplace-based approach, whether that is at the earliest stages of clarifying the concerns, at the most complex intervention of assessment across the full scope of practice, or in building an action plan to get back on track. Second, one of the most important building blocks of a successful process is an open and constructive relationship with the relevant professional association. Practitioners should be strongly encouraged to engage the support of their professional association, and employers or contractors should work with them as constructively as possible. This will significantly streamline the process and may well result in a much earlier and more amicable resolution. And finally, at each stage of the process, it is essential to keep all parties engaged. Premature or inappropriate use of adversarial interventions is likely to stiffen attitudes and even drive key parties away. In that setting, the first to suffer may well be the patients, closely followed by the practitioners themselves.

Summary

❑ Year on year, only 1 per cent of doctors get into difficulties sufficient to need help outside of their team or organization, whether from NCAS or the regulator.

❑ The experience of NCAS over its 10 years has consistently demonstrated that what lies behind concerns about professional practice is frequently more deep-seated and complex than at first sight: in essence, 'what you think you are looking at may not be what you are seeing'.

❑ Tackling concerns with a view to resolving them must be built on the practitioner in context: the team, the organization and the relationship between these and the practitioner's working and personal life.

❑ The most successful resolution of concerns will be built on a workplace-based approach, whether that is at the earliest stages of clarifying the concerns, at the most complex intervention of assessment across the full scope of practice, or in building an action plan to get back on track.

❏ One of the most important building blocks of a successful process is an open and constructive relationship with the relevant professional association.

❏ At each stage of the process, it is essential to keep all parties engaged. Premature or inappropriate use of adversarial interventions is likely to stiffen attitudes and even drive key parties away.

References

1. Donaldson LJ (1994). Doctors with problems in an NHS workforce. *Br Med J* 308, 1277.
2. National Clinical Assessment Service (2011). *Concerns about Professional Practice and Associations with Age, Gender, Place of Qualification and Ethnicity – 2009/10 Data*. Available from: http://www.ncas.nhs.uk/
3. Paice E, Orton V (2004). Early signs of the trainee in difficulty. *Hosp Med* 65, 238–40.
4. National Clinical Assessment Service. Website: http://www.ncas.nhs.uk
5. Department of Health (2004). *Maintaining High Professional Standards in the Modern NHS*. Available from: http://www.dh.gov.uk/
6. *Mezey v South West London & St George's Mental Health NHS Trust* [2007], EWHC 62.
7. National Audit Office (2003). *The Management of Suspensions of Clinical Staff in NHS Hospital and Ambulance Trusts in England*. London: The Stationery Office.
8. National Clinical Assessment Service (2011) *Use of NHS Exclusion and Suspension from Work amongst Doctors and Dentists. 2010/11 Mid-year Report*. Available from: http://www.ncas.nhs.uk/
9. Department of Health (2004). *Primary Care Medical Performers Lists. Delivering Quality in Primary Care. Advice for Primary Care Trusts on List Management*. Available from: http://www.dh.gov.uk/
10. Department of Health (2004). *Maintaining High Professional Standards in the Modern NHS*. Part IV, para 6. Available from: http://www.dh.gov.uk/
11. See, for example, *Kulkarni v Milton Keynes Hospital NHS Foundation Trust and Another* [2009] EWCA (Civ) 789 and R on application of Secretary of State for Health v Knowsley NHS PCT [2006] EWHC 26 para 68.
12. Wu A (2000). Medical error: the second victim. *Br Med J* 320, 726–7.

Chapter 15

Medical education and training

Simon Gregory

Introduction

It is sometimes easy to think of medical education as an add-on, something that happens by osmosis alongside patient care. In truth, medical education and training are key to the safe and effective delivery of both current and future patient care. As Sir John Temple wrote in his 2010 review of the impact of the European Working Time Directive on the quality of training: 'Training is patient safety for the next 30 years.'[1] And as the Goodenough report stated many decades before that, in 1944: 'Properly planned and carefully conducted medical education is the foundation of a comprehensive health service.'[2]

Medicine is a highly popular and respected profession, with applications to medical school continuing to be very high despite the long, and now very expensive, university course, and the difficulty of gaining entry. To be responsible for and to guide their development are considerable privileges. Medical management in education and training is about service: service to patients and service to those who serve them. We manage this by common consent and while we do this as part of the NHS and in accordance with the expectations of the UK regulator of medicine and medical education, the General Medical Council (GMC), it can only be achieved due to the generous efforts, goodwill and support of all who are involved in medical education. Thus leadership in medical education is 'servant leadership'. This chapter seeks to help those readers who aspire to serve and to encourage others to consider serving in education roles.

Teaching, training or education?

The terms teaching, training and education are often used interchangeably, but it is important to differentiate them if we are to truly understand the role of the medical manager in the pedagogical realm of developing doctors, or, more accurately, in assisting and supporting their development. Teaching typically refers to a didactic imparting of knowledge. As Moore wrote:[3]

> Training … means a narrowly focused programme that leads to high proficiency in a specific skill. It prepares a student for a particular job or activity but provides neither broad perspective nor flexibility of approach. Education enables students to see the forest and the trees.

The volume of medical knowledge is so vast that it is impossible for individuals to ever learn it all. Indeed the rate of publication of research, and thus the creation of new knowledge, is such that no one person will have the capacity to keep up to date. Education is the development of a knowledge base. As Samuel Johnson said: 'Knowledge is of two kinds. We know a subject ourselves, or we know where we can find information on it'.[4] It is not sufficient merely to train doctors. While that training is vital, they must also have a sound knowledge base and a desire and ability always to adapt and challenge this with new information in order to strive to be the best doctor that they can be. In short they must be continually educated. The role of the manager is to provide the environment in which this education is possible and to ensure that students/trainees are provided with sufficient learning opportunities, that they are supported, that their progression is managed and, where necessary, that performance issues are identified and addressed. Medical education and training are based on a pedagogical model and the management of this education and training builds upon that pedagogy.

History

It is not within the scope of this chapter to consider the entire history of medical education, not least because this will be as old as the history of medicine, but there are key developments in the twentieth and twenty-first centuries which form the basis for much of current medical education and therefore its management. While there have been significant developments on both sides of the Atlantic, even at UK medical education conferences the most commonly quoted report into medical education is the Carnegie Foundation's Flexner report of 1910. This report, among other achievements, led to the regulation of American medical schools and the creation of a science-based curriculum with pre-clinical and clinical elements.[5] But there have been numerous reports, reforms, initiatives and consequent developments in the UK.

These started in 1881 with the GMC's report on education and examination, which outlined requirements for medical schools in the UK, including the subject areas to be included in the undergraduate curriculum. Among many reports, the Goodenough report[2] of 1944 made seminal recommendations about the structure, organization and funding of medical schools and their curricula. It was this report that initiated the pre-registration year, which continues as the first year of the Foundation Programme. It also highlighted the importance of high-quality teaching staff and the organization of teaching as a clinical division with an academic head. The GMC further reviewed medical training in 1957. This signalled a change in emphasis from the memorization of factual data to encouraging critical study and thought.

With the advent of the NHS in 1948 came reform of postgraduate training, including regional training centres under the leadership of postgraduate deans (deaneries). These are often seen as arising from the Christchurch Conference in 1961, although the first deanery was created in 1945. It is perhaps not surprising that this was in the same city that the Christchurch Conference took place: Oxford.

In 1968 a Royal Commission issued the most significant, and perhaps the most lengthy and thorough, report on medical education in the UK, the Todd report.[6] This report was way ahead of its time and many of the recommendations took decades to be fully implemented. This report stated a need for significant curriculum reform. It also advocated speciality registration, noted the establishment of the Central Committee for Postgraduate Medical Education (in 1967) and proposed that the GMC take on responsibility for postgraduate medical education as it had for undergraduate medical education. This latter recommendation was finally fully realized in April 2010.

Undergraduate medical education has been transformed during the last 20 years, for two reasons. First, as the wealth of medical knowledge has expanded, it has exceeded that which it is possible to include in the undergraduate curriculum. Second, it was observed that students entering medical school as bright young individuals were rapidly becoming disillusioned.[7] As a result of these things, the GMC has led reforms of undergraduate medical education and facilitated the incorporation of modern methods of teaching and learning with the publication of *Tomorrow's Doctors* in 1993 (with two revision documents in 2003 and 2009),[8] in which it set the standards for knowledge, skills and behaviours that medical students should learn at UK medical schools and the outcomes they should achieve.

Postgraduate training has undergone radical reform over the last 18 years, beginning with the changes brought in by Kenneth Calman in 1993 when he was Chief Medical Officer. These changes created focused specialist training with competitive entry, national training numbers, continuity of training, trainee supervision, performance assessment and certification at the end of training. These reforms were built upon with the advent of 'Modernising Medical Careers' (MMC) and its subsequent revisions after the 2007 Medical Training Application Service (MTAS) debacle, the ill-fated national junior doctor recruitment process that saw many junior doctors (and their families and supporters) distressed and which caused a national outcry. MMC sought to reform medical education and training to speed up the production of competent specialists based upon the Foundation Programme and, among many other changes, centralized selection into 'run-through' specialist training. The 2007 review under the leadership of Sir John Tooke[9] made many recommendations, which, like the Todd report, seem to be slow in their implementation but offer much wisdom about the general direction of postgraduate training.

These recommendations and subsequent developments are shaping the role of management in postgraduate medical training, including professional leadership, an accountability structure, a broad-based platform and increased flexibility. This latter recommendation is very much needed, as the current systems are inflexible, constraining doctors in training and lacking adaptability to the changing needs of the NHS and the patients it serves. The challenge for the next decade for medical education is to ensure the highest quality of medical graduates and specialists while also ensuring that, as far as possible, they are adaptable and continually developing.

Key points

History

- Medical education is the foundation of a comprehensive health service.
- The volume of medical knowledge is too vast for individuals to retain it all.
- Medical education and training have undergone considerable reform over the last century, in particular during the last three decades.
- Greater flexibility is required to adapt to the needs of health services.

Structure of training

The current structure of medical training in the UK is complex. Figure 15.1 illustrates this complexity. In some ways this brings diversity of opportunity, but in postgraduate education the reforms have stalled and the intended flexibility has not yet materialized. Undergraduate education is normally of 4–6 years' duration with the shorter length of training being undertaken by graduate entrants and the longer training being undertaken by students doing an intercalated Bachelor's degree or a preclinical course in the format of a medical and veterinary sciences tripos.

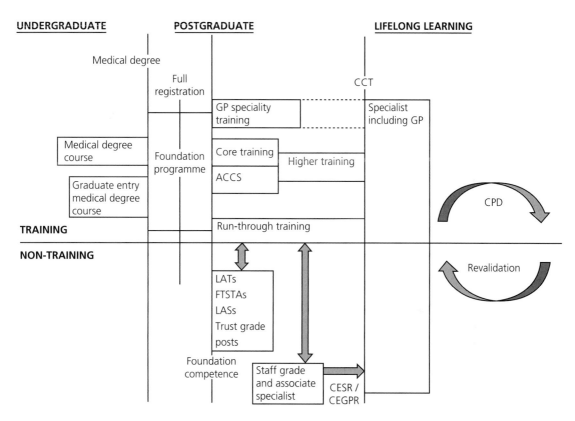

Figure 15.1 The structure of medical training in the UK in 2011. ACCS, acute common core stem; CCT, Certificate of Completion of Training; CESR, Certificate of Eligibility for Specialist Registration; CEGPR, Certificate of Eligibility for General Practice Registration; CPD, continuing professional development; FTSTA, fixed term specialist training appointment; LAS, locum appointment for service; LAT, locum appointments for training.

Upon qualification, new doctors enter the Foundation Programme, a 2-year programme with a defined curriculum and assessments. While full registration is normally gained at the end of the pre-registration year, successful completion of the full programme is required to be eligible to enter speciality training.

Since the Tooke review, speciality training has been in two formats. One format is 'run-through training', in which, once selected and subject to successful progress, trainees continue in this

training programme until they gain their certificate of completion of training (CCT), e.g. obstetrics and gynaecology or general practice. The other format came about after the MMC/MTAS problems, when some specialities 'uncoupled'. These specialities have separate curricula for core and higher training, e.g. surgery, medicine and psychiatry. They have competitive selection into both core and higher training with no guarantee of progression between the two and, in some cases, there is currently a significant numerical mismatch between the two. It should be noted that there is a common core curriculum (acute common core stem) that permits progression into anaesthetics, acute medicine and emergency medicine. There are plans for other core curricula but progress towards these has been painfully slow.

Not all doctors are in training programmes or specialists holding a CCT; some may be in non-training grades. These include service posts at equivalent pay levels to doctors in training, often referred to as 'trust grade posts', locum appointments for service (LASs), locum appointments for training (LATs) and fixed term specialist training appointments (FTSTAs). The latter were created for the transition to MMC and were originally only intended to exist for 2 years. But some remain, which has impeded the necessary decisions required to rebalance training numbers to future workforce need and perhaps given some junior doctors unrealistic expectations of career progression in their chosen speciality. LAT and FTSTA posts can contribute, under certain circumstances, to progression towards a CCT, but service posts may not. Many doctors continue to provide excellent service to patients in staff grade and associate specialist posts (SAS). While not part of recognized training programmes, if doctors in non-training grades wish to gain the equivalent of a CCT, they can apply to the GMC for equivalent recognition.[1] Deaneries now receive some funding to support SAS doctors, which may include continuing professional development or support in preparing for equivalent recognition (although it cannot fund the costs of that process).

Medical revalidation is apparently soon to be upon us although there have been many delays in its implementation and it is clear that the systems proposed are still not fit for purpose (see Chapter 16). But already this and the introduction of appraisal (especially NHS appraisal) have brought a renewed focus on continuing professional development. This renewed focus, roles in revalidation and the need to support those who cannot readily revalidate will create new training and support responsibilities for both educators and medical managers, including those who are managing medical education.

Roles

There are many roles available to doctors (and other professions) who wish to be involved in medical education. Although there is a hierarchy of careers in medical education, it would be folly to think that this implies greater importance of the roles higher up the structures. Returning to the model of servant leadership and leadership by common consent, it should be recognized that the most vital roles are those of the teachers and trainers in immediate contact with medical students and junior doctors. It is in these roles that the real impact on the development and careers of our charges is achieved. However, these roles are not within the remit of this chapter, as the focus of this book is on medical management.

In each role the medical educator, in fact, balances three roles: those of manager, leader and educator (Fig. 15.2). At different times, various elements need to be to the fore, but to be a successful medical educator, all three have to be present and developed. Furthermore, in each of these three roles there will be many mundane roles to be fulfilled that can be formulaic and monotonous, yet are vital. But these should not overpower the need for passion and vision if medical education is to be continually

refreshed to adapt to developments in medicine and to our changing society. In short, managers in medical education need to be both 'mechanics and prophets'.[2]

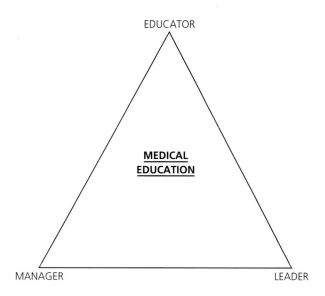

Figure 15.2 The medical education professional triangle.

The wide variety of roles differs greatly between medical schools and deaneries and between the primary and secondary/tertiary care arenas. Stylized versions of the career paths are shown in Figures 15.3–15.5 in order to illustrate the opportunities available. From the bottom to the top of each diagram, the balance between educator and manager/leader changes, with the more pure educator roles at the bottom.

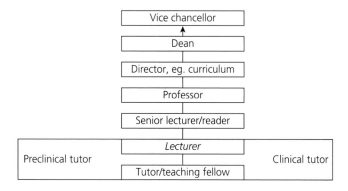

Figure 15.3 The undergraduate medical educator career pathway.

There has long been a clear career structure within undergraduate medicine and in the primary care elements of postgraduate medicine. But a career structure within secondary care postgraduate medicine has only gained greater clarity over the last 5 years with the development of career pathways within deaneries supported by thinking from the National Association of Clinical Tutors[10] and the Postgraduate Medical Education and Training Board (PMETB, now subsumed into the

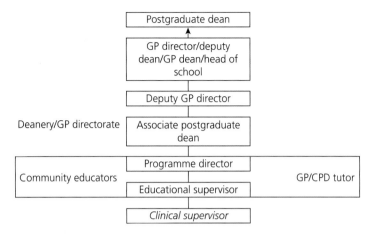

Figure 15.4 The postgraduate GP medical educator career pathway.

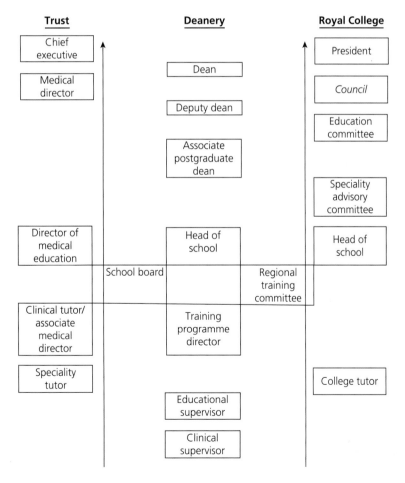

Figure 15.5 The secondary and tertiary care postgraduate medical educator career pathway.

GMC following the merger of the two organizations in April 2010). The roles of clinical supervisors, educational supervisors and training programme directors (TPDs) are summarized within the *Reference Guide for Postgraduate Specialty Training in the UK*.[11] Details of the person specifications and job descriptions for TPDs, heads of school and associate postgraduate deans are available from many deanery websites.

The management and leadership elements of the senior educator roles are increasing with many competing pressures, including the need to ensure robust selection, curriculum delivery, rotation planning, assessment and progression management, handling of performance concerns, alignment with the needs and workings of the wider NHS (not least service provision) and budgetary management (often of many millions of pounds). This budgetary role will become increasingly hard given the impact of the current financial ischaemia, which is manifested in the changes to undergraduate funding, including increasing student fees and 'flat cash' for postgraduate training budgets, which will effectively mean real-term reductions in trainee numbers. Additionally there are the pressures of educating and managing within an increasingly litigious society. Many medical schools and deaneries are now on the receiving end of threats and actual litigation, including lawsuits, employment tribunals and judicial reviews.

Key points

Structure of training

- UK medical training is complex.
- There are many different career paths that do not all lead to a common end point.
- There is a wide variety of medical education roles.
- The roles of clinical and educational supervision are especially important.
- Managers in medical education need to be both prophet and mechanic.

Medical education as a discipline

With increasing structure and complexity there has been an increasing recognition that the role of the educator and the role of the medical manager in education are professional roles in themselves. As such medical education is developing as a discipline in its own right. There are many associations, societies and groups seeking to support medical educators and to advance medical education (see Table 15.1).

Recognizing the greater complexity and professionalization of the educator role, the Academy of Medical Educators (AoME) was established in 2006 with the aim of providing a focus for all concerned in the education of medical students and doctors. Its aims are to advance medical education by the development of a curriculum and qualification system, undertaking research for the continuing development of professional medical education and the promotion and dissemination of best practice in medical education.

Table 15.1 Organizations that support and develop medical education

Organization	Website	Synopsis	Journal
Association for the Study of Medical Education (ASME)	www.asme.org.uk	Forum for debate and exchange of information, to promote knowledge and expertise in medical education	Medical Education Clinical Teacher
Association for Medical Education in Europe (AMEE)	www.amee.org	International organization for medical educators and researchers	Medical Teacher
National Association of Clinical Tutors (NACT UK)	www.nact.org.uk	An association for those involved in postgraduate training of doctors, mainly secondary care focus	Clinical Tutor
National Association of Primary Care Educators (NAPCE)[a]	www.napce.net	A multi-professional network of primary care educators	
UK Association of Programme Directors (UKAPD)[a]	www.ukapd.org	The national body of GP Specialty Training Programme directors	
United Kingdom Conference of Postgraduate Educational Advisers in General Practice (UKCEA)	www.ukcea.net	The membership body of GP associate postgraduate deans (associate advisers) and GP directors/deans	
Medical Schools Council	www.medschools. ac.uk	Forum and cooperation body representing UK medical schools	
Conference of General Practice Education Directors (CoGPED)	www.cogped.org.uk	Forum of GP directors, GP deans and GP heads of school	
Conference of Postgraduate Medical Deans of the United Kingdom (COPMeD)	www.copmed.org.uk	Forum of postgraduate deans	
Academy of Medical Educators (AoME)	www.medicaleducators. org	The professional organization for all involved in medical education	

[a] UKAPD and NAPCE have announced their intention to merge.

Standards in medical teaching and training

In the pursuit of its objectives, the AoME has developed professional standards.[12] These apply to medical educators and equally to those who manage medical education. These have been mapped to the standards of the GMC and the Higher Education Academy. These standards are divided into six themes with the central purpose of 'improving clinical care through teaching excellence' (see Box 15.1). Theme 6 – the educational management and leadership theme – includes descriptors of three levels of standards of educational management, educational leadership and educational governance.

> **Box 15.1** Academy of Medical Educators – professional standards
>
> - Theme 1 – Values of medical educators
> - Theme 2 – Educational scholarship
> - Theme 3 – Teaching and supporting learners
> - Theme 4 – Assessment and feedback to learners
> - Theme 5 – Design and planning of learning activities
> - Theme 6 – Educational management and leadership

These professional standards have the potential to form the basis of a curriculum for a discipline of medical education – and, in the context of this chapter, theme 6 in particular forms the focus for the professional standards of those involved in educational management and leadership. The standards also form the basis of the current GMC work on developing the accreditation standards the council will require for the approval of educators (GMC trainer approval). These professional standards fit well with the Medical Leadership Competency Framework (see Chapter 3).

As mentioned earlier, since April 2010 the GMC has taken over regulatory responsibility for the continuum of medical education. As the GMC itself states: 'The GMC is responsible for the regulation of education and training throughout a doctor's career, from medical school, through the Foundation Programme and specialty training, including general practice training programmes, to continuing professional development.'[13] It hopes to ensure consistency of expectations and standards.

The GMC sets out the duties of a doctor. In so doing, it is explicit that these duties apply equally to roles in medical education and training, and that those who are in educator and managerial roles are personally responsible for their professional practice and must be able to justify their decisions and actions.

In *Tomorrow's Doctors*,[8] the GMC sets out the standards expected of medical schools and encourages medical educators to develop the future doctor as a scientist and a scholar, as a practitioner and as a professional. In *The Trainee Doctor*,[13] the GMC outlines the standards expected of postgraduate training. In both documents the GMC sets out its expectations and standards within nine domains (see Table 15.2). As can be seen from the table, while there are subtle differences of wording, there is more in common than there are differences between the AoME and GMC standards. Although the bulk of the standards are mandatory, the documents also include developmental standards. It is clear not only that high standards are expected but also that there is an explicit expectation of continuous quality improvement.

In addition to meeting these GMC standards, we should expect and uphold the standards required of all doctors as outlined in *Good Medical Practice*.[14] As medical managers leading medical education, we have a duty to link with other quality systems. The plethora of standards expected of doctors in general, and medical educators in particular, can be overwhelming but many of these overlap as they centre on maintaining high professional standards. Table 15.3 illustrates areas of similarity.

Table 15.2 General Medical Council standards

Domain	Undergraduate	Postgraduate
1	Patient safety	Patient safety
2	Quality assurance, review and evaluation	Quality management, review and evaluation
3	Equality, diversity and opportunity	Equality, diversity and opportunity
4	Student selection	Recruitment, selection and appointment
5	Design and delivery of the curriculum, including assessment	Delivery of approved curriculum, including assessment
6	Support and development of students, teachers and the local faculty	Support and development of trainees, trainers and local faculty
7	Management of teaching, learning and assessment	Management of education and training
8	Educational resources and capacity	Educational resources and capacity
9	Outcomes	Outcomes

Table 15.3 A comparison between the standards required by the General Medical Council (GMC) of all doctors and of educators and the Academy of Medical Educators' (AoME) professional standards [a]

AoME professional standards [12]	Good Medical Practice 2010 [14]	The Trainee Doctor, 'standards for postgraduate training' [13]
1.1 Professional integrity	Paras 56–59 – Being honest and trustworthy	
1.2 Respect for patients	Paras 20–21 – The doctor–patient partnership	Domain 1.1 – Care of patients is first concern, 1.2–1.3 and 1.10–1.11 Supervision
1.3 Respect for learners	Paras 17–19 – Teaching and training, appraising and assessing	Domain 1.2–1.3 – Supervision
1.4 Continuing professional development	Paras 12–13 – Keeping up to date	Domain 6 – Support and development of trainees, trainers and local faculty
1.5 Equality of opportunity and diversity	Para 46 – Respect for colleagues (paras 7–10 [b] – Decisions about access to medical care)	Domain 3 – Equality, diversity and opportunity Domain 4 – Recruitment, selection and appointment
1.6 Commitment to medical education	Para 14 – Maintaining and improving your performance	Domain 6 – Support and development of trainees, trainers and local faculty

Continued

Table 15.3 Continued

AoME professional standards[12]	Good Medical Practice 2010[14]	The Trainee Doctor, 'standards for postgraduate training'[13]
2 Educational scholarship	Paras 12–14 – Keeping up to date and maintaining and improving your performance Paras 70–71 – Research	
3 Supporting learners	Paras 15–17 – Teaching and training, appraising and assessing	Domain 5 – Delivery of approved curriculum including assessment Domain 6 – Support and development of trainees, trainers and local faculty
4 Assessment and feedback to learners	Paras 15 and 17–19 – Teaching and training, appraising and assessing	Domain 5 – Delivery of approved curriculum including assessment
5 Design and planning of learning activities	Para 16 – Teaching and training, appraising and assessing	Domain 8 – Educational resources and capacity
6 Educational management and leadership	Supplementary guidance – management for doctors paras 35–39	Domain 2 – Quality management, review and evaluation Domain 7 – Management of education and training
		Domain 5.3 – Specific requirement that all delivering education and training should reinforce good medical practice

[a]Since this chapter was written, the AoME has revised its standards and the GMC has consulted on the approval of trainers. This table is based upon the original AoME standards.

[b]Standards shown in parenthesis (e.g. paras 7–10) denote standards that apply to patient care that are sufficiently similar to standards for educators to warrant inclusion. The standards the GMC requires of undergraduate and postgraduate education are very similar to those shown in Table 15.2. Only the standards for postgraduate training are shown in this table for clarity. They are very similar to the 'Standards for the delivery of teaching, learning and assessment' as specified in *Tomorrow's Doctors*.[8]

Key points

Medical education as a discipline

- Medical education is developing as a discipline in its own right.
- The Academy of Medical Educators has developed professional standards for medical education.
- The GMC has outlined nine domains of quality in medical education, including the management of teaching, learning and assessment/education and training (domain 7).

Revalidation

With the advent of revalidation for all doctors comes an added responsibility for postgraduate deans. Whereas medical directors will be the responsible officers (ROs) for non-training grade doctors in their trusts/primary care trusts (PCTs), deans are to be the RO for all doctors in training. (Note, however, that the successor to RO once PCTs are abolished is yet to be determined.) This RO role is a mammoth responsibility. While there are already systems in place for assessment, including workplace-based assessment (WPBA), and for evaluation of progression in training (Annual Review of Competence Progression (ARCP) including ARCP panels), these will need to be much improved if they are to satisfy the requirements of the GMC with the educational supervision meetings and reports delivering the required elements of enhanced NHS appraisal. In addition, the transfer of information between medical schools and deaneries, from deanery to deanery, employer to employer, and especially between employers and the deanery (two-way), will be essential. The integrity of any information pertaining to performance, conduct and health will be vital if the processes are to be trustworthy and competent. As the professional registration of the deans and the medical directors will be dependent upon their RO role, and no doubt lawyers will be circling, we must all work together to achieve the best systems that we can.

There will be an increasing focus on identifying performance concerns and on remediation. The handling of under-performance is rapidly becoming a role in its own right. Aspects of the role will include identification of issues of under-performance, exclusion of alleged under-performance, remediation and support. These roles will link closely to the support of continuing professional development of all doctors.

Career guidance

There is a mismatch between the career expectations and aspirations of sixth-form students, medical students and junior doctors and the current and future needs of the NHS. This is further complicated by the historical poor quality of workforce planning. That said, workforce planning is always going to be difficult. Twenty years ago there was advice that respiratory medicine was going to shrink considerably with the decline of tuberculosis and that cardiothoracic surgery would expand due to the impact of ischaemic heart disease and an ageing, obese population. Both predictions have been proved wrong, as was the workforce planning linked to them.

Application and selection data over recent years have shown a considerable mismatch between aspirations and vacancies/national training numbers. In particular, far more junior doctors wish to pursue surgical careers than are needed, and far too few apply for psychiatric training. This mismatch leads to under-provision in what are termed shortage specialities and increasing disappointment and disillusionment among doctors aspiring to over-subscribed specialities. The NHS cannot afford to train doctors it does not require in certain specialities while there are vacancies in other specialities. Any doctor can aspire to be what they desire, but it is the responsibility of a tax-funded education system to train, as best as can be predicted, only those numbers and specialities that are needed by the NHS. It is a considerable task helping students and doctors to understand the career choices available to them and supporting them in making informed decisions.

Career decisions need to be based upon robust workforce planning. It is hoped that the relatively new Centre for Workforce Intelligence will provide robust data and predictions upon which to plan the future workforce.

Some doctors make career choices that, for a variety of reasons, are not appropriate or become inappropriate. It is currently too difficult to transfer between specialities and there is insufficient support for making such changes. This is wasteful and an inability to admit inappropriate career choices or to remedy them makes disillusionment and litigation more likely.

There is clearly a need for robust careers guidance and management.

Educator career development

Historically, any consultant could reasonably expect to have a firm of junior doctors attached and therefore to be an educator. In reality, some consultants were educators but many junior doctors only experienced apprenticeship-style learning. Although this approach has its strengths, it is not sufficient. The firm structure has largely disappeared thanks to changes associated with the New Deal and the European Working Time Regulations (formerly Directive) and the expansion of the consultant workforce. Similarly, there has been a considerable expansion in medical student numbers and of the requirements of the curriculum. There has also been much greater use of non-teaching hospitals and community placements.

These changes and the increasing expectations of medical educators are leading to a necessary professionalization of the medical educator workforce. This was led by innovative GP trainer courses but is now widespread, with many 'teaching the teachers' courses and the development of courses encouraging study at Master's level (Box 15.2).

Box 15.2 Examples of medical educator and manager learning opportunities

Medical education courses

- Teaching the teachers (www.londondeanery.ac.uk)
- Teaching the teachers to teach (www.eoedeanery.nhs.uk)
- Effective teaching skills (http://events.rcplondon.ac.uk/)
- Medical education – MMEd, MA/MSc/PG Dip (www.dundee.ac.uk, www.dmu.ac.uk, www.beds.ac.uk, www.keele.ac.uk, www.cardiff.ac.uk)

Leadership in medical education courses

- Developing leaders in healthcare education (www.asme.org.uk)
- Leading innovations in healthcare and education (www.harvardmacy.org)

Similarly the expectations of medical managers have increased, including managers of medical education, and development opportunities for those managers have similarly increased. While some have undertaken Master's in Business Administration (MBA) courses and other higher degrees with management elements, others have participated in leadership programmes (examples of these are also shown in Box 15.2).

For those not wishing to undertake formal study or a dedicated educator course, there are many other resources available, including many excellent books (see Box 15.3) and the many journals and websites listed in Table 15.1.

> **Box 15.3** Additional medical education resources
>
> - *Medical Education and Training: from Theory to Delivery*. Carter Y, Jackson N (Oxford University Press)
> - *Cost Effectiveness in Medical Education*. Walsh K (Radcliffe)
> - *Educational Leadership*. McKimm J, Swanwick T (www.asme.org.uk)
> - *Understanding Medical Education: Evidence, Theory and Practice*. Swanwick T (Wiley-Blackwell)
> - *Medical Education: Theory and Practice*. Dornan T, Mann K, Scherpbier A, Spencer J (Churchill Livingstone)
> - *A Practical Guide for Medical Teachers*. Dent JA, Harden RM (Churchill Livingstone)

Key points

Career guidance

- There is a considerable mismatch between the career aspirations of doctors in training and the needs of health services.
- Workforce planning is notoriously difficult.
- High-quality career guidance, trainee flexibility and adaptable career structures will be vital.
- Educator professional development will also be increasingly important, given the ever-increasing expectations of them.

Quality

Ensuring a high quality of education and of patient care is key to the role of managers in medical education and training. These managers work under the auspices of the GMC's Quality Improvement Framework,[15] which covers medical education and training. Through this framework and using a variety of evidence and processes, the GMC assures education and training but makes explicit the duty of medical schools and deaneries to manage the quality of their courses and programmes, and of local education providers to ensure robust quality control.

But the quality responsibility of medical education managers is broader than this. Education and training do not occur in isolation. Quality as it relates to medical education can be considered under the following headings:

- the quality of the training course or programme regarding curriculum delivery and support
- the quality of care provided by students or trainees and their fitness to practise
- the quality of the educational environment
- the quality of patient care achieved by the service and educational provider.

There is rightly an increasing focus on the links to the quality of care provided to patients. There is a two-way quality relationship. Medical education quality processes provide valuable insights into the quality of the healthcare environment and the service provided therein. Healthcare provider quality assurance processes similarly can provide information about the care provided for students/trainees and their educational environment and opportunities.

Research and evidence base

Thanks to the efforts of medical education researchers supported and encouraged by the Association for the Study of Medical Education (ASME) and the Association for Medical Education in Europe (AMEE), among others, there is an increasing evidence base supporting medical teaching and training. Similar to the evidence-based medicine movement, medical education is supported by the Best Evidence in Medical Education (BEME) collaboration (www2.warwick.ac.uk/fac/med/beme). However, the evidence base is much smaller and weaker than is required. There is insufficient funding and infrastructure for medical education research, too much medical education is delivered purely on a historical basis and perhaps too much has been changed on a fashionable whim rather than being an evidence-based decision. As Prystowsky and Bordage[16] stated: 'An important mission of medical education is to educate trainees to provide excellent patient care, yet there is little research published on the effect of medical education on patient outcomes.' They further state that 'leading journals in medical education contain limited information concerning the cost and products of medical education' and conclude: 'It behoves medical education researchers to evaluate more fully the effects of medical education on the entire spectrum of participants and outcomes.' The standards and scope of research into medical education are not yet sufficient. As medical managers responsible for the use of vast sums of public funding and the careers of current and future doctors, the challenge, despite the current financial climate, or perhaps because of this climate, is to raise the standards of this research and to strive to continually raise the standards of medical teaching and training. We must apply the same academic rigour as we apply to medical treatments given that those medical treatments are in the control of those for whom we are responsible.

Challenges

Many of the challenges that face managers in medical education have already been mentioned, including the pressures of financial restrictions and the consequent impact on training numbers, the impact of medical revalidation and the greater responsibility to identify and deal with performance concerns.

A greater and ongoing challenge is that medicine, and therefore medical education, needs to adapt to meet the needs and expectations of those whom we serve and therefore must seek to understand and reflect societal change and ensure an appropriate medical workforce while maintaining our professional ethics and standards.

In common with other medical managers, one of the greatest challenges managers of medical education face, especially in the postgraduate sector, is the frequent, indeed almost continual, reorganization, and the uncertainty and inertia that this creates. While the ideal would be a significant period without such reorganizations, where we would be able to focus on delivery and assuring high-quality teaching and training, it would be naïve to expect that ever to be the case. The reality is that the taxpayer funds our roles and purpose, which are therefore subject to a control that is itself subject to the views of the electorate. As current leaders we must learn, and help our successors to learn, to cope with this constant change and uncertainty. Leadership in medicine is about providing vision and purpose in a constant state of flux.

> **Key points**
>
> Challenges
>
> - Quality of care and quality of education and training are interlinked and co-dependent.
> - The current medical education evidence base needs to be built upon with more high-quality research.
> - In common with healthcare in general medical education is continually challenged by financial stringency and relentless reorganization and reform. The skill of the exceptional leader in medical education is to deliver in spite of these or even using these as catalysts.

Conclusion

The scale of medical knowledge is too great for human recall. Medical education takes the brightest and the best our education system has to offer and normally helps to shape them into excellent doctors. Medical education is complex, with many different career paths and often aspirations that differ from what is realistic or achievable. Medical students and doctors in training need highly professional, well-managed educational programmes and environments which are quality-assured to the highest standards if they are to reach their full potential. To achieve this, professional medical educators led by excellent clinical leaders must support them. The responsibility for developing current and future doctors to be the best public servants that they can be and to provide the best healthcare that they can is a great privilege. It carries considerable responsibility and many challenges, but builds upon a proud tradition and strong foundations. It is a fabulous discipline in which to serve and ultimately to maximize the potential for high-quality care by the NHS.

> **Summary**
>
> ❏ Medical teaching and training are vital to the delivery of safe patient care both now and in the future.
> ❏ Medical training in the UK is complex and there are many roles involved in delivering and supporting it.
> ❏ Medical educators balance roles as managers, leaders and educators.
> ❏ There is increasing recognition that medical education is a discipline in and of itself.
> ❏ There are many opportunities for professional development, and while there are many challenges, medical education is a most rewarding area of medical management.

References

1. Temple J (2010). *Time for Training: A Review of the Impact of the European Working Time Directive on the Quality of Training*. London: HMSO.
2. The Goodenough Report (1944). *Report of the Inter-Departmental Committee on Medical Schools*. London: HMSO.
3. Moore JW (1998). Education versus training. *J Chem Educ* 75, 135.
4. Boswell J (1998). *Life of Johnson*. USA: Oxford University Press.

5. Flexner A (1910). *Medical Education in the United States and Canada: a Report to the Carnegie Foundation for the Advancement of Teaching.* New York: The Carnegie Foundation.

6. Todd (1968). Royal Commission on Medical Education (1965–1968). *Report to Parliament.* London: HMSO.

7. Fraser RC (1991). Undergraduate medical education: present state and future needs. *Br Med J* 303, 41–3.

8. General Medical Council (2009). *Tomorrow's Doctors: Standards for the Delivery of Teaching, Learning and Assessment.* London: GMC.

9. Tooke J (2007). *Aspiring to Excellence: Findings and Recommendations of the Independent Inquiry into Modernising Medical Careers.* London: HMSO.

10. National Association of Clinical Tutors (2007). *Proposals for the Organisation of Postgraduate Medical Education at Provider Level.* London: NACT.

11. NHS Medical Specialty Training (England) (2010). *The Gold Guide: A Reference Guide for Postgraduate Specialty Training in the UK*, 4th edn. Available from: www.mmc.nhs.uk/

12. Academy of Medical Educators (2009). *Professional Standards.* London: AoME.

13. General Medical Council (2011). *The Trainee Doctor: Foundation and Specialty, including GP Training.* London: GMC.

14. General Medical Council (2010). *Good Medical Practice.* London: GMC.

15. General Medical Council (2010). *Quality Improvement Framework.* London: GMC.

16. Prystowsky JB, Bordage G (2001). An outcomes research perspective on medical education: the predominance of trainee assessment and satisfaction. *Med Educ* 35, 331–6.

Chapter 16

Appraisals and revalidation

Jayaraman Thiagarajan

Introduction

The General Medical Council (GMC) was established as a registration and regulatory body for doctors by an Act of Parliament in 1858.[1] An attempt to review the functioning of the GMC in the modern era was undertaken in the 1970s by the Merrison Committee,[2] establishing the principles of self-regulation. The impetus for changes to medical regulation, in recent times, came through a series of highly publicized medical scandals, culminating in the watershed report of the Bristol Enquiry.[3-7] Introducing the concept of revalidation, this latter report stated:

> Periodic revalidation, whereby healthcare professionals demonstrate that they remain fit to practise in their chosen profession, should be compulsory for all healthcare professionals. The requirement to participate in periodic revalidation should be included in the contract of employment.

These inquiries and reports highlighted inadequacies on the part of individual doctors, systems of governance and regulation, resulting in failures of quality and safety of care. In 1997 the Labour government introduced the concept of clinical governance[8] in a move to improve quality and standards of care in the NHS. In 1999 the GMC took the first step towards revalidation, by stating that 'all doctors must be able to demonstrate regularly that they continue to be fit to practise in their chosen field'.[9] The clinical governance initiatives and early GMC revalidation arrangements were predicated on producing evidence and regular assessment through formal review of practices and clinical performance. An amendment of the Medical Act 1983 was passed in 2002 to permit revalidation as one of the functions of the GMC.[10] The fundamentals of how revalidation should be implemented and the concept of quality-assured formative and summative appraisals as the basis for revalidation were set out in the Chief Medical Officer's report, *Good Doctors, Safer Patients*.[11] The legal basis for the implementation of revalidation, including the concept of responsible officers (ROs) and GMC affiliates, was contained in the white paper *Trust, Assurance and Safety: The Regulation of Healthcare Professionals*.[12] The GMC's statement of intent[13] sets out the period for implementation of revalidation from autumn 2012. This chapter sets out what organizations and ROs need to have in place for revalidation to go live from next year.

The roles and responsibilities of the RO

The provisions of the Medical Profession (Responsible Officers) Regulations 2010 came into effect on 1 January 2011 (MPR).[14] It mandated that every designated body (i.e. organization) employing doctors in any role appoint a RO. Responsible officers have to be medical practitioners at the time of appointment with a minimum of 5 years' experience and remain as medical practitioners in order to discharge their duties as an RO.

Prescribed connection

The RO will be the vehicle through which doctors are revalidated. Regulation 12 of the MPR identifies the prescribed connections between an individual doctor and the RO of the appropriate designated body (see Fig. 16.1).

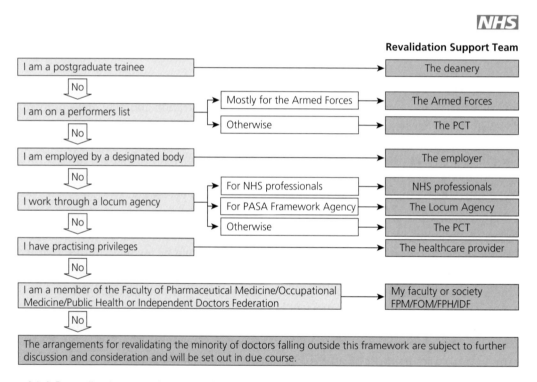

Figure 16.1 Prescribed connections – as described by the Revalidation Support Team. FOM, Faculty of Occupational Medicine; FPH, Faculty of Public Health; FPM, Faculty of Pharmaceutical Medicine; IDF, Independent Doctors Federation; PASA, Purchasing and Supply Agency.

A minority of doctors will fall outside the framework shown in the figure. The GMC in conjunction with Department of Health will issue guidance on how these doctors can be revalidated. The ROs will, in turn, relate to the strategic health authority (SHA) RO for the purposes of revalidation. The structure of prescribed connections as it stands today can be seen in Figure 16.2. This will be subject to change because of proposed organizational changes arising as a result of publication and subsequent modification of the white paper, *Equity and Excellence: Liberating the NHS*.[15]

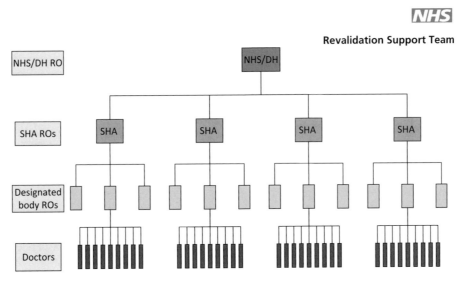

Figure 16.2 Structure of prescribed connections – as described by the Revalidation Support Team. DH, Department of Health; RO, responsible officer; SHA, strategic health authority.

Responsibilities of the RO

The RO's role straddles many functions. In effect, the RO sits at the interconnection between clinical governance and human resource functions as they relate to an individual doctor. The RO's responsibilities are outlined below.

In relation to *contracts of employment or contracts for the provision of services with medical practitioners*, the RO:

- ensures that medical practitioners have qualifications and experience appropriate for the work to be performed
- ensures that appropriate references are obtained and checked
- takes any steps necessary to verify the identity of medical practitioners
- where the designated body is a primary care trust, manages admission to the performers list in accordance with the regulations.

In relation to *communicating with the GMC*, the RO:

- cooperates with the GMC in carrying out its responsibilities
- makes recommendations to the GMC about doctors' fitness to practise, taking all relevant information into account
- where appropriate, refers concerns about the doctor to the GMC
- monitors a doctor's compliance with conditions imposed by or undertakings agreed with the GMC.

In relation to *monitoring medical practitioners' conduct and performance*, the RO:

- reviews regularly the general performance and quality information held by the designated body
- ensures relevant information relating to all the doctor's roles is available for monitoring fitness to practise and appraisal
- maintains records of all fitness-to-practise evaluations, including appraisals, investigations and assessments

- establishes a system for collating patient and colleague feedback for all doctors which complies with GMC requirements.

In relation to *appraisal*, the RO:

- ensures that the designated body maintains an appraisal system which complies with national guidance and requirements
- ensures that doctors can undertake annual appraisals
- ensures that appraisals take account of relevant information relating to all the doctor's roles.

In relation to *responding to concerns*, the RO:

- responds appropriately when variation in individual performance is identified, including:
  - taking any steps necessary to protect patients
  - establishing procedures to investigate concerns about the conduct, performance or fitness to practise of a doctor
  - initiating investigations with appropriately qualified investigators and ensuring that all relevant information is considered
- ensures that appropriate measures are taken to address concerns, including but not limited to:
  - requiring the doctor to undergo training or retraining
  - offering rehabilitation services
  - providing opportunities to increase the doctor's work experience
  - addressing any systemic issues within the designated body which may contribute to the concerns identified
- recommends to the designated body, where appropriate, that a doctor should be suspended or have conditions/restrictions placed on his or her practice
- ensures that any necessary further monitoring of the doctor's conduct, performance or fitness to practise is carried out
- ensures that a doctor who is subject to these procedures is kept informed about progress.

The RO:

- maintains records of all steps taken
- transfers relevant information and records to a new RO in a timely manner.

Second RO

The RO Regulations 2010 have provisions for the appointment of a second RO under the guidance and approval of the SHA RO. This is necessary where a designated body has identified issues of conflict of interest or appearance of bias between the RO and a medical practitioner in respect of whom the RO has responsibilities. The second RO will need to be from an external organization and will take on the role of RO for the doctor in question.

Resourcing and supporting the RO

The RO Regulations call for the provision of sufficient funds and other resources in discharging their duties as ROs. This will depend on current systems in place within a designated body, and on what needs to be in place to get the system ready for revalidation. Resources and support fall into three groups:

- intra-organizational
- regional – RO Network
- national – Revalidation Support Team (RST), GMC, Academy of Medical Royal Colleges (AOMRC).

Intra-organizational

To assess and plan organizational needs, the RST has requested designated bodies to complete an Organisational Readiness Self Assessment (ORSA).[16] Completing this enables a gap analysis, and an action plan to be produced. All designated bodies are expected to complete the ORSA on an annual basis, and both submit a board report and provide this for external inspection by bodies such as the Care Quality Commission (CQC). The ORSA can also be used by ROs as supporting documentation for the purposes of their own appraisal and revalidation and for external validation of the revalidation arrangements in place.

Meeting the new standards of appraisals that are subject to quality control both internally and through external agencies means that the numbers of appraisers in an organization will need to increase. The appraisers' role will become professionalized. This will necessitate a clear job description, selection and continued training, and support and development appraisers in their role. Revalidation will work or fail on the basis of how well appraisers do their job. This will therefore need resources in terms of personnel, time and money.

The functioning of clinical governance systems and their interaction with the appraisal process will require clear strategies in place. This includes the ability of the organization to provide individual practitioners with information pertaining to their practice that can be included in their appraisal folder, such as information pertaining to individual and team performance, serious incidents, complaints and compliments, audits, implementation of speciality-specific guideline/protocols and so on. Current systems may not be able to do this in a comprehensive manner. Designated bodies may need to invest in systems that can support individual doctors in this way.

Where designated bodies do not have a system of colleague and patient feedback, there is a need to roll this out and ensure that it integrates seamlessly with the appraisal process.

These requirements call for the provision of an electronic platform to make the process easier for individual doctors, for the organization and, ultimately, for the RO. As the current Department of Health toolkit is withdrawn and a plethora of private providers is in the market, a designated body will need to make a choice regarding this issue. A standard for the toolkits is expected to be issued by the RST in 2011 and will be helpful in making this choice.

All of the above necessitates making a business case for the roll-out of revalidation and identifying what is required internally within a designated body to implement it. This will be dictated by a gap analysis and an action plan derived from completing the ORSA.

Regional – RO Network

The role of the SHA RO is both to oversee the performance of ROs in the region and to support and help develop the ROs in their roles (see Box 16.1). The RO Network is the vehicle through which this will be delivered. The RO Network will include all the ROs of designated bodies in the SHA and the GMC employment liaison officer (ELO). The network will help ROs both to share the issues that concern them as regards revalidation and to deal with identified issues early, with peer support and expert advice as necessary. In particular, the ELO is expected to play a key role in helping ROs deal with issues pertaining to individual doctors. The ELO is also expected to advise on referral to the GMC when an RO feels they cannot safely recommend a doctor for revalidation. The RO Network will provide ongoing help and support to ROs in difficult areas and as issues crop up with the implementation of revalidation.

Box 16.1 Responsibilities of the strategic health authority's responsible officer (SHA RO) – as described by the revalidation support team

In relation to the RO's appraisal, the SHA RO takes reasonably practicable steps to ensure that:

- the RO undergoes regular appraisals
- appraisals are carried out by the body for which the medical practitioner is the responsible officer
- appraisals involve obtaining and taking account of all available information relating to the RO's fitness to practise during the appraisal period

In relation to monitoring the RO's conduct and performance, the SHA RO:

- ensures that the RO has established systems and procedures which will enable them to carry out their responsibilities effectively
- reviews regularly the general performance information held by the SHA, including clinical indicators relating to outcomes for patients
- takes all reasonably practicable steps to ensure that the designated body addresses issues arising from that information

In relation to evaluating the RO's fitness to practise, the SHA RO:

- takes all reasonably practicable steps to investigate concerns about the RO's fitness to practise raised by the RO's organization or arising from any other source
- where appropriate, refers concerns about the RO to the GMC
- monitors the RO's compliance with conditions imposed by or undertakings agreed with the GMC
- makes recommendations to the GMC about the RO's fitness to practise taking all relevant information into account
- maintains records of the RO's fitness to practise evaluations, including appraisals and any other investigations or assessments
- cooperates with the GMC in carrying out its responsibilities

In relation to responding to concerns about the RO, the SHA RO takes reasonably practicable steps to ensure that:

- procedures are in place to address concerns raised about the RO arising from any source
- the body for which the medical practitioner is the RO initiates investigations with appropriately qualified investigators
- any investigation into the conduct or performance of the RO takes into account all relevant matters
- any necessary further monitoring of the RO's conduct, performance or fitness to practise is carried out
- an RO who is subject to these procedures is kept informed about progress and their comments are taken into account where appropriate

In relation to responding to concerns about the RO, where appropriate the SHA RO:

- takes any necessary steps to protect patients
- recommends to the RO's employer that the RO should be suspended or have conditions or restrictions placed on his or her practice
- identifies concerns and ensures that appropriate measures are taken to address these, including but not limited to:
  - requiring the RO to undergo training or retraining
  - offering rehabilitation services
  - providing opportunities to increase the RO's work experience

National

Revalidation Support Team

The RST aims to support NHS organizations in the effective provision of revalidation and to support individual participation in appraisal and revalidation. It does this through partnership working with the Department of Health, the GMC and designated bodies. The RST's Programme of Work describes two key projects, including the production of a final medical appraisal guide (MAG) which will underpin revalidation and a project to support organizational readiness (ORSA) in England. In addition, there are two cross-cutting projects to support delivery of the RST's programme: Testing and Piloting (TaP) and Communications and Stakeholder Engagement.

General Medical Council

As a medical regulatory body, the GMC issues guidance pertaining to revalidation, such as *The Good Medical Practice Framework for Appraisal and Revalidation* and *Supporting Information for Appraisal and Revalidation*.[17,18] The GMC's statutory function also allows it to deal with fitness-to-practise issues that may arise from failure or non-engagement of a medical practitioner with respect to revalidation.

Academy of Medical Royal Colleges (AOMRC)

The AOMRC seeks to work with all the Royal Colleges and faculties to promote the sharing of skills, experience and knowledge on revalidation. It seeks to facilitate the Royal Colleges in setting up speciality-specific standards that will guide medical practitioners in developing their core skills and competencies in the discharge of their duties. This will also inform the appraisal discussion that is at the heart of revalidation.

Organizational responsibilities in getting to state of readiness

The GMC Revalidation: A Statement of Intent,[13] published in October 2010, outlines the need to test organizational readiness in summer 2012 before the formal launch of revalidation in late 2012. The role of the ORSA in helping designated bodies to identify priorities, develop action plans and a business case was described in the previous section.

RO appointment and training

All designated bodies had to have an appointed RO in place as of 1 January 2011. The ROs must also have attended mandatory introductory training offered by the RST through the SHAs. The core elements of the RO job description have been identified by the RST and are described in responsibilities of the RO. This needs to be incorporated into the job description of ROs developed by trusts and/or SHAs.

Appraisal system and appraisal policy

This will be the area subject to greatest change and subject to regular scrutiny, both internally and by external organizations. As all doctors will be subject to revalidation proposals, designated bodies need to identify all doctors employed who have a prescribed connection to the RO. This will include doctors who may never have been subject to appraisals in the past, such as trust doctors.

Appraisal policy

All designated bodies should have an appraisal policy in place. The core content of what should be in the appraisal policy is contained in documents produced by the RST and comes with the ORSA questionnaire. This needs to take note of the requirements of GMC's publication, *Good Medical Practice*.

Clinical governance and 360-degree feedback

Responsible officers have statutory responsibilities for clinical governance. Information from this needs to feed into the appraisal process described in the previous section. A key part of proposals to strengthen medical appraisal is the introduction of colleague and patient feedback. A patient and colleague feedback exercise using structured feedback questionnaires will need to be carried out for most doctors at least once in each 5-year revalidation cycle. GMC guidance on this has been issued recently.[19] Commonly agreed guidelines on this aspect of medical appraisal will be a key priority area.

Appraiser training and selection

The number of appraisers needed to meet the requirements of enhanced appraisals for revalidation requirements will increase. Appraisers need to have a clearly defined job description. They must be selected to their posts and provided with initial training and ongoing support in order to meet the requirements of enhanced appraisal. The initial training for medical appraisers should cover the competencies and skills required for the organization's appraisal process, but, to inform revalidation, should also include:

- understanding the purpose of appraisal and revalidation and the links between these processes and other systems for improving the quality of medical practice in the organization and the wider health system
- competency in assessing supporting information that informs the appraisal and revalidation process, speciality aspects of appraisal
- skills to conduct an effective appraisal discussion, including all the elements necessary for revalidation
- the ability to produce consistently high-quality appraisal documentation, sufficient to inform the revalidation recommendation, as well as informing personal development.

Appraisers should also have leadership and support in their role. Support for appraisers may include:

- access to leadership and advice on all aspects of the appraisal process from a named individual (e.g. appraisal lead)
- periodic review of performance in the role of appraiser, including suggestions for inclusion in their personal development plan (PDP), which address their development needs
- access to training and professional development resources to develop appraiser skills
- provision of peer support, speciality support (if required) and discussion of difficult areas of appraisal and significant events in an anonymized and confidential environment
- some appraisers may need access to external peer support because of their role within the organization (e.g. the medical director or appraisal lead) and/or their relationship to the other appraisers
- organizations may choose to satisfy these requirements in different ways, but there is evidence that a well-structured appraiser support group led by a suitably skilled appraisal lead or facilitator can meet these needs.

Appraisers need regular feedback on their performance in their role and mechanisms need to be in place to make this happen. Performance review may include:

- assessment/evaluation after training or after a probationary period
- feedback from appraisees on the appraiser's performance in the role
- review of outcomes of completed appraisals (e.g. PDPs, summaries of appraisal discussion)
- review of any complaints or significant events relating to the appraiser
- periodic structured evaluation of specific areas of knowledge, skills and attributes (e.g. handling of patient safety issues arising in appraisal, portfolio evaluation, speciality aspects of appraisal and communication).

Exception audits of missed or incomplete appraisals

Responsible officers need to be informed of all missed and incomplete appraisals and exception audits needs to be done on a regular basis. Appraisals may need to be rescheduled and completed at the earliest opportunity.

Further developments

This chapter highlights what a medical director/RO should know and do to get to a state of readiness for the introduction of revalidation. Continuing developments and guidance are in the offing from the RST, the GMC and the AOMRC that will describe in detail some of the processes that underpin appraisal and revalidation. Continuing structural changes in the NHS will also have an impact in most sectors. Issues to do with doctors who are deemed unsuitable for revalidation and their remediation requirements are outside of the scope of this chapter but will need to be addressed.

Summary

❏ To ensure that organizations are ready to introduce revalidation the following need to be in place:

  ❏ RO, appointed and trained
  ❏ completed ORSA and identified action plans
  ❏ draft of an appraisal policy to support the introduction of revalidation
  ❏ selection and training of appraisers to support the introduction of revalidation
  ❏ implementation of new guidance and amendments to the revalidation process as issued by the GMC and/or RST.

References

1. The Medical Act (1858). London: Crown.
2. Merrison AW (chairman) (1975). *Committee of Inquiry into the Regulation of the Medical Profession. Report.* London: HMSO.
3. Pauffley A (chairman) (2004). *Independent Investigation into how the NHS Handled Allegations about the Conduct of Clifford Ayling.* Cmnd 6298. London: The Stationery Office.

4. Matthews S (chairman) (2004). *To Investigate how the NHS Handled Allegations about the Performance and Conduct of Richard Neale*. Cmnd 6315. London: The Stationery Office.

5. Pleming N (chairman) (2005). *The Kerr/Haslam Inquiry: Full Report*. Cmnd 6640. London: Crown.

6. Ritchie J (chairman) (2000). *An Inquiry into Quality and Practice within the National Health Service Arising from the Actions of Rodney Ledward*. London: The Stationery Office.

7. Kennedy I (chairman) (2001). *The Report of the Public Inquiry into Children's Heart Surgery at the Bristol Royal Infirmary 1984–1995: Learning from Bristol*. Cmnd 5207. London: The Stationery Office.

8. Department of Health (1997). *The New NHS: Modern, Dependable*. London: Department of Health.

9. Department of Health (1999). *Supporting Doctors, Protecting Patients*. London: Department of Health.

10. The Medical Act 1983 (Amendment) Order 2002. Available from: http://www.legislation.gov.uk/

11. Department of Health (2006). *Good Doctors, Safer Patients. Proposals to Strengthen the System to Assure and Improve the Performance of Doctors and to Protect the Safety of Patients*. London: Department of Health.

12. Department of Health (2007). *Trust, Assurance and Safety: The Regulation of Healthcare Professionals. White Paper*. London: Department of Health.

13. General Medical Council (2010). *Revalidation: A Statement of Intent*. Available from: http://www.gmc-uk.org/

14. The Medical Profession (Responsible Officers) Regulations 2010. Available from: http://www.legislation.gov.uk/

15. Department of Health (2010). *Equity and Excellence: Liberating the NHS*. London: Department of Health.

16. NHS Revalidation Support Team. *Organisational Readiness Self Assessment Tool*. Available from: http://www.revalidationsupport.nhs.uk/

17. General Medical Council (2011). *The Good Medical Practice Framework for Appraisal and Revalidation*. Available from: http://www.gmc-uk.org/

18. General Medical Council (2011). *Supporting Information for Appraisal and Revalidation*. Available from: http://www.gmc-uk.org/

19. General Medical Council (2010). *Revalidation: The Way Ahead. Annex 3 – GMC Principles, Criteria and Key Indicators for Colleague and Patient Questionnaires in Revalidation*. Available from: http://www.gmc-uk.org/

Chapter 17

Public health

Paul Cosford

- Introduction
- The three domains of public health
- Public health doctors as managers
- Management and leadership skills for doctors working in public health
- Public health roles for all medical managers
- Conclusion
- Summary
- References

Introduction

One of the most attractive features of public health is the ability to combine a specialist medical career with medical management. This allows the doctor working in public health to, for example, manage outbreaks of infectious disease, address environmental health concerns (such as the health effects of landfill sites), implement strategies to improve health in local communities (often with a focus on those with the poorest health, such as children in deprived communities), and work with senior health and local authority managers to improve the quality of health and social care. To tackle the breadth of issues that are necessary to improve the public's health, most doctors working in this field will need considerable management expertise to influence clinical, political and managerial systems in the NHS, local authorities and other public and private sector organizations, as well as to manage the team of public health specialists, practitioners and other staff who support them.

The doctor working in public health therefore needs to be armed with a wide range of management skills and expertise. The approach taken in this chapter is to outline the three domains of health improvement, health protection and improving health and social care quality within which doctors working in public health operate, and to highlight the management aspects required to work successfully in these areas. The chapter then outlines the generic aspects of management and leadership which are required of doctors working in public health, but which are relevant, too, for all doctors. Recognizing that in influencing the health of individuals, all doctors have a role in improving the health of the public, the chapter finally highlights some opportunities that all medical managers have to improve the public's health overall.

The three domains of public health

The most widely accepted definition of Public Health was coined by Sir Donald Acheson in 1988. He was the Chief Medical Officer writing a report on the future of the public health function following high-profile failings in the control of an outbreak of gastro-intestinal disease in Stanley

Royd Hospital,[1] and of Legionnaire's disease in Stafford.[2] He described public health as 'The science and art of improving health and preventing disease through the organised efforts of society'.[3]

This is a very broad definition, but there are three commonly described 'domains' within which specialists in public health work to achieve the overall aim that this definition reflects: health improvement (acting on the lifestyle, economic and social determinants of health such as smoking, poverty and inequalities); health protection (protecting individuals and communities from infectious disease and environmental hazards); health and social care quality (ensuring people receive safe and effective health and social care that meets their needs).

Health improvement

This involves acting on the underpinning determinants of health to reduce the incidence of disease and improve the quality and length of life. Box 17.1 demonstrates the breadth of the determinants of health. These include behavioural risk factors because people who do not smoke, who drink within sensible limits, eat five portions of fruit and vegetables daily and who are physically active live, on average, 14 years longer than those who do none of these.[4] Much public health effort as a result goes into strategies to improve these. The factors affecting health also include underpinning social, environmental and economic risk factors.

Box 17.1 Factors affecting health

Fixed

- Genes
- Sex
- Ageing

Social and economic

- Poverty
- Employment
- Social exclusion

Environment

- Air quality
- Housing
- Water quality
- Social environment
- Green space

Lifestyle

- Diet
- Physical activity
- Smoking
- Alcohol

- Sexual behaviour
- Drugs

Access to services

- NHS
- Social care
- Transport
- Leisure

Figure 17.1 shows that people in deprived communities live substantially fewer years than those in wealthier communities, with even more years lived with disability. Although this is partially underpinned by differences in lifestyle,[5] it is also significantly underpinned by wider social factors, such as poor housing, environment and employment, among others. The role of the doctor working in public health is to develop evidence-based strategies to act on these determinants of health which often require the combined actions of more than one agency, and to use their leadership, managerial and influencing skills to implement that strategy with the collaboration of those other agencies. As an example, Table 17.1 shows the elements of a strategy to reduce prevalence of tobacco use, and the organizations that need to be influenced in order for it to be successful.

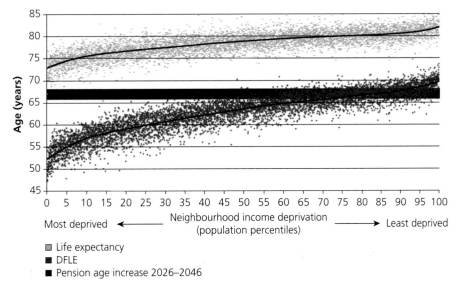

Figure 17.1 Life expectancy and disability-free life expectancy (DFLE) at birth, persons by neighbourhood income level, England 1999–2003. (*Source*: The Marmot Review.[6])

Health protection

Infectious diseases and environmental hazards are a significant risk to poor health, and form the bulk of the health protection work of doctors working in public health. A good, albeit international,

Table 17.1 Elements of a local tobacco control strategy

Action required	Individuals and organizations that need to deliver the action
GPs to provide evidence-based support (including brief advice) to stop smoking within their practices	GPs Local medical committees Primary care trusts (and their successor bodies)
Hospital trusts to refer cardiac, respiratory and maternity patients for specialist stop smoking support	Trust medical and clinical directors Trust nurse directors Cardiac and respiratory clinical network lead clinicians Trust managers Commissioners
Improve the effectiveness and targeting (to groups with high smoking rates) of specialist stop smoking services	Providers of specialist stop smoking services Commissioners of specialist stop smoking services
Reduce the uptake of smoking in young people by implementation of evidence-based programmes in schools	Schools (head teachers) Local authority directors of children's services
Reduce the availability of illicit tobacco by disrupting the local illicit tobacco market	Police UK Borders Agency Local authority trading standards department
Improve enforcement of tobacco legislation (smoke-free public places, underage sales, plain packaging)	Local authority trading standards department Police
Effective publicity campaigns	Those running national and local campaigns

example is the outbreak of *Escherichia coli* O104 in Germany in May 2011, in which 809 people developed haemolytic-uraemic syndrome and 2717 more developed gastroenteritis (a total of 3526 cases, including 47 deaths) as a result of infection with a rare organism not previously recognized as causing human disease.[7] Figure 17.2 demonstrates the epidemic curve, which gives the typical picture of cases from a point source outbreak.

The roles of the doctor working in public health in this instance are to identify outbreaks through disease surveillance systems (such as laboratory reports), to investigate and control the cause of the outbreak, and to ensure that the individuals affected are identified and followed up. In this example, a case–control study provided an initial epidemiological link with salad consumption (initially lettuce, tomatoes and cucumbers); further epidemiological and microbiological investigation later definitively identified the cause as sprouting seeds (fenugreek) which enabled appropriate control measures to be put in place.[7] The public health doctors in the team established to address any consequences for the UK required particular management expertise in leading the team which brought together all the different aspects of outbreak investigation and control. At the same time they worked closely with the UK government and food standards agencies in the UK and throughout Europe to understand the measures needed to control the source of the outbreak, ensure they were in place in the UK and keep the public informed of actions to minimize risk.

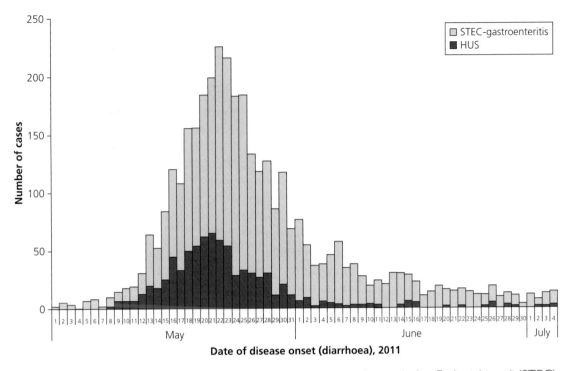

Figure 17.2 Cases of haemolytic-uraemic syndrome and Shiga toxin-producing *Escherichia coli* (STEC) due to *E. coli* O104 infection in Germany, 2011. (*Source*: Robert Koch Institute, Berlin.)

Improving health and social care quality

This is an area of considerable overlap with the roles of other doctors and medical managers. A typical example is improving the quality of care in respect of venous thromboembolism (VTE), in which there is good evidence of an effective treatment to prevent hospital patients getting VTE, but this is not systematically implemented.[8] The public health doctor's interest here is that every patient should get the right treatment all the time, and that this will have a significant impact on the outcomes of hospital care. Indeed, moving from the 40 per cent current coverage of effective care to 80 per cent would prevent approximately 5600 cases of VTE in England annually,[9] with consequent benefits to their health and capacity to return to normal life. This is a further example where the doctor working in public health will need considerable management skill, and a working knowledge of the theory and practice of achieving change in complex organizations such as the NHS. One well-described framework for this is Kotter's[10] eight steps to achieving change. Their application to the reduction of VTE and other scenarios such as healthcare-associated infection are described in detail elsewhere.[11]

Public health doctors as managers

These examples make it clear that many of the routine roles of doctors working in public health are management-focused. It is true that the technical and scientific expertise of drawing up a strategy to reduce the prevalence of smoking, conducting a case–control study to identify the source of an outbreak, or identifying the evidence-based medical interventions to reduce VTE are fundamental to public health practice. Nevertheless, the application of this expertise to improve or protect the health of patients and communities requires a breadth of managerial and leadership skills, including the negotiating and influencing skills needed to achieve the changes that are being sought. Implementing the strategy to reduce tobacco prevalence outlined in Table 17.1, for example, requires, among other things:

- working with medical and managerial colleagues in the NHS to ensure that GPs provide brief advice with pharmacological support where appropriate
- ensuring that patients receiving treatment in hospital settings for respiratory or cardiac conditions, and pregnant women, are routinely asked and offered appropriate support to stop smoking
- that effective and evidence-based specialist smoking-quitting services are commissioned and provided
- collaborative working with local authorities (trading standards) and law enforcement agencies to reduce the availability of illicit and smuggled tobacco within communities.

Each of these requires key management and leadership skills, including giving clarity to the vision of what the services could achieve; identifying key leaders within these services who need to support the changes required; an understanding of how to achieve change in service delivery; the ability to influence those individuals who need to act to achieve the change; and an ability to monitor and report on progress, and exert influence where change is not taking place.

As well as the ability to influence and achieve change in the practice of clinicians and managers in the NHS, local authorities and other organizations, the doctor working in public health will usually be the leader and manager of a team. This is likely to include medical, scientific and managerially trained staff who deliver the complex range of activities required to improve public health. In this context the leader/manager's role is to know the characteristics of high-quality healthcare teams and to develop them within the team that they manage. Key among these characteristics of high-quality teams are:[12]

- strong leadership
- a focus on delivering health outcomes that the team members agree are important for them, and which they monitor to check the effectiveness of their team
- a focus on the development of staff in their skills and competencies
- appropriate sharing of clinical and health information to support the effective work of the team
- a clear understanding of who their external stakeholders are and what these stakeholders think of the strengths and weaknesses of their work.

Along with many medical managers, therefore, the doctor working in public health needs to understand how to manage and lead a team to deliver the objectives of that team.

Management and leadership skills for doctors working in public health

The Faculty of Public Health has defined 10 areas of specialist public health practice within which those practising public health operate. Each has a number of competencies within it, many of which include managerial and leadership skills, such as understanding different types of leadership and being able to identify the steps required to implement change.[13] They are the subject of the public health specialist training curriculum and constitute the basic skills required for the practice of public health. Bearing in mind the complexity of the managerial and leadership roles that public health doctors often have, however, it is worth considering further what is meant by 'management' and 'leadership'.

Management

A particularly important requirement for public health doctors as managers is to bring simplicity and order to what at first sight appears to be a complex managerial task. Without this it is impossible to convert a management challenge into a set of achievable actions. Ten practical functions have been described by Gillam[14] as follows:

- Defining the task – this converts the overall aims into achievable and specific tasks.
- Planning – this identifies the options for achieving the task, evaluates them and converts the favoured option into a work plan. The more creative one can be in planning, the more likely it is that an effective plan will be developed.
- Briefing – the communication through meetings with relevant individuals and organizations, presentations and written briefing documents of the task and the plan. To be successful this must bring the plan to life for the audience.
- Controlling – this involves monitoring key elements of the plan to make sure it is on track, and to make sure the elements meet appropriate standards.
- Evaluating – having a method to evaluate the success of the interventions with regular reporting on progress.
- Motivating – people must be motivated to deliver the plan, and this can involve identifying incentives such as personal recognition of people who have successfully implemented the plan, promotions and other rewards.
- Organizing – making sure that the facilities and equipment required to deliver the different elements of the plan are in place and work appropriately.
- Setting an example – successful managers demonstrate the values and behaviours they espouse in their own work, and this is obvious to those who work with them.
- Communicating – good managers are clear and effective communicators, whether they are using verbal or written forms of communication.
- Housekeeping – good managers are able to manage their time and workload and are good at recognizing and acting to manage stress in themselves and in others.

These functions are critical for all medical managers, not just those working in public health, and yet doctors rarely receive formal training in this area. Management development is therefore a fundamentally important aspect of training and development for any doctor working in public health.

Leadership

Management skills are insufficient on their own to enable doctors working in public health to influence the breadth of individuals and organizations that need to act in concert to achieve the complex changes that may be required. They also need to be good leaders, able to describe a compelling vision and able to gain support for that vision from those whom they lead, as well as those in other organizations with whom they work. Leadership is not the same as management, but there is a considerable overlap. Some of the critical features of leadership are that it aims to achieve specific goals by the actions of the leader, who is able to influence the thoughts, emotions and actions of others, in order to support the achievement of these goals.[15] In the USA, a study of healthcare workers suggested that leadership has four key features:[16]

- the provision of strategic direction
- instruction to team members

- monitoring of team performance
- assisting team members when necessary to achieve the outcomes.

This list again demonstrates the overlap between management and leadership, but the most important messages are that managerial and leadership skills:

- are essential elements in the armoury of doctors working in public health
- are not accidental – they need to be a specific part of specialist training and post-training personal and professional development.

Public health roles for all medical managers

This chapter would not be complete without some consideration of the role of medical managers who are not public health specialists in improving the health of the public. The public's health is clearly the accumulation of the health of the whole population, and so improving each individual's health and well-being will lead to a cumulative improvement of the overall health of the public.

Taking the domain of health improvement as an example, smokers who present to hospital as patients are often surprised, when asked about their smoking status, that this rarely leads to advice or support on stopping smoking. Indeed, referrals of hospital patients to stop smoking services are surprisingly infrequent. This is despite there being good evidence that receiving hospital treatment for a cardiac or respiratory illness and being pregnant are times when people are more likely to wish to give up smoking.

So what is the role of medical managers here? It has to be to use their management and leadership skills to raise awareness of and create a climate within which hospital treatment is seen as an opportunity to support people to live more healthily, and where it is understood that all opportunities should be used to support people – in this case, to stop smoking. It is a legitimate aim for every contact with the NHS to be a health-promoting one. The manager's role is then to create a management process that will lead to achieving this climate. For example, a manager might create a programme called a 'health-promoting hospital' and seek a small group of staff from different parts of the hospital to work together to consider what this means in practice and how it should be implemented. In the case of patients who smoke, this might, for example, involve establishing a base within the hospital for evidence-based stop smoking services and then monitoring the numbers of referrals by ward or clinic. In terms of the management and leadership functions described in the previous section, this process would involve creating a vision of how a health-promoting hospital might look, creating an appropriate team to develop the plan, supporting its implementation, monitoring its success and helping the team to sort out difficulties as they arise.

This is just one example of how medical managers, whatever their background, can contribute to the public's health. There are many similar examples in the other domains of public health; in health protection, for example, medical managers often lead a hospital's contribution to multi-agency emergency planning, which ensures an adequate health sector response to major emergencies.

Conclusion

Public health as a speciality includes many management and leadership roles. This chapter has described the key skills in management and leadership that doctors working in public health require to be able to practise effectively. In addition to these, all medical managers have a significant impact on the health of the public, and for this reason a population health perspective needs to underpin the practice of medical management more generally.

Summary

❏ Public health doctors need a wide range of management and leadership skills to tackle the breadth of issues necessary to improve the health of communities.

❏ Public health doctors work in three main areas: health improvement, health protection and health and social care quality improvement. All three require strong management and leadership skills.

❏ It is possible to describe the key features of management and leadership, as well as the characteristics of high-quality (and therefore effective) teams. Understanding these helps individuals and teams to develop these characteristics.

❏ All medical managers have a significant influence on the public's health through their medical management roles. Understanding the service for which they are responsible in the context of the health of the local community is a critical step to enhancing this impact.

References

1. Department of Health and Social Security (1986). *The Report of the Committee of Inquiry into an Outbreak of Food Poisoning at Stanley Royd Hospital*. London: HMSO.

2. Badenoch J (1986). *First Report of Inquiry into the Outbreak of Legionnaire's Disease in Stafford in April 1985*. London: HMSO.

3. Committee of Inquiry into the Future of the Public Health Function (1988). *Public Health in England*. London: HMSO.

4. Khaw KT, Wareham N, Bingham S, Welch A, Luben R, Day N (2008). Combined impact of health behaviours and mortality in men and women: The EPIC-Norfolk Prospective Population Study. *PLoS Medicine* 5, 518.

5. Lakshman R, McConville A, How S, Flowers J, Wareham N, Cosford P (2011). Association between area-level socioeconomic deprivation and a cluster of behavioural risk factors: cross-sectional, population-based study. *J Pub Health* 33, 234–45.

6. The Marmot Review (2010). *Fair Society, Healthy Lives. The Marmot Review. Strategic Review of Health Inequalities in England Post 2010*. Available online: http://www.instituteofhealthequity.org

7. Robert Koch Institute (2011). *Technical Report: EHEC/HUS O104:H4 outbreak Germany* May/June 2011 as of 30 June 2011. Berlin: Robert Koch Institute,.

8. House of Commons Health Committee (2005). *The Prevention of Venous Thromboembolism in Hospitalised Patients*. 2nd Report of Session 2004–2005. London: The Stationery Office.

9. Chief Medical Officer for England (2009). *Annual Report of the Chief Medical Officer*. London: Department of Health.

10. Kotter J (1996). *Leading Change*. Cambridge, MA: Harvard Business School Press.

11. Gillam S, Cosford P (2011). Scenarios. In: Gillam S, ed. *Leadership and Management for Doctors in Training*. London: Radcliffe Publishing, pp. 92–108.

12. Cosford P, Thomas J (2010). Safer out of hours primary care. *Br Med J* 340, c3194.

13. Faculty of Public Health of the Royal College of Physicians (2004). *Public Health Training Portfolio.* London: Faculty of Public Health.

14. Gillam S (2011). *Leadership and Management for Doctors in Training.* London: Radcliffe Publishing.

15. Pointer D, Sanchez JP (2003). Leadership in public health practice. In: Scutchfield FD, Keck CW, eds. *Principles of Public Health Practice.* New York: Thomson Delmar Learning, pp. 140–60.

16. Klein KJ, Ziegert JC, Knight AP, Xiao Y (2006). Dynamic delegation: shared, hierarchical and de-individualised leadership in extreme action teams. *Admin Sci Quart* 51, 590–621.

Chapter 18

Medical management in mental health services

Sylvia Tang and Geraldine O'Sullivan

- Introduction
- The changing role of the medical manager
- Mental health medical director's portfolio
- Medical management structure supporting the medical director
- The management of the multidisciplinary team in mental health
- Managing partnerships
- Managing change in mental health services
- Managing external relationships
- Training and education in mental health
- Summary
- References

Introduction

Medical management of today's mental health services in the UK has come a long way since the first official role of medical superintendent of mental asylums, a role which began in the mid- to late-1800s and lasted through to the demise of the asylums, more than a century later. Today medical management is very different and much more complex, with its emphasis on quality, patient experience, performance management, financial controls and strong external regulation, including professional regulation.

Following de-institutionalization, mental health services were embedded in a variety of acute trusts, community trusts and some continuing as asylums until the mid-1990s. In 1999, *The National Service Framework for Mental Health*[1] transformed the mental health services, aided by significant investment. This led to new models of care, which have been evaluated and shown to improve the quality of care and outcomes for mentally ill patients. However, it has also led to a greater number of teams, all of whom are competing for resources, and can sometimes lead to fragmentation of services unless closely managed with clear articulation of the different contributions and roles of various teams. Closure of beds has continued to be the trajectory for mental health services as a result of community developments, providing better ongoing care in the community, thereby preventing relapse, and also providing meaningful alternatives to in-patient care. The evidence base for service models and interventions and a holistic multiprofessional approach have brought greater credibility and a scientific basis to the speciality.

The formation of mental health trusts has led to the growth of strong medical leadership in mental health services and this mirrors the improvements that have come about as a result of the development of services provided by mental health and learning disability trusts.

The medical leader cannot over-emphasize the developmental journey of mental health and the transformation of care models that has not been readily replicated by many other medical specialities. Indeed, this impressive journey in mental healthcare since the closure of the asylums provides a good model for other specialities in relation to the management of long-term conditions. The years of providing mental health services in community trusts or acute trusts were probably aimed at de-stigmatizing and reintegrating both patients and psychiatrists, but unfortunately this often led to a 'Cinderella service', plagued by poor funding and a lack of priority.

Therefore the development of separate mental health trusts in the last decade has meant that the speciality has benefited from a culture of robust management and innovative practice. Along with the task of creating new ways of working, this has led to a high number of mental health organizations meeting the challenge to become foundation trusts. A tough governance and financial regulatory structure means professionals in the field have had to become acutely business-minded and capable medical leaders and managers. Ironically, however, mental health foundation trusts are increasingly absorbing other organizations, namely community provider trusts. This is an interesting turnaround in the progression of this 'Cinderella service' and is lending an increasing sense of pride to the role of mental health medical manager.

The changing role of the medical manager

While psychiatry and mental health services were embedded within multispeciality organizations, the medical leader within the psychiatry department was often the representative of the doctors acting as head doctor and defender of mental health services. The main aim of the medical manager was frequently that of advocate for mental health services within an environment with a poor understanding of, and a lack of interest in, mental health and learning disability services. The development of mental health trusts as separate, 'uni-speciality' trusts led to the growth of the role of the mental health medical manager and medical director, usually a psychiatrist by background. The traditional perception of the medical director as 'head doctor' or as the representative of doctors on the board persisted for most medical staff and possibly most medical directors. There was little perception of the executive director's responsibilities and accountabilities as part of a trust board. However, this changed with the development of foundation trusts.

Changes in the role of the medical director came to the fore during the mid-2000s when many trusts were aspiring to become foundation trusts. The process of preparation, training and board development would not allow any medical director to continue in the 'head doctor' role. The focus on strategy, business planning, risk identification and the unitary board (where all directors are equally accountable) is one of the great strengths of British business and the expectation that the medical director should understand financial risk ratings and information technology made the role more complex than simply being a manager and professional lead for doctors. However, interestingly, in most organizations many of the traditional roles remain assigned to the medical director, such as Caldicott Guardian and director for infection control and prevention, and some medical directors still carry out their managerial responsibilities on a part-time basis.

Lord Ara Darzi played a key role in raising the status of the medical leader, which led to medical directors becoming more influential, with responsibilities not only for the direction of clinical services within the trust but also beyond organizational boundaries. Clinical leadership and management of services have been further reinforced by Monitor, the financial regulator promoting service line management and leadership by clinicians as managers supported by a service manager.[2] More recently, the requirements for significant cost improvements turned 'salami slice' cost efficiencies into wholesale service redesigns under the direction of clinical leaders. These changes have had a significant impact on the crucial role of the medical manager in mental health.

In most mental health trusts, there is now a medical management structure which supports the medical director, consisting of associate medical directors and clinical directors who require adequate management time in their job plans with sufficient administrative support to be able to meaningfully manage what are often complex day-to-day issues arising from the management of services.

Mental health medical director's portfolio

The medical director has an interesting and crucial role on the board of mental health organizations and is often relied on to be the guardian for safety and quality, including at board level.[3] The traditional role of the medical director was to lead and manage all medical staff in the provision of a safe and effective clinical service. In recent times, the quality agenda has taken precedence and the link between finance and quality of service has been thrust into the limelight on a national scale following various scandals such as that which occurred at the Mid-Staffordshire NHS Foundation Trust.[4] This has been attributed particularly to boards not recognizing the potential impact on quality of plans for financial savings. The role of the medical director in safeguarding quality, patient safety and clinical effectiveness in the light of such financial efficiency savings cannot be over-emphasized. It is the medical director's responsibility to highlight such situations where clinical safety and quality of care can be compromised and this has made the role on the board an extremely important and high-profile one.

This is of particular relevance in mental health services where outcome measures that are used in acute care, such as infection rates, postoperative complications and mortality rates, are not the best and most relevant measures of quality. Instead a more complex matrix of measures is required to translate quality into quantitative measures. This is being made even more complex by the increasing emphasis on the inclusion of social care targets, such as measuring the proportion of people in contact with secondary mental health services in employment and with good housing. Furthermore, with the commitment by the Department of Health to extend Payment by Results into mental health, the development of clear outcomes will be crucial to the new payment system. The medical director in mental health has the task of explaining to clinicians the need for data collection, which, over the last five years, has become an increasing burden as the number of performance targets and outcome measures has expanded.

The medical director's portfolio often spans the agendas of regulation, governance and operational matters, which is certainly wide-ranging. The operational management of medical staff may continue to sit with the medical director – and even in trusts where this has been devolved to operational managers, the regulatory requirements for doctors, including revalidation, mean that the operational management of doctors is usually linked to the role of medical director and is different from the operational management of other professionals. This is highlighted by national policies for managing doctors such as *Maintaining High Professional Standards*,[5] and by the fact that medical consultants have a separate contract, 'the new consultant contract'.[6]

Medical management structure supporting the medical director

Clinical engagement at all levels is key in supporting any agenda and the medical director plays a crucial role in bridging that gap between frontline clinicians and senior management. Good engagement of the general medical body is more likely to be achieved if the medical director has earned the respect of both medical and non-medical colleagues.

Given the importance of the executive role of the medical director, it is essential that mental health organizations have an operational medical management structure sufficient to manage day-to-day operational issues, so that the medical director's time is protected for board and leadership functions.

The training and development of the medical workforce in relation to management roles, line reporting and responsibilities, and appropriate delegation have been, and will continue to be, one of the principal tasks of the medical director in ensuring there is adequate capacity within the organization to provide clinical leadership across what is often a dispersed service.

Time management is often a challenge for any medical director, particularly for those who are part-time. The email traffic to the medical director alone can be considerable, as it covers the entire spectrum of corporate, operational and clinical issues, as well as strategy and the medical workforce. The broad portfolio of the medical director, spanning strategic, operational and clinical responsibilities, often leads to an easy pattern of escalation and referral of issues both from medical and non–medical staff unless this is dealt with appropriately. This requires perseverance, and a clear, unambiguous job description for the medical director is a first step in the right direction.

The supporting medical management structure will vary from one organization to another. Most mental health organizations have clinical directors who work alongside a general manager overseeing a specific geographical area or sub-speciality. Given that these directorates generally manage large budgets of £20 million–£60 million, clinical directors are often supported in their role by medical leads who will carry out job planning and appraisals for medical staff and manage on-call rotas and the like. This enables clinical directors to focus on managing the budget and the strategic direction of the business unit, as well as the increasingly important role of linking closely with general practitioners who will be the commissioners of the services provided by the directorate.

The clinical directors have an important role in overseeing the annual cycle of job planning, linking personal consultant objectives to the organizational strategic objectives. The alignment of job planning and personal development plans with organizational strategic objectives is probably still not fully achieved or accepted but any business would want this to be routine, especially for its most expensive staff group.

Relationships between medical managers and general managers

The clinical director and general manager are generally jointly accountable for the financial and performance management of the directorate, both in terms of the quality of the service and in terms of meeting key performance indicators, of which there are many in mental health. A good working relationship, where both work together to achieve these aims, is essential.

The management of the multidisciplinary team in mental health

Mental health trusts are currently at the forefront of multiprofessional team-working where a host of responsibilities and tasks are delegated to non-medical staff. The clinical director in mental health will typically oversee the management of doctors in their directorate and work alongside the general manager. Other disciplines are typically managed through general line management. This distinction in terms of day-to-day management is related to the strong professional voice of doctors and the reluctance of general managers to manage them, as this is often regarded as being quite a challenge.

There are now many different multidisciplinary teams in mental health services. Each team should have a clearly defined function, against which it should be monitored. The manager will need to monitor the team's effectiveness and have a core set of measures and performance indicators by which to judge this. Consultant psychiatrists play an important part in multidisciplinary teams through their role in providing leadership to the team.

It is clear that well-functioning multidisciplinary teams with a clearly defined role around the treatment and care of a particular group of patients offer the optimal way to deliver care to vulnerable individuals in acute and community settings. Diversity within these teams enriches the care they deliver and they need strong day-to-day clinical leadership, which is usually provided by the consultant psychiatrist so that complex and difficult clinical issues can be safely managed.

In community mental health teams, which are the main access point to secondary mental health services and form the buffer between primary and secondary mental healthcare, the management of demand and capacity by managers and leaders of the team, including the medical manager, is essential as these teams are often inundated with referrals. Planning and prioritization of activity are important and caseload management for all staff is essential, ensuring that there is an entry and discharge process in operation within the team, so that patients don't get stuck in a service where there is no active care plan. Similarly, the management of the psychiatrist's caseload is important to make good use of the consultant's skills, ensuring that there is not a preponderance of routine follow-ups in outpatient settings instead of a focus on the more complex and risky patients. Therefore monitoring of caseloads and turnover should be in place, with prioritization of the more complex and needy patients. Good job planning that is linked to team and directorate objectives is an important task for the medical manager in these settings.

The distinction between medical and other clinical staff is, of course, further accentuated by contractual issues, different unions and differences in training, roles and functions, levels of responsibility and salaries. This is often at the core of difficulties that arise in multiprofessional teams. It is important that the varying tasks and roles of different professionals are clearly articulated, with an acceptance among staff of the different roles and responsibilities of the medical consultant versus other senior clinicians, so that there is efficient and judicious use of the medical workforce and resources. The Royal College of Psychiatrists[7] has described the role and responsibilities of the consultant psychiatrist in these settings. This was particularly useful in stating that the consultant does not need to see and be responsible for every patient. In a service that delivers care within multidisciplinary teams, it is essential that the distinctive role of the consultant psychiatrist is articulated and understood within the organization and at board level. The unique role of consultant psychiatrists is related to their breadth of experience and depth of knowledge, which enable them to effectively manage complexity. For example, the nurse prescriber has an important role in implementing treatment plans covering the pharmacological treatment of a straightforward mental illness, but a severe, treatment-resistant mental illness needs to be managed by a clinician with a good knowledge of pharmacology. This is not to undermine the crucial roles played by other disciplines.

On the frontline, the consultant psychiatrist plays a crucial role in providing clinical leadership to the multidisciplinary team and should work alongside the team leader who will typically be a nurse, or occasionally a social worker who has become a general manager. Problems arise when a medical colleague is unable or unwilling to meet these obligations.

Managing partnerships

Most mental health trusts in England are partnership organizations with social care. Formal agreements, arising from the Health Act 1999, have enabled health and social care organizations to have pooled budgets. As a result, mental health trusts often have partnerships with the co-terminous county council to deliver health and social care to mentally disordered patients. The underlying aim is to deliver integrated health and social care in a joined-up way that should facilitate the delivery of seamless care with less duplication for patients. However, it has also meant that two very different cultures have come together to achieve a common goal: better outcomes from mental health services for users and carers.

In the establishment of any partnership, it is essential to clarify from the outset shared goals and objectives for collaboration. In this context there is a need for the senior managers to develop a shared vision which specifies what is to be achieved with clear roles and responsibilities and an accountability framework for joint working.[8] There is also a need for clear policies and procedures, agreed between both agencies, to ensure that good-quality, safe care is delivered, including, for example, protocols for sharing patient information. Managers working in a partnership organization therefore need to manage the sometimes conflicting cultures and to clarify the roles and responsibilities of health and social care clinicians reporting to them.

One consequence is that multidisciplinary teams made up of health and social care staff have been created, and this is the setting within which the psychiatrist usually works. As a result, the medical manager in mental health services has become responsible for delivering performance targets related to social aspects of living that may seem unrelated to healthcare. For example, housing and employment are frequently used indicators of improvement in and recovery from mental illness. These are influenced by much more than the mental health of an individual and will depend on factors other than the well-being of the individual, such as socioeconomic factors and attitudes within society towards mental illness. This has the effect of broadening the remit of mental healthcare services, and in these circumstances the medical aspects of care can sometimes be questioned and challenged. The medical manager will be responsible for managing the doctors within these teams. Problems can arise when concerns are raised about the prioritization of the social aspects of care to the perceived detriment of the health aspects.

Barriers to good partnership working include the different performance targets, different IT systems, and cuts in one budget putting more pressure on the other partner. Managing partnerships is not easy and formal partnerships between health and social care agencies are in some areas being scrapped following disagreements between partners. Shrinking budgets in one or both agencies often test the endurance of these partnerships and there is no doubt they are easier to manage at times of growth in health and social care spend. Tait and Shah[9] describe the advantages and challenges of partnerships between mental health organizations and social care and the voluntary sector and also outline important steps that boards and their managers need to put in place to ensure good governance and operational management. In particular, they argue that it must be clear where the boundaries of responsibility and accountability lie.[8]

Managing change in mental health services

Reorganization and change seem to be core to all healthcare systems, with mental health services being no exception. Currently, at this time of austerity, there is the challenge of meeting very significant cost reductions with significant 'cost improvements plans' required annually for four years. The underlying principle that the public sector can become more efficient year on year is a challenge which requires the closest quality assurance processes overseen by the executive team. This is especially so given increased activity, population growth and nationally agreed contracts. Change can have an impact on staff morale and overall work output and it is important that clinicians are inherently involved in developing and leading transformation programmes. This is apparent in the King's Fund 2011 report, *The Future of Leadership and Management in the NHS*.[10] This report makes an interesting point that the proportion of overall budget in NHS management systems is but a tiny fraction of that in any other industry, putting into perspective the criticism that managers in the NHS are on the rise. On the contrary, it suggests that this proportion needs to be considerably bigger in order to achieve effective management. Action is needed on several fronts if the goal of transforming the NHS into a truly world-class system is to be met.

As a result many mental health organizations are planning major service transformation to avoid the negative effects of serial salami slicing. It is essential that medical managers and consultant psychiatrists are central to this transformation to ensure that quality and safety of clinical services are safeguarded and that the new models of care do not neglect important aspects of treatment. Strong medical management that is built into the organization will help to ensure that doctors are inherently involved in innovating and leading change and will facilitate safer transformation and good leadership of change.

An important aspect of change is to 'quality assure' them. The clinical governance department will play a role in this, often led by the medical director. Doctors with research experience also play a crucial role in the evaluation of services and can assess their effectiveness scientifically, including the outcomes for patients. The NHS has a responsibility to evaluate implementation of service models, including effectiveness and outcomes, satisfaction and cost-effectiveness in order to provide the best outcomes for patients at the least cost – that is, to ensure optimal value for money. One of the drawbacks of research into service change is that research outputs often lag far behind the changes, and so quality assurance needs to be built into the change programme.

The job of the senior medical manager is to be principled and to evaluate the evidence, look at strategic issues of safety, best outcomes and satisfaction and make difficult decisions within the financial constraints, governance and monitoring requirements of the external world. The challenge to the medical manager and medical director is to translate the application of the requirements of governance and regulations, to make sense of the measurements and to turn quantitative measures into meaningful qualitative measures.

The improved engagement of senior clinicians through service line management has the potential to overcome many obstacles. When clinicians are closely involved in change, they can manage the difficulties that arise with engagement, attention to detail and careful treatment of the messages. However, owing to the complexity and the challenging nature of these tasks a programme of organizational and personal development, as well as supervision, is required.

Managing external relationships

The advent of health authority or cluster QIPP (quality, innovation, productivity and prevention),[11] the need to engage clinicians and the idea of clinical senates spanning provider and commissioner clinicians have resulted in the medical leader being invited to a range of external meetings. The focus on quality has also led to the medical director being invited to contract monitoring and commissioning meetings to discuss contracts, quality and performance. The role of the medical director in these instances can be to translate, interpret and explain data in meaningful terms and to identify appropriate clinical, quality and performance data for future measurement. This engagement has been particularly helpful in identifying meaningful and achievable CQUIN (commissioning for quality and innovation) targets.[12] The escalation of the clinical commissioner agenda has led to an increase in the responsibilities of the mental health medical manager in terms of relationship management with commissioners and future commissioners, in representing both the effects of service changes and the impact of cuts on the quality of mental health services. For example, the cost of ongoing maintenance treatment of low- to medium-need patients will have to be carefully understood and balanced against the desire of some GPs that patients continue under shared care agreements while otherwise stable. This is absolutely crucial to the management of a block budget that is ever shrinking.

The transition to a Payment by Results tariff model for a 'needs-based' care pathway will have no transitional funding and will have to be carefully managed. This will require a collaborative approach between partners to manage a fundamental change in funding and commissioning, alongside a parallel attempt in the acute sector to try to cap spend, decrease tariff and move more activity back to community or primary care.

Training and education in mental health

The role of any NHS medical leader must consider education in terms of both the future workforce, such as medical students and postgraduate doctors in training, and the substantive workforce, with attention to the development of successors for leadership positions. These aspects are covered in other chapters in this book.

However, within mental health services, traditional considerations for training are now far broader, with a recognition that doctors are leaders in their teams and service areas but have not traditionally received any training other than modelling that would equip them for this role. The focus of training has traditionally been on clinical management, teaching skills, presentation skills and, more latterly, on managing difficult trainees. However, managing agendas such as productivity, change and the information revolution are all skills that need constant updating. The challenge in the deeply multiprofessional world of mental health is that the traditional relationships between consultants and their teams have changed. The consultant, although the clinical leader of the team, is often challenged by competing agendas, such as social care agendas, mental health legislation or human resource rules and regulations. The role of the consultant psychiatrist is therefore much broader than was previously the case and current trainees need to be prepared for these wider roles.

Recruitment into psychiatry is diminishing in the UK, something that may be related to the lack of clarity about the medical role of the doctor within psychiatry and the multidisciplinary team. The medical model within mental healthcare is continually being challenged by other professional groups. Medical leaders in psychiatry need to articulate the need for good medical care as the first step on the road to recovery of a patient with a severe mental illness. Stigmatization continues to be a major issue in mental health, and it may not have been helped by the separation of mental health from physical health in the early 2000s. However, there have been many benefits from the separation, such as improved funding and an emphasis on quality and performance of mental health services in their own right.

Like medical managers in other branches of medicine, those in mental health are sometimes on the receiving end of personal attacks from clinical colleagues, adversity that can be difficult to manage. The skills needed to deal with these complexities and to engage consultants both in strategic thinking and in the minutiae require a great deal of thought and training – although it does get easier with experience.

There is no going back and while there may be some brief moments of relief, pleasure and even personal recognition and a sense of achievement, these cannot be relied upon. For every one of these, there are plenty of the other more difficult interactions. The most important thing is to enjoy one's work and to gain personal reward simply from doing the job, and not necessarily from any recognition one gains in doing so.

Summary

❏ Medical management in mental health services has developed and evolved considerably since the creation of independent mental health trusts, leading to strong medical leadership and management in this area across the UK.

❏ Mental healthcare is usually delivered within a multidisciplinary team and the consultant psychiatrist plays a crucial role in providing clinical leadership to the team and enabling effective management of complexity.

❏ The medical manager in mental health has a crucial role in leading and managing change, and this is especially true at times of financial austerity necessitating major service transformation and redesign.

❏ Medical management in mental health is complex, with the need to manage what are often varied and dispersed services across various settings and with different partners.

❏ Mental health services are often delivered by partnership organizations. When formal partnership arrangements are created, it is important to define the expected benefits from the outset. These should be met and monitored within a clear accountability and responsibility framework.

References

1. Department of Health (1999). *National Service Framework*. Available from: http://www.dh.gov.uk/

2. Monitor (2009). *Service Line Management: An Overview*. Available from: http://www.monitor-nhsft.gov.uk/

3. Deuchar N, Atkinson E (2009). The role of the medical director in mental health. *Adv Psychiatr Treat* 15, 404–10.

4. Francis R (2009). *Independent Inquiry into Care provided by Mid-Staffordshire NHS Foundation Trust*. Available from: http://www.wirral.nhs.uk/

5. Department of Health (2004). *Maintaining High Professional Standards in the Modern NHS*. Available from: http://www.dh.gov.uk/

6. Department of Health (2002). *Consultant Contract Framework*. Available from: http://www.dh.gov.uk/

7. Royal College of Psychiatrists (2006). *Roles and Responsibilities of the Consultant in General Adult Psychiatry* (Council Report CR140). London: Royal College of Psychiatrists.

8. Hudson B, Hardy B, Henwood M, Wistow G (1997). *Inter-agency Collaboration: Final Report*. (Commissioned by Department of Health). Leeds: Nuffield Institute for Health.

9. Tait L, Shah S (2007). Partnership working: a policy with promise for mental healthcare. *Adv Psychiatr Treat* 13, 261–71.

10. The King's Fund (2011). *Report on The Future of Leadership and Management in the NHS*. London: The King's Fund.

11. Department of Health (2010). *Quality, Innovation, Productivity and Prevention (QIPP)*. Available from: http://www.dh.gov.uk/

12. Department of Health (2008). *Using the Commissioning for Quality and Innovation (CQUIN) Payment Framework*. Available from: http://www.dh.gov.uk/

Chapter 19

Medical management in acute care

Ed Neale

Introduction

The more formal management structures, and hence the development of the medical manager, were introduced into the NHS in the late 1980s under the heading of resource management. This was the first concerted attempt by government to give doctors responsibility and accountability for what they spent on healthcare for their patients. It was soon followed by the new funding concept of the 'purchaser–provider split', with hospitals being funded for the patients they treated instead of being given a funding allocation based on previous expenditure. A clear assessment of the original concept is given by Shackley and Healey.[1]

Over the last 10–15 years the funding structures and format have been refined, but they still follow the same basic pattern for acute hospitals. More recently, however, those same funding streams have been increasingly used to force delivery of quality targets, such as improved waiting times and better outcomes. Thus the role of the medical manager in the acute setting has changed over the last 20 years from one that was largely to do with being accountable for financial delivery to one where the manager is held to account not only for meeting financial targets, but also for patient safety, clinical outcomes, delivery of national targets, meeting statutory obligations and ensuring ongoing compliance with the various regulatory frameworks that now govern work in the NHS and healthcare in general.

Medical management in acute care

Acute trust structures

Acute hospitals are hierarchical in their nature. The days of a hospital run by 'the head administrator', the matron and the senior surgeon and physician are long gone. Health service management is a career path in its own right, with a defined structure for the professional manager that goes from management trainee to chief executive. This creates several tiers of management that sit alongside the clinical teams that deliver healthcare. Medical managers must work with their professional management colleagues to ensure delivery of the highest quality care. Unfortunately while there is training available for the interested clinician in management principles and techniques, it is by no means uniform across the country and there was no recognition of experience and achievement after the demise of the British Association of Medical Managers in 2010 until the creation of the Faculty of Medical Leadership in late 2011. In addition, management for clinicians is yet to be fully integrated into the undergraduate curriculum. Finally, time spent as a clinical manager in an acute trust is often temporary, with clinicians reverting to an exclusively clinical role after three to five years. This can lead managers to temper their dealings with colleagues in view of the fact that their roles could soon be reversed.

Thus there are two competing forces that can determine the final management structure of an organization: the managerial imperatives and the clinical associations. The advent of foundation trusts and the influence of the regulator, Monitor, have pushed organizations towards more clinically based structures. The key to good health management is to ensure these tiers support healthcare delivery by the clinicians, and do not put barriers in its way.

A very small proportion of medical managers give up their clinical careers and become full-time managers. Although it was the stated aim of the government that one-third of chief executives should be medically qualified, this has not been achieved for various reasons.[2] In this chapter I will discuss the managerial roles undertaken by doctors who maintain, to at least some degree, their clinical role.

The management structure varies from trust to trust, with many having very complicated organizational diagrams, but they all follow the same basic principles. The hospital will be divided into speciality- or service-based areas, usually headed by an experienced clinician, often known as the clinical lead. These are often called service lines or directorates. A number of these may then be grouped into a division or business unit, headed up by a clinical or divisional director. The number of divisions or business units will vary depending on the size of the organization. Leading these clinical managers will be a medical director who will have overall responsibility and accountability for the delivery of high-quality care by all clinicians, and will sit on the board as an executive director of the organization. As an example the structure of the Bedford Hospital NHS Trust, my own organization, is shown in Figure 19.1.

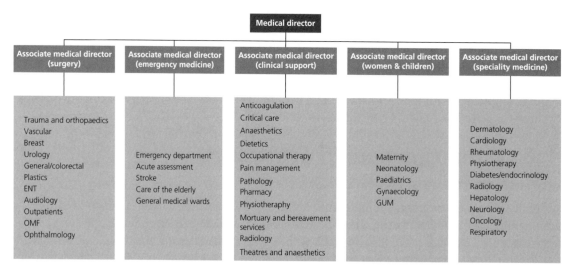

Figure 19.1 Medical management structure for business units, Bedford Hospital NHS Trust. ENT, ear, nose and throat surgery; GUM, genito-urinary medicine; OMF, oral and maxillofacial surgery.

Over the past 10 years there has been a significant increase in the role of and demands on the medical director. Responsibilities arising from the Care Quality Commission (CQC), revalidation, government targets, General Medical Council (GMC), educational requirements for both undergraduate and postgraduates, clinical governance, the Human Tissue Authority, Caldicott guardianship and many other areas mean that the medical director's portfolio has grown considerably. This is not sustainable for a single individual, so the role has to be delivered by delegating the responsibility and accountability to a number of deputies or assistants.

The acute trust medical management career

Every consultant appointed to a post in an acute hospital will be a medical manager to a greater or lesser extent. A significant part of the consultant role is leading a clinical team, but this is often not recognized as medical management. Within the clinical team there will probably be junior doctors, nurses, other health professionals, secretaries, clerks and administrative assistants. Whether they recognize it or not, the members of this team will look up to the consultant for leadership and direction, and how the consultant interacts with team members and others in the hospital will have a significant impact on the overall clinical quality and output of the whole team.

In addition, if the consultant has junior doctors, there will be a further managerial role, including education and other aspects of the junior's role such as ensuring compliance with the European Working Time Directive and pastoral care.

Department management/clinical lead

The department head or clinical lead is usually responsible for a single speciality, which could range in size from an anaesthetic department with 20 consultants and all the associated theatre and intensive care staffing and costs to a single-handed department (such as rheumatology). In either case the needs are the same, though of a different magnitude, and comprise management of the medical staff as well as leadership of other clinical staff (such as nurses and allied health professions) and non-clinical staff (such as secretaries, porters and clerks).

Service clinical director

An alternative management structure used by some hospitals is to group a small number of related specialities together with a clinical director at their head – for example, specialist surgery might include ophthalmology, ear nose and throat, and urology. The responsibilities would be similar to those of a department lead, but they are more likely to need general management support, such as finance, governance and human resources, due to economies of scale.

Head of division/clinical business unit

Recently, particularly with the development of business unit structures,[3] there has been a move to amalgamate many related services into much larger groups with a well-defined internal management structure, such as a division or business unit. These can follow speciality lines or they might follow the patient pathway more closely. The current Bedford Hospital NHS Trust structure, for example, has moved from a three-division structure – where one division included all medical specialities, all pathological and imaging diagnostic specialities and the accident and emergency (A&E) department – to the structure in Figure 19.1 where one business unit covers acute medicine and A&E (the majority of the hospital's emergency work), one covers speciality medicine, and all diagnostic services have been grouped together with theatres and anaesthetics as a single support services business unit.

The exact structure that is best for any organization will depend on local circumstances. When designing any structure, the key is first to decide what is to be achieved in managerial terms, in particular from the medical managers' perspective as they will need to have time to manage (which is often insufficient) as well as to maintain their clinical skills. The support that will be available to the medical manager will also need to be addressed. Each area will require general managerial, human resources (HR), finance and clinical governance support if it is to fulfil all its objectives and contribute fully to the overall aims of the organization. Within a large business unit, however, the lead (in the case of Bedford Hospital NHS Trust this is designated the associate medical director) will delegate roles such as audit or risk management to a single individual, not just for that person's speciality, but for the whole business unit.

Other management roles

Education and the clinical tutor

Educational roles have become far more formalized over the last five years. Speciality educational requirements have become more stringent as postgraduate training has become more formalized. The skills needed to deliver the training requirements are no longer those of the average consultant, and increasingly additional training must be undertaken to fulfil the role. Deaneries, Royal Colleges and regional Schools will monitor the performance of speciality tutors to ensure they deliver.

In addition to the speciality role, there are also broader trust educational roles to be filled such as Foundation Years programme director or clinical tutor. It was the advent of the latter in the late 1960s, who then needed training for their educational role, that led to the introduction of study leave to ensure senior doctors remained up to date. Now, 40 years on, all consultants with responsibility for junior doctors are required to have educational training.

Do not underestimate the experience that can be gained from educational roles that will be invaluable in a future clinical management role. Clinical tutors (also called associate medical directors for education in many trusts) not only act to ensure the availability and assure the standards of educational and pastoral support for the trainees, but often also have to manage the postgraduate centre and its staff. In doing so they may find themselves involved in non-medical appraisal, managing budgets, dealing with health and safety, security and many other issues. They frequently have to manage both senior and junior doctors as well as non-medical personnel. The well-defined but often limited nature of education can be a good training ground for consultants who later take on more formal medical management roles with much bigger portfolios. In my own organization, three of the last eight clinical tutors have gone on to become divisional clinical directors, two to be speciality leads, three to chair the Medical Staff Committee and one medical director. In addition, the last undergraduate sub-dean has also become a divisional clinical director.

Clinical governance or audit lead

Clinical governance was introduced in 1999[4] following a proposal by Scally and Donaldson in 1998.[5] Its inception formalized many informal processes of clinical review within each service. It has now grown to encompass all aspects of quality, risk management and assurance and it will be the cornerstone of revalidation once it is introduced (see Chapter 16). While individual clinicians all have a role to play, coordination and direction are needed within any service to ensure that all aspects of quality are addressed, including audits required by commissioners, regulatory bodies, educational bodies and the National Health Service Litigation Authority. Local risk management processes need to be overseen, and any resulting investigations conducted quickly and efficiently, with clear documentation of lessons learnt and action plans to address all issues raised.

This whole process will be repeated in every area of the organization and should be brought together in order to provide the central assurance needed by the board to discharge its responsibilities, and to be ready for any regulatory inspections.

Information governance and the Caldicott Guardian

Information governance and data protection are areas that are often unfamiliar to the medical profession, yet they are fully aware of patient confidentiality, which is not only a GMC requirement but also a fundamental part of the Hippocratic Oath. The reality is that healthcare is now a massive industry and it is all too easy to forget that not all organizations we communicate with need, or have a right to, all the personal information they would like. The Caldicott Guardian is the protector of personal data for the organization on behalf of patients and staff. A typical example of the types of issue to be addressed is data on a neonatal unit's clinical IT system. The clinicians at a local tertiary centre might request that a baby's information is transferred to them electronically at the same time that they accept the baby, which would be perfectly acceptable. However, if they then use this data in a subsequent research project, this would not be acceptable, unless either the parents have given permission for their baby's data to be used or the researchers have requested a separate, anonymized data set.

The acute medical director's portfolio

The acute medical director's role has grown considerably and is today as broad and time-consuming as one allows it to be. The role should not be undertaken lightly and while more junior medical management roles may be seen as stepping stones, it remains unique in management terms. Prospective medical directors, in order to be effective, must ensure that their colleagues understand that the role is appointed by the board, and is not the gift of the medical staff as a whole. The medical director is not, and never should be, the 'representative' of the consultant body. The medical director is, however, an almost unique position on the board as the guardian, alongside the director of nursing, of clinical standards and practice, as many boards today have few or no other clinically qualified members.

Medical directors may have varying degrees of formal management training, which will help in the day-to-day delivery of their duties, but by far and away the most important help they will need and the area they will feel most lacking in will be HR advice. The issues facing a medical director may vary from ensuring high-quality clinical care to modernizing clinical practice, or from dealing with dysfunctional departments where doctors do not speak to each other to delivering an effective hospital-at-night system, but behind almost every task to be tackled lies an HR issue. Often these issues require behaviour modification, capability assessments or even disciplinary proceedings and to do so will be almost impossible without good HR advice – and preferably advice that is not 'risk averse'. Figure 19.2 gives a simple algorithm which can be applied to almost any problem that is brought to your attention.

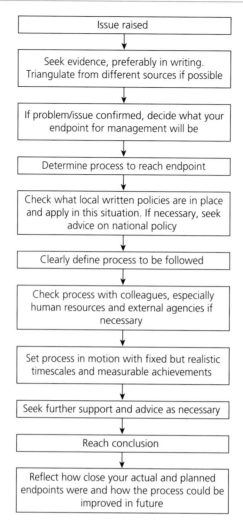

Figure 19.2 An algorithm for the management of most problems and issues.

The more senior the medical management role, the more crucial the relationship with the HR department (or 'organizational development' as it is now often known) becomes. The relationship not only relies on personal contact, for advice and help, but also, and possibly more crucially, on the availability of local and national policies and guidelines with which we can manage, surprisingly, many colleagues.

Management and regulation

The NHS is increasingly regulated, and each regulatory body has the right to carry out inspections. Box 19.1 gives an indication of the number of bodies who have a right to inspect an acute trust in one form or another. Increasingly this regulation requires evidence of processes, procedures and outcomes to be available for immediate scrutiny when they inspect. Hence the recording and archiving of non-clinical data, such as the minutes of governance or risk management meetings, assume an importance comparable to keeping accurate data on clinical outcomes.

Box 19.1 Organizations that have the authority to inspect an NHS acute trust

Human Tissue Authority (HTA)
A Quality Network for Inpatient Child and Adolescent Psychiatry
Accreditation scheme for tissue banks
Auditors' Local Evaluation (ALE)
Audit Commission
Breast cancer quality assurance review
Cancer Peer Review
Cancer Screening QA
Care Quality Commission
Child Health Informatics Centre
Clinical Pathology Accreditation Ltd
Council for Healthcare Regulatory Excellence
General Chiropractic Council
General Dental Council
General Medical Council (GMC)
General Optical Council
General Osteopathic Council
Health Professions Council
Nursing and Midwifery Council
Pharmaceutical Society of Northern Ireland
Royal Pharmaceutical Society of Great Britain
Environment Agency (waste management licensing)
Fire authorities
Health and Safety Executive
Health Information Accreditation Scheme
Health Promoting Hospitals
Health Protection Agency (HPA)
Health Quality Services (the HQS has joined with the CHKS and become the HAQU)
Hospital Accreditation Programme
Information Commissioner
Investors in People
Local authority environmental health departments
Local Involvement Networks (LINks) and the Commission for Patient and Public Involvement in Health
Medicines and Healthcare Products Regulatory Agency

Monitor (independent regulator of NHS foundation trusts)

National Audit Office

National Institute for Innovation and Improvement

National Patient Safety Agency (NPSA)

National Treatment Agency for Substance Misuse

NHS Business Services Authority

Counter Fraud and Security Management

Dental Practice Division programmes

Pensions Division

Prescription Pricing Division

Supply Chain Management Division

Hosted and Managed Services

NHS Estates – general

NHS Estates – patient environment action teams

NHS Litigation Authority – includes risk management standards and clinical risk management standards

North Central London Strategic Health Authority library accreditation

Overview and scrutiny committees of local authorities

Primary care trust commissioners

Peer Review of Cancer Registries

Postgraduate Medical Education and Training Board

Human Fertilisation and Embryology Authority (HFEA)

Deanery School of/Royal College of Anaesthetists

Deanery School of/Royal College of GPs

Deanery School of/Royal College of Midwives

Deanery School of/Royal College of Nursing

Deanery School of/Royal College of Obstetricians and Gynaecologists

Deanery School of/Royal College of Ophthalmologists

Deanery School of/Royal College of Paediatrics and Child Health

Deanery School of/Royal College of Pathologists

Deanery School of/Royal College of Physicians

Deanery School of/Royal College of Psychiatrists

Deanery School of/Royal College of Radiologists

Deanery School of/Royal College of Speech and Language Therapists

Deanery School of/Royal College of Surgeons

Deanery School of/Royal College of Surgeons – Faculty of Dental Surgery

Deanery School of/Royal College of Surgeons – Faculty of General Dental Practice

Deanery School of/Royal Pharmaceutical Society

Strategic health authority (SHA) – in their role of local monitoring on behalf of the healthcare commission

SHA Local Supervising Authority Annual Audit

Skills for Health

The National Autistic Society

Postgraduate Medical Education and Training Board (PMETB)

Eastern Deanery Monitoring Visit for the Foundation Training Programme (on behalf of the GMC)

Cambridge Clinical School – annual monitoring visit for service level agreement (SLA) for provision of undergraduate clinical placements and accommodation

Helicon Library Accreditation (new for trust and voluntary)

GMC Annual Survey of Trainees and Trainers

Resuscitation Council UK – Resus Service

Resuscitation Council UK – Accredited Course Centre

Advanced Life Support Group (ALSG) – accredited course centre

Counter Terrorism Security

Commission for Equality and Human Rights

JobCentrePlus (for annual renewal of Two Ticks symbol)

The primary inspecting agency will be the CQC. This body has taken over the responsibilities of the Healthcare Commission and now validates and triangulates information available from various sources and inspections about the organization against a set of publicized outcome measures.[6]

All organizations who undertake postmortems will now also be licensed by the Human Tissue Authority. This body was set up in the wake of the Alder Hey scandal to oversee the postmortem sector and ensure that facilities are appropriate and up to date. Like many organizations they require a nominated lead, the 'designated individual', who has to be at an appropriate level of the organization. The need for a board-level lead is a frequent requirement of many regulatory bodies and national policy documents, and it will therefore often fall to medical or nursing directors to take on these roles.

Another area requiring a board lead is children's services and safeguarding, the latter of course including vulnerable adults. This role carries with it responsibility not only for the service, and ensuring there is no repeat of the Victoria Climbié or Baby P scandals, but also for liaison with many other agencies such as local authorities and the police.

General employment requirements are also part of the remit of the medical director. As an executive director, the medical manager is as accountable for health and safety lapses as the director of finance or the director of HR. These are legal and statutory requirements that have to be accepted as part of the accountability aspects of any senior management post.

The role of the medical director or responsible officer is covered in Chapter 16. Suffice it to say that revalidation should not increase the work of medical directors significantly if they are already fulfilling their role and addressing all performance issues appropriately. The new medical director will, however, be surprised at the number of contacts that are made with both the GMC and the National Clinical Assessment Service (NCAS) in the management of doctors who are either in difficulty or have come to the attention of the GMC for a variety of reasons. In managing these situations, the GMC publication *Good Medical Practice*[7] and the Department of Health's *Maintaining High Professional Standards in the Modern NHS*[8] are invaluable aids to prevent process mistakes which may come back to haunt you if an appeal against one of your decisions is made.

Job planning and clinical excellence awards

Unique to secondary care is the process of job planning. This was not new when the new consultant contract was introduced in 2003, but has become far more sophisticated than it used to be originally, which was little more than a weekly timetable for consultants.

Job planning is a contractual requirement for consultants and non-consultant career grade staff. There is clear guidance from both the Department of Health and the BMA on the process; however, much can be gained by locally agreed implementation plans to ensure transparency of the process. Nothing is likely to engender more bad feeling than the presumption that a consultant has 'got away' with a much lighter job plan for a bigger salary.

At a practical level there are now commercial electronic packages to support the process. It is an annual requirement and is, *de facto*, a form of performance management. Most organizations work on an annual commitment of 42 weeks (52 weeks per year, less six weeks' annual leave, 10 days' study leave and eight bank holidays). A well-structured job plan will not only include a weekly timetable of clinical duties, but also clear objectives for how many of a particular activity will be delivered (e.g. at one clinic per week, a minimum of 42 clinics will be delivered).

In addition, it clearly states the non-clinical time the consultant will be employed for, and what activities are to be done during that time. Thus there will be time for activities related to revalidation, but in addition time spent as audit or risk management lead will be identified, with clear objectives such as organizing five audit meetings per year, with every trainee presenting at least once.

If performed well and consistently, job planning can be used to improve efficiency and productivity among consultants as well as improving clinical standards through objective setting. If persuasion and discussion fail to change culture and approach by an individual, the use of the pay cheque in the form of the job plan and clinical excellence awards can be a great motivator.

Clinical excellence awards are another area almost unique to secondary care. Like job planning they require consistent and transparent processes that have been agreed with the local negotiating committee, but which follow the guidance as issued annually by the Advisory Committee on Clinical Excellence Awards. Though often chaired by a non-executive director, the local awards committee will seek the advice and knowledge of the medical director, who, it must be remembered, sits there as a manager, not as a clinician. Whatever the processes, it is important that all members of the committee remain clear that the award is not for doing one's job, but for providing excellence over and above what would be normally expected.

Support structures for acute medical managers

The support structures in place for acute hospital medical managers generally follow the hierarchical nature of the organization. In addition, however, there is extra support for those in certain positions.

Consultants can look to their clinical or divisional director for support or help with problems. As medical director, on the other hand, in-house support may be limited. If you are lucky, your predecessor will have stepped aside rather than retiring, in which case help is at hand – do not be afraid to ask for it. Former medical directors know exactly what the role is like and will have the benefit of prior knowledge to help you. The medical director also has their executive director colleagues for professional managerial support. They are often more skilled and experienced in management techniques, but frequently lack the medical director's clinical insight. Increasingly, as chief executive roles are filled with doctors, they too may be able to offer clinically sound advice.

The medical director should also have further support from the regional medical director, and in future their responsible officer. In addition, there are other organizations available for support, such as NCAS, the defence organizations (e.g. the Medical Defence Union, the Medical Protection Society) and the GMC. Many of these, if contacted for support, will often not give hard advice, but will offer support for what you intend to do in a given situation, perhaps fine-tuning the plan, or alternatively will request formal referral, taking the issue you had hoped to manage supportively internally to a much higher level.

Many regions in the NHS have a medical directors' forum, or similar, where medical directors can gather on a regular basis to discuss common issues. This may be seen by regions (while they remain) as a means of performance-managing medical standards across many trusts, but do not underestimate the informal network that is created between acute trust medical directors as a result. This is further enhanced by the use of email groups and there are times when these can be extremely useful. The new or concerned medical director then has the option of contacting a more experienced colleague, who will have nothing to gain or lose and will thus give sound impartial advice, or of asking a number of colleagues how they may be dealing with a particular problem they all face.

What is governance?

Governance is a word much used in business and which is increasingly being understood in the clinical context by clinicians. In a management context, however, the *Oxford English Dictionary* defines it as the 'act, manner, fact or function of governing'. In other words, governance underpins management. Governance is not just the structure through which the organization is managed, but also the processes that are in place to ensure the organization is working well, that its outcomes are good, and that where outcomes are less than ideal these are identified and systems are put in place to ensure continuous improvement.

Once the correct structure has been put in place to support management, good governance also requires the ongoing collection of evidence to prove to the board and the organization, as well as to relevant external regulatory bodies, that the organization is well run by a team who understand the issues they are facing and have the ability to improve them.

Executive and board roles

Medical directors are in a unique position in both an executive team and on a board. In most cases they are the sole practising clinician, and frequently, by the very nature of the fact that few clinicians move regularly between organizations for management promotion, they will be the longest serving member of the organization at this level. As a direct result, they will be able to provide a wealth of organizational experience and memory, explaining processes that the organization tried before and, in particular, giving a perspective on how to engage the consultant body to gain maximal organizational change.

This can be even more evident at board level, where many non-executive directors, upon their appointment, will have little or no understanding of the working of an acute organization and may look to the medical director for guidance, often with lesser challenge on clinical issues than to other non-clinical executive colleagues.

It can, however, be a lonely role, and a close working relationship with the director of nursing is essential. Although on paper all boards are run on democratic principles, with the chair having a casting vote (though this is rarely needed) the reality is that the medical director and the nursing director have a virtual veto, as they are expected to provide assurances that patient safety and experience will not be compromised by each decision. Standing up to a compelling financial argument can be difficult and daunting, but medical directors have to be sure of their opinions and understand which decisions are safe and which are not. They must never be afraid to seek help from other colleagues when coming to a decision, but ultimately that decision will be theirs and theirs alone.

The development of the revalidation agenda gives a clear example of how the medical director is expected to stand alone as a voice for clinical standards and patient safety. When revalidation was first proposed, the original guidance suggested that any recommendations for revalidation or not would have to be a board decision. But boards, particularly non-executive members, felt unable to make this decision, and argued they would look to the medical director/responsible officer for advice. The final regulations in law[9] now clearly state that the responsible officer (who initially in most organizations will be the medical director) will make the recommendation alone. The board is now only responsible for ensuring the necessary resources are in place to deliver the role.

External relationships

The medical director role and that of the medical manager have varying commitments in terms of external relationships. Medical managers have to demonstrate all kinds of skills, from diplomacy when, for example, selling services to the local GPs or primary care trusts (PCTs) through to negotiation during the annual contracting round; they have to be tactful when appearing before a local overview and scrutiny committee but firm if clinical standards may be compromised.

The nature of the NHS is such that, although over the last decade or so there have been many reorganizations at regional and local levels (strategic health authorities, primary care trusts), from the perspective of the acute trust, patients keep coming and there is often little evidence of demand management. The latest proposal creates the concept of clinical commissioning boards in each locality to answer those critics who say that previous systems were driven by managers and not clinicians.[10] These reorganizations can lead to 'pathway redesign' and even mergers between organizations. At such times medical managers have to exhibit considerable leadership skills, seeing the 'big picture' as well as the needs of the organization which they lead. This can lead to potential conflicts of interest, but the secret to success is to always keep the needs of the patient clear in your mind. The acid test is: would you be satisfied with the service being provided if it were yourself or your family? If not, then it is essential that you do something to change it.

The most important external relationship in the acute sector, and this must never be forgotten, is that with the GPs. They, too, are usually long-standing local servants of the NHS, and also frequently good friends. Professional relationships must be nurtured and maintained. The purchaser–provider split appears to be here to stay, but reorganizations will be a regular occurrence in the NHS as long as it is seen as a political challenge by each successive government. The medical profession cannot afford to allow itself to be undermined. Only two groups know what is best for patients: doctors and the patients themselves. Ensuring ongoing discussions on the best pathways for patients and how to deliver them using all the medical skills at our disposal is the only way to achieve optimum care for our patients. After all, it could be said that if we got the clinical discussions right 100 per cent of the time, and to the satisfaction of our patients, we would not need many of the managers, clinical and non-clinical, that we have.

The relationship between the health service manager and the medical staff

The relationship between career managers and clinicians is often supportive, fruitful and productive, but all too often it can lead to conflict and problems if not handled well.

Career managers, particularly from recent NHS management training schemes, often do not understand the basis of clinical training in the 1980s and 1990s, the period when today's senior clinicians were trained. Clinical training then was based on fully understanding the principles of normality in order to be able to analyze and correct any abnormality for a good clinical outcome. Doctors were trained to be confident and self-reliant. They were trained to constantly question established practice in order to move medicine forwards. They cross-checked each other's work and trusted no one in order to provide a safe service for patients. These doctors are now the established leaders in many hospital departments. All too often managers will go to senior clinicians having finally found data on which to base their argument for change, only for clinicians to challenge the origin of the data, and even produce their own to support continuing to practise as they have done for many years.

The clever manager understands the senior consultant and as a result can achieve great things. Consultants are used to a hierarchical 'firm' structure, in which they head up a team of nurses and junior doctors. As such, they believe they have risen to the top of their profession and many see their equivalent, in management terms, as the chief executive, also at the top of their career, leading a team of 'junior managers'. The consultants might not perceive the speciality business manager, or even the chief operating officer, as being on a par with them and may feel, therefore, that any discussions they have on how to move any particular service forwards should be with the chief executive.

The astute manager will quickly realize that reasonable discussions and compromises, keeping patient safety and good clinical outcomes at the forefront of the conversation rather than finance or targets, interspersed with appropriate social niceties, will soon bring individual consultants round, and that once some start to change, others will follow suit – assuming they can see the benefits. Many new initiatives start as a 'pilot', often not in the true research sense, but because one member of a department agrees to try it and subsequently achieves success, so others are persuaded to join in. As a former turnaround director in our organization once put it: 'Change the silent majority to isolate the clinical terrorists.'

The position of the senior medical manager can be slightly different. Their colleagues will often expect them to understand the clinical viewpoint and the reasons why a new system is unlikely to work. Equally, and possibly more importantly, medical managers understand the objections, are often well respected clinicians in their own right and can more clearly explain the need for change. It is for this reason that it is important, no matter how big the management portfolio becomes, that medical managers maintain some regular clinical practice, so they will always 'know what it is really like'. On the other hand, senior managers (and even medical directors) expect the senior clinical managers to understand and follow the corporate view, and to be able to convince their colleagues of its validity and of the case for change. One of the most obstructive types of senior manager is the person who appears to understand corporate policy at a senior manager level, but who, upon returning to the department, immediately supports his or her colleagues in their resistance to change.

Conclusion: the acute medical director – the buck stops here

All medical management is about accepting responsibility and accountability. Doctors do this every day in their clinical work, but many find it difficult to do it in the managerial context. For those who can, medical management can be a fulfilling short- or long-term challenge running alongside a satisfying clinical career. Aspiring medical directors must realize that, in this post, they are not being appointed by their colleagues to 'fight their corner', but are being appointed by the trust board as executive directors in the first instance, but also as guardians of clinical care for the organization. They are in a unique position and, if successful, they should be able to look back and see significant changes they have made to services for patients. In their clinical role they will strive to provide high-quality care for their patients, but in their management role they should be able to see the part they have played in ensuring others are able to provide the best possible care for the patients – past, present and future – in their own locality.

In dealing with staff, and consultants in particular, it is important that medical managers are consistent in the standards they apply and transparent and proportional in the action they take. They must maintain confidentiality at all times, not start rumours around the hospital, and beware of inadvertently giving information away by confirming that a rumour is true or untrue. Above all, however, they must maintain a sense of humour or they will be at risk of being overwhelmed by the workload.

Traditionally the medical director role was one taken up before retirement, and certainly it is not one for the newly appointed consultant, but increasingly they are being appointed at a younger age, prompting the question: 'What comes next?' The skills and experience that will have been acquired in the post can be used in many other areas of the health service, be it locally, regionally or nationally. Equally, good-quality medical managers will in future find themselves being recruited to other organizations as medical directors, or even making the transition to chief executive.

One thing is for certain, while in post and afterwards, the medical director's portfolio is always expanding, and the ability to say no to new requests and even to new roles is one of the most difficult to master! Yet despite that, those medical directors who continue to work clinically at the end of their term of office will often find a queue outside their door of people with jobs for them to do, both within and outside their organization.

Summary

❏ The medical manager role is an ever-changing one but it is here to stay, and the good medical manager will have the flexibility to meet these changes.

❏ Acute organizations have a defined hierarchical structure which provides developmental career opportunities for those with an interest in medical management.

❏ The acute medical director portfolio, while ever expanding, is, and always will be, based around ensuring (and assuring) standards of care in the organization as well as standards of practice by individual doctors.

❏ The acute medical director requires a supporting team to be in place for all areas, but above all will need high-quality HR/employment advice.

❏ Networks exist outside any organization to support the medical director and these should be regularly tapped for help and advice – there will always be someone else who has had to deal with a very similar problem to the one you currently face.

References

1. Shackley P, Healey A (1993). Creating a market: an economic analysis of the purchaser-provider model. *Health Policy* Sept 25, 153–68.

2. Ham C, Clark J, Spurgeon P *et al.* (2010). *Medical Chief Executives in the NHS: Facilitators and Barriers to Their Career Progress*. NHS Institute for Innovation and Improvement. Available from: http://www.institute.nhs.uk/

3. Monitor (2009). *Service-line Management: An Overview*. Available from: www.monitor-nhsft.gov.uk/

4. Department of Health (1999). *Clinical Governance: Quality in the New NHS*. HSC 1999/065. Available from: http://www.dh.gov.uk/

5. Scally G, Donaldson L (1998). Clinical governance and the drive for quality improvement in the new NHS in England. *Br Med J* July, 61–5.

6. Care Quality Commission (2010). *Essential Standards of Safety and Quality*. Available from: http://www.cqc.org.uk/

7. General Medical Council (2006). *Good Medical Practice*. Available from: http://www.gmc-uk.org/

8. Department of Health (2005). *Maintaining High Professional Standards in the Modern NHS*. Available from: http://www.dh.gov.uk/

9. The Medical Professional (Responsible Officers) Regulations 2010. Available from: http://www.legislation.gov.uk/

10. Department of Health (2010). *Equality and Excellence: Liberating the NHS*. London: Department of Health.

Chapter 20

Medical management in private healthcare

Duncan Empey and Sheila Peskett

Introduction

Although medical managers in the independent healthcare sector have usually worked previously in the NHS, there are significant cultural and governance differences between the two sectors which can present some specific challenges. We shall address these in this chapter.

Context: UK private healthcare

The NHS is the principal provider of healthcare throughout the UK, accounting for more than 95 per cent of activity, with an expenditure of £103.8 billion in 2010. The independent (or private) sector (IS) expenditure on acute healthcare accounted for £7.5 billion, an increase of 5 per cent on the previous year. The majority is funded by private medical insurance (PMI), premium expenditure on which reached £3.67 billion in 2010. The remainder is self-funded by patients or by companies for their staff.

There are five large companies in the UK that provide around 85 per cent of medical care in the private sector, and many smaller organizations that own fewer facilities providing a wide range of services. The NHS also has private patient units (PPUs), which generated £421 million in 2008/09, limited by a cap on the proportion of total income allowed to be generated from private care. NHS patients now account for almost half the activity in some of the larger IS organizations, but this is only a small fraction of healthcare provision in NHS organizations.

Sometimes observers question why private healthcare provision is continuing and even expanding when the NHS has reduced waiting lists and provides high-quality services. There is no single factor, but consumers wanting to choose their own consultant, to choose the timing of operations and the environment in which to have them, together with an increased demand for procedures not often available in the NHS, such as cosmetic and obesity surgery, ensure that the desire for private medicine is always there.

Private medical insurance

The PMI market in the UK is competitive, with the majority of policies being taken by companies for their staff, but a large number being individual subscriptions. PMI policy income has increased between 3 and 7 per cent each year since 2006, with a 3 per cent increase in 2010. Such an increase in the face of a recession suggests that many consumers prioritize expenditure on private healthcare before other calls on their income.

Workforce

Doctors who work in the IS come from six categories:

- Those who are NHS employees who have practising privileges (PPs) with, but who are not employed by, one or more of the independent hospital groups. These are most commonly consultants who undertake private practice in their spare time and provide the majority of medical care in the IS.
- Those who are not NHS employees who have PPs with, but are not employed by, one or more of the independent hospital groups. These are people who have usually worked previously in the NHS but now work entirely in the IS.
- Those who are not NHS employees but are employed by one or more of the independent hospital groups. The majority of these doctors work in the independent sector treatment centres (ISTCs). They frequently come from the European Union. They are on a specialist register with the General Medical Council (GMC) and have been selected for having an appropriate level of training and experience to be able to perform at the same level as NHS consultants.
- Those who are NHS employees but have been seconded to an IS organization to undertake specific work for the NHS, usually in the ISTCs.
- Those who are not NHS employees but are self-employed practising in the IS and have no PPs.
- Resident medical officers (RMOs) who are either employed by an IS hospital group or by the RMO supplying organization. These doctors provide 24-hour emergency cover for the private hospitals.

Nursing and other healthcare professionals are mainly employees of the hospital provider although some may be independent contractors.

ISTCs

These were established in 2004 as part of the Department of Health's Independent Sector Treatment Programme in order to reduce waiting times for patients with common conditions needing medical interventions such as joint replacement surgery, hernia repairs and endoscopic examinations. They allowed organizations without any previous activity in the UK to establish centres as well as the main private providers which used their own facilities, or more commonly purpose-built units. Because of the 'additionality clause' in the first phase, whereby clinicians who were either working or had been working in the NHS in the previous 6 months were excluded from working in the ISTCs, consultants were recruited from abroad. The original contracts have expired or are about to do so, but other methods whereby patients may have care in private hospitals, such as 'choose and book', have been developed.

IS as NHS provider

As indicated earlier, 5 per cent of NHS patients are treated in private facilities which have been accredited through the 'Any Willing Provider' (now 'Any Qualified Provider') process. Despite some political anxiety about 'privatization' of the health service and pulling back on encouraging plurality of provision and competition, it is likely that the IS will remain as a significant alternative provider for NHS patients.

Regulation

The sector is regulated by the Care Quality Commission (CQC) according to the regulations currently in place. Medical staff are regulated by the GMC and a recent change is the legal requirement for IS providers to appoint a responsible officer (RO) for medical revalidation of doctors who do not work in the NHS and have PPs (discussed later in this chapter).

The Human Fertilisation and Embryology Authority (HFEA) regulates private provision of fertility services. The Human Tissue Authority (HTA) and the Medicines and Healthcare Regulatory Authority (MHRA) are involved in many aspects of provision of private pathology services, and the Health and Safety Executive (HSE) oversees the safety of hospital sites, staff and patients. Non-medical health professionals are regulated by the Nursing and Midwifery Council (NMC) and the Health Professions Council (HPC).

Key points

Private health in the UK

- The IS accounts for less than 5 per cent of expenditure on health in the UK, but provides useful additional capacity for provision of some NHS services and a flexible alternative for patients who choose to be treated privately.
- Most services are provided by NHS consultants who also work in the NHS, but the IS also employs doctors in the NHS ISTCs.
- The sector is regulated by the CQC and health professionals within it by the relevant regulator.

Governance and the medical director role

There is no common management or governance structure for private healthcare providers as there is, say, for NHS foundation trusts. The constitution of boards varies according to the type of organization. IS providers consist of commercial organizations, some of which are owned in whole or in part by overseas healthcare organizations, by charities of all types and sizes and some by religious foundations. There is no statutory requirement for the executive board or team to include a medical director, although all private healthcare organizations do have mechanisms for seeking medical advice. With phase two of the Department of Health's Independent Sector Treatment Programme, however, private providers were obliged to demonstrate three levels of medical leadership – corporate, local for the scheme and local for the speciality – for successful procurement of a contract to deliver services to the NHS. With re-tendering of 'wave one' contracts, primary care trusts (PCTs) have also demanded similar degrees of medical leadership at corporate and local level. Appointment of medical directors in the IS has become more the norm, although some are not employees but are engaged on a consultancy basis, and not all are board members or part of the executive team, wherein lies potential tension.

The main purpose of the role of medical director is similar to that in the NHS – i.e. it is to provide medical leadership on all professional issues relating to medical practice in the organization, including recruitment and selection, appraisal and professional development, where appropriate; PPs, performance issues and related clinical governance management; and now most IS medical directors are also the appointed RO for revalidation. The incumbents should ensure that there are effective systems and processes in place for all these functions. Ensuring that there are effective and appropriate governance arrangements in place for doctors working in the organization, whatever their status, is paramount. This requires clarity about terms of engagement, reporting and accountability lines and having systems for ensuring competence.

How much support there is for the medical director varies from organization to organization. Providers with hospitals or treatment centres that have employed consultants will usually have local medical directors. Some IS providers also have external specialist advisers. The bedrock of support in individual hospitals, however, lies in the medical advisory committee (MAC) system and its chairmen, and local clinical governance committees. The medical director relies on the effective working of local systems and reporting mechanisms to keep abreast of all the medical professional issues that may arise. With hospitals from Aberdeen to Truro this can present logistical problems.

Medical advisory committees

Most IS providers have local MACs in each of their units to advise the hospital executive director or general manager on medical matters. This will usually include the awarding and limiting of PPs, clinical governance (often by a subcommittee) and facilitating links with the local healthcare community. The MAC chairman is an important role, but does not fit with the description of a medical manager. The post is usually unremunerated and the ultimate decisions usually lie with the hospital executive director or general manager, who will often also take advice from the group medical director.

Practising privileges

For those non-employed consultants undertaking private practice, the system of engagement with the organization is through the granting of PPs. Although the details vary between IS providers, the general principles are the same. Eligible doctors applying for PPs must go through a credentialing process to demonstrate that they are qualified, trained and experienced to the level of a consultant; that they are fit to practise within their proposed scope of practice; and that they have appropriate registration and indemnity. They must also provide criminal records disclosure and appropriate occupational health certification. They must agree to comply with the organization's policies and procedures, particularly around clinical governance, and must submit evidence of satisfactory annual appraisal. They must also inform the organization if they become the subject of a GMC referral or investigation by another organization, if they are restricted or suspended by another organization, or if there is any other reason to give cause for concern about their practice. In return the organization undertakes to provide an appropriate environment and infrastructure for consultants to practise safely and effectively.

The PPs agreement is very clear about the scope of practice of any individual doctor, and anyone wishing to introduce a new technique or treatment must submit a proposal according to the organization's policies on such matters. The same applies to anyone wishing to do research using patients seen privately and/or the organization's facilities. The local MAC is critical in monitoring and advising management on all these matters.

Hellenic Project

The Hellenic Project was initiated in 2009 by the Independent Healthcare Advisory Service (IHAS) and the NHS Partners Network (NHSPN) working with Dr Foster. The five largest and many smaller IS groups are contributors. Phase 1 (2011) included data on activity, mortality, readmissions, length of stay, day-case rates and benchmarks. Phase 2 gathered data on transfers, returns to theatre and infection control indicators, and Phase 3 gathered data on patient-reported outcome measures (PROMs) and patient survey results. For 2012 it is planned to publish risk-adjusted indicators (mortality, readmissions) based on *International Classification of Diseases*-10 (ICD-10). This project will enable for the first time accurate outcome information, comparable to that in the NHS, from most of the IS to be made available to commissioners and patients.

Key points

Corporate governance

- Independent sector providers have varied models of corporate governance.
- Medical management is by a medical director working with a network of local MACs.
- Most doctors are consultants who are not employees but have PPs.
- The Hellenic Project will provide quality and outcome information comparable to that in the NHS from the majority of the sector.

Challenges for the medical director

The challenges of the role range from the mundane to the more esoteric. For many, the role is part-time so there is an imperative to prioritize and to allocate time and effort most effectively.

Numbers and geography

Most private providers have hospitals or facilities across the country providing a range of services. Geography is, therefore, one challenge, but aiming for common standards and policies is another. The number and variety of medical staff working in a private organization create their own issues. As we have said, the medical director may have oversight for independent, private consultants, employed doctors, seconded doctors and those from agencies, needing to ensure that they are all fit for purpose with appropriate systems in place for performance management. Ensuring that governance systems cover this variety while maintaining common standards for all is like holding the reins of four or more horses pulling a single chariot.

Stakeholders

The scope of healthcare provision in the UK has changed with the increase in plurality of providers for NHS patients with the resultant impact for private providers that they have to interact and negotiate with a wider variety of external stakeholders than in the past. These include the Department of Health, local commissioners, local NHS trusts, strategic health authorities (SHAs), subcontractors and other independent providers, regulators, as well as the public and patients. Most medical directors in the IS have a background in the NHS at clinical and managerial or leadership levels with an extended healthcare network. This has given them an intimate knowledge and understanding of the UK healthcare system, but this is not always appreciated by their commercial colleagues and can lead to frustration that their expertise is sometimes not used to advantage.

The political influences around healthcare cannot be underestimated. The IS, although now recognized as a member of the healthcare community in the UK, is still regarded with suspicion by many. Maintaining an objective approach about what could and should be achieved exercises the minds of medical directors as well as their organizations. Helping to develop the strategic approach to engagement with the NHS and government is an important contribution the medical director can make.

Clinical governance

Clinical governance systems and processes are very similar to those in the NHS, although the details of data collected may not be exactly the same as in the NHS. Work is under way, however, to ensure that information and data provided by the IS match those in the NHS, so that true comparisons can be made between the two sectors (see the earlier discussion on the Hellenic Project).

All private hospitals or facilities in the main IS providers have local clinical governance committees, whereby the usual performance indicators, such as complaints, adverse events, returns to theatre, prolonged lengths of stay, unplanned readmissions and PROMs, are monitored and reported to the corporate clinical governance or risk management committees. Scrutiny of such data is taken very seriously so that appropriate and timely action can be taken. Individual practitioners are provided with their own performance measures. This will be very important for revalidation and whole-practice appraisal.

Clinical governance can be particularly challenging for the IS medical director because of the increased numbers and varying terms of engagement of doctors they have to deal with, and their relative inaccessibility, as well as the fact that they may be working in a number of organizations. Making arrangements to meet people can, in itself, be difficult. This is particularly apparent when addressing concerns about poor performance.

The fact that consultants are almost always not employees also means that the relationship between consultants and the local hospital manager or MAC chair or with the group medical director is quite different from that in NHS trusts. Work is planned and scheduled by the consultant and facilities provided by the hospital rather than activity being directed by the hospital. When things go wrong, there are no disciplinary procedures as such available for non-employed doctors, although the MAC may conduct a professional performance review in order to advise the general manager on further action, but informal discussions possibly followed by limitation or removal of PPs are the usual options. The IS organization will not usually undertake the responsibility for remediation in cases of bad behaviour or performance in the same way that an NHS trust would for one of its doctors, unless the doctor in question is employed by the IS provider. Where consultants work in both the NHS and the IS, close communication and cooperation between medical directors can lead to a solution, but for purely independent practitioners many problems can arise (see Case study 20.1).

Case study 20.1

An anaesthetist was noted to have his name associated with a case reviewed at almost every monthly company clinical governance meeting over a 5-month period – not serious problems, but investigated because of the relatively frequent occurrences. It transpired that he had PPs at several hospitals all owned by different IS providers over quite a wide geographical area. Further investigation showed that there had been minor to moderate concerns at each of them, but as he did no more than one or two sessions at each per month the numbers had not been large. He had not had an appraisal for 4 years, and that had been done by a colleague in another speciality. Advising him to reduce his spread of commitments, appointing a mentor and appraiser at the hospital he chose as his main base, and ensuring information exchange between the providers resulted in significant improvements.

Despite clinical governance systems and policies for raising concerns, the problems of a doctor in difficulty are often slow to come to light. Advising from a distance is often less than satisfactory but sometimes necessary. It is essential, therefore, to minimize risk to patient safety and organizational reputation, to have sound systems and processes in place for monitoring performance, dealing with complaints and serious incidents, and to investigate concerns properly.

General managers are responsible for clinical governance locally and for the performance of doctors working in their hospitals. They can be supported and empowered by the corporate medical director and local medical leaders through provision of professional guidance, but the challenge is to ensure that they are competent and confident in this aspect of their roles and so, reciprocally, they can support the medical director.

New techniques, innovation and research

Most large IS providers have policies on how new therapeutic techniques will be introduced into their hospitals, on how innovation will be managed, and on research. In each case the local MAC will review the proposal, but usually outside advice (including research ethics committee approval) is also required. Medical managers need to be sure that robust procedures are in place for these developments to ensure that patient safety is not compromised.

Complaints

It is a current requirement of the Essential Standards of Quality and Safety (the standards in use in England), which the CQC uses to assess the IS healthcare providers, to ensure that each provider has in place appropriate arrangements for individuals not funded by the NHS who wish to complain about the services provided. IS providers mostly subscribe to the Independent Sector Complaints Adjudication Service (ISCAS), which advises on a two-stage procedure for the provider to follow, and a third stage involving an independent adjudicator who may recommend an award to a complainant as well as advising the organization on lessons to be learned. Complainants may also choose to refer doctors to the GMC in some cases.

Where clinical negligence is alleged, doctors will also involve their defence organization, but usually the IS provider has to complete the initial investigation to handle the complaint.

Investigations

When there are serious untoward incidents which involve concerns about clinical competence, the IS medical manager may choose to have an independent investigation. Most of the medical Royal Colleges offer, for a fixed fee, a service whereby colleagues in the speciality will visit a unit and interview those involved, eventually producing a report which guides the doctor and the provider on the next steps. There are several private companies that provide a similar service, which can be specifically focused on issues concerning the provider, but may be more or less expensive as they are charged on a time basis. Through an agreement between the IHAS and the National Clinical Assessment Service (NCAS), IS providers can also seek advice from the latter organization, but this also incurs a fee for item of service.

Professional vs commercial

There is an understanding in most cases that the medical director will contribute to strategic discussion and business development, where appropriate, but this can lead to a potential clash of values for the medical director when working in a commercial organization.

The primary ethical concern for a commercial organization is to enhance the value of the business for the benefit of its owners/shareholders, whereas for a medical director the primary ethical aim is usually to provide high-quality healthcare for the benefit of the patient. The two aims are not mutually exclusive, but their order of importance could lead to internal or external conflict. Doctors, however, are not unused to this ethical dilemma in that, as practitioners, they often have to balance the benefit for individual patients against the benefit for the wider population. The challenge of a possible clash of values, however, has to be recognized and dealt with – doing so successfully is the mark of a good medical manager.

There is also the issue of encouraging income-generating activity. Surgeons who have a high conversion rate of referrals to surgery will not only earn more money for themselves but also for the organization. The challenge for the medical director is to ensure, through clinical governance systems and oversight, that best, evidence-based practice is undertaken and that patients are not operated on unnecessarily (see Case study 20.2).

Case study 20.2

At one hospital, a shoulder surgeon had a high operative rate. When he retired, his practice was largely taken over by another surgeon who was much more conservative in his approach to the management of patients with shoulder problems. This resulted in a noticeable fall in income for the hospital. The tension that this sort of problem creates between management and the profession is not always easy to deal with, as there could be many factors affecting the different practices of these two surgeons. Open and frank dialogue, however, helps to gain better mutual understanding by all parties. The responsibility of the medical director remains to protect patient safety and to ensure high-quality care.

At the business level, the challenge for the medical director is to gain a better understanding of the commercial world so as to be able to contribute more effectively to the strategic direction and business development of the organization. There is a whole other dimension to risk management to be appreciated and comprehended. With commercial nous comes the need to learn how to employ marketing and advertising, not only effectively but also ethically. Within all this, too, are the issues around protection of organizational reputation.

Supporting the executive team appropriately by fostering an integrated approach to governance at the corporate level can help to ensure that the core business of healthcare drives business decisions, while at the same time maintaining the right balance between commercial and clinical imperatives.

Commercial factors, marketing and advertising

The IS and the NHS have important differences and similarities. Obviously the scale of the facilities, the range of services offered and the requirement for payment in private hospitals are big differences, but the basic aim of providing safe and high-quality healthcare to patients is common to both.

Sometimes people wonder if the pressures of running a commercial business lead to a temptation to cut corners and reduce quality or safety. This is not the case. The NHS also has to work within its budgets, and for both NHS and private hospitals, quite apart from the imperative on clinical grounds to provide an excellent service, the risk to reputation is too great to allow any fall in standards. No business ever flourished by providing unsafe or poor services. Even the most budget of budget airlines pride themselves on good time-keeping and safety.

Often the IS has advantages in its provision of quality services – for example, most accommodation is in single rooms with en suite bathrooms which greatly reduces the potential for cross-infection.

Independent healthcare companies are usually run by a small number of business people and a very large number of clinical staff. The business managers need an understanding of healthcare, as they would need an understanding of any field in which they were working, even though they are not clinical. Part of the role of medical managers is not only to give clear advice on clinical matters but also to improve our managers' understanding of our approach, just as they help us to understand the basics of balance sheets and project flow charts.

Advertising is as important to IS healthcare providers as it is to those who provide other services in a marketplace. The medical manager often contributes to the approval of copy to ensure no errors creep in in relation to claims about outcomes or overall quality. However, most referrals will come to hospitals through their consultants who, in turn, have patients referred to them by GPs. It is usually services such as health screening or sports clinics that are directly marketed to companies or patients, and some providers have associated businesses such as health clubs.

Political issues

Private healthcare can evoke very strong opinions from doctors, patients and the public, not to mention politicians of all stripes and the press. The NHS is a great success on so many levels that some see alternative provision as undermining that success. This is not the case, as the provision of £7.5 billion of healthcare without any call on the public purse will have an overall effect of reducing demands on the NHS.

Another concern is the NHS paying private providers to perform operations and treatments on NHS patients. This might be a problem if prices were high, but the IS is paid the same tariff price as any NHS organization for that procedure or episode of care. When ISTCs were set up to ensure that doctors were not tempted away from the NHS, the rules excluded employment of any doctor currently in the NHS or who had worked in the NHS in the previous 6 months. This has been relaxed recently to allow NHS consultants to operate on a sessional basis in private facilities on NHS patients, the job plan system which consultants follow ensuring that they are working in their own time.

These tensions can impact on the medical manager who may receive complaints and criticisms from doctors or members of the public opposed to private healthcare who seek to use perceived failings to damage the sector's reputation. Patient confidentiality often constrains the responses which may be made.

Key points

Challenges

- Multiple sites spread over a wide geographical area require effective processes to be in place for the medical directors to fulfil their responsibilities.
- Clinical governance is well developed in the IS, although the large numbers of doctors with PPs can require particular vigilance.
- Balancing the requirements of the business and professional aspects of service provision is an important part of the medical director's work.

The IS medical director job description

As previously stated, the main purpose of the medical director in an IS healthcare organization is to provide medical leadership to the organization on all professional issues relating to medical practice in the organization, and to contribute to strategic discussion and business planning with the senior management team or board.

The person specification requires the individual to be on the GMC Specialist or General Practice (GP) Register with a licence to practise. A minimum of 5 years' experience as an NHS consultant or GP principal is usually required, with experience of medical management roles being highly desirable. The usual personal attributes and skills, such as drive, integrity, communication, networking and influencing, are also prerequisites.

Responsible officer

The duties of the medical director have been described in previous sections but there is a new role now, with added responsibility, with the appointment of responsible officers (ROs) for revalidation. IS healthcare organizations are 'designated bodies' (DBs) and medical directors working in such organizations have been appointed as their ROs. As for all DBs and ROs there are statutory conditions that must be met to ensure that the overarching purpose to protect patients by ensuring the GMC's standards are met is fulfilled. These are set down in the Medical Profession (Responsible Officers) Regulations 2010 which became law on 1 January 2011, and in the Department of Health's document *The Role of the Responsible Officer – Closing the Gap in Medical Regulation*.[1]

All ROs in the IS will have responsibility for a number of doctors, ranging from the few to the hundreds, for whom they will be making recommendations to the GMC about their revalidation. Doctors working in the IS have sometimes had difficulty in identifying their RO. The following gives guidance on this:

- Anyone with any sort of contract (even those with no defined PA sessions) with an NHS designated body will relate to that organization's RO.
- Doctors on a GP performers list will relate to the PCT.
- Trainees will relate to the deanery – this is not usually an issue for the IS, although some ISTCs do have training contracts for placement of doctors in training.
- Doctors with more than one employer will relate to the one where they work the majority of their time or, if equal, to the one nearest their registered address.
- Doctors who work independently will relate to a non-NHS DB if they have PPs with that organization or, if not, the following organizations have been designated and they may relate to them if they are members:
  - Faculty of Public Health
  - Faculty of Occupational Medicine
  - Faculty of Pharmaceutical Medicine
  - Independent Doctors Federation.

The NHS Revalidation Support Team (RST) has developed a tool: Organisational Readiness Self Assessment (ORSA)[2] for all DBs and ROs, NHS and IS, to complete and return. The assessment form requires:

- details of the DB
- details of training and support for the RO
- information on the appraisal system, including policy, audit and training and support for appraisers

- organizational governance arrangements
- systems for raising and investigating concerns
- policy for remediation and further training.

Appraisal

The bedrock of revalidation will be the strengthened whole-practice appraisal. It will be key to the overall success of re-licensing. While IS providers have always required their doctors to undergo annual appraisal to maintain their PPs or contract of employment, there are now additional responsibilities around appraisal and scrutiny of such.

Revalidation for doctors practising in both the NHS and the IS needs to take account of their work in both sectors. Annual appraisal will take place in the sector within which they do the bulk of their work. This may not necessarily be their DB and IS ROs may find themselves responsible for arranging appraisals for people with ROs in another organization. It is the responsibility of individual doctors to be appraised annually, but it is the responsibility of the DB and RO to support this and to have appropriate systems in place to do so. Doctors who practise privately must determine how the private component of their practice is included in their annual appraisal, but, again, the DB and RO must provide performance data for all its doctors. The framework for whole-practice appraisal is modelled on the GMC Practice Framework for Appraisal and Revalidation.[3]

This means that IS ROs must ensure not only that there is an appraisal policy and management system in place for those doctors relating to them, but also that the quality of the appraisal can be assured if it is not being undertaken by the organization. This is an additional challenge for IS medical directors/ROs and their organization.

Other challenges for the IS are those that have been highlighted previously, that is that hospitals in any one organization may be geographically widely spread and that an IS organization may have large numbers of purely private practitioners, emphasizing the importance of having strong management systems, both technologically and in personnel, in place to be confident that the performance of doctors and systems are being monitored properly. Applying consistency is essential.

Identifying and investigating concerns about performance is a responsibility of the organization and the medical director. This may be quite straightforward, but supporting remediation of below-standard performance presents further challenges for the IS. Organizations have a fairly clear responsibility for their employees, including employed doctors, but the situation is not so clear-cut for those with PPs, who, as private practitioners, have a responsibility for maintaining their own professional competence and dealing with situations where that may be brought into question.

Training and education

Consultants working in both the NHS and IS usually arrange excellent continuing professional development (CPD) for themselves under the guidance of their NHS appraiser and through their personal development plan (PDP). Consultants who are fully private will in future be appraised by the DB that is the IS provider where they mainly work. The provider will appoint their RO, who will oversee the appraisal cycle and make recommendations for revalidation to the GMC.

However, most IS providers also arrange study days, evening lectures, workshops and clinical meetings for their consultants and local GPs.

Legal aspects and indemnity

Independent service providers cover their employed staff with insurance and indemnity for all their activities, but not for consultants with PPs. Consultants must (as a condition of their PPs) have indemnity for clinical negligence claims at all times, and this must be of a sufficient amount to cover the value of possible claims. Traditionally this requirement has been covered by membership of one of the three UK medical defence organizations (the Medical Defence Union, the Medical Protection Society and the Medical and Dental Defence Union of Scotland), but recently various insurance-based options have entered the market. They offer lower premiums, but may not all be able to offer a similar level of professional support to clinicians who may need help in facing allegations made to the GMC. Also, the cover must be adequate, which can be hard to judge, with an award exceeding £6 million in a recent case. 'Run off' insurance is also required to cover claims after ceasing to practise.

The cover for NHS patients being operated upon in an IS hospital is complex, and changing, but sometimes they are included in the Clinical Negligence Scheme for Trusts (CNST).

Maintaining professional relationships

Medical managers in the IS function best if they are in close touch with the medical professional community as much as possible. If they are an RO, they must be a licensed doctor, but not all undertake clinical work. This is not a hindrance as they are usually experienced clinicians by background. It is important, however, that they network with individual clinicians and other medical managers in the IS and NHS. The NHS medical director has generously invited medical directors in the IS to attend the Annual NHS Medical Directors Conference, which has greatly improved the opportunities for mutual understanding and exchange of knowledge.

The medical Royal Colleges are also important stakeholders in the IS, particularly in their work on setting standards and providing/supervising CPD. Also many senior members of the Royal Colleges are active clinicians in the IS. The British Medical Association (BMA) has a Private Practice Committee and interaction with that is a valuable activity for the medical manager in the IS, both to learn the views of users on a national level and to provide accurate information on the sector. There are also revalidation network boards, where ROs from both sectors meet to share experience and expertise.

Key points

Medical directors in the IS

- Medical directors becoming ROs for revalidation increases the scope of the role and will change the relationship IS providers have with their doctors.
- Appraisal of fully private consultants and the provision of data to inform the whole-practice appraisal of NHS-based consultants will be an important service provided by the IS to consultants' revalidation.
- Maintaining professional relationships with colleagues and professional bodies is important for medical directors to sustain their role.

Summary

❏ The IS in the UK is a small but significant part of healthcare provision.

❏ Standards are high and there are many opportunities for innovation and practice development.

❏ For the medical manager, challenges include a large geographical span of responsibilities, large numbers of practising clinicians and the management of relationships with commercial colleagues and non-employed doctors in an environment which differs significantly from NHS organizations.

❏ Fortunately the context for practice provided by IS hospitals is usually excellent and consultants are highly skilled and motivated to provide outstanding care for their patients, so the number of problems is small and the satisfaction of patients is extremely high.

References

1. Department of Health (2010). *The Role of the Responsible Officer – Closing the Gap in Medical Regulation – Responsible Officer Guidance.* Available from: http://www.dh.gov.uk/

2. DH Revalidation Support Team (2011). Organisational Readiness Self Assessment Tool (ORSA). Available from: http://www.revalidationsupport.nhs.uk/index.php

3. General Medical Council (2011). *The Good Medical Practice Framework for Appraisal and Revalidation.* Available from: http://www.gmc-uk.org/

Chapter 21

Medical management in primary care

Paresh Dawda

- Introduction
- The structure of practices
- High-level processes
- Core practice processes
- Management of support processes
- Conclusion
- Summary
- References

Introduction

Effective primary care is internationally recognized as being essential and core to sustainable healthcare[1] and has been firmly established in the NHS since its inception in 1948. Primary care is defined as the first contact of a patient with a healthcare provider, usually a GP, dentist, optician or pharmacist in a given episode of illness, and over 90 per cent of the contacts with the NHS are provided by these services. Primary medical care in the UK is provided by general practice and the volume of activity provided amounts to over 300 million consultations a year. The nature of general practice has changed over the years through a series of reforms and, indeed, at the time of writing, the NHS is undergoing a further radical reform.

The nature of the reforms since 2004 has led to general practice being delivered through a number of different contractual routes and this has led to an increase in the heterogeneity of providers in the primary care medical market. The range of these heterogeneous providers varies from single-handed practices to 'corporate' providers managing and running a number of practices. Hence, there are practices of different complexity, different skill mixes and varying levels of management support. Policy driving care closer to home and the need to contain costs have led to a further layer of complexity, with some practices offering services beyond those considered to be traditional general practice. These include services previously considered to be within the scope of secondary care, but with the advent of health practitioners with special interests, there has been a shift into primary care.

The changes have seen an expansion of the role of practice managers, as well as nurses, and healthcare assistants. The changes have also seen a change in the profile of employment status of GPs, with an increase in the proportion of non-principals and those holding a salaried role rather than as a GP principal, which historically was the most prevalent model of delivering general practice.[2] The breadth of the practice manager role can be seen by a review of the competency framework published with the new General Medical Services (nGMS) contract.[3] The exact role will vary depending on a number of factors, and will encompass operational, tactical and strategic components to varying degrees. It must also be remembered that essentially general practices are small businesses and therefore the role of the clinician in management in general practice will be wide and varied. The exact role will depend on a number of factors, including the size of the practice and the level of support from the practice manager, with whom the medical manager will need to have an extremely close working relationship. The role may also be either the responsibility of one clinician (e.g. an executive partner) or, as is often the case, it may be distributed among several GPs or partners.

The structure of practices

The profession's leadership has consistently highlighted that the future of general practice will be to deliver a patient-centred service that provides high-quality, safe and needs-based care,[4] and to do so the strategic and organizational development of general practice must be increased.

The organization of most practices takes the form of a traditional organizational structure (Fig. 21.1). Reviewing the structure of a practice in this way provides a useful overview of the hierarchy. However, it does not provide a functional representation of the processes involved in running a practice and service provision. Figure 21.2 shows the structure of the practice as a system, illustrates the different processes that operate within a practice and provides a useful functional representation. It views the structure, particularly the core processes, from the perspective of a patient.

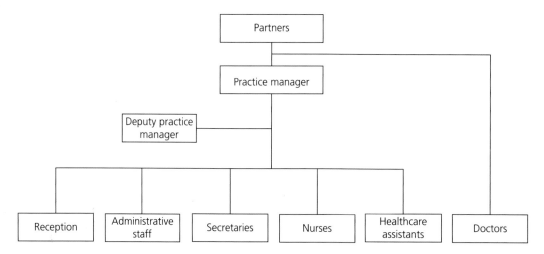

Figure 21.1 The traditional practice organizational structure.

High-level processes

Business vision, mission and strategy

A good business, even a small one, should have a vision, mission and strategy. Often in small businesses or solo practices this is not formalized and may be the case in many general practices. However, as practices grow and their dynamics change, the need to have a unified and shared vision, mission and strategy becomes more important. A key role of the medical manager is to contribute to that process and provide leadership in execution of that strategy.

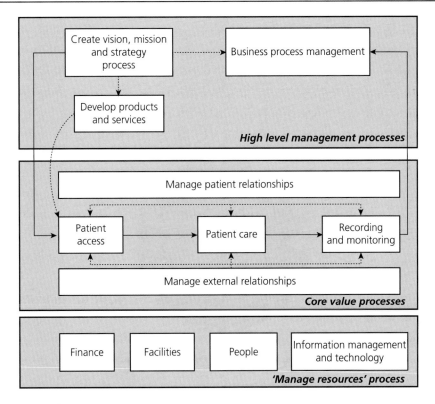

Figure 21.2 The practice as a system.

A key aspect of developing mission and vision is to consider the perspectives of the different stakeholders. These will often represent different views and perspectives and so, in formulating a strategy, a balanced approach is necessary to ensure that no one area alone is being neglected.

The balanced approach may include the following dimensions:

- patient experience
- staff
- quality and safety
- financial.

Box 21.1 shows an example of the process one practice went through to develop their mission and vision.

Box 21.1 Developing a mission and vision

An example of a mission statement for one practice is 'Delivering excellence in healthcare', which is simple and easy to remember. Their vision statement is: 'A well-managed practice with a clear leadership in a pleasant environment with time to think and less stress, with more time to practice clinical skills for the benefit of the patient.'

The process of developing this included the whole team, and during the workshop to do this, the team in small groups identified words to articulate and express their feelings (see below). The words used by the practice are now symbolized in their logo: a sunflower with three layers (the core, an inner layer of petals and an outer layer of petals), surrounded by their mission statement.

Words used by the practice

How we are seen (outer layer):

- Excellence in patient care – high quality and safe care
- Professional
- Accessible
- Innovative
- Broad range of services
- 'Value for money'
- Excellence as an employer
- Friendly environment

The team works because of our (middle layer):

- Teamwork
- Cohesion
- Commitment
- Fairness
- Fun/enjoyment
- Compassion
- Support

- Flexibility
- Vision
- Sense of achievement

Our core values that support this are (inner layer):

- Trust
- Honesty
- Integrity
- Respect
- Belief

Business process management

Management requires the regular monitoring of processes of care. The active monitoring of the practice performance in each of the above areas would be a joint role between the practice manager and the medical manager. The monitoring of performance may be considered along these four dimensions.

The purpose of this process is to monitor the other processes at a high level to ensure that practice performance is stable and as planned. The high-level monitoring requires regular review of key outcomes from each of the other component processes illustrated in Figure 21.2. However, at the component process level, the number of measurements would be greater and would include a mixture of outcome and process measures. This approach is consistent with the NHS Quality and Outcomes Framework (QOF), which has identified that the NHS will be monitored through a series of outcomes grouped into five domains:[5]

- preventing people from dying prematurely
- enhancing quality of life for people with long-term conditions
- helping people to recover from episodes of ill health or following injury
- ensuring that people have a positive experience of care
- treating and caring for people in a safe environment and protecting them from avoidable harm.

It has been explicitly specified that providers will be expected to have a series of more 'granular' measures that include process measures, where granularity refers to the breaking down of processes into sub-processes, each with its own set of detailed measures.

The role of the medical manager in this area will include identifying key measures from the component process that need to be monitored at a higher level and hence align it to the NHS Quality and Outcomes Framework. The use of metrics in these four dimensions provides a balanced viewed of the practice's performance. Figure 21.3 shows a sample of measures that could be used for the patient care process, and a selection of key performance indicators may be selected from this process to view regularly at this higher level.

These metrics should be updated and monitored frequently. There is no specific recommendation on the frequency of monitoring. The measurements should be plotted in a time-based series with a run chart or statistical process control chart. This allows the data to be viewed visually and simplifies the interpretation. Essentially the purpose is to understand the variation within the data and decide whether it is 'common cause variation' or 'special cause variation'. This will enable good management decisions to be made on the data. If a process is stable, i.e. exhibiting common

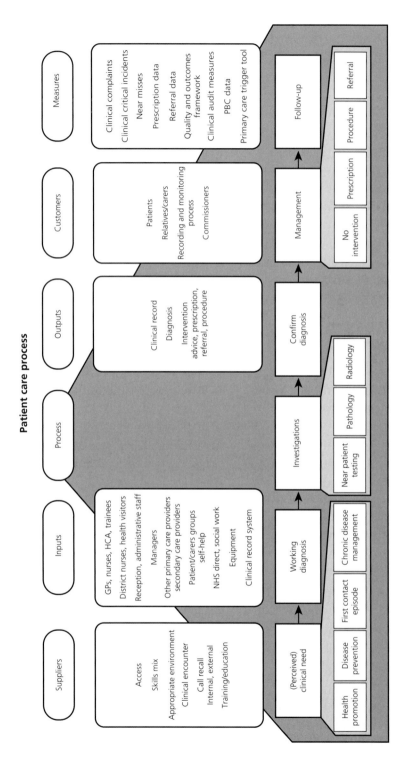

Figure 21.3 The SIPOC (suppliers, input, process, output, customer) patient care process. PBC, practice-based commissioning.

cause variation, and it is meeting the required specification, then all that is required is ongoing monitoring. If, however, a stable process is not meeting the requirement, the process will need to be redesigned and the frequency of monitoring should be more frequent. Where a process shows special cause variation (assignable cause), the cause should be explored and evaluated in detail to identify the learning and causes. If the direction of change is desired, then consider making the identified cause a part of the process. If the change is not in the desired direction, the process needs to be reviewed to prevent such causes occurring again. The understanding of variation of data in this context is critical and fundamental to making good management decisions and further information is available from www.institute.nhs.uk.

Consider the example of patients who do not attend for their appointment. The chart in Figure 21.4 shows a weekly breakdown of the number of patients who did not attend for their appointment. It shows that it varies from week to week, but that the level of variation is stable and predictable so long as the system is not changed, i.e. it shows common cause variation.

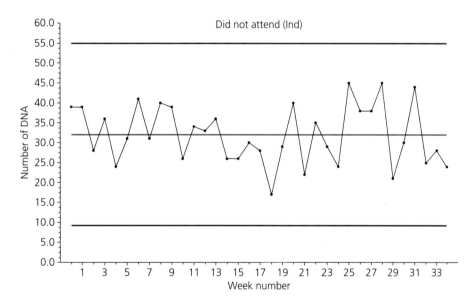

Figure 21.4 Example of common cause variation. DNA, did not attend.

Now consider some more data points from subsequent weeks (see Fig. 21.5). We know the process was stable, but after week 36, there is special cause variation. This is identified in a number of ways using rules. In this example, after week 36 there are seven consecutive data points all above the average line. In addition, there are also data points above the upper control limit. Both of these are examples of a number of rules that show special cause variation. An increase in the number of non-attendances is clearly not desired.

Reviewing the reason showed that this was because at week 32 a change was made to the appointments system. This change allowed patients to book appointments up to two months in advance, rather than the two weeks that was allowed under previous systems. The decision now would be to either return to the previous system or to test new ideas, e.g. a mobile phone text reminder system, to try to reduce the number of non-attendances.

281

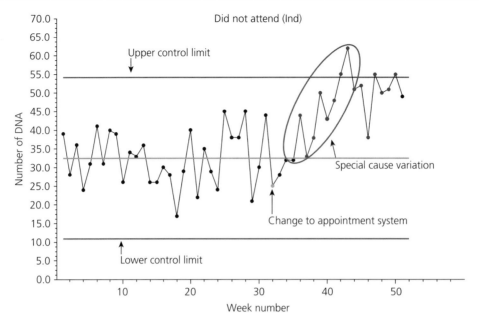

Figure 21.5 Example of special cause variation.

Key points

High-level processes

- A balanced set of measures should be identified and used to monitor the performance of the practice.
- The measures should be aligned with the NHS Quality and Outcomes Framework.
- The measurements should be frequent and viewed graphically using run charts or statistical process control charts to identify either common cause variation or special cause variation.

Core practice processes

Patient access

The reforms over the last few years have prioritized the need for improved patient access. This was originally audited in 1998 and then subsequently regularly reviewed with the Quality and Outcomes Framework and the data is publicly available.

Access is an overarching term used to describe a range of functions and can be summarized into five dimensions:[6]

- physical access to services
- timeliness of access
- access to a practice and GP of choice
- access to a range of quality service, i.e. the appropriate level of expertise and onward referral as appropriate and necessary
- equity of access, described as system-wide dimensions to access.

There have been a number of policies and strategies driving the access agenda in general practice. The NHS Plan[7] introduced targets to increase the number of GPs and to improve the timeliness of access to see a GP or primary healthcare practitioner by 2004. The new contract for GPs that was introduced in 2004 aligned incentives to improved quality, including access. There is a strong correlation between the number of GPs per head of population and mortality, and such evidence has been a key driver for the more recent policies to improve access, e.g. equitable access centres.[8] The healthcare changes occurring in England at the time of writing have removed those access targets, but an expectation that access to care needs to be improved and maintained has been mandated.

The medical manager in general practice has a clear role in defining the policy, strategy and subsequent implementation of approaches to improving access. However, many of the operational aspects may subsequently be managed by the non-clinical manager.

National guidance[9,10] has identified approaches and possible solutions that primary care trusts (PCTs) and practices could adopt to improve access. These solutions have been varied. However, they cannot necessarily be implemented in all practices without first testing and refining them. These approaches require the support of the clinician and medical manager. For example, the improvement to telephone access may require investment in new technology, e.g. online appointments or a telephone system, as well as a change in the procedures for call handling. The medical manager will have a role in engaging peers and other partners in a partnership.

Improvements in access may also lead to a change in the mode of service delivery. This may include, for example, a greater degree of remote assessment and management, such as telephone consultations or online consultations. Telephone consultation training and standard operating procedures would require a clinical perspective, which needs to incorporate risk assessment and management issues. Medical indemnity organizations are often able to provide guidance with conducting risk assessments.

Improved access may also include a change in the skills mix of staff providing services, e.g. advanced nurse practitioners, nurses and healthcare assistants or perhaps an even more innovative skills mix. The implications of this include training, up-skilling, recruitment, mentoring and coaching staff. The medical manager has a role in specifying the training needs and job descriptions as well as in appraisal of those clinical staff with new roles. Depending on the type of change and skills mix, there would be a need to coordinate and write practice-based protocols for staff in the new roles, to monitor these services and to ensure quality and safety.

GPs and patients alike value continuity of care. This has been associated with greater patient and staff satisfaction, reduced costs and better health outcomes.[11] The type and definition of continuity of care vary. There have been competing priorities, e.g. extended opening hours and the demand for same-day appointments have eroded relationship continuity.[11] The medical manager needs to consider what the practice's needs for continuity are, how they may be achieved and to balance some of the changes mentioned above with maintaining continuity of care. A key aspect is to listen to and understand the needs of the patients and this is discussed further in the following section. For example, increasing the number of same-day appointments without really understanding the patients' needs may result in a worsening of patient experience.[12]

Equity of access is a critical area for the whole of the NHS. The variation in access, particularly for vulnerable groups, can be great and is compounded by the difficulty in researching this area.[13] The role of the medical manager here may be to identify the local issues, identify vulnerable groups within the practice area and then engage the wider team and stakeholders in improving access for these groups.

Key points

Patient access

- Many aspects of patient access can be managed by the non-clinical manager.
- Changes to improve access may threaten quality, safety and continuity of care and it is the role of the medical manager to identify and manage these risks.
- The changes to access may create new roles and ways of working and the medical manager will need to support the changes in roles and responsibilities of staff, as well as the new way of working.

Patient care

The patient care process refers to aspects of care that are directly related to the provision of clinical care. An example of the aspects involved in the patient care process, from the author's own practice, can be seen in Figure 21.3 showing the SIPOC (suppliers, input, process, output, customer) diagram.

Components included here may be driven by commissioned services, e.g. QOF and enhanced services, but should extend beyond just what the commissioners specify. The King's Fund, in its recent inquiry into the quality of general practice, identified a number of dimensions[14] of quality, some of which would be included in this process:

- diagnosis
- referral
- prescribing
- acute illness
- long-term conditions
- health promotion
- end-of-life care
- maternity care.

Research into the provision of care has identified that optimum care with evidence-based interventions is delivered only 55 per cent of the time.[15] Care delivery problems are frequent in general practice and there is a wide variation in many areas, as identified and discussed in detail in the King's Fund inquiry. The clinical indicators of the QOF are an attempt to reduce variations of care and its success has been the subject of much debate. The reliability of provision of clinical care can be improved by focusing on the structures and systems with which care is delivered. These include approaches that go beyond the foundation of education, training and vigilance and use the principles of deliberate reliable process design. All clinicians, and particularly the medical manager, should lead the design of clinical care processes so they are reliable.

Aspects of clinical governance, including education, training and quality improvement, are part of the patient care process. The medical manager will need to be involved in the practice's clinical meeting programme and in aligning the programme with the practice's development plan. The quality and safety of care delivered can be analyzed and monitored using a holistic approach to care, which may include:

- staff event reporting
- leadership walkaround
- staff surveys
- patient surveys
- review of patient complaints
- monitoring and measuring a number of metrics such as the trigger tools for measuring safety
- routine data, e.g. referral data and prescribing data.

The medical manager needs to review and analyze these different sources of information and lead meetings to discuss them, e.g. significant event analysis (SEA) and review of patient complaints. It is particularly important for the clinical manager to understand how to manage and investigate events. The quality of significant event auditing is variable and generally has much scope for improvement. The causes of adverse events are multifactorial[16] and in most SEAs the focus is on the care delivery problem, where the error or violation occurred. However, there are a range of factors described as 'error-producing conditions'[16] that may contribute to the adverse events, including:

- patient factors
- individual doctor factors
- teamwork
- environment factors
- task factors.

These in turn may be influenced by cultural and organizational factors. The same model may be used and considered in a proactive way to prevent adverse events. The medical manager has a duty to improve the quality of event analysis by exploring areas beyond the care delivery problems. Where there are specific issues related to an individual clinician, the medical manager will need to be involved in managing them.

The prescribing of drugs and referral of patients to other agencies are common and frequent interventions in general practice, and practices are increasingly performance-managed by the commissioner against these areas. They need to be actively managed, with regular review of the data, understanding the variation and making appropriate system changes that are clinically sound to be able to meet the needs of patients and the commissioner. The management of QOF is another area where the clinical manager will take a proactive role together with the practice manager. The QOF and new standard setting are now in the remit of the National Institute for Health and Clinical Excellence (NICE). NICE also continues to produce guidance on a range of areas and it recommends that the practice 'identifies a person to be responsible for developing a system and process for identifying guidance that is relevant and for making decisions and liaising with the most appropriate people, to ensure that the relevant recommendations are implemented'. It also suggests that if this is the practice manager then it is important that a 'clinical advisor is available to discuss the relevance of each piece of NICE guidance soon after it is published.'[17]

Many clinicians, including nurses, will be involved in the different aspects of providing patient care. Hence, medical managers may not necessarily be directly involved in all the areas this process encompasses. However, the leadership and coordination of workstreams in this area very much remain their responsibility.

Key points

Patient care process

- The patient care process is a core process encompassing many aspects and the medical manager needs to be involved in leading and managing it.
- Patient care is about delivering good, reliable evidence-based care and putting in place systems and structures to enable this to be done.
- The use of metrics, as well as soft measures, will help to monitor the quality and safety of clinical care.

Recording and monitoring

The recording and monitoring of care have become increasingly important as practice revenue has become increasingly aligned with being able to demonstrate achievement in a series of process and outcome measures of care. The standardized recording of key clinical data and the ability to extract the information in a timely and meaningful way directly affect practice revenue.

Over and above that, standardized clinical recording facilitates patient care and can be considered to be part of 'management continuity' of care. Good record-keeping is an attribute of being a good medical doctor and is it strongly recommended not only by medical indemnity organizations but also by the General Medical Council (GMC). As well as recording at the point of clinical care, recording of clinical information occurs at various other points, e.g. when a new patient registers at the practice and the medical records are received and when correspondence about patient care is received from other clinicians involved in the delivery of care. The Primary Care Information Management Service (PRIMIS) has defined five attributes of a high-quality clinical record as follows:

- completeness
- accuracy
- relevance
- accessibility
- timeliness.

The medical record may be electronic, on paper, or mixed. The majority of recording in UK general practice is electronic. Electronic medical records have coded and non-coded components. It is the coded components that facilitate data retrieval, either in the consultation or during monitoring searches, e.g. for the recall system. The current coding system that is used are 'read codes', although there have been plans to move to an alternative coding system. For those aspects of care remunerated through QOF, national guidance published in the business rule set determine the read codes to be used and the monitoring searches that are subsequently developed by clinical system providers. However, for other aspects of clinical care, there is no national direction on the use of coding and individuals and individual practices are free to determine their own coding approach and strategy. The codes used may be variable and wide and this can have an impact on the ability to retrieve the data regarding a particular condition or episode of care. For example, a review of read code usage at the author's practice identified that 5439 different codes have been used, of which 184 were used at least 100 times or more. It is therefore useful for the clinical manager to determine, influence and limit the number of codes used and develop a coding strategy. This coding strategy should include guidance and a policy for identifying which aspect of the medical record, for new patients and external correspondence, should be summarized and coded into the clinical record. There is national guidance available on good practice in keeping GP electronic records on the Department of Health's website.[18]

One risk of requiring overly intensive recording and coding is that it can distract doctors from the patient sitting in front of them and there is evidence that GPs are spending less time talking to patients and more time attending to computers. However, the IT infrastructure may facilitate the standardized entry of records, e.g. through the use of templates, and thus make it easier for clinicians to record the data.

This coding policy and strategy can then be monitored and PRIMIS helps GP practices monitor their data by providing tools that enable them to benchmark their data against other anonymized GP practices at local, regional or national levels.

Coded data provides the ability to undertake searches and to develop registers of morbidity that, in turn, facilitate the provision of clinical care. This includes, for example, call and recall systems, which again need to be managed and monitored through this process. While the administration of this process may be undertaken by the non-clinical manager, the clinician will need to be involved in decisions regarding appropriate recall time-frames. Coded data also facilitates a range of other activities, such as clinical governance and audit, as well as claim procedures for a range of commissioned services, e.g. immunizations and minor surgery.

As well as the recording of clinical data, there is a need to support the recording of information and data not directly related to patient care. For example, this may include significant events, complaints and personal medical attendants' reports. Practice systems to manage the recording of these areas are variable and range from having no structured system, to paper systems, spreadsheets and databases, and comprehensive web-based systems. In its 2006 guidance *Management for Doctors*,[19] the GMC states:

> As well as keeping patients' clinical records, about which Good Medical Practice gives advice, you must keep financial, employment, research and other records for which you are responsible in good order. Good records are part of good management: you should keep paper or electronic audit trails to demonstrate good management decision-making. This is particularly important if you manage a healthcare business.
>
> You should keep clear, accurate and legible management records of relevant decisions and transactions in line with the law, local procedures and good practice. These records should be made at the same time, or soon afterwards. These records must be compiled and stored securely and used honestly, with proper regard for patient and staff confidentiality, and made available to anyone authorised to see them. When disposing of records, you must do so with similar care and in line with relevant guidelines. You should take professional advice as necessary.

Key points

Recording and monitoring

- The IT infrastructure, through use of templates, supports standardized record-keeping.
- Regular data quality searches will help to maintain data quality.
- Standardized record-keeping and coding allow clinical information to be retrieved more easily. This will support improved quality of care, audit and clinical governance as well as claim procedures.

Patient relationships

Customer relationships management is considered to be a critical process in most commercial organizations. The components of the process may be reactive, e.g. management of complaints, but some should also be proactive. This may include supplying patients with a range of information on healthcare and services, e.g. through the website and patient newsletters. The engagement of patients in the services provided by the practice and in redesigning aspects of care would also be included in this process, e.g. patient satisfaction surveys, patient participation groups and patient focus groups.

Patient complaints

A national NHS and social care complaints procedure exists which requires complaints to be investigated and dealt with in a timely fashion. The complaints procedure is a two-stage one, the first of which aims to create a local resolution. However, if complainants remain dissatisfied after this stage, their complaint can be referred to the Health Service Ombudsman.[20] The administration and management of patient complaints are often the responsibility of the practice manager or administrator. However, where the complaints are related to a clinical rather than an operational matter, the medical manger will be required to investigate and explore the clinical nature of the complaint, seek medico-legal opinion as necessary and respond accordingly.

The QOF requires that 'the practice conducts an annual review of patient complaints and suggestions to ascertain general learning points which are shared with the team'. This is good practice and a review may identify recurring themes, such as those in Figure 21.6. Having identified such themes, it is important to address the care processes to improve them, and in future practices will need to specify the learning and subsequent improvements in annually produced quality accounts.

Patient and public engagement

Patient engagement and involvement may include a variety of aspects. Patient engagement may be defined as 'engagement in one's own health, care and treatment'.[21] The literature on patient engagement generally shows high levels of satisfaction, although patients consistently suggest they want to be more involved in their own decision-making. In terms of quality improvement in this area, the challenges facing practices and those GPs involved in managing them include:[21]

- addressing training needs to extend beyond basic consultation skills
- developing a culture valuing patient engagement
- active care planning
- improving consultation lengths
- a sense of loss of ownership following referral to other providers.

Patient involvement means 'involvement in design, planning and delivery of health services'.[21] The recent review on the subject by the King's Fund found limited evidence and the most prevalent mode of involving patients appeared to be patient participation groups.

Patient influence lies along a spectrum, ranging from a review of complaints, giving information, listening and responding, to consulting and advising. Experience-based design extends this continuum to include co-design of services with patients, which has at its centre storytelling as a powerful method to provide an appreciative understanding of the qualities of a service.[22] These are

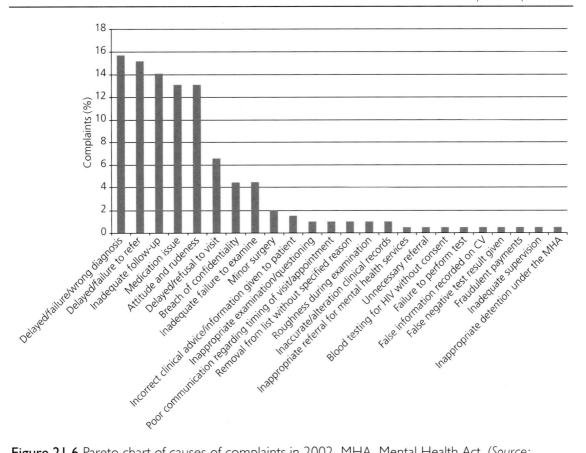

Figure 21.6 Pareto chart of causes of complaints in 2002. MHA, Mental Health Act. (*Source: MDU.*[20])

clearly important at a practice level and the need to understand the voice of the patient is critical, if the service is to deliver improvements in patient experience. For example, access initiatives have often been targeted to improve same-day access, whereas many patients say they want greater choice in the time of their appointment. Hence, increasing the number of same-day appointments may not improve the patient experience and could, in fact, be associated with a reduction in patient satisfaction. The role of patient involvement will become even more critical as the role of commissioning consortia develops, and indeed commissioning may be the vehicle to increase meaningful patient involvement.

Both patient engagement and involvement require a series of tools that can be used at practice level, which may include suggestion boxes, surveys, patient interviews, focus groups, patient participation groups and citizens juries.

There is a broad range of regulation and legislation in place to safeguard patients' interests, including the Data Protection Act, the Access to Medical Reports Act, the Freedom of Information Act and the Mental Capacity Act. Guidance is available from the GMC, the British Medical Association and the medical indemnity organizations on the requirements for practices to fulfil their obligations under these pieces of legislation. The role of the medical manager is to ensure that these obligations are met by working with the practice manager to create reliable administrative systems. Failures may be detected through a review of complaints.

There is an increasing drive in all health services for transparency and accountability, and in future practices will have to produce a set of quality accounts. The Department of Health has produced guidance on the expectations of what will be contained in such accounts. It includes three parts: a statement on quality; priorities for quality improvement; and a review of quality performance together with who has been involved. The National Patient Safety Agency (NPSA) has produced guidance on the principles behind being open and communicating with patients when an incident occurs. The medical manager must, under this process, consider the implementation of these guidelines and lead the practice in developing a culture conducive to the needs for greater transparency and accountability in the NHS.

Management of external relationships

Effective primary care has an organizational and coordinating role. GP practices interface with many areas within primary care and secondary care. For example, they regularly interface with local chemists, care homes, community nursing services, intermediate care services, acute care providers and trusts, dentists, opticians, other practices, local medical committees, localities and PCTs. The introduction of commissioning consortia increases the level of interface practices will need to have with commissioning bodies. In order to improve and expand the range of services provided by the practice to patients, practices will need to interact with local authorities and voluntary sectors as well as those already mentioned. This may be more effectively done through commissioning consortia; however, practices will need to also do this at a practice level.

Management of support processes

The management of the premises and facilities will often be done by the practice manager. The level of management will depend on the nature of the premises and the terms of occupancy. The medical manager will need to be involved in the procurement of supplies, e.g. disposable minor surgery equipment, emergency drugs and medical equipment.

Human resources processes involve a range of activities, including recruitment, induction, training and staff development, appraisal and performance management procedures. The practice manager will manage most of these processes, but the medical manager will need to be involved, particularly in relation to clinical staff. This involvement may include assistance with writing job descriptions, interviewing clinical staff, involvement in their inductions and appraisals. The role in training and development and in planning clinical meetings that are aligned to practice development plans has already been discussed.

All medical staff in general practice are required to have NHS appraisals and, as such, it may be the case that medical staff and medical partners do not have a separate practice appraisal. It would, however, be a good human resources policy to ensure that all medical staff also have a practice appraisal. The management of performance, particularly poor performance, among medical staff requires a strong and firm input from the medical manager. The National Clinical Assessment Service (NCAS) has suggested that managers pay particular attention to three steps: identification, recognition and management. A health component to performance issues is present in almost a quarter of cases that come before NCAS (see Chapter 14 on doctors in difficulty) and it is therefore important for GP practices to have access to occupational health services. Historically, however, this has not always been the case; often practices managed their own occupational health issues. This is not considered best practice as it often causes conflicts of interest. Practices should therefore ensure that staff health is managed by an occupational health service rather than by the practice.

Other aspects of support processes, such as health and safety, information management and technology and finance, are usually managed by the practice manager. Some of these areas are also discussed elsewhere in this book. However, the clinician would need to contribute to these processes when and as required, e.g. by writing standard operating procedure for needlestick injuries or budgeting. Another example where the clinician may need to be involved is in the risk assessment of specific issues or groups, e.g. children. There is national guidance from the Department of Health[23] recommending that the environment should be safe, suitable and young people-friendly. Reception, waiting and treatment areas should be accessible, comfortable and welcoming, with a range of recreational activities, e.g. appropriate reading books, and these should comply with health and safety regulations. A risk assessment would need to consider the balance of providing these with the risk of cross-infection, and indeed the risk may change during outbreaks of infectious diseases, as was the case during the pandemic influenza outbreak of 2009. During that period it was advised that all waiting rooms be cleared of toys, books, newspapers and magazines. The inquisitive nature of children may increase the risk of needlestick injury from sharps boxes not at a suitable height, or from sharp corners of desks. Clinical input in these situations will help to reduce the risk as far as is reasonably possible.

Key points

Support processes

- Many of the support processes will be managed by the practice manager but may require input from the medical manager for specific issues.
- The medical manager will need to be involved in the management of clinical staff and peers, and further advice and guidance are available from http://www.ncas-uk.org/resources/good-practice-guides.
- Practices should use occupational health services where these are required rather than try to manage the clinical aspects of occupational health issues themselves.

Conclusion

General practices are variable in size, but they are generally small to medium-sized enterprises and so the role of the medical manager is very wide and all-encompassing. The duties may also be distributed among a number of individuals. This creates the potential risk that key roles and functions may be overlooked and not fulfilled. Using a structure that organizes the practice as a system makes the functions more transparent. In a dispersed role, different leads may be assigned to each of the component processes. The use of tools such as the SIPOC provides a lot of information about that process in a simple way, including the key steps, the customers of the process and the key measures with which that process may be monitored. This chapter has provided a high-level overview of the wide-ranging roles for the medical manager in primary care. Many of the operational and day-to-day aspects are managed by practice managers and therefore the emphasis on a close working relationship is absolutely critical.

Summary

❏ General practice is varied and mixed with many different types of practices and it is evolving in its structure and complexity as the NHS undergoes further reform.

❏ The focus of this chapter is the medical management of general practice as providers of health services (rather than as commissioners which is discussed further in Chapter 5).

❏ Recognizing the practice as a system facilitates a focus on processes of care and provides a structure through which a practice can be managed as a system.

❏ A key component of the systems approach is to have objective measures that align to the practice's mission and vision (and also the wider requirements of the NHS).

❏ Understanding data and variation is essential for good management decisions. The use of graphical representation and process control charts is a powerful tool in understanding variation.

❏ The medical manager will be key to managing core processes, particularly patient access, patient care and patient relationships and recording and monitoring.

❏ The systems approach to assessing significant events is a useful tool not only to assess significant events but also to manage risk proactively.

❏ The growing role of practice managers and other members of the team provides invaluable support to the medical manager.

References

1. WHO (2008). *The World Health Report 2008 – Primary Health Care (Now More Than Ever).* Available from: http://www.who.int/

2. Gerada C (2009). Changing Partnerships Discussion Paper. Available from: http://www.rcgp.org.uk/

3. British Medical Association (2007). *Annex C: Competency Framework for Practice Management.* Available from: http://www.bma.org.uk/

4. Lakhani M, Baker M, Field S (2007). *The Future Direction of General Practice A Roadmap. General Practice.* Available from: http://www.rcgp.org.uk/

5. Department of Health (2011). *The NHS Outcomes Framework.* Available from: http://www.dh.gov.uk/

6. Boyle S, Appleby J, Harrison A (2010). *A Rapid View of Access to Care.* London: The King's Fund.

7. Department of Health (2000). *The NHS Plan.* Available from: http://www.dh.gov.uk/

8. Department of Health (2007). *Our NHS Our Future: NHS Next Stage Review – Interim Report.* Available from: http://www.dh.gov.uk/

9. Department of Health (2009). *Primary Care and Community Services: Improving GP Access and Responsiveness*. Leeds: DoH.

10. Practice Manager Network (2009). *Improving Access, Responding to Patients*. London: Department of Health.

11. Freeman G, Hughes J (2010). Continuity of care and the patient experience. London: The King's Fund. Available from: http://www.kingsfund.org.uk/

12. Sampson F, Pickin M, O'Cathain A, Goodall S, Salisbury C (2008). Impact of same-day appointments on patient satisfaction with general practice appointment systems. *Br J Gen Practice* 58, 641–3.

13. Dixon-Woods M, Annandale E, Harvey J, Olsen R, Riley R, Arthur A, Katbamna S, Smith L (2005). *Vulnerable Groups and Access to Health Care: a Critical Interpretive Literature Review*. Available from: http://www.netscc.ac.uk/

14. Goodwin N, Dixon A, Poole T (2011). *Improving the Quality of Care in General Practice: Report of an Independent Inquiry Commissioned by The King's Fund*. London: King's Fund.

15. McGlynn EA, Asch SM, Adams J, Keesey J, Hicks J, DeCristofaro A *et al.* (2003). The quality of health care delivered to adults in the United States. *New Engl J Med* 348, 2635–45.

16. Vincent CA, Taylor-Adams SE, Chapman EJ, Hewett D, Prior S, Strange P *et al.* (2000) How to investigate and analyse clinical incidents: Clinical Risk Unit and Association of Litigation and Risk Management protocol. *Br Med J* 320, 777–81.

17. National Institute for Health and Clinical Excellence (2012). A Simple Practice System. Available from: http://www.nice.org.uk/

18. Department of Health (2011). *The Good Practice Guidelines for GP Electronic Patient Records – version 4*. Available online: http://www.dh.gov.uk/

19. General Medical Council (2006). *Management for Doctors – Guidance for Doctors*. Available from: http://www.gmc-uk.org/

20. The MDU (2003). *Complaints in General Practice 2001 and 2002*. Available from: http://www.the-mdu.com/

21. Parsons S, Winterbottom A, Cross P, Redding D (2010). *The Quality of Patient Engagement and Involvement in Primary Care: a Research Report for the King's Fund*. London: The King's Fund.

22. Bate P, Robert G (2006). Experience-based design: from redesigning the system around the patient to co-designing services with the patient. *Qual Saf Health Care* 15, 307–10.

23. Department of Health (2011). *'You're Welcome' – Quality Criteria for Young People Friendly Health Services*. Available from: http://www.dh.gov.uk/

Index